GREEN & BLUE

CONFLICTING WORLDS

New Dimensions of the American Civil War

T. Michael Parrish, Series Editor

GREEN & BLUE

Irish Americans in the Union Military 1861–1865

DAMIAN SHIELS

LOUISIANA STATE UNIVERSITY PRESS
BATON ROUGE

Published by Louisiana State University Press
lsupress.org

DESIGNER: Michelle A. Neustrom
TYPEFACE: Adobe Caslon Pro

COVER ILLUSTRATION: 164th New York Volunteers of Corcoran's Irish Legion going up the Confederate earthworks at Cold Harbor, June 1864, by Alfred R. Waud. Prints and Photographs Division, Library of Congress.

LIBRARY OF CONGRESS CATALOGING-IN-PUBLICATION DATA

Names: Shiels, Damian, author.
Title: Green and blue : Irish Americans in the Union military, 1861–1865 / Damian Shiels.
Description: Baton Rouge : Louisiana State University Press, 2025. | Series: Conflicting worlds : new dimensions of the American Civil War | Includes bibliographical references and index.
Identifiers: LCCN 2024033312 (print) | LCCN 2024033313 (ebook) | ISBN 978-0-8071-8370-0 (cloth) | ISBN 978-0-8071-8426-4 (pdf) | ISBN 978-0-8071-8425-7 (epub)
Subjects: LCSH: United States—History—Civil War, 1861–1865—Participation, Irish American. | Irish American soldiers—Correspondence. | Irish American soldiers—Biography. | Irish Americans—History—19th century. | United States—History—Civil War, 1861–1865—Social aspects.
Classification: LCC E540.I6 S54 2025 (print) | LCC E540.I6 (ebook) | DDC 973.7/473—dc23/eng/20250108
LC record available at https://lccn.loc.gov/2024033312
LC ebook record available at https://lccn.loc.gov/2024033313

for the staff and volunteers of the U.S. National Archives Civil War Widows' Pension Digitization Project, without whom this book would not have been possible

CONTENTS

ACKNOWLEDGMENTS

This book has its earliest origins in the online world, one that has transformed both access to historical sources and the capacity of scholars based far from the archives to engage with them. The extraordinary work that archivists, educators, institutional staff, and curators across the United States have put into the digitization of primary and secondary materials has been of incalculable benefit in investigating Irish American Civil War servicemen. The great majority of the correspondence that features in *Green and Blue* became accessible and identifiable as a result of the U.S. National Archives Civil War Widows' Pension Digitization Project. That digitization facilitated the interrogation of pension material on a scale that simply would not have been feasible or achievable in the predigitization age. I owe an enormous debt to the staff and volunteers of the National Archives who worked with such dedication on the project. A heartfelt thanks is particularly due to NARA Archives Specialist Jackie Budell, who supervised so much of the initiative. Jackie's knowledge of the files is unrivaled, and I am fortunate that my many years working with this material has also resulted in her becoming a firm and valued friend.

In multiple ways, this book is the dénouement of the online project I commenced in 2010 at www.irishamericancivilwar.com. Many of the arguments that follow initially began to form on its pages, and it was as an early research initiative of the site that the daunting task of systematically combing the digitized pension files for "new" Irish correspondence began. I am deeply thankful for the engagement and interaction of all the blog's readers over the years; they have both supported and helped to positively shape my research. An example of the scholarly contribution such public online dialogue can engender lies in a series of comments left on the blog in 2013 by Jim McManus.

Jim consistently maintained that the figure of 150,000 Irish serving in the Union military was too low, and that the source on which it was based represented only a portion of the real figure. It was that exchange which prompted the decision to reassess Irish numbers for service in the conflict, the results of which form an important element of this book.

The world of Civil War blogging brought me into direct contact with a host of fellow researchers of both the conflict and the Irish experience of it. The conversations, exchanges, and collaborations that resulted have contributed greatly toward how I have come to think about and consider Irish service. Among them are fellow scholars of the Civil War Irish, Dr. Catherine Bateson and Brendan Hamilton, who I am fortunate to now call irishamericancivilwar.com editorial colleagues as well as friends and contributors. Particular thanks are also due to Pat Young of the *Immigrant's Civil War,* Harry Smeltzer of *Bull Runnings,* 90th Illinois historian and author Jim Swan, 154th New York historian and author Mark Dunkelman, the inspirational John Hennessy, formerly chief historian of Fredericksburg and Spotsylvania National Military Park, and Dr. Myles Dungan, who has done so much to highlight the experience of the Irish military diaspora. Particular mention is due to my late friend, battlefield companion, and dedicated preserver of the Irish soldier's wartime experience, Joe Maghe. It is a great sadness to me that Joe was unable to see this project come to fruition. His loss is much lamented.

The realization of this book is indebted to the longstanding guidance, advice and friendship of Professor David Gleeson, whose scholarship has so enhanced our knowledge of the Irish in the Civil War era. His suggestions and counsel were vital in helping transform a database of letters and an idea into a completed analytical monograph. I am also grateful to Dr. Ann-Marie Einhaus, Dr. James McConnel, Professor Brian Ward and Professor Aaron Sheehan-Dean for their input in reading and offering thoughtful suggestions at different stages of the work. Thanks are likewise due to Northumbria University for their support through key stages of the process in producing this book.

The team at Louisiana State University Press have been a joy to work with. From the moment I first broached the potential of publication, the engagement, enthusiasm, and advice of editor in chief Rand Dotson and series editor Professor T. Michael Parrish were second to none. I am likewise grateful for the support of James Wilson, Neal Novak, Sunny Rosen, and all the production, design and marketing team at LSU for their commitment to the project. Particular mention is due to the expert copy-editing work of Derik Shelor, from which the finished manuscript benefitted greatly. I would also like to express my gratitude to the anonymous reviewers who gave of their time to help improve the book and advance it towards publication.

Beyond the immediate world of Civil War history, there are many individuals who have provided support on the journey toward *Green and Blue.* In that regard I would like to acknowledge Andrew Hankinson, Dr. Mark Clinton, Alison Kelly, Deka Nylund, Ken Budell, Jenny Liljestrand, Patrick Mulcahy, George Morgan, and Dr. Louise Nugent to name but a few—and of course Ben, Ivra, and Macha. My final thanks are reserved for my mother, Angela Gallagher, and my partner, Sara Nylund, who have always been my greatest supporters and advocates. Sara's companionship and counsel have been indispensable to me in both my personal and professional life over the years. So too has her expertise as an accomplished specialist in the field of historical and heritage-related graphics and I am fortunate she agreed to produce the graphs and map which feature in this book. Aside from anything else, Sara's understanding of the seemingly endless amount of time I spend in the company of long-dead nineteenth-century Irish Americans is remarkable. Without a shadow of doubt, there would be no *Green and Blue* without her.

A NOTE ON CONVENTIONS

The terms "Irish" and "Irish American" are used interchangeably throughout the text, and in the context of this book they have the same meaning—namely, either those who were born in Ireland, or those born outside of Ireland to a parent or parents born in Ireland. The reasoning behind this is set out in chapter 1.

The reader will encounter dozens of individuals in the pages that follow. Unless expressly stated otherwise, each of the men whose experiences are utilized were members of the rank and file. In order to avoid unduly cluttering the text with repeated rank and unit designations, these are used variably throughout. Those seeking information on the specifics of each man's unit, service, and fate can find it in the appendix, where brief military biographies of the soldiers and sailors are presented.

A number of chapters in the book are built around the original correspondence of working-class Irish immigrant servicemen, many of whom struggled with their literacy. In order to maintain the historical authenticity of their voices, the quotes utilized present their words as they were originally written. They so frequently stray from spelling and punctuation conventions that to employ [ ], *sic,* or similar strategies throughout would serve only to confuse their meaning, and so are utilized only sparingly. For more difficult examples, the key to comprehension lies in the phonetics of the letters the correspondent utilized; in such instances the reader will profit from approaching the passage by reading it aloud. An exception to this approach has been made with respect to the widespread use of the "N-word" by the correspondents when referencing African Americans, where en dashes have been employed in its place.

GREEN & BLUE

Introduction

The "Irish" in the Civil War

The early hours of 1 July 1862 had been tough for Patrick Dooley. Indeed, it had been a pretty harrowing week. For six days he and his comrades in the Army of the Potomac had been under arms, caught in a seemingly ceaseless pattern of move, fight, move, then fight again. Along the way there had been little time for food, never mind sleep. Finally, having trudged about the heavily wooded Virginia countryside all through the hours of darkness, they reached their destination. A few days later Patrick would recall it. He remembered "a large Open Country abounding with corn and fruit," where the "wheat was in stacks," an image that conjured for him memories of the "Old Country."[1] The name of the place was Malvern Hill. On that day Patrick Dooley, a twenty-six-year-old stonecutter from Clonmel, Co. Tipperary, was among roughly 57,000 Union and Confederate soldiers who would engage in one of the most ferocious engagements of the war on its slopes. In the aftermath, Patrick wrote two letters to his mother describing what he had seen. He had been particularly struck by the awe-inspiring sight of the whole army drawn up in line of battle, with "different Banners fluttering in the Breeze." One stood out, he assured his mother, for "of all the old green-flag was most admired." Beneath its folds, the Irish Brigade "looked most cheerful," while their leader, Brigadier General Thomas Francis Meagher—the former Young Ireland leader and darling of Irish America—was being "most admirably gazed upon by all the yankees he looked splendid."[2] As Patrick Dooley told it, in that moment of martial splendor before the breaking of the storm, it had been the Irish Brigade who drew the rapt attention of all present. He garnered immense pride from the fact that the Irish had afterward backed up their rousing appearance with their actions on the field. Having recounted the harrowing particulars of his personal experiences, Patrick offered an appraisal of the Irish performance: "all our Irish Regiment took a most prominent part in the Fight and Suffered Severely the Splendid 9th Massachusetts Regt lost Severely, also the Irish Brigade and the 37th Irish Rifles, and other Irish Regiments."[3]

Given his bursting Irish pride, it might be expected that Patrick Dooley had stood shoulder to shoulder with Meagher's boys under the Irish Brigade's green banner, or had endured the maelstrom among his countrymen of the 9th Massachusetts. But like the majority of Irish Americans in uniform, he had served with neither of them. Instead, he had faced the Confederate onslaught alongside comrades in a nonethnic, mixed unit—the 40th New York Infantry. Patrick may have picked a different path, but he recognized that it was the ethnic regiments of the Army of the Potomac who were seen as the ultimate expression of Irish commitment to the Union. He understood that their performance was centrally important in shaping how Irish Americans were perceived by others in the United States. He knew that because of all this, those at home were always eager to learn of their fate. These perceptions have stood the test of time. Just as the Irish Brigade captivated the attention of the massed ranks on Malvern Hill that summer in 1862, they and the other ethnic regiments have been captivating the memory and historiography of the Irish in the American Civil War ever since. Across 160 years, the Irish American experience of the conflict has been judged and defined through the prism of that minority of men who served beneath those green flags, and through the words of an even smaller cohort—largely officers in those same ethnic regiments—who committed their experiences to paper. The seemingly irretrievable experiences of the vast majority—men like Patrick Dooley—have long been lost in their wake.

This book is the first scholarly investigation of Irish Americans that seeks to examine their experience throughout the armies and naval squadrons of the wartime United States. Whereas previous studies have taken as their primary focus the Irish Brigade and other ethnic Irish regiments, *Green and Blue* aims to look beyond, to reincorporate the stories of the tens of thousands of men like Patrick Dooley into our conceptions of Irish American service. In the pages that follow, readers will find new consideration of just what constituted an Irish American, new insight into how many of them fought in the conflict, and where they did so. They will be provided with an account of these men's origins and of the influences that held sway over them before their enlistment. Perhaps most significantly, they will encounter the fruits of a newly identified source, which for the very first time provides direct access to the words of hundreds of Irish American enlisted men—working-class voices like that of Patrick Dooley—previously thought not to have survived. The book's ultimate goal is to provide the most detailed understanding yet possible of Irish Americans who served in Union blue during the American Civil War: who they were, where they came from, what shaped them, what they experienced, and what some of them thought. Aimed primarily at those concerned with Irish American Civil War service and Civil War soldiers' studies, it is also hoped *Green and Blue* can have utility for those with an interest in aspects of social history, Irish history, and the history of the Irish diaspora. This is in large part due to the richness of the primary material discussed, which furnishes unparalleled access into 1860s tenement Irish communities in places like New York's Five Points and Boston's North End, offering a window on how those within identified, interacted, and survived. The perspectives this material provides on the men who left those communities for the seat of war challenge a number of our existing concepts of Irish American soldiers and sailors. Not the least of them is the emergence of evidence that thousands of Irish Americans marched off to battle in the firm belief that the United States, not Ireland, was now their home and their country—and a place they were willing to die to defend.[4] In the final reckoning, many of those who answered Abraham Lincoln's call are revealed not simply as "Irish" or even "Irish American," but as distinctly "American Irish."

These Irish servicemen made a major contribution toward securing U.S. victory during the American Civil War. The benefits they provided to the Federal military were accentuated by the overwhelming weighting of their participation on the side of Union, where the Irish-born likely outnumbered their brethren under Confederate arms by a factor of approximately nine to one.[5] It was such disparity in representation that caused secessionist commentators to consistently attack the prominence of immigrants in the U.S. military throughout the course of the conflict. Typical were the May 1862 sentiments of Virginia's *Daily Richmond Examiner*, which characterized U.S. forces as a "hired army" filled with the "hateful Dutch and Irish scum that infest the North."[6] The *Examiner*'s focus on the Germans and Irish was a recognition of the position these two ethnic groups held as far and away the most consequential immigrant manpower pool in the wartime United States. Between them, men born in Ireland and the German states contributed in the region of 400,000 men to northern armed forces between 1861 and 1865.[7]

While German Americans likely served in slightly larger numbers, where Irish Americans stood apart was in the range and extent of their distribution through the Federal military. The Irish did not exhibit the same degree of preference for enlistment in ethnically affiliated regiments that appears to have marked out much of the German experience, and as a result the great majority of Irish Americans went to war in units that carried no ethnic affiliation.[8] The Irish were the bedrock of the U.S. regulars, and they contributed thousands of sailors to the war on the waters. They marched off as volunteers on foot, on horseback, and on gun limbers from every state that sent men to the front. It was a rare regiment indeed that went to the defense of the Union without counting at least one Irish American among its ranks. These men may have been everywhere, but their story is not. As a group, they were some of the poorest whites to enter northern service, with many of them being at best semiliterate. After the conflict, those who survived were reabsorbed into the working-class urban societies from whence most had come, their recollections left unwritten. With the passage of time they became hard to identify and even harder to trace in the historical record, factors that have combined to frustrate and confound efforts at broad analysis.

On the surface, these men's absence from the narrative of Irish Americans in the Civil War is not readily apparent. It is a deficiency that has been almost completely masked by the all-encompassing folds of the green flags borne by the Irish Brigade and other ethnic volunteer regiments. This was a process that began even as the Civil War still raged. As the most recognizable and visible manifestations of Irish commitment to the cause of Union, it was these ethnic regiments that people talked about, wrote about, championed, and celebrated. It was their deeds that were recounted through the pages of the Irish American press and which enriched the speeches of Irish American leaders. It was their units that bore the prefix "Irish" in the nation's most widely read publications, and it was their officers' renderings of the Irish in bivouac and battle that were the most sought after by Irish at home and abroad. As the war descended from gloried procession into bloody slog, maintaining the high visibility of these ethnic units took on even more urgent meaning. The apparent waning of Irish American support for the war from late 1862 onward, as manifested through their prominent visibility in draft opposition, their leading role in the July 1863 New York City draft riots, and their continued support for the Democratic Party and animosity toward the Emancipation Proclamation, saw them fending off increasingly vocal charges of disloyalty.[9] Calling attention toward the ongoing service and sacrifice of units such as the Irish Brigade was an important counter to such allegations. The ethnic regiments continued to perform that role even after 1865, when despite wartime service Irish Americans frequently faced widespread anti-immigrant nativism. The guns barely had time to cool before journalist and veteran David Power Conyngham published his hugely influential volume *The Irish Brigade and Its Campaigns* in 1867. Apart from wishing to remember those he had served beside, Conyngham was seeking to make a clear and unambiguous statement about Irish commitment to Union victory. Tellingly, he dedicated his book to those who "fell sustaining the cause of their adopted country" and to "the courage and fidelity of the Irish race."[10] Across the next four decades, histories of ethnic Irish regiments such as the 9th Massachusetts, 69th Pennsylvania, 116th Pennsylvania, and 9th Connecticut followed, as did a number of collections focusing on Thomas Francis Meagher and memoirs such as those of Irish Brigade chaplain Father William Corby.[11] As time passed and new waves of immigrants arrived from the Mediterranean and Eastern Europe, the highly visible commemoration and celebration of ethnic formations like the Irish Brigade and its veterans helped to confirm Irish America's pedigree in having contributed during the country's greatest struggle. Even fifty years on from the fighting, there remained an appetite for veterans of the Irish Brigade to share stories to represent their community's participation, recalling a time when the "men of Erin" had met their Confederate foe to the sound of "wild Irish 'Hurroos.'"[12] By the time the last American Civil War veterans finally passed from the stage, the sway that the Irish Brigade and the ethnic regiments held over both the popular memory and written record of the Union Irish was complete.

The privileged position held by the Irish Brigade and ethnic units in the memory and historiography of the Civil War is in large part entirely reasonable. They were, after all, a vitally important and intrinsic element of the story of Irish American participation in the conflict. Yet for all that, they were the minority Irish experience. Rather than dominating the entire story, they should be regarded as just one, albeit significant, component. Yet every major scholarly publication on the Irish in the Federal military has been left with little option but to place a dominant focus on these atypical and exceptional ethnic formations. The reason for this lies in source survival, or rather the lack of sources. Ordinary enlisted Irish Americans seem to have left little in the way of written records behind, an absence that presents the single greatest obstacle for those who wish to study them. Lawrence Frederick Kohl has characterized this absence as a handicap that afflicts all who work on Irish American service during the Civil War.[13] It is a deficit recognized and repeatedly underscored by all scholars of the Civil War Irish, who despite extensive research efforts have had to accept the restricted source base and develop alternative approaches built around what material is available.[14] As the most recognizable and visibly "Irish" units in the historical record, those approaches have necessarily centered around the ethnic regiments, together with references to the war in the contemporary Irish American press, in the printed speeches of Irish American community leaders, and in the memoirs and correspondence of ethnic Irish officers. Inherently top-down in nature, these sources have forced a reliance on the experience of ethnic regiments and officers to act as proxy representatives for the Irish American whole. This creates its own problems, as in the absence of alternatives that facilitate a more wide-ranging, bottom-up assessment of Irish American service, we can have little surety regarding just how representative they are. Take for example ethnic newspapers like the *New York Irish American* and *Boston Pilot,* both vitally important sources for 1860s Irish America. Their pages promoted Irish exceptionalism, consistently reproduced wartime letters relating to the Irish revolutionary Fenian Brotherhood, and carried speeches and statements from community leaders that linked different views on the Civil War to Irish interests.[15] Taken on their own, it is reasonable to infer from them that the causes of Ireland, Irish revolution, and Irish interests were dominant concerns for all Irish Americans. But without a wider source base to draw from, it is difficult to be sure of the extent to which Irish nationalist views expressed in such newspapers were deeply shared by all Irish in Federal uniform.[16] In the absence of details on the life priorities of the ordinary Irish recruit, it is challenging to determine the extent to which they read such papers because of a fervent ideological belief in their political message, or because of their more mundane coverage of local and Irish news. There is a lack of evidence to facilitate a critical examination of how many Irish American servicemen may have chosen to get their information from different, nonethnic publications. Indeed, there are scant indicators as to how many Irish Americans in the military could even read such newspapers in the first place. By pursuing the wider experience of all Irish American troops, both inside *and* outside the ethnic formations, *Green and Blue* sets out to test the understanding we have built upon the scaffolding of sources like the ethnic newspapers and ethnic regiments, and to explore the extent to which new evidence and new analyses support, challenge, or complicate our existing assumptions.

The current understanding of Irish American service has been developed by a small and dedicated cohort of Civil War historians who have devised distinctive and often highly innovative frameworks through which to approach the topic of Irish American service. Like many wider studies of the Civil War soldier, one of the primary objectives of this work has been to gain deeper insight into the ideological motivations and sense of identity of the Irish American Union volunteer, topics which remain the subject of considerable debate. The first to examine these issues in a modern context was William Burton. In his 1988 *Melting Pot Soldiers: The Union's Ethnic Regiments,* Burton argued that the Irish went to war "to support their friends and comrades and to preserve the Union." Stressing how similar they were to other Federal troops, he concluded that "the best-kept secret of the ethnic regiments is how truly American they were."[17] In her seminal 2006 book *The Harp and the Eagle: Irish American Volunteers and the Union Army, 1861–1865,* Susannah Ural disagreed. In what remains the most influential work on Irish Americans in U.S. service, Ural focused primarily on the Irish communities of New York, Philadelphia, and Boston and on ethnic units like the Irish Brigade. She discerned in them evidence for a dual loyalty to Ireland and America, a loyalty that increasingly favored Ireland as the Irish grew disillusioned with the conflict in the aftermath of the Emancipation Proclamation and the battlefield losses of 1862. Ural argued that as "a population largely comprised of recent immigrants, the need to see the war in terms of what it could provide them as Irishmen was greater than the need to see it in terms of their American identity."[18] Taking as his foil the question of citizenship, Christian Samito also focused primarily on the ethnic units in his 2009 *Becoming American Under Fire: Irish-Americans, African-Americans and the Politics of Citizenship During the Civil War Era.* In his assessment, the conflict was a transformative one for Irish

Americans, who he argued were increasingly viewing their ethnic culture from within an American context. He deemed them broadly loyal to the Union and the Constitution, and regarded their experience of the war as something that significantly reinforced their ties to American identity and aided their inclusion as citizens.[19] Ryan Keating turned his focus beyond the New York-Philadelphia-Boston heartlands for his 2017 *Shades of Green: Irish Regiments, American Soldiers, and Local Communities in the Civil War Era,* which focused on three ethnic regiments in Connecticut, Wisconsin, and Illinois. Keating's was also the first to incorporate a bottom-up analysis, combining traditional sources with assessment of military, pension, and census records.[20] His work highlighted the differences between distinct Irish groups in the northern states and identified the importance of local community and defense of the Union as motivators for enlistment. Keating also perceived dual allegiances among the Irish, but argued that their service solidified their relationship with their adopted country, seeing them emerge as American soldiers.[21] The latest monograph to tackle wider issues of Irish American service has come with Catherine Bateson's 2022 *Irish American Civil War Songs: Identity, Loyalty and Nationhood,* in which the wartime songs composed about Irish participation are examined for their meaning. Bateson sees in them an Irish American commitment to "fight, serve, and defend the American Union and the nation's ideals of freedom and liberty." In contrast to some of the other scholarship, she argues that a pattern of distinctly American identity existed before the conflict, rather than being something that developed as a result of it.[22]

The ideological emphasis many Irish Americans placed on themes such as preserving the Union is something that has emerged in my own work on www.irishamericancivilwar.com, a website dedicated to exploring the impact of the Civil War on Irish Americans.[23] As the years have passed, the research focus of the site has increasingly moved away from concentrated analysis of the ethnic units and toward a broader examination of Irish American service through the microanalysis of individuals and individual family groups. Scrutiny at this scale can forcefully demonstrate the power that the practical often held over the ideological when it came to life choices, and it complicates our understanding of who these people were and how they viewed themselves. Showcasing the potential of such analysis for investigations of Irish America informed my 2016 book *The Forgotten Irish: Irish Emigrant Experiences in America,* which examined the microhistory of thirty-six immigrant families.[24]

The primary resource that facilitated this work came in the form of pension applications by the widows and dependents of men who served during the American Civil War, held at the U.S. National Archives.[25] Known colloquially as the "Widows' Pensions," they have formed the primary focus of my research for well over a decade. Early on, it became apparent that a small but significant number of these files held that rarest of Irish American Civil War sources: wartime letters composed by enlisted men. The potential such letters held to transform our understanding of the Irish experience of the Civil War was immediately apparent. It prompted the decision to engage in a long-term project to search the available files and compile a "new" corpus of these writings, with the hope that it could one day contribute toward a broad-ranging analysis of Irish American service. *Green and Blue* is the result.

RECOVERING THE UNION IRISH

A central component of this book is analysis of the lives and correspondence of 395 Irish American soldiers and sailors drawn from across the full breadth of Union arms. They emerged through the systematic analysis of approximately 168,000 chronologically arranged pension files that were reviewed over an eight-year period. This number represents the digitized portion of the roughly 1.28 million case folders of the widows, dependent parents, siblings, and minor children of servicemen and veterans housed at the National Archives in Washington, D.C.[26] These men are the most fully representative group of Irish American servicemen ever gathered together for analysis. They saw service in the forces of twenty-two different states and districts, in more than 260 distinct units, and in every theater of war in which the United States was engaged. Almost 98 percent of them entered the military in the enlisted ranks. Among their number are representatives of the Irish Brigade and the ethnic regiments, but, reflecting the reality of Irish American wartime distribution, the majority are volunteers, substitutes, draftees, sailors, and regular soldiers who went to war beyond the green flags.

In total, 1,135 letters composed by or for these 395 Irish American servicemen were uncovered within the widows' and dependents' files. An additional 297 pieces of wartime correspondence associated with servicemen but not written by them were likewise identified. Largely notifications of illness, injury, or death, this latter grouping also included letters from wives and family.[27] These inclusions added a further 173 individuals to the body of men with associated letters, making for a total of 568 Irish American soldiers and sailors with identified associated wartime correspondence. This represents the most important corpus of ordinary Irish American wartime writing yet gathered together.[28]

Given the significance of these men and their correspondence, it is useful to explore precisely why their letters came to be contained within these pension files, and why the trove of contextualizing documentation that surrounds them is so important for elucidating Irish American service. The origin of the depositions can be traced back to 14 July 1862, when Congress passed a new act to provide for all men who were disabled by wounding or disease during their Civil War service. Sections 2–4 of that legislation made specific provision for the families of those who had died, with wording that proved critical in precipitating the subsequent submission of servicemen's correspondence as part of the pension application process. It stated that a soldier's or sailor's:

> widow, or, if there be no widow, his child or children under sixteen years of age, shall be entitled to receive the same pension as the husband or father would have been entitled to had he been totally disabled, to commence from the death of the husband or father, and to continue to the widow during her widowhood, or to the child or children until they severally attain to the age of sixteen years, and no longer . . . [if the serviceman] shall not leave a widow nor legitimate child, but has left or shall leave a mother who was dependent upon him for support, in whole or in part, the mother shall be entitled to receive the same pension . . . [if the serviceman] has not left or shall not leave a widow, nor legitimate child, nor mother, but has left or may leave an orphan sister or sisters, under sixteen years of age, who were dependent upon him for support, in whole or in part, such sister or sisters shall be entitled to receive the same pension.[29]

This 1862 act created a pension system that was expanded and modified in the decades that followed the Civil War, and on which hundreds of thousands of widows and dependents came to rely.[30] Unsurprisingly, the primary goal of all applicants was to prove to the Bureau of Pensions that they were entitled to pension payments. For widows, those efforts usually centered around authenticating their relationship with a serviceman, while for parents it tended to focus on demonstrating they had been financially supported by their son. Most turned first to affidavits to achieve these aims. These were usually supplied by the applicant and, if necessary, by a range of other individuals supporting the application. Those who provided these affidavits could include, among others, family members, friends, neighbors, acquaintances, employers, landlords, shopkeepers, physicians, and current/former servicemen. At the heart of each of these affidavits was the provision of evidence required by the Bureau, and they were often supplemented by other documents, such as official copies of marriage and baptism records, military papers, and medical appraisals. When an applicant struggled through other means to provide a piece of evidence, or simply wanted to reinforce their connection to a serviceman, they resorted to including original letters. Although these were often valuable to the families—and they sometimes requested that they be returned—once they had been submitted as part of an application they became official Federal records. Although this has ensured their survival, parting with them must have been a severe emotional wrench for many. This is one of the reasons that only a small percentage of files contain such correspondence—it tended to be a measure of last resort.

When correspondence was submitted, it was sometimes just a single letter. Other files contain an entire series that spans months or years of service. The letters were always included for a specific reason associated with the claim—for example, if a soldier mentioned sending money home to his parents, or if they proved a familial relationship (e.g., if the man had enlisted under an alias). This selection process by the family member is significant, as there was no censorship with respect to the remainder of a letter's content. The Pension Bureau was entirely uninterested in the sentiments expressed in a letter once it provided them with the specific facts they required to make a determination on an applicant's pension eligibility. Applicants could submit any letters they possessed that satisfied those narrow requirements.

The value of these wartime letters is exponentially enhanced by the array of documentation surrounding them in the files. This provides a vast amount of personal contextual information for each of the servicemen and their families, often spanning decades, and often allowing them to be traced both pre- and post-immigration. Each element serves as a building block for reconstructing some of the life experiences of these Irish Americans, revealing rare detail and providing unique insights into broader aspects of the immigrant experience. For example, dependent parents who needed to demonstrate that their son had financially supported them often described where he had lived, where he had worked, what he earned, and what he had spent his money on. Dependent mothers who could not rely on living husbands for support might outline to the Pension Bureau a history of violence or alcoholism that led to abandonment, or describe how their husband was broken down by age and a life of hard labor. Widows and dependents seeking to prove events in Ireland—be it a marriage or financial support—often revealed information on chain migration, step migration, maintained links across the Atlantic, and remittances. It is inclusions such as these that mark the pension files out as a unique and invaluable source of data for the Irish American experience, and which greatly heighten the already significant historical value of the wartime correspondence contained within them.

There can be no doubt that these assembled letters provide us with a remarkable opportunity to explore Irish American soldiers and sailors as never before, but it is worth recalling that their preservation came at significant cost. In the vast majority of instances, they survived the conflict only because the men who had them composed did not. That melancholy fact is a reminder of the conflict's impact on Irish America, and its often life-altering consequences for individual families, repercussions that linger as a constant backdrop to these men's words. For those interested in exploring their service and fate in more detail, short military biographies of each of the men featured in *Green and Blue* are supplied as an appendix.

The chapters that follow seek to build and expand on the existing scholarship to construct a more complete and representative view of Irish American service than has heretofore been possible, encompassing what Ryan Keating has termed the different "Shades of Green" found in Irish American communities across the North.[31] While the correspondence of the soldiers and sailors forms a major focus in a number of chapters, their primary employment is as a tool to examine the entirety of the Irish American experience in the Federal military. The wide-ranging perspective this book seeks to adopt provides both an opportunity and a necessity for the detailed foregrounding of the Irish experience of the conflict. This includes gaining deeper appreciation of who these men were, where they came from, and what societal and political influences played on them prior to their entry into service. It also requires a sweeping reappraisal of where they fought and how many of them did so, the answers to which hold fundamental import for assessing deeper questions regarding their service.

The book's first two chapters go in pursuit of an understanding of these origins, initially by examining the antebellum society that produced and shaped Irish American servicemen, and then through the first detailed modern analysis of Irish American numbers and distribution through the Union military. This portion of the book concludes by considering the contextual information gathered on the "new" correspondents, illustrating the degree to which they are representative of Irish America. The final three chapters are dedicated to giving the correspondents fuller voice. Each chapter explores several themes through a detailed assessment of the letters themselves, critically examining and analyzing the men's words with reference to existing scholarship on the Civil War Irish and Civil War soldiers studies. Specifically, they hone in on Irish American life and experience in uniform, the men's contemporary reputation and interactions on the issues of race and politics, and finally their sense of identity and personal motivations for service—so fundamental to understanding why hundreds of thousands of Irish Americans chose to risk their lives in order to preserve the American Union. Before exploring what these men did, said, and experienced during the Civil War, it is necessary to first consider where they came from and what influenced them in the years before the cannons commenced to roar.

1
The Union Irish on the Eve of War

Union sailor Denis Horgan fits the archetypal image of the Irish immigrant in Federal service. A recent arrival, he had landed at Manhattan's Castle Garden in the spring of 1857 following a seven-week journey from his native Cork, Ireland's most populous county. Though he had lost his father, Danny, at the height of the Great Famine, he and his fruit-seller mother, Mary, had toiled hard to make sure they were not among those at the very bottom of Irish society. As a boy in the early 1850s he had taken what work he could around their Shandon home, filling positions as a common laborer, a porter, and in the local stables. As a dutiful and responsible son, he had handed his earnings over to his mother each Saturday night to put toward the running of the household. Slowly, as he grew older and more experienced, Denis's weekly wages rose from a low of 2s 6d to a respectable 7s. This provided the cushion he needed to save for passage to America, and so he requested that his employer put a shilling a week aside for his transatlantic journey.[1]

Like many other Irish emigrants, Denis's status as a single passenger belied the commitments he maintained in Ireland. Upon his arrival in America he was expected to remit some of his earnings back to Cork and to gather the funds needed for his mother to join him. Neither was he traveling into the unknown. Once in New York, Denis wasted little time in writing to his uncle and grandmother, both residents of Boston. Having overspent on the voyage in an effort to supplement his meager on-board rations, Denis asked them to send "some help to take me to Boston please god I would Be grateful to you and not to let me starve in a strange land."[2] They duly obliged, and Denis Horgan set out for Massachusetts. Once there he tried his hand at laboring and as a teamster, but the work was too temporary. Eventually he headed for New Bedford, and new opportunities. Denis signed on to the crew of a whaler, a job that brought big risks, but potentially big rewards. In 1862, he was returning from his second trip aboard a fully laden vessel when disaster struck, and the ship went to the ocean floor along with her precious cargo. He survived to return to Boston, but was left penniless. On 23 May—the day after he came ashore—Denis Horgan presented himself at the Boston Naval Rendezvous and became a U.S. sailor.[3]

Denis Horgan's pre-service background in Ireland and the United States provides a contextual framework that is crucial in seeking to understand his decision to serve the Union. It illustrates in microcosm the necessity of examining the personal and societal environments of the men who would enlist during the American Civil War, and the background of the Irish communities that produced them. Just as they were shaped by their individual histories, they were also products of their societies, and of influences both within and without Irish America. On the eve of war, these Irish American men had a lot in common. Their cultural background, cohesive communities, and working-class status ensured that was the case. Most of them had originated from similar Irish backgrounds, shared the same faith, held a broadly comparable political outlook, and faced the same prejudices. As a result, they have largely been treated as a homogenous block. To be sure, all these factors played a vitally important role in forming their personalities, outlook, and behavior—but there was much more to them as individuals. Many who went on to Federal service had not even been born in Ireland—enough in itself to complicate perceptions of the "typical" Irish American. Even men of Irish nativity showed considerable divergence. Those who had immigrated before the Famine carried with them a different set of life experiences than those who arrived during and immediately after that great exodus. Likewise, those who landed in the midst of the conflict did not necessarily share the perspectives of those who had known life in the antebellum United States. The men who first arrived in America as children had grown up in markedly different environments than those who stepped ashore as adults, often just a handful of years behind them. They were the same, but they were different, too. All were Irish American, and all need to be included and considered in any analysis of Irish American service during the Civil War. Understanding their origins and their society is a vital prerequisite to engaging with their wartime experiences, as is forming a clearer concept of just who was "Irish American" in the 1860s United States.

IMMIGRATION AND DEMOGRAPHICS

The popular image of the Irish who fought in the American Civil War is one of adult men who immigrated to the United States as a direct consequence of the Great Famine. However, there were also thousands in uniform whose American origin story began with earlier nineteenth-century mass migration from Ireland. That transatlantic movement had accelerated exponentially in the three decades from 1815 to 1845, when between 800,000 and 1,000,000 Irish set out across the Atlantic, almost double the number who had undertaken the same journey over the preceding two centuries.[4] Nevertheless, there can be no doubt that it was the exodus instigated by the Great Hunger of 1845–1852 that contributed most overwhelmingly to the number of Irish Americans who would eventually take up arms. In a movement unparalleled in Irish history, between 1845 and 1855 almost 1.5 million Irish left for the United States alone, with more than 2 million finding a new life overseas—almost a quarter of the island's pre-Famine population.[5] As many as a third of all these Famine-era emigrants were native Irish speakers; it would later be claimed that some members of the Irish Brigade "spoke nothing but Gaelic" at the time they enlisted.[6] The transformative impact of the Famine on Ireland has been aptly characterized by Kerby Miller as a time when "an entire generation virtually disappeared from the land . . . only one out of three Irishmen born about 1831 died at home of old age—in Munster only one out of four."[7] The great majority of these Famine-era emigrants held the United States as their preferred destination. Every year between 1847 and 1854 over 100,000 Irish flooded into American ports, with still more making their way to what they hoped would prove the Promised Land via Canada.[8]

Though the number of Irish arrivals abated somewhat from 1855 onward, the figures remained impressive. Between 1856 and 1860 almost 250,000 more Irish landed in the United States, an annual average of nearly 50,000.[9] Adverse events in America did have a demonstrable impact on Irish immigration. For example, the financial panic of 1857 saw Irish numbers drop to 31,500 in 1858, while the coming of the American Civil War saw the 1861–1862 average fall to less than 31,000.[10] However, immigration surged again in 1863–1864. In those years, poor economic conditions in Ireland coincided with strong monetary inducements to serve the U.S. war economy and military, with the result that more than 94,000 Irish arrived in each of those years.[11]

Irish emigration in the years prior to the Famine was dominated by single men, most often drawn from the ranks of groups such as the middling farmers (ten to thirty acres), smallholders (two to nine acres), and artisans. During the 1830s, these male emigrants outnumbered females by a factor of two to one.[12] The coming of the Famine significantly reduced the already precarious financial condition of those crossing the Atlantic, but the very poorest still struggled to escape the catastrophic conditions in Ireland—or could make it only as far as Britain. Nevertheless, the Irish who washed up on America's shores during the Famine were significantly worse off both in terms of finances and skills than those who had gone before.[13] The cataclysm also impacted the demographics of those who were choosing to leave Ireland, with an increase in the number of female emigrants and family groups. The typical male immigrant from this period was likely to identify as a laborer and be aged between twenty and forty-five.[14] Many—particularly those who arrived as children, teenagers, and young adults—would be of prime military age by the coming of the American Civil War.

Although the majority of Irish immigrants were from rural backgrounds, once they arrived in the United States they congregated in towns and cities, becoming, in the analysis of David Doyle, "urban pioneers."[15] By 1860 almost 44 percent of all Irish-born immigrants lived in major cities with populations in excess of 20,000, and even those living in rural counties were most commonly there to work in industries such as mining and milling.[16]

By 1861, largely urban Irish communities of various sizes had established themselves across the states from which the majority of Union forces would be drawn, ensuring the heavy concentration of Irish in units raised among metropolitan populations. Some of the communities that produced them had started to take shape even before the Famine migration, particularly in cities like New York, where areas such as the Sixth Ward had begun to develop an Irish character by the 1820s.[17] However, it was the influx after 1845 that had the most impact. By 1860, many northern cities accommodated colossal numbers of Irish-born immigrants; Boston in excess of 45,000, Brooklyn (a separate city from New York in this period) in excess of 56,000, Philadelphia in excess of 95,000.[18] Even more telling were the proportionate figures. In many cities, one in every five of the total populace—in some, one in every four—were Irish-born. By far the most significant Irish enclave in the United States at the outbreak of the American Civil War was New York City. The Manhattan

TABLE 1. American Cities with Populations of More Than 10,000 Irish-Born in 1860, Ordered by Size of Irish-Born Populace

City	*State*	*No. Irish-Born*	*Total Population*	*% City Foreign-Born*	*% City Irish-Born*
New York	New York	203,740	805,651	47.62	25.29
Philadelphia	Pennsylvania	95,548	585,529	28.93	16.32
Brooklyn	New York	56,710	266,661	39.22	21.27
Boston	Massachusetts	45,991	177,812	35.88	25.86
St. Louis	Missouri	29,926	160,773	59.76	18.61
New Orleans	Louisiana	24,398	168,675	38.31	14.46
Chicago	Illinois	19,889	109,260	49.99	18.20
Cincinnati	Ohio	19,375	161,044	45.71	12.03
Baltimore	Maryland	15,536	212,418	24.71	7.31
Albany	New York	14,780	62,367	34.66	23.70
Newark	New Jersey	11,167	71,914	37.02	15.53

Source: Adapted from statistics supplied in Kennedy, Population of the United States in 1860, xxxi–xxxii.

metropolis was home to more than 200,000 Irish-born in 1860; 25 percent of the city's total population and more than double the size of the next largest Irish population in Philadelphia.[19] Indeed, the Irish-born of New York City accounted for 13 percent of all Irish immigrants in the United States.[20] When considered in conjunction with the Irish populations of the city of Brooklyn and the adjacent communities in New Jersey, the dominance of the New York region as the heartland of 1860s Irish America is apparent. When war came, it was this area that sent far and away the most Irish Americans to the front.

Although the bulk of the Irish made their homes in the industrialized cities of the North Atlantic seaboard, there were also sizable numbers to be found in the major population hubs of the Midwest, particularly St. Louis, Chicago, and Cincinnati, all of which would prove profitable future recruitment centers for Irish troops. By 1850 there were in the region of 150,000 Irish-born living in the Midwest, again mainly in major urban centers.[21] Some Irish did break free from these built-up areas to make their homes in rural

America, but even here the Atlantic seaboard dominated, with the most significant Irish rural populations located around New York, New Jersey, and Massachusetts.[22]

Within their urban communities the Irish had a particular tendency to congregate in specific wards, serving to further enhance the Irish character of many districts within northern cities but also complicating their integration into the wider United States. These Irish American communities were extremely cohesive, and ethnic cohesion was a feature that those who came from them brought into the military. Within their communities, the men had usually married by their late twenties, overwhelmingly choosing to do so with fellow Irish immigrants.[23] Younger men tended to leave the family home between the ages of nineteen and twenty-five, but even then they remained firmly embedded within the local community fabric. They usually became boarders in the homes of other Irish families, a pattern of "ethnic exclusivity" that has been identified in numerous Irish American communities and which is repeatedly seen among large numbers of Irish servicemen.[24]

The Irish in the United States tended to live in large numbers together, but this does not mean that they necessarily formed a single undifferentiated mass. Those from different parts of Ireland often gravitated toward different cities. For example, Philadelphia proved attractive for many northeastern and northwestern Ulster immigrants, who were especially prominent among wartime volunteers from that city, while 20 percent of the entire populations of Meath and Cavan at the time of the Famine made for New York.[25] The regional and community identities and affiliations that immigrants carried with them to America could also endure within major Irish enclaves. For example, in Manhattan's Five Points district of the Sixth Ward in 1860, 84 percent of Kerry immigrants confined themselves to just two of the neighborhood's twenty blocks.[26] Similarly, many Cork people elected to make their homes together in New York City's Seventh Ward. Established by the late 1830s, the area would become known as the "Cork Ward."[27] Interestingly, when it came time to enlist, these transplanted regional ties did not necessarily cause men to serve together in the same units, but they did greatly influence the sense of identity, place, and responsibility they carried through their service. The existence of such familial and regional ties in Irish American communities was an almost inevitable consequence of the process of chain migration, which engendered both constant contact with—and continuous new arrivals from—

the "Old Country."[28] That this occurred is evidenced by the scale of financial remittances to Ireland, much of it to enable passage to America. Between 1850 and 1855 alone, an average of more than £1.2 million (roughly $6 million) was being sent back across the Atlantic each year.[29] Continuing the process of chain migration and financial remittances would remain central to the lives of many Irish Americans even after they had gone off to war.

The urban concentration points of Irish communities were often also the poorest areas, dominated by slums—locations such as the Five Points in New York City, Moyamensing in Philadelphia, and the North End and Fort Hill in Boston.[30] Life for the Irish poor in these districts was unquestionably tough. They were overrepresented in the criminal justice system, apparently suffered from illness more frequently, and were susceptible to higher mortality rates than other groups.[31] The inevitable result of this reality was that Irish immigrants became intrinsically linked in the minds of many native-born white Americans with poverty and slums, a stigma that remained attached to them even after they entered the military.

The economic condition of Irish America and the economic opportunity the Civil War presented is an oft-quoted characteristic of Irish American service, but the want of sufficient detail on the financial realities of life for enlisted men has led to its neglect in favor of concentrated discussion on ideological aspects of Irish wartime participation. What sources such as the pension files make plain is that a thorough understanding of these men's economic background and circumstance is essential to considerations of what shaped them and the decisions they made between 1861 and 1865. Throughout, the precarity of working-class Irish American existence looms large. Most of the men who went off to the military did so from rented homes, with relatively few enjoying the security of property ownership. Immigrant Irish men in general were less likely to own property than native-born whites, a symptom of their more unstable occupational profile.[32] Although the degree to which they occupied unskilled positions is sometimes overstated, as a workforce the Irish had the most limited prospects for upward mobility of any immigrant group.[33] By the time of the 1855 census in New York City, some 27,000 Irish-born men were employed as skilled and semiskilled artisans—51 percent of the Irish-born male workforce.[34] Still, laboring was the primary occupation for most. Handlin's analysis of the Boston Irish in 1850 found that 48 percent of the Boston Irish working population were laborers.[35] Laboring also dominated in 1860 Philadelphia, with weaving and tailoring the next most common Irish-born male pursuits.[36] There were some signs of the intergenerational upward mobility that many Irish American families aspired toward. In 1855 Buffalo, Irish-born men in their twenties were considerably less likely to be laborers than older pre-Famine immigrants.[37] Nonetheless, as an overwhelmingly urban working-class population, progress was often slow and rarely linear.[38] The forms of employment the Irish could secure were often short-term and precarious, while the areas of the economy they operated within were particularly vulnerable during financial downturns. Significantly, as the American Civil War loomed, just such downturns arrived—first in 1857, when some 100,000 people lost their jobs in New York City and Brooklyn, and again in 1860–1861.[39] Downturns such as these went on to have weighty influence on not only why some men enlisted, but also where they did so.

ANTEBELLUM IRISH AMERICAN SOCIETY

The migrant, economic, and community backgrounds of the men who would become the Union Irish provide essential context with which to consider their service. So, too, do some of the major societal and political issues that concerned Irish Americans on the precipice of the Civil War. A brief foregrounding of their immediate antebellum positions, particularly surrounding religion, politics, nativism, and race, sets the scene for later consideration of what they said and did while wearing the uniform of the United States.

The exponential growth of the Irish presence in the antebellum United States produced profound changes and profound challenges for Irish and native alike. These were nowhere more noticeable than in the spheres of religion, politics, and race. For the Catholic Church, the influx of Famine-era migrants irrevocably altered both its size and makeup. Across the United States as a whole, the Catholic population soared from 663,000 in 1840 to 3,103,000 in 1860, an increase driven by Irish (and German) immigration.[40] Unsurprisingly, the waves of Catholic immigrants in the late 1840s and 1850s also had the consequence of irrevocably intertwining Irish American identity with Catholicism, largely at the expense of Irish American Protestants, a factor that contributed toward the continued divergence of the two groups.[41]

Significantly for future soldiers and sailors, this period also bore witness to a sustained effort on the part of the Catholic Church in Ireland and America to improve the somewhat lackluster devotional and sacramental performance of their Irish flock. A "devotional revolution" embarked upon by the Church on both sides of the Atlantic accelerated as a result of the Famine, transforming Irish Catholic worship and ensuring that practicing Catholicism became a core element of "Irish" identity.[42] As part of this, the Church particularly concentrated on increasing rates of confession and communion (which had usually only been focused on during Easter in pre-Famine Ireland), on promoting devotions such as the rosary, and on the use of devotional aids like scapulars, catechisms, and Agnus Dei.[43] These efforts proved extremely successful; by 1861 it had become imprinted to such a degree that thousands of young Irish American men would regard devotions as fundamental to their religious engagement.[44]

The numbers of Irish immigrants arriving on American shores, combined with their relative poverty and the fact that the vast majority were Catholic, provoked an almost inevitable nativist reaction.[45] Though anti-Irish sentiment had been prevalent prior to the Famine migration—Irish Catholics had been attacked in Philadelphia, Richmond, and Charleston in 1844 and 1845 for example—the late 1840s and early 1850s saw nativism intensify.[46] Many native-born white Americans were concerned that these new migrants would change the face of the United States, viewing the Catholic religion and the competing allegiance its followers owed to the pope in Rome as a threat to their vision of the American Republic. So it was that only a few years prior to the outbreak of the Civil War Irish immigrants were forced to face their greatest nativist threat. It came in the form of the political movement commonly referred to as the Know Nothing Party, or the American Party. Emerging in the wake of the 1854 Kansas-Nebraska Act, it attracted members who tended to hold anti-slavery sentiments but were also anti-immigrant and, particularly in the northern states, strongly anti-Catholic.[47] It was no coincidence that among their early political successes were the capture of the mayoralties of Boston, Philadelphia, and Chicago, all cities with sizable Irish populations.[48] Though their period in the American spotlight was brief and their political power had waned irretrievably by 1860, nativist sentiment was still a major fact of life for Irish Catholic immigrants during the American Civil War. By the late 1850s, many nativists had moved their support to the new Republican Party, contributing toward the Irish distrust of those who supported that political organization. Despite efforts by some Republicans to distance themselves from more extreme nativist views in advance of the 1860 election, it was a distrust that extended into the administration of the new president, Abraham Lincoln.[49]

The Irish were far from passive in the face of the opposition they faced, and indeed it was their growing political influence that caused some of the greatest concern to nativists. The bulk of the Catholic Irish population in the United States were faithful adherents to the Democratic Party, a political affiliation that the majority of enlisted men carried to the war. The Whigs—and later the Republicans—were seen by many Irish Americans as promoting a culturally Protestant agenda, as being suspicious of immigrants, and of seeking to place strictures and controls on activities such as school education and alcohol consumption.[50] In contrast, the Democrats had come to recognize the potential voting power of groups like the Irish and actively pursued their support. In the years prior to the Civil War, they cultivated the Irish vote in cities like New York by appealing to them on issues such as culture, class, and civil liberties, and particularly through the positions they ultimately adopted on issues important to the Irish working class.[51] The political machine that the Irish began constructing in the antebellum period was fundamentally linked to the fabric of the communities they had built. At its heart were locations such as saloons and grocery shops, which served as vital political gathering points, while employment within fire companies or in police departments often served as initial staging posts for the politically ambitious.[52] As Hasia Diner points out, this loyalty to the Democrats did not mean that the Irish were entirely homogenous within the party, and they often aligned themselves to different factions.[53] In some instances this factionalization was carried into the Civil War. An example of this can be seen in the 40th "Mozart" and 42nd "Tammany" New York Infantry Regiments—both of which proved highly attractive to Irish Americans—which were affiliated with the rival Mozart Hall and Tammany Hall organizations.

Another characteristic of Catholic, Democratic Irish America was the views many within the community held on the issue of slavery and toward African Americans. There has been a significant amount of work carried out in the United States seeking to ascertain why Irish Americans in the North held such strongly anti-Black views. The most influential thesis has been put forward by Noel Ignatiev, who argued it was a response to anti-Irish racial discrimination, which caused Irish immigrants to feel a need to prove themselves by "becoming white" at the expense of African Americans.[54] This assertion that the Irish were responding to not being considered racially white has increasingly been recognized as problematical, and has been challenged.[55] For other scholars, such as David Roediger, the rise of intense racism among Irish Americans should be regarded in more practical terms, as an issue that was primarily inflamed by circumstance and perceived economic threats.[56] Chapter 4 will explore this issue in detail, demonstrating how analysis of enlisted Irish in the wartime military adds much fresh insight, particularly with respect to these Irish American servicemen's unshakable belief in their own white supremacy.

Like the political party to which they adhered, Irish Americans were solidly anti-abolition. Many Irish Americans viewed emancipationists as anti-Catholic (and by extension anti-Irish), felt they were more concerned with the welfare of the slaves than with the appalling conditions of poor urban whites, and furthermore considered them willing to risk the future of the United States in pursuit of their radical agendas.[57] The Irish American political position was supported by the Catholic Church in the northern states, which opposed abolitionism. Though the Church preached of the evils of abusing slaves and of the slave trade itself, they defended the institution as legitimate, particularly as they judged enslaved African Americans to be significantly better off than those who remained free in Africa.[58] Irish Americans, many recently arrived from a country where they had enjoyed few rights, were also fervent believers in the sanctity of the American Constitution, which had provided them with the freedoms they enjoyed in the United States. Viewing that document as sacrosanct and intrinsic to the Republic, they passionately opposed abolitionists, who sought to challenge the Constitution's enshrinement of slavery.[59] At a more individual and practical level, Irish Americans undoubtedly saw African Americans as a labor threat, something that caused considerable animosity. Where perception became reality—such as when Black workers were brought in to replace striking white stevedores in New York in 1855—violence soon followed.[60] For working-class Irish Americans, the particularly virulent views many held toward African Americans was something many ultimately carried with them into the Union military.

DEFINING THE IRISH AMERICAN SERVICEMAN

Men like Denis Horgan, whose story was told at the beginning of this chapter, have come to be regarded as the archetypal "Irish American" Civil War serviceman. A native of Ireland, he was both a recent immigrant and a Catholic, with economic imperatives that may have influenced his decision to enlist and seemingly scant reason to have an emotional connection to his new American home. To be sure, there were many who had very similar backgrounds to that of Denis Horgan—but there were many more who did not. As Catherine Bateson has noted, scholars of the Civil War have traditionally struggled to define just what constituted an "Irish American," raising questions as to precisely which "Irish Americans" are actually being assessed.[61] Before any broader discussion of Irish Americans in uniform can usefully be pursued, we must look beyond the archetypal Irish-born, Catholic, recently arrived adult immigrant, and go in search of a more complicated and nuanced impression of what constituted an Irish American in 1861.

The most obvious deviation from the stereotypical Irish servicemen comes in the form of the thousands of Protestant Irish who fought for the Union. The overpowering dominance of Irish Catholic immigration during the Famine era has served to mask the story of Irish American Protestants during the same period. These men came from all over Ireland, but those from Ulster were by far the most numerous. Although Ulster Protestant immigration into the United States has traditionally been associated with the eighteenth century, Patrick Fitzgerald has demonstrated that the outflow of Protestants to America in the nineteenth century was many times greater in terms of real numbers.[62] Indeed, by the outbreak of the American Civil War there were more first- and second-generation Irish Protestants living in the United States than at any previous period in the nation's history, and large numbers of them answered Abraham Lincoln's call.

It is the exclusion of the second-generation Irish, be they Protestant or Catholic, that has proved the most problematic with regard to defining Civil War Irish America, and by extension Irish American wartime service.[63] Civil War scholarship has customarily employed nativity to delineate Irish American participation, particularly when endeavoring to assess the scale of the Irish community's military contribution. Somewhat paradoxically, the lack of source material has compelled some of the same scholars to include non-Irish-born men when seeking out representative voices from the Irish community.[64] The reality is that within the context of wartime Irish America, nativity is of extremely limited utility as a measure of ethnicity. It is rendered so by the practicalities of the Irish emigration experience and the demonstrable intergenerational ethnic cohesiveness of Irish migrant communities. It is also one of the most striking aspects of the Civil War widows' and dependents' pension files, where time and again applications relating to non-Irish-born ethnic soldiers and sailors overflow with evidence of their place within their Irish American community.

By 1860, the ethnic Irish community extended significantly beyond the 1.6 million people of Irish nativity recorded on the census.[65] Tens of thousands of young men born into the tight-knit Irish communities of the United States in the 1830s and 1840s undoubtedly regarded themselves as distinctly Irish American. They were further augmented by thousands more who had been born to Irish immigrant parents and into Irish communities in Britain and Canada. These latter cohort were products of the Irish tendency to step-migrate, with family groups regularly spending months, years, or even decades in another country prior to proceeding on to the United States.[66] The scale of the antebellum Irish community in Britain was captured by the census, which recorded 415,000 Irish-born in 1841, a figure that rose to 806,000 by 1861.[67] In Scotland alone, Irish-born individuals accounted for 4.8 percent of the population in 1841 and 7.2 percent by 1851.[68] As a result, there is no doubt that a considerable proportion of the 585,973 English-, Scots-, and Welsh-born enumerated on the 1860 Federal census were ethnically Irish.[69] The ghostly traces of the contribution Britain's Irish communities made toward Union manpower are observable in postwar American military pensions that were claimed in England and Scotland, a significant number of which were being paid to Irish families.[70] Precisely the same holds true for Canada. Aside from those who had step-migrated through or permanently settled in the Canadian provinces, many Irish Americans in states such as Maine and Michigan had family on both sides of the border, and regularly moved back and forth between the two countries. This ensured that many of the 249,970 individuals of Canadian birth making their homes in the United States by 1860 were also ethnically Irish, as were still more of those who crossed over the border during the war.[71] This has been recognized by Donald Akenson, who argues that a significant proportion of those whom we term "Irish American" at this period had come from Canada, and were of Canadian nativity.[72] By 1861, the scale of this largely invisible block of American-, British-, and Canadian-born Irish had become highly significant. It has been postulated that they may have added as much as 50 percent to the ethnic Irish population of America's largest cities.[73]

While they regularly shared home communities and other societal traits, as individuals the Irish Americans who went off to fight were a surprisingly varied lot. Among them were the thirty-something American-born sons of pre-Famine immigrants, and teenagers who had spent their earliest years among the Irish of England or Canada. There were Irish-born boys who had grown to men in the United States, and new immigrants who had reached their majority in the fields and country lanes of Ireland. When they eventually went to war, the scale and breadth of their service was every bit as diverse as their individual stories.

2

In Search of the Irish American Serviceman, 1861–1865

The decades-long road to war and the clashes over slavery that led to it were punctuated by a number of bloody signposts, none more dramatic than John Brown's effort to incite a slave rebellion at Harper's Ferry, Virginia, in October 1859. Encapsulating the majority Irish opinion, New York City's ethnic weekly the *Irish American* described Brown as a "fanatic" and "blood-stained bandit" whose radical abolitionist views were "antagonistic to the very existence of the Republic."[1] Brown's efforts at Harper's Ferry reached their denouement when a Marine detachment—commanded by a certain Colonel Robert E. Lee—crashed through the doors of the engine house, where the raiders had barricaded themselves. Shots rang out as the Marines entered the building, and Irish immigrant soldier Luke Quinn crumpled to the ground, mortally wounded. Luke Quinn would be the first of tens of thousands of Irish Americans to lose their lives in a U.S. uniform in the years to come.[2]

Less than two years after Harper's Ferry, Confederate artillery opened the American Civil War by firing on the U.S. garrison in Fort Sumter, one of the defensive fortifications of Charleston Harbor, South Carolina. The bombardment began on 12 April 1861 and forced the surrender of Sumter the following day, apparently bringing to a relatively bloodless conclusion an action that had profound repercussions. On 14 April, Private Daniel Hough from Co. Tipperary was working one of the fort's guns as the departing garrison fired a one hundred-gun salute in honor of the Stars and Stripes. As he rammed home a cartridge, an errant spark ignited the charge, causing a premature explosion that ripped through him, his gun, and the remainder of the gun crew. Hough was one of six men caught in the blast, and the first of two to die from their injuries. He and his comrade—Skibbereen native Edward Gallway—gained the unwanted distinction of becoming the first official U.S. fatalities of the American Civil War. Of the six men who were wounded, only one had been born in America. All the rest, including Hough and Gallway, were Irish.[3] The origins of those who died at Fort Sumter did not escape the attention of those still in Ireland, generating foreboding at the potential bloodletting to come. In what proved a prescient prediction, one Irish newspaper warned that the impending conflict "threatened as much sorrow, widowhood and affliction to the home of Ireland, as of America itself," foretelling that it would witness "the lives of her exiled children . . . offered in thousands."[4]

There is no doubt that thousands of Irish immigrants lost their lives fighting for the United States during the American Civil War. But just how many of these men were there, and where did they serve? Notwithstanding the excellent existing scholarship on the Irish in the American Civil War, the concentration of focus on the ethnic regiments has meant that these are questions that have not yet been addressed in any comprehensive way. As a result, there has been a significant underappreciation of the true scale of Irish American service, resulting in the erroneous assessment that they were proportionately underrepresented in the U.S. military. This in turn has had major ramifications for how the Irish contribution and commitment to the conflict has been perceived.

IRISH SERVICE: DISTRIBUTION AND FREQUENCY

One of the favored places Irish Americans went to war was in the ranks of the regulars. In April 1861, the Federal garrison at Fort Sumter had contained eighty-six soldiers. Of them, at least thirty-eight had been born in Ireland, accounting for almost 44 percent of the total.[5] In contrast, just twenty-three had been born in the United States. This was a pattern replicated across the regular army. Of the slightly more than 14,500 professionals on the rolls in January 1861, almost 37 percent were Irish-born.[6] When ethnic men not born in Ireland are considered, it may be that closer to 50 percent of the U.S. Army was Irish American. The Irish dominated the prewar regulars because it was a highly unattractive form of employment, and as a result it relied on those drawn from the poorer and less-skilled strata of American society, particularly immigrants. Three out of every five of these regular Irish soldiers enlisted from the Mid-Atlantic states—a third of them from New York alone—mirroring the patterns of Irish urban settlement in the United States. The scale of the Irish presence in the regulars was guaranteed by the army's concentration on the urban centers where they lived for its recruitment efforts.[7] The practice of using the army as an economic refuge was something Irish immigrants had brought with them to America. Back in Ireland, the early nineteenth century had witnessed the development of a service tradition that by 1830 saw more Irishmen than English serving in the British Army.[8] This trend continued despite the Famine migration and resultant falloff in population; the Irish proportion of the British military remained over 30 percent in 1868.[9] In America, the U.S. regulars proved a continuing attraction for the Irish through the period of the Civil War, as the professional branch of the Union military sought to expand to meet the Confederate threat. During the course of the conflict some 50,000 new recruits were taken into the regulars, and of them more than 20 percent have been estimated as Irish-born; again, significantly more would have been Irish American.[10]

As is discussed in further detail below, none of these regulars are included in the standard estimate of Irish American service. This is despite the fact that, in practical terms, it was frequently the case that regular units were among the most "Irish" to take to the battlefields of the American Civil War. The professionals who fought in the vicinity of Gettysburg's Wheatfield on 2 July 1863 serve to illustrate the point. While the actions of the Irish Brigade understandably dominate memory of the Irish American contribution to the fighting in that sector on the battle's second day, it is almost certain that more Irish Americans perished in Colonel Sidney Burbank's 2nd Brigade, Second Division of the V Corps. The Irish Brigade went into the Wheatfield with just over 530 men, thirty-two of whom were killed or mortally wounded. Burbank's regulars entered the fight with a little over 900 men, losing 134 to mortal wounds. Analysis indicates that a minimum of thirty-two were Irish natives, and a number of others were certainly Irish American. Given that the Irish American character of Burbank's force was unlikely to have exceeded 50 percent, the regulars' losses in the Wheatfield sector inflicted a greater real and proportionate loss on Irish America than those of the Irish Brigade.[11] The great majority of Irish American casualties in the four years of war were "hidden" in units such as these. They may not have had the same impact on politics, popular perception, or memory as those sustained in ethnic regiments, but they brought very real suffering into the Irish American communities forced to endure them. The cumulative negative impact such widespread, sustained, and repeated losses had on ethnically cohesive and tight-knit populations should not be underestimated.

While Irish American regulars may have been the first to taste action during the Civil War, they were followed closely by another branch of service that proved particularly attractive to Irish Americans: the navy. Irish American sailors were prominent among the relief vessels that witnessed the firing on Fort Sumter on 12 April 1861.[12] Between 1861 and 1865, more than 118,000 men enlisted in the Union naval service, some 20 percent of whom are estimated to have been Irish-born.[13] As with the regulars, these men have been excluded from standard estimates of how many Irish Americans served during the war. The navy had many parallels with the regulars. It proved popular with the Irish working class, especially those who found employment difficult to come by; and as with the regulars, foreigners were overrepresented among its prewar ranks.[14] The navy also offered a distinct advantage over service in the army: it was perceived as less arduous and markedly safer. With the advent of the draft later in the war, naval enlistment offered an opportunity to escape forced service on the battlefield.[15] The navy also dangled the prospect of financial reward. Aside from the monthly pay, the navy offered the potential of a share in prize money realized from captured vessels. Perhaps even more significantly, the service had a policy of providing salary advances of between two and three months' pay to the often cash-strapped new recruits.[16]

When war came in 1861, among the first to answer the call to defend the Union were those who had served in prewar militia units. By far the most famous Irish American example was the 69th New York State Militia, which had achieved notoriety in 1860 when its colonel, Michael Corcoran, had refused to parade them on the occasion of the visit of the prince of Wales. Although they initially took the field for ninety days' service in 1861, they also saw hard fighting later in the war as part of Corcoran's Irish Legion.[17] A number of other antebellum militia organizations formed the nucleus for ethnic volunteer companies and regiments, such as Boston's Columbian Artillery, whose membership was at the core of what became the 9th Massachusetts Volunteers. Disbanded during the nativist purge of foreign militia companies in 1855, the Columbians survived by reorganizing as a civic organization.[18] Irish militia companies answered the call across the North. In Pennsylvania, patriotically named antebellum groups such as the Meagher Guards, the Hibernia

Greens, the Shields Guards, and the Emmett Guards came together to form companies in the 24th Pennsylvania Volunteers, the three-month antecedent of the Irish 69th Pennsylvania Volunteers.[19]

The great bulk of Irish American service during the Civil War was undertaken in the ranks of the state volunteers. The distribution of Irish-born volunteers—and by extension Irish American volunteers—largely conformed to their prewar distribution across the northern states (see table 2). Nowhere could rival New York for its distinctly Irish American character. Whenever a regiment raised in an urban part of that state suffered on the battlefield, it was usually a bad day for New York's Irish communities. These concentrations of Irish American servicemen in the Mid-Atlantic and New England states also had a knock-on impact on where most of them fought their war. Irish Americans were significantly more concentrated in the forces that operated in the Eastern Theater, such as the Army of the Potomac, than they were in the armies of the West.

Understandably, the story of Irish American service during the Civil War has been overwhelmingly focused on the activities of these volunteers, and most particularly on the two- and three-year volunteer regiments that adopted an ethnic Irish character. The data suggests that Irish-born participation may not always have been uniform across different states. An example of this is Massachusetts, where the Irish-born represented over 15 percent of the white population but apparently furnished less than 10 percent of white volunteers.[20] It is tempting to suggest that the depressed numbers were influenced by local Irish disenchantment following the hardships experienced during the Know Nothing rise of the 1850s. However, it is perhaps more likely a result of difficulties with nativity data, anti-Irish bias in the compilation of the figures, and/or the fact that a considerable number of early war Irish volunteers from Massachusetts served in units from outside of the state, most particularly in New York. Conversely, while the Irish-born accounted for just below 4 percent of New Hampshire's population in 1860, they contributed almost 10 percent of that state's white volunteers, likely a consequence of the financial inducements on offer to those willing to serve in the state's units during the later war years. But by far the most significant figure is that for New York, given that it was the state that by some distance furnished the most Irish-born men for the war effort. The figures suggest that, despite incidents such as the New York City draft riots, the Irish were disproportionately represented among state troops,

TABLE 2. U.S. Sanitary Commission Figures for Volunteers as a Proportion of the Irish-Born Population in 1860, Organized by Size of Irish Population

State	*Irish Pop. (1860)*	*White State Pop. (1860)*	*Irish as % White State Pop.*	*No. Irish Vols. (USSC)*	*No. White State Vols. (USSC)*	*Irish as % White State Vols.*
New York	498,072	3,831,590	13	51,206	337,800	15.16
Pennsylvania	201,939	2,849,259	7.09	17,418	271,500	6.42
Massachusetts	185,434	1,221,432	15.18	10,007	105,500	9.49
Illinois	87,573	1,704,291	5.14	12,041	216,900	5.55
Connecticut and Rhode Island	80,730	622,153	12.98	7,657	54,900	13.95
Ohio	76,826	2,302,808	3.34	8,129	259,900	3.13
New Jersey	62,006	646,699	9.59	8,880	5,9300	14.97
Wisconsin	49,961	773,693	6.46	3,621	7,9500	4.56
Missouri	43,464	1,063,489	4.09	4,362	85,400	5.11
Michigan	30,049	736,142	4.08	3,278	72,000	4.55
Iowa	28,072	673,779	4.17	1,436	56,600	2.54
Maryland	24,872	515,918	4.82	1,400	27,900	5.02
Indiana	24,495	1,338,710	1.83	3,472	156,400	2.22
Kentucky	22,249	919,484	2.42	1,303	43,100	3.02
Maine	15,290	626,947	2.44	1,971	54,800	3.60
Vermont	13,480	314,369	4.29	1,289	26,800	4.81
Minnesota	12,831	169,395	7.58	1,140	20,000	5.70
New Hampshire	12,737	325,579	3.91	2,699	27,800	9.71
District of Columbia	7,258	60,763	11.95	698	12,000	5.82
Delaware	5,832	90,589	6.44	582	10,000	5.82
Kansas	3,888	106,390	3.66	1,082	16,800	6.44

Note: For Connecticut and Rhode Island, the Sanitary Commission report presented the totals for these two states as a combined figure.

Source: The table is an amalgam of data from the U.S. Sanitary Commission and the nativity statistics from the 1860 Federal census. In the Sanitary Commission report, its author, Benjamin Apthorp Gould, went to some length to explain the significant obstacles he faced in attempting to establish nativity, due to the substantial gaps in the available information, which forced him to extrapolate. These gaps impacted states with high Irish enlistment: e.g. there was no nativity information for 104,391 of the 337,800 white New York volunteers, for 139,132 of the 271,500 white Pennsylvania volunteers, and for 34,631 of the 105,500 white Massachusetts volunteers. This calls into serious question the reliability of the overall figures, but they are, and will remain, the best available estimates. See Gould, *Investigations in the Military and Anthropological Statistics of American Soldiers,* 15–16, 25–26.

furnishing over 15 percent of white volunteers while accounting for 13 percent of the 1860 white population.

As has been demonstrated, the mantle of the most famed formation of the war, then as now, was worn by the Irish Brigade. Unquestionably the most important Irish unit to see service, the Brigade was a lightning rod for attention during the conflict.[21] Thomas Francis Meagher received authorization to form the Irish Brigade in August 1861, and went on to serve as its first brigadier general.[22] Initially consisting of the 63rd, 69th, and 88th New York Volunteers, it was later joined in the field by the 28th Massachusetts Volunteers and 116th Pennsylvania Volunteers, although the latter regiment was less ethnically Irish American than the others and did not carry a green flag into battle.[23] During the first years of the conflict the Irish Brigade earned a reputation for hard fighting, something borne out by its casualty figures; although fewer than 3,000 men took the field at any one time, it sustained more than 4,000 casualties during the course of the war.[24] Given its contemporary position as the preeminent expression of Irish loyalty to the Union, it is unsurprising that the devastating losses it sustained also influenced wider Irish enthusiasm for the war on the home front.[25] The most spectacular example of this came with the impact and fallout of the Brigade's fate at the December 1862 Battle of Fredericksburg, Virginia, where they sustained horrendous casualties. Susannah Ural has pointed to the Brigade's losses in that engagement as a major prompt for increasing Irish American doubts about "the direction of the war and their place it."[26] Although the degree to which that was universally the case is debatable, there is no doubt it did influence contemporary Irish American opinion on the progress of the conflict and especially on how their men were being employed on the battlefield. The Irish Brigade's experience at Fredericksburg also led to that engagement's near immediate positioning as the most powerful exemplar of Irish sacrifice during the Civil War. Their ordeal caused both the town and battlefield to became indelibly linked to the memory of Irish American participation, a position Fredericksburg continues to hold to this day.[27]

The Irish Brigade has significantly overshadowed the only other brigade-level ethnic Irish formation of the war, Corcoran's Irish Legion. Raised in the late summer and fall of 1862 and led by Michael Corcoran, it consisted of the 155th, 164th, 170th, and 182nd (otherwise known as the 69th New York National Guard Artillery) New York Volunteers.[28] Noted for its Fenian links, many of the men in the Legion had eschewed enlistment in the Irish Brigade in order to wait for the release of their much loved leader from Confederate prison. Corcoran, who had been captured while leading the 69th New York State Militia at the July 1861 Battle of First Bull Run, had been held for potential reciprocal execution if the United States carried out a threat to execute Confederate privateers. He died while serving as brigadier general following a fall from his horse in December 1863. Up to that point the Legion had escaped the worst of the war, but that changed with their transfer to the Army of the Potomac in 1864, and they suffered considerable casualties during the Overland Campaign and around Petersburg, Virginia.

The majority of ethnic Irish regiments served outside of these two brigade formations, marching to the guns as individual representatives of their ethnicity. Across the loyal states in 1861 and 1862, Irish communities sought to explicitly signpost their dedication to the Union by sending an ethnic unit into the field. While many successfully established Irish American "green flag" regiments, others were forced to dilute the ethnic makeup of their outfit in order to reach the requisite numbers or abandon the effort altogether. As a result, not all ethnic regiments that were mustered in were completely Irish in character. This could create friction, particularly where ethnic delineations occurred along company lines. Pride in identity was not the exclusive purview of Irish American troops; for example, when two native white American companies from Cattaraugus County were joined with the ethnic 37th New York "Irish Rifles," tensions quickly manifested between the two groups.[29]

No two ethnic Irish regiments shared exactly the same demographic profile, and each was reflective of the communities, circumstances, and moment in time that produced it.[30] Patently, enlistment in such units allowed soldiers both to serve among their own and to express their self-identity by acting as highly visible representatives of their ethnicity on a national stage. Nonetheless, the fact remains that despite the overwhelming prominence of ethnic Irish regiments in both the memory and historiography of Irish service, the vast bulk of Irish volunteers did not serve in them. For many this was an accident of scale. Numerous Irish American communities formed company-level units, which then marched to war as a component of nonethnic regiments. Typical were the efforts of the Irish in the upstate New York town of Seneca Falls, who formed the "Irish Volunteers," who went on to represent them as Company K of the 33rd New York "Ontario Regiment." These Irish American volunteers departed for the front with as much fanfare among their local community as that provided for the Irish Brigade regiments in New York City.[31] Some companies had large Irish contingents without having the numbers to be wholly Irish American. Depending on the ratios, some still successfully expressed an Irish identity. Company A of the 13th Vermont Volunteers, the "Emmett Guards," contained Irish Americans from Burlington, Rutland, and Westford (many drawn from among the marble quarrying community) but also included a number of native white Americans and French Canadians.[32] Other formations who had at their inception been overtly ethnic do not appear to have carried their Irish appellations into service, despite strong Irish American numbers. In Boston what had begun recruitment as the "Irish Brigade of Volunteers" eventually found its way into service as Company F of the 20th Massachusetts Volunteers, the "Harvard Regiment."[33]

A number of regiments attracted the Irish at levels not dissimilar to those enjoyed by green flag formations. Some of these outfits carried affiliations that naturally aligned them with Irish America, as was the case with the strongly Irish 42nd New York Volunteers, tied to the city's Democratic Tammany Hall organization, and the 11th New York Volunteers—the "First Fire Zouaves"—drawn from among the city's firemen. Despite not being a green flag unit, the 42nd New York also contained a number of prominent Fenians, with Young Irelander and Fenian founder Michael Doheny playing a role in its organization.[34] The 3rd Rhode Island Heavy Artillery, the largest body to serve from that state during the war, drew significant numbers of Irish Americans from the manufacturing industries, particularly into Companies I and K. They apparently had opted for this regiment because a sufficient number of Irish officers could not be found to form a distinctly ethnic unit, and—according to the regimental historian—because of opposition to "all appearances of caste" among the state volunteers.[35] In a recruitment system that was centered around the ability of ambitious and patriotic community leaders to organize their own companies, personal loyalties often proved decisive. James Cullen, an Irish contractor in Detroit, Michigan, undoubtedly drew on the connections he had made as an employer to speedily raise men for what became Company E of the 24th Michigan Volunteers, and as a result it had a distinctly Irish character.[36]

Equally important were the economic incentives on offer, even early in the war. It was almost certainly the promise of attractive terms that enabled an officer of the 40th New York Volunteers to poach an entire company of Irishmen from Lawrence, Massachusetts, and secure them for service in his own regiment.[37] However, even at company level, it was most common for Irish Americans to serve in numbers where they did not make up the majority ethnicity.[38] It was a rare Union formation that did not have a sprinkling of Irish Americans on its roster, particularly if it had recruited from among urban populations. While some of these Irish served as the only representative of their ethnicity, it was more common for Irish Americans to form small groups within larger mixed companies. It is apparent that once they had chosen to enlist, a range of often interwoven factors influenced each Irish American's decision regarding with whom he served. In 1861 and 1862, the majority based their choice on a combination of personal friendships, community affiliation, economic incentivization, officer standing, and unit character. As the war progressed, economics became more and more dominant as the major determinant in the selection they made. But in the heady days of the conflict's first months, many likely chose their unit in much the same way that William Carroll of the 61st New York Infantry seems to have—on the spur of the moment. When his parents asked him why he had joined a New York City regiment and not one from their Brooklyn home, he explained, "I listed in the new York park I was not in Brooklyn the day that I listed."[39]

The story of early war volunteers has dominated analyses of Irish American servicemen just as it has dominated the wider field of Civil War soldier studies.[40] But immigrants and Irish Americans were so associated with late war recruiting that any broad analysis of their participation must seek to incorporate those who entered the military from mid-1863 onward, particularly if early and late war enlistees are to be compared. It is instructive in that context to examine the means and methods by which Irish Americans entered the military during the late war period, and how they have historically been perceived.

As the fighting dragged on through the bloody confrontations of 1862, the Union's escalating need for manpower ran up against a growing reticence among those of military age in the United States to commit to what was clearly going to be a protracted and deadly struggle. By the autumn and winter of that year, few were under any illusions about both the hardships and risks that accompanied military service. In an attempt to solve the issue, Federal authorities instituted the draft. Their first efforts were embodied in the Militia

Act of 17 July 1862, which empowered the secretary of war to draft militiamen for nine months' service, with each state assigned quotas they were required to meet.[41] The need for a more extensive conscription program led to the Enrollment Act of 3 March 1863. This required all male citizens and immigrants who had declared an intent to become citizens aged between twenty and forty-five to be enrolled for the draft. Those enrolled were split into two classes. Class One was composed of single men aged between twenty and forty-five and married men between twenty and thirty-five; Class Two was married men between thirty-five and forty-five. Class Two were only to be drawn when Class One had been exhausted.[42] Each draft district (which equated to congressional districts) was assigned a quota, with the draft required only if the number of men supplied fell short. Once drawn, an individual could avoid service by claiming exemption, by furnishing a commutation fee of $300, or by supplying a substitute. The commutation fee option was repealed in July 1864, a move that led to an explosion in the cost of securing a substitute.[43] All told, four drafts were held in the North between the summer of 1863 and the close of the war.[44]

The draft and the substitute industry it created significantly muddied perceptions of Irish American wartime service, particularly because in the eyes of many northerners the Irish were synonymous with it. Irish American efforts to evade or resist the draft and to cheat the bounty system were seized upon by many of their opponents. As early as August 1862 *Harper's Weekly* in New York was running cartoons satirizing efforts to avoid the draft, choosing Irish Americans in characteristically simian form to represent two of their three "dodgers" (the third being a member of the upper class).[45] It is noteworthy that within a week of its publication the same New York City Irish Americans targeted by these racist caricatures were receiving word of the major losses their communities had sustained at the August 1862 Battle of Second Bull Run, Virginia, where the city's units had taken a battering.

The draft was extremely unpopular, particularly among the lower classes. The commutation fee appeared to offer credence to the belief that this was a rich man's war but a poor man's fight. Opposition to the draft was most savage in New York City, where it manifested itself in the infamous orgy of violence that characterized the Irish-dominated New York City draft riots of July 1863. The fact that this and a number of other incidents of unrest—such as the draft opposition in Pennsylvania's anthracite coal region—were dominated by the Irish led to lingering questions about the nature of Irish American loyalty to

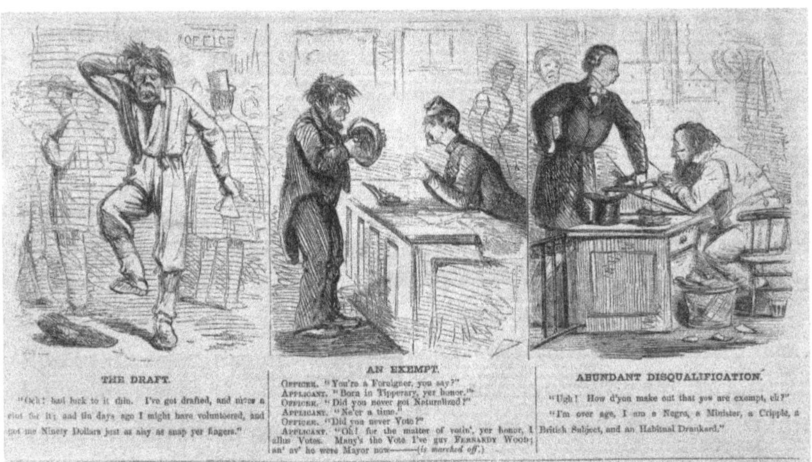

FIG. 1. Depictions of men seeking to avoid the draft, from the 23 August 1862 issue of *Harper's Weekly*. The cover of the following issue ran with a full-page image of Michael Corcoran to celebrate his release, demonstrating the role class and social standing played in depictions of the Irish. (Library of Congress.)

the Union.[46] Irish Americans did prove particularly adept at obtaining draft exemptions, and were more than happy to claim foreign citizenship as one method of doing so.[47] Indeed, as Tyler Anbinder has demonstrated, the Irish American ability to avoid being held to service meant that they and other immigrants appear to have been less likely to end up in uniform due to the draft than native-born working-class whites.[48] Nevertheless, it remained the case that only an unlucky (or willing) few ever ended up at the front as a result of having their name pulled from the draft wheel. Of the 776,829 men who were officially drafted during the American Civil War, only 46,347 ever donned uniform.[49] Instead, it was the draft substitutes and bounty volunteers who provided the vital manpower the United States required during the war's final years—and among their ranks, Irish Americans were extremely plentiful.

While just over 45,000 drafted men went into the military, 73,607 were paid to act as substitutes.[50] Tens of thousands more took their pick from the local and state bounties and financial inducements that were offered by towns and districts throughout the northern states in an effort to fill their quotas and stave off the draft. While it has been argued that Irish Americans began to abandon their support for the war after 1863, this was not reflected in their willingness to enter the military during this period.[51] In fact, what evidence exists suggests that they likely proved proportionately more willing to enlist than native white Americans. In 1863, immigrant men made up 77 percent of substitutes in New York's Fifth District, 84 percent in Massachusetts's Third District, 74 percent in Concord, New Hampshire, and 60 percent in Pennsylvania's Eighth District. These figures were often multiples of their proportion in the general local population.[52] Similarly, analysis of nonresidents who enlisted in the towns of Claremont and Newport, New Hampshire, found that almost 60 percent were foreign-born, of whom almost 20 percent were native to Ireland.[53]

Monetary inducements were central to enticing the majority of these Irish American substitutes and bounty volunteers into the service, and (often unscrupulous) brokers targeted newspapers that were widely read within the Irish American community. Typical were advertisements that ran in the 5 June 1864 edition of the *New York Herald*. They promised that "ALL IRISHMEN, GERMANS AND ENGLISHMEN who want employment will be paid a large amount cash to go as substitutes for drafted men. Best chance ever offered." Another proclaimed "SUBSTITUTES CAN GET $500 CASH.—100 IRISHMEN, Germans and Englishmen wanted immediately. Recruits also wanted. Choice of artillery and cavalry. Boardinghousekeepers and agents please apply."[54] The working-class Irish responded in droves. The financial rewards were enough to entice hopeful men directly from Ireland, and contributed toward the rebounding of Irish immigration that saw inward numbers triple in 1863.[55] American consuls in Ireland were inundated with requests for passage to the United States in return for enlistment in Federal forces.[56] While there is no evidence that the consuls ever acted upon these requests, many men did enter into agreements with third parties to have their passage paid to America in return for either laboring services or military enlistment.

The corrupt systems that developed around the substitute and bounty system became legion, and Irish Americans were highly visible among both the exploiters and the exploited. Their reputation was not helped by the high-profile serial desertion of men such as John O'Connor, who claimed to have jumped thirty-two times before he was caught in 1865, and Thomas Ryan, who was executed for jumping some thirty times.[57] Nevertheless, there was relatively little evidence for the openly prejudicial and nativist views of men such as Provost Marshal General James Barnet Fry, who confidently charged that it was "a notorious circumstance that the great mass of the professional bounty jumpers were Europeans."[58]

The quality, motivations, and commitment of these late war recruits can be called into question, particularly among those who enlisted following the removal of the commutation clause in July 1864. But they are all too often dismissed en bloc as unscrupulous and unreliable mercenaries. Civil War scholarship has frequently demonstrated a bias toward the study of the early war "ideological" volunteer, often implicitly marking such individuals out as having been somehow better and more admirable men than their late war counterparts.[59] The lack of ideological motivation to enlist in a war or a failure to show the same willingness to die or be maimed for a cause does not make men lesser, or correlate with moral inferiority. Indeed, many of these late war recruits played a crucial role in the Union's final push toward victory in 1864 and 1865. There is a need for a corrective in how they are perceived. Rather than contrasting them with the early war volunteer, it is time to examine these men in the wider context of wartime northern society. As J. Matthew Gallman's research has demonstrated, military service was not necessarily seen as a prerequisite for being deemed a loyal and patriotic Union man during the Civil War. Nevertheless, these late war recruits elected to serve in a war that about 60 percent of the white men of military age in the United States chose to avoid.[60] As the most willing enlistees ran out, it was left to immigrants and other working-class men to decide if the potential once-in-a-lifetime economic windfall that service offered outweighed the by then all too apparent risks. There undoubtedly were those among their number who sought to exploit the system and who shied away from battle, but the fact remains that the majority did not.

Given the breadth, scale, and variance of Irish American service through the course of the conflict, seeking to establish as accurate a baseline as possible for how many of these men may have served in the U.S. military during the Civil War is essential. The traditional estimate of about 150,000 most commonly used in the field of Civil War history is too low.[61] It is difficult to overstate the ramifications the persistence of this figure has had on perceptions of Irish service, given that it has led scholars to argue that the Irish were proportionately underrepresented in the U.S. military, and in turn to seek explanations for that supposed underrepresentation.[62] Given its interpretive import, teasing out the origin of this figure, why it is flawed, and seeking to establish a more accurate impression of proportionate Irish representation becomes especially necessary.

In 1869 the U.S. Sanitary Commission produced what remains the most reliable estimate for how many Irish-born men entered volunteer regiments, suggesting that approximately 144,221 Irish-born men volunteered in the East and Midwest.[63] This was followed in 1889 by William F. Fox's highly influential *Regimental Losses in the American Civil War*, which sought to present the Commission's figures "in round numbers," i.e. 150,000 men.[64] This figure has become fossilized as the total for Irish American service ever since. Yet in the small print of the Sanitary Commission's original calculations lies the evidence as to why it is only a partial tally. That report was explicit that the estimate was inclusive only of Irish-born volunteers from the eastern and midwestern states. It specifically *excluded* men who served in the navy or the regulars, as well as volunteers who had served the states of the Pacific coast, or the territories, or those who had enlisted in units raised in former Confederate states, such as heavily Irish Louisiana.[65]

Patently, these excluded men need to be reintegrated into estimates of Irish numbers, yet even when omitted there is no compelling evidence for the underrepresentation thesis. The distribution of volunteers across the United States presented in table 2 takes the Sanitary Commission estimates for Irish-born white volunteers from eastern and midwestern states and compares them with nativity data from the 1860 census. Of the twenty-one states and the District of Columbia for which such comparable estimates are possible, the Irish-born made up 7.12 percent of the 1860 white population, and provided an estimated 7.2 percent of the white wartime volunteers.[66] While the use of the 1860 census figure does not account for wartime immigrants, the resultant percentages are still likely an underestimate. For example, analysis of microdata from the 1860 census by Cormac Ó Gráda suggests that there were significantly more Irish women in the United States than men, at least in the major cities. This female dominance is particularly pertinent when assessing the proportionate scale of Irish American military representation from northern cities, given that up to 60.9 percent of the Irish-born population of New York City may have been female, a figure that stood at 58.4 percent in Philadelphia and 51.1 percent in Boston.[67] When one further considers the thousands of sailors, regulars, and other Irish Americans that these figures exclude, there is a high likelihood that rather than being underrepresented, Irish men actually served in greater proportion than their percentage of the population.

Drawing on the latest scholarship to assess nativity in the different branches of the military, it becomes possible to offer a reappraisal of the numbers of

Irish-born in Federal service that reincorporates the branches and volunteers that have for so long been excluded (see table 3).

Given that a proportion of the naval recruits had likely seen army service prior to their enlistments, and allowing for other transfers and duplication, a reasonable figure for Irish-born service in the Union military might be around 180,000 men. Yet even this does not represent a true figure of Irish American service. As explored in chapter 1, Irish nativity was not a reliable marker of ethnicity or identity during this period. Given the nature of the surviving records, seeking to integrate the non-Irish-born sons of Irish immigrants into the total is extremely difficult to accomplish with any certainty. One of the few

TABLE 3. Estimate of Total Number of Irish-Born in the United States Military during the American Civil War

Group	*Estimate of Irish-Born*
Union Volunteers from East & Midwest	144,221[1]
Union Navy	23,608[2]
Regulars in 1861	5,425[3]
New Regular Enlistments 1861–1865	10,000[4]
Union Volunteers from Pacific Coast and Territories	6,440[5]
Total	189,694

[1] Gould, *Investigations in the Military and Anthropological Statistics of American Soldiers,* 27.

[2] Michael Bennett's analysis indicates that 118,044 men enlisted in the Union naval service between 1861 and 1865, and his statistical sample produced a figure of 20 percent Irish-born. This would represent some 23,608 men. Bennett, *Union Jacks,* 5, 9.

[3] Mark W. Johnson's analysis indicates that of the slightly more than 14,500 professionals on the rolls in January 1861, almost 37 percent were Irish-born. His sample of more than 2,000 antebellum regulars found that 36.64 percent had Irish nativity, with the next highest proportion being those born in the United States, at 33.68 percent of the total. See Johnson, "'Where Are the Regulars?,'" 150, 295.

[4] Mark W. Johnson calculates that about 69,000 men served in the regulars during the Civil War. During the course of the conflict some 50,000 new recruits were taken in. His sample of new wartime enlistments indicated that 20.53 percent, or some 10,000 men, were Irish-born. See Johnson, "'Where Are the Regulars?,'" 2, 150, 295, 306.

[5] Gould excluded the 92,000 volunteers from the Pacific Coast and territories. His figure of 144,221 Irish-born represents slightly more than 7 percent of the total number of white volunteer soldiers among his study group (2,018,200). If they served in the same proportion among the 92,000, that would represent an additional 6,440 men.

efforts to do so comes from Don H. Doyle in an estimate based on his reading of the Sanitary Commission data. Doyle places the number of American-born men of Irish parentage in the Union military at roughly 90,000.[68] If accurate, this would mean the total Irish American contribution to the northern war effort could have been in the vicinity of 270,000 men—and this without considering Irish Americans of British or Canadian nativity. To again adopt a conservative approach, a total figure of roughly 250,000 would seem a reasonable one to put forward for total Irish American participation.

The transformational implications of such a reappraisal are readily apparent. Rather than considering 150,000 Irish Americans and discussing what caused these men to be underrepresented in the northern military, it becomes necessary to fundamentally reframe our analysis. In its place we are left to consider why upward of a quarter of a million Irish Americans decided to fight for the United States during the American Civil War. The hundreds of ordinary men for whom correspondence has now been identified provides us with a means to do so.

A REGIMENT OF REPRESENTATIVES: THE CORRESPONDENTS

From the early war volunteer to the late war substitute, and from the Irish Brigade private to the Mississippi Squadron landsman, Irish American representation in the Union military was vast and varied. Gaining comprehensive insight into the service of this quarter of a million men requires the examination of as broad and diverse a representative group as possible. The regiment worth of Irish American correspondents gathered together for this book are the most fully representative grouping of Irish Union servicemen ever examined. The words they left behind prove invaluable, but so too is the exceptional detail available regarding their backgrounds, demographics, and service, which itself reveals significant new insights into Civil War Irish American service.

Enlistment of the Correspondents

Of the 395 writers identified among the pension files, almost 50 percent "listed" in 1861, while nearly 75 percent were wearing Union blue by the end of 1862.[69] This rush to the colors was not uniform, but came in a series of waves (see Graph 1). The first and largest occurred in the six months between May

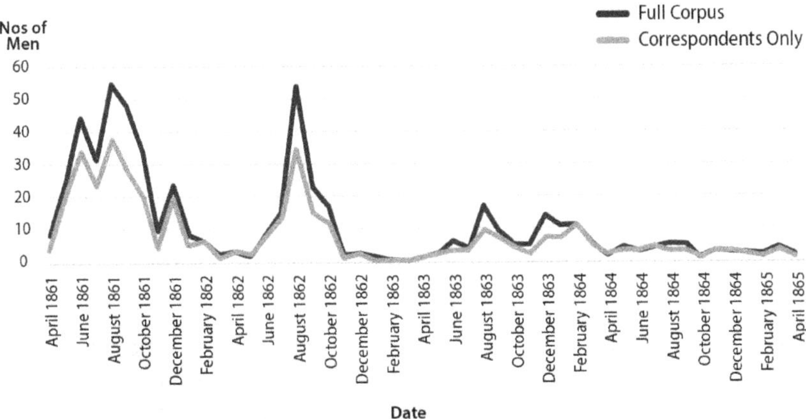

GRAPH 1. Identifiable pattern of enlistment for men examined in *Green and Blue*. The "Full Corpus" represents 551 men who had any wartime correspondence in their files, the "Correspondents Only" the 386 whose files contained correspondence they had composed.

and October 1861. Most intensive across June, July, August, and September, only the defeat at First Bull Run intervened to put a temporary dampener on recruitment. These men were answering the first in what became a series of calls made for long-term volunteers during the conflict.

The first summer of the war had not taken hold before the government realized that their April request for 75,000 ninety-day militiamen would be insufficient, in both scope and duration.[70] On 3 May 1861, Lincoln called for 42,000 three-year volunteers, 18,000 sailors, and an enlargement of the regular army.[71] Congress confirmed the president's request on 6 August, which, when combined with acts of 22 and 25 July, increased the required number to 500,000 men. It was a mark of the enthusiasm prevalent in those early months that 700,680 troops were ultimately furnished.[72] Among the Irish American correspondents, this 1861 drive reached its crescendo in August. But once the pool of willing men was exhausted, enlistments fell away precipitously and—a slight recovery in December excepted—the numbers would not rally again for many months. The impact of this 1861 recruitment drive on the size of the Federal military was dramatic, and this was the most intensive period of enlistment for the Irish Americans. On 1 July 1861, as the momentous fight at First Bull Run approached, the army's strength stood at 186,751. By 1 January 1862, its numbers had exploded to 575,917 men.[73]

In April 1862 the government suspended recruitment, but before long it was once again appealing for men.[74] By the summer of 1862 the heavy attrition of the conflict and its insatiable requirement for manpower had left the Union in desperate need. A call for 300,000 three-year enlistments came on 2 July 1862, followed on 4 August by a demand for 300,000 militia for nine-month service.[75] This prompted the second major wave of Irish American enlistment, between July and October 1862, which again reached its zenith in August. The wider impact of this recruitment was once more visible in army numbers, which increased from 637,126 on 31 March 1862 to 918,191 on 1 January 1863.[76] The efforts to entice men into the military in the summer and fall of 1862 witnessed an increase in the state and federal inducements on offer, and also brought about the Militia Act, the forerunner of the draft that would become the dominant feature of recruitment efforts from 1863 onward. As with the previous year, the correspondent data indicates that once all those willing to sign on in response to this call had entered the service, recruitment all but dried up. The final, and smallest, wave of Irish American recruitment among the correspondents came in the late summer of 1863 and winter of 1863–1864. This was sparked initially by the first draft held under the Enrollment Act in July 1863, with many of those enlisting at this time able to benefit from increasingly generous financial inducements.

It is apparent that whatever their ultimate motivations for enlistment, Irish Americans made their decision to enlist in the context of specific government calls and drives to increase numbers in the military. Their personal ideologies and circumstances played a major role in the choices they made, but the climate created at the local, state, and national level as the Union voraciously pursued men for service was intrinsic to the process that transformed them into soldiers and sailors. Conversely, in those months where that climate was absent or diminished, few Irish Americans threw their lot in with Uncle Sam.

Employment of the Correspondents

Analysis of the preenlistment occupations of the 395 correspondents demonstrates that they were overwhelmingly drawn from among the lower classes, ranging from skilled artisans to unskilled laborers. Almost 92 percent of the letter writers worked in blue-collar or agricultural positions, or had no employment (see table 4).[77] The largest cohort, almost 37 percent, were drawn from the ranks of the skilled, men such as carpenters, blacksmiths, tailors, and painters. Slightly under 19 percent were semiskilled, such as those identified as factory workers or men who made their living off the sea, while a little less than 10 percent worked in agricultural positions, either as agricultural laborers or farmers. One in four were unskilled, largely seeking work as laborers and day laborers. Of the white-collar correspondents, most worked as printers, clerks, or peddlers—proprietorial positions were rare. Their low representation is also a symptom of the pension application process, as dependents from the upper echelons of society (be they Irish or otherwise) rarely had to resort to the submission of correspondence to prove their entitlement.[78]

The occupations of the correspondents are broadly in line with what might be expected from an urban Irish population. The one deviation comes with the apparent underrepresentation of the unskilled, though (as will be explored later in this chapter) the age profile of the letter writers meant that they were less likely to be unskilled than those even a few years older than them. Detailed analysis of the working histories of individual soldiers and sailors indicates the fluidity (and precarity) of Irish American employment, with men frequently advancing and regressing back and forth through unskilled/semiskilled/skilled positions during the course of their working lives. An example is James Briody, the American-born son of immigrants from

TABLE 4. Occupational Status of Irish Americans from the "Full Corpus" and "Correspondents Only" Databases

	% *Unskilled*	% *Semi-Skilled*	% *Skilled*	% *Low White-Collar*	% *High White-Collar*	% *Agricultural*	% *None*	*Total*
Correspondents Only	24.93	18.40	36.80	7.42	0.89	9.20	2.37	337
Full Corpus	30.11	16.84	35.37	6.74	0.63	8.42	1.89	475

Note: The table excludes those for whom no occupation data could be ascertained. Occupational classifications are adapted from Stephan Thernstrom, *The Other Bostonians: Poverty and Progress in the American Metropolis 1880–1970* (Cambridge, Mass.: Harvard Univ. Press, 1973), 289–292, and David T. Gleeson, *The Irish in the South, 1815–1877* (Chapel Hill: Univ. of North Carolina Press, 2001), 195–196.

Castlerahan, Co. Meath, who was described as a stonecutter when he enlisted in the 20th Massachusetts Infantry in August 1862.[79] Yet James was not employed in that capacity at the time he joined up. He had spent the six months prior to enlistment driving an express wagon, and before that he had tried his hand as a seaman.[80] Irish-born James McGee is recorded as a stage driver on the muster roll of the 132nd New York Infantry, but according to those who knew him he was a laborer in a soda water manufactory when he took up his gun.[81] Galway native Patrick Kelly was listed as a shoemaker in his compiled military service record, but he is entered as a laborer on the Massachusetts state roster.[82] In fact, Kelly was an apprentice at the time of his enlistment.[83]

The evidence suggests that some Irish Americans may have been seeking to put their "best foot forward" when describing their employment to recruiters, and that their listed occupations may not necessarily have always been what they did, but what they intended or hoped to do. The projection of future occupation has previously been noted in other nineteenth-century Irish emigrant records. One example identified by Breandán Mac Suibhne relates to Donegal schoolteacher Patrick McGlynn, who left Ireland for Australia's goldfields in 1857. On his outward journey his occupation was recorded as "miner" even though he had never been one, he just intended to be so upon his arrival.[84] Even for those who had previously worked in skilled positions, it did not mean they were employed in those areas at the time they chose to become soldiers or sailors. Further complicating matters is the fact that Civil War military records are plagued by inconsistencies in how occupations were recorded. For example, while men like Barney Carr, Michael Daly, John Fitzpatrick, and Richard Flynn were entered on the rosters as "farmers," all were in fact farm laborers.[85] Similar issues surround men with apparently skilled employment who in reality worked in semiskilled factory positions.

Many of the correspondents also exhibited signs of the intergenerational upward mobility that was a major attraction of the United States for Irish immigrants. Future 3rd New Hampshire Infantry private John Crowley was a tinman's apprentice in 1860, when his father was employed as a laborer.[86] John Hennessey held a position as a clerk in Troy, New York, while his older brother and father were common laborers—though on his 1863 enlistment he gave his occupation as bartender.[87] Another laborer's son, Patrick Dunnican from Co. Roscommon, was a groom in 1860 and a blacksmith by the time he was drafted into the ranks of the 32nd Massachusetts Infantry in 1863.[88] Mathew

McCourt, the New York-born child of an Irish laborer father in Ann Arbor, was a mason when he became a soldier in the 1st Michigan Infantry.[89] Prior to the upheaval created by the Civil War, many of these men were on track to begin the long and uneven climb that would come to characterize social advancement in Irish America.

Distribution of the Correspondents

The geographic concentrations and military distribution of the letter writers confirms their viability as representatives of total Irish American service. New York dominates among them just as it dominated Irish American service as a whole. Men who were credited to the Empire State represent more than 40 percent of the correspondents (see table 5). This figure dwarfs the slightly more than 16 percent of correspondents each who entered the fight as representatives of Massachusetts and Pennsylvania, the next largest contingents. Taken together, these three states account for greater than 73 percent of all the correspondents. A little over 5 percent served Illinois, and all told just under 14 percent of the writers served in units that hailed from the Midwest or Confederacy (in the latter case represented solely by Louisiana). These figures are broadly comparable to the proportionate distribution of the Irish population in the 1860 North, with a slight bias toward New York, Pennsylvania, and Massachusetts, and a commensurate slight underrepresentation of smaller states. It also compares favorably to the general pattern of Irish volunteer enlistment estimated by the U.S. Sanitary Commission.[90] The distribution reinforces the fact that it was eastern communities who sustained the vast bulk of Irish American losses during the Civil War.

The state of affiliation of Irish Americans was not necessarily the same as their community of origin. In an effort to ascertain the latter, an examination of the county and state where the pensions were initially claimed was undertaken. Of the 395 correspondents, this detail was available for 387. A total of nine addresses were in Ireland, with two in England and two in Canada. The remaining 374 were initially being paid out in America (see table 6). That so few pensions were claimed outside of the United States is itself a measure of the low return rate of Irish emigrants after their departure across the Atlantic.[91]

The United States county analysis further confirms the overwhelmingly urban origins of Irish American servicemen, conforming with what is known

TABLE 5. State Affiliation of All 395 Correspondents, Expressed in both Numbers and Percentages

State	*Percentages*	*No. of Correspondents*
New York	40.51	160
Massachusetts	16.71	66
Pennsylvania	16.46	65
Illinois	5.32	21
Ohio	2.53	10
Rhode Island	2.53	10
Connecticut	2.03	8
New Jersey	2.03	8
New Hampshire	1.77	7
Maine	1.52	6
Michigan	1.52	6
Kentucky	1.01	4
Vermont	1.01	4
Wisconsin	1.01	4
Indiana	0.76	3
Louisiana	0.76	3
Missouri	0.76	3
Delaware	0.51	2
Kansas	0.51	2
District of Columbia	0.25	1
Iowa	0.25	1
Maryland	0.25	1

Note: In the case of naval service, state of assignation was based on location of enlistment.

about Irish population distribution in the 1860s North. Almost one in five of the correspondent pensions were claimed in New York City alone, with significant concentrations around Philadelphia, Boston (Suffolk), and Brooklyn (Kings). The Greater Boston area and manufacturing centers such as Lowell and Providence are also among the best represented (Middlesex and Provi-

TABLE 6. American Counties Where Pensions of Irish American Civil War Correspondents Were Claimed

State	*County*	*Percentage*	*No. of Correspondents*
New York	New York	18.45	69
Pennsylvania	Philadelphia	14.17	53
Massachusetts	Suffolk	7.75	29
New York	Kings	5.88	22
Massachusetts	Middlesex	3.74	14
Rhode Island	Providence	3.21	12
Massachusetts	Essex	2.67	10
Pennsylvania	Allegheny	2.41	9
New York	Niagara	2.41	9
New York	Monroe	2.14	8
Massachusetts	Norfolk	1.87	7
Massachusetts	Worcester	1.87	7
Illinois	Cook	1.60	6
Ohio	Hamilton	1.34	5
New York	Rensselaer	1.34	5
Connecticut	New Haven	1.07	4
Maine	Penobscot	1.07	4
New York	Columbia	1.07	4

Note: Only counties representing 1 percent and above are included. Derived from pension location information for 374 American based correspondents. No pension address was available for a small number of the correspondents because their letters were included in files that did not directly relate to them (e.g. they were submitted in support of another Irish American's claim).

dence counties, respectively).[92] Fewer pensions were active in the Midwest. One of the chief reasons behind this was the recent migration of many of the correspondents to the region, younger generations who had moved westward in search of opportunity, particularly following downturns such as the Panic of 1857. For example, the pensions of Barney Carr, Michael Daly, James Fitzgerald, John Fitzpatrick, and John Lynch were all secured by parents in New York even though each had served in Illinois regiments.[93]

The concentration of pensions in the major eastern urban Irish American enclaves provides some indication as to the extent of losses those communities suffered during the conflict. These fatalities were tied to the fortunes of a wide array of units, and not singularly bound to attrition in marquee formations like the Irish Brigade. When one considers the overrepresentation of Irish Americans in the Union military in places like New York City, the scale and consistency of death notifications must have quickly become an overwhelmingly frequent occurrence among what was a highly cohesive group. The ramifications of this both politically and in terms of potential community resentment serves to add further context and nuance to our understanding of factors that contributed toward manifestations of Irish American disaffection, not the least of which are seismic events such as the July 1863 New York City draft riots.

The Irish Americans who donned Federal uniforms were distributed more widely through the Union military than any other ethnic group. This range

TABLE 7. Final Branch of Service of the 395 Irish American Correspondents

Branch of Service	*Number of Correspondents*
Volunteer Infantry/Militia	272
Volunteer Cavalry	28
Volunteer Light Artillery	6
Volunteer Heavy Artillery	14
Volunteer Engineers	4
Volunteer Pontoniers	1
Sub-Total Volunteers	325
Regular Infantry	13
Regular Cavalry	3
Regular Artillery	5
Sub-Total Regulars	*21*
United States Navy	43
United States Marine Corps	6
Sub-Total Navy	49

Note: As some men had served in multiple units, sometimes across different branches of service, the unit in which their main Civil War service was rendered was selected.

and diversity in experience is borne out by the fact that the 395 men served in more than 270 different units, credited to twenty-one different states and the District of Columbia.[94] The majority (more than 68 percent) were members of volunteer infantry or militia regiments, with a little over 82 percent being members of a volunteer formation of one form or another (see table 7). Just under 13 percent were in naval service, with slightly more than 5 percent in the regulars. A total of sixty-four servicemen, or 16 percent, were identified as members of ethnic Irish regiments; at least four men who died having moved on to nonethnic outfits had previously seen ethnic service.

Nativity of the Correspondents

Analysis of the backgrounds of the letter writers—undertaken in order to confirm Irish ethnicity—revealed the nativity makeup of the group. As has been highlighted, the Irish America to which they belonged was a community founded on familial and ethnic affiliation rather than on place of birth. Slightly over 35 percent of the correspondents for whom nativity could be established were born into Irish families outside the island of Ireland (see Graph 2). Unsurprisingly, most of them had entered the world in America, with those from the United States representing a little under 28 percent of the letter writers of known nativity. Interestingly, this correlates precisely with the estimate that some 70,000 of the roughly 250,000 Irish American Union

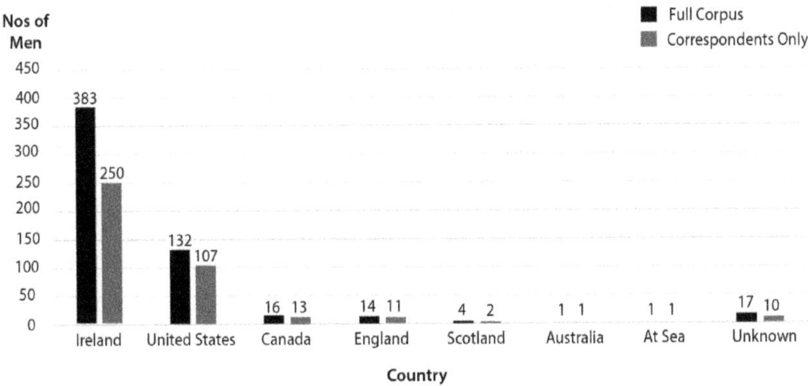

GRAPH 2. The countries of nativity of the soldiers and sailors (Full Corpus and Correspondents Only).

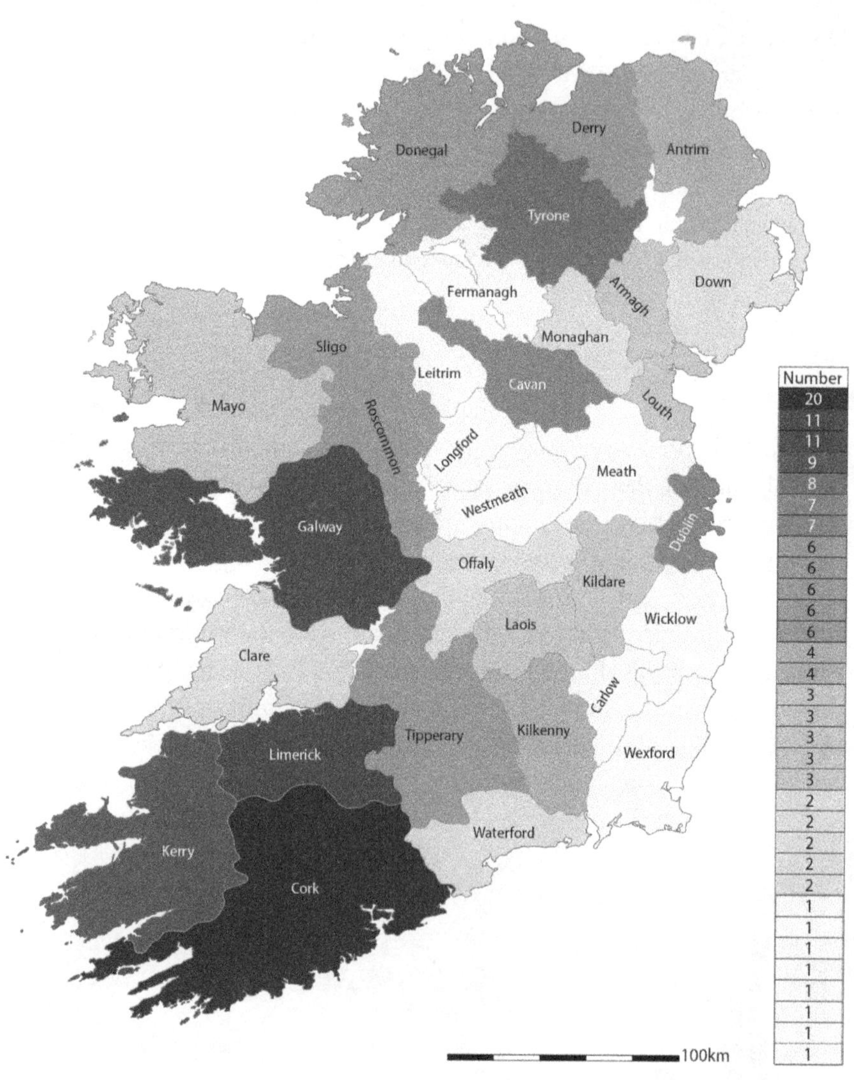

The known counties of nativity of the Irish American correspondents, shaded by density.

servicemen had been born in America, which similarly represents 28 percent of that total. A little more than 7 percent of the correspondents had been born elsewhere: in Canada, England, Scotland, Australia, or while their families were crossing the Atlantic. Of those identified as born in the United States, state of nativity was established for just over 91 percent. Again New York (41.84 percent) dominates, followed by Massachusetts (22.45 percent) and Pennsylvania (20.41 percent).

Those born in Ireland represented just under 65 percent of the writers for whom nativity was established.[95] County of origin is notoriously difficult to confirm for Irish-born servicemen, given the propensity for birthplace to be listed simply as "Ireland" during the American Civil War. Nonetheless, county of nativity was established for 209 of the Full Corpus (just under 55 percent) and 151 of the Correspondents (or just over 60 percent). County Cork, Ireland's most populous county and the one which sent out the highest number of emigrants in the years immediately prior to 1861, dominates (see map).[96] At least one letter writer was identified from each of the thirty-two counties on the island.

From a provincial perspective, the largest body of correspondents could be traced to Munster (34.44 percent), followed by Ulster (26.49 percent), Leinster (21.19 percent), and Connacht (17.88 percent).[97] The ratios are generally comparable with relative levels of outward migration from those provinces that can be traced through the 1850s, with the exception of Connacht, where the proportion of correspondents outstrips that figure (see Graph 3). However, Connacht had been a major source of immigrants at the height of the Famine, when detailed origin statistics were not being gathered, and this likely goes some way toward explaining the discrepancy.[98] Taken together, these figures provide further evidence of the representative nature of the correspondents, who hailed from all over Ireland in similar proportions to the known levels of provincial immigration to the United States.

As with the occupation data, all is often not what it seems with respect to nativity. Detailed analysis reveals frequent discrepancies between place of birth as stated on the census and that recorded on military records. The overwhelming majority of these inconsistencies are unidirectional—a soldier or sailor recorded as Irish-born on the census was entered as American-born when joining the military. The instances of altered nativity seem to be particularly prevalent among those who chose naval service, but it was a common

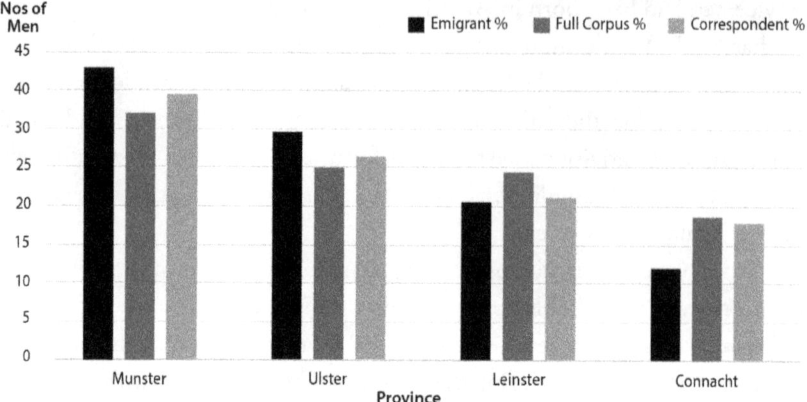

GRAPH 3. Proportion of Irish immigrants to the United States from each of Ireland's four provinces from May 1851 to 1860 (immigrant %) compared with proportion of Irish correspondents identified from each province (Full Corpus % and Correspondents Only %). Provincial emigration proportions from May 1851 to 1860 are based on figures supplied in table 2 of Miller, *Emigrants and Exiles*, 570–571.

practice throughout the northern military. The U.S. Sanitary Commission report admitted as much, stating that in many cases "place of residence was frequently given in the stead of place of birth."[99] Such widespread underrecording of Irish nativity has significant implications when it comes to considering the scale of Irish American service within the Union military. The frequency with which these discrepancies are encountered suggests the probability that large numbers of soldiers and sailors who were recorded as American-born were actually native to Ireland. Whether intentional or otherwise, this has served to further suppress the true totals for Irish-born in Union service, adding still more evidence in support of the argument that Irish Americans were overrepresented within the northern military during the American Civil War.

Age and Marital Status of the Correspondents

Perhaps the youngest correspondent identified in the corpus was William Carroll of the 7th Connecticut Infantry, who was no more than fifteen years old when he enlisted, and may have been as young as fourteen.[100] The oldest was Felix Mooney. The 61st New York Infantry soldier was approximately fifty-four years old when he succumbed to wounds and disease in 1862.[101] They represent either end of the age spectrum among the correspondents (see

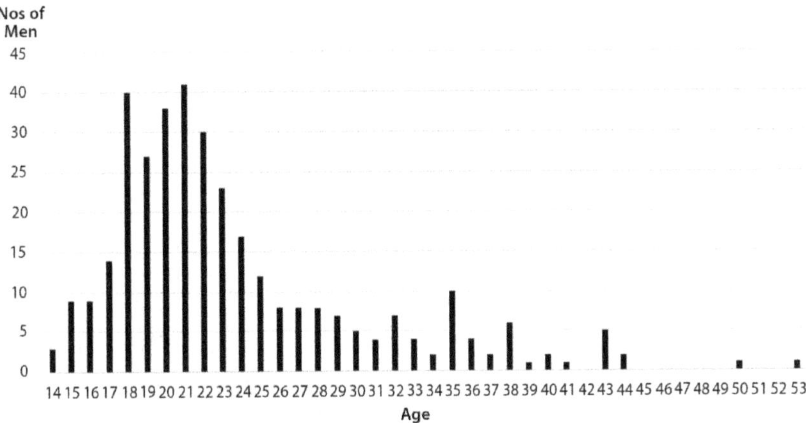

GRAPH 4. The age of the Irish American correspondents at enlistment.

Graph 4). As their cases suggest, there is little doubt that many Irish American boys and men who were both under and overage lied in order to enlist. Overall, the typical Irish American letter writer during the American Civil War was relatively young. While the average age of white Union volunteers was 25.8 years, that of the Irish American correspondents was 24.16.[102]

A little less than one in four of the correspondents were married, with the remainder entering military service as single men.[103] The figures for Irish Americans who had spouses at home is below the estimated 30 percent provided for Union soldiers as a whole.[104] Given the Irish tendency to marry later, this discrepancy is explained by the younger average age of the correspondents, a lower age profile that can be explained by the greater rates of literacy prevalent among more youthful Irish Americans. This is borne out by the marital status figures for the Full Corpus, which indicate that almost 37 percent of the entire group were married, with just over 63 percent being single. The Full Corpus includes men with contemporary correspondence they had not themselves sent, much of it in the form of death notifications written to their families by comrades and medical staff.

THE QUESTION OF CLASS

Historiographical discussion and debate on Irish American participation in the American Civil War is consistently—sometimes exclusively—framed around ethnicity. Invariably, when seeking to explain Irish American enlistment and motivations, it is toward ethnicity that historians have primarily turned.[105] Likewise, it is in issues of ethnicity that explanations for a supposed flagging of Irish American commitment to the cause of Union have chiefly been sought.[106] It goes without saying that ethnicity was and is a fundamental element of the Irish American story. But there was another factor that was just as influential at shaping these men's Civil War experience, one that is hammered home consistently by the economic data and demographic profile of the correspondents: class. Although it has received only scant attention, many of the challenges and prejudices Irish Americans faced during their service and many of the decisions they made were the product not just of who they were, but where they sat on the social spectrum of the United States.

The identified correspondents are overwhelmingly working class in origin. Indeed, among those white groups most commonly delineated in northern service, Irish Americans were almost certainly the most uniformly working class. In a wider sense, the lower classes are perhaps the least understood of all northern demographics during the Civil War, largely because their voices are greatly underrepresented in the surviving historical record. This is despite the fact that they made up 60 percent of organizations like the Army of the Potomac, a force where 40 percent of the rank and file had worked in unskilled occupations.[107] Their absence has been recognized in major analyses of Union correspondence, such as James McPherson's important and influential study *For Cause and Comrades: Why Men Fought in the Civil War,* in which he acknowledges that the work was heavily biased toward American-born white soldiers from the middle and upper classes.[108] Though there has been some notable recent scholarship that has begun to redress this imbalance, there remains a long way to go.[109] In particular, little analysis has been undertaken on what motivated these northern working-class whites to enlist—particularly those from urban backgrounds.[110] Similarly, there is much to be done on what influenced their decisions to remain in or depart from the service, or on how their commitment ebbed and flowed through time.

This prompts a recognition that Irish Americans arguably represent the largest and most readily delineated urban working-class white group in northern service. It also forces a consideration that a more complete understanding of the actions and reactions of Irish Americans during the conflict may lie not in examining the influence of their ethnicity, but their class. Without confidently being able to determine the extent to which Irish Americans differed from other urban working-class comrades during the conflict, the degree to which their ethnicity made them exceptional remains open to significant debate. Unless and until further work is undertaken on the urban working poor in the Union military, it will remain extremely difficult to determine the degree to which their experience was an outlier based on ethnicity or conformist in terms of social position. Similarly, it will remain challenging to confidently identify potential areas of contrast and alignment.

It was from among the lower classes of cities like New York and Brooklyn that the largest Irish American contribution to the war effort came, and it was those Irish communities that commensurately suffered the greatest losses of any Irish communities in the United States. Their pervasiveness in the ranks of urban regiments saw them quickly become a target for those with southern sympathies. Typical were the sentiments of Adalbert Volck, a pro-Confederate artist, who complained that many of the early war Union volunteers came "mostly from the very dregs of the people," forcing the "best blood" of the South to "fight the scum of the North."[111] In 1863 Volck visualized these "dregs" in an etching entitled "Enlistment of Sickles' Brigade"—a brigade filled with Irish Americans—that depicts a largely Irish group of ne'er-do-wells congregating around the Five Points (see Fig. 2).

FIG. 2. "Enlistment of Sickles' Brigade" by pro-Confederate artist Adalbert Volck. (Met Museum, Harris Brisbane Dick Fund.)

Neither is it necessary to look toward southern utterances to reveal the significance of class for Irish Americans during the Civil War. Its importance is evidenced by commentary from within the Irish community itself, further underlining the variance that existed within the 250,000 men who saw service. When Lieutenant John Conway was killed with the Irish Brigade at the September 1862 Battle of Antietam, Maryland, his brother-in-law Charles Brady counseled his newly widowed sister in Brooklyn "to keep away from all the low Irish and not be lead away by them you may think they are for your good they will bring you to ruin."[112] As a successful farmer with a real and personal estate valued at $2,550, Charles Brady no doubt felt in a position to offer such words of wisdom.[113] His greatest fear was that his sister, in remaining connected to Irish culture and community, would be led astray by the multitudes of working-class Irish Americans who surrounded her in Brooklyn and New York City. The upwardly mobile farmer was giving voice to the stratification in Irish American society that would later see individuals defined as either "lace-curtain" or "shanty" Irish.[114] Captain John Lynch of the Irish Brigade, who firmly considered himself part of the refined middle class, further articulated this class distinction—and how he viewed the working-class men under his charge as fundamentally different—in an 1861 letter home:

> we have the men under our thumbs and as docile as lambs as for Company "C" I make the *fellows* jump like young Kittens the *Hard ones* can hardly understand it they thought me a *milk sop* only fit to be tied to your apron strings (in fact I understand they made use of that expression) but faith they caught a *Tartar* Lieut Ryan himself thought I was too fine gentleman to make a good Camp Soldier and says he is most agreably disappointed both him and the Company think me *now* a good *officer*, since I have brought them to their senses.[115]

The lack of working-class Irish American correspondence from the American Civil War has necessitated an overreliance on the words of the Irish officer classes to represent the ethnic experience of the conflict. But as correspondence such as that of John Lynch suggests, these two sets of men, though they shared ethnicity and were aligned on many issues, were not the same. In this regard, the most important aspect of the newly identified correspondence is not the extent of its regional representativeness or the fact that it includes both Irish and foreign-born "Irish Americans." Though both are significant, the greatest strength the corpus possesses is its overwhelmingly working-class makeup. Through the remainder of this book, it is the voices of these ordinary Irish American men that will be heard.

3

Life in Uniform

The last letter Barney Carr ever wrote came from Georgia. It was headed "in Front of they Enemys Brest works and they are a shooting at us all they time, This date June they 20th 1864." Partway through the lines he was penning to his mother, he was forced to stop. When he next had a chance to take up his pen, Barney vividly portrayed the reason for his abrupt hiatus: "I have had to stop writhing we are a Lying on they Line battle and there are *12* Pices of Canons in front of us and they are a shelling they Rebs and that draws they Rebles fire and it is a horrible Plase to be in Canonballs are a flying thick round us and they shells are a screaming in they air and through the woods Cuting they timber and Earth in all directions." Weeks of hard campaigning and almost constant exposure to death had been wearing away at Barney's psychological well-being, and his letter oscillated between reassurances—"by grace god I still live yet and am well and harty in they bargin"—and exhausted resignation—"Dear mother theses are hard times nothing but fighting Everey day and killing of men I am a geting Tired of it."[1] Seven days later, Barney Carr became the only member of his regiment to lose his life in the assault on Kennesaw Mountain.

Without an awareness of Barney Carr's origins, there is nothing in his letter that marks him out as an Irish American. It betrays nothing of his poverty-stricken Co. Derry beginnings, his assisted emigration across the Atlantic, or his subsequent placement in institutional care due to want. What emerges is an impression of a war-weary teenager facing his own mortality on the firing line, pouring out his thoughts to his mother, lest it be his last opportunity to do so.[2] They are words that could have been written by any number of servicemen, of any background, Federal or Confederate. When we raise our gaze beyond the ethnic units to encompass the full breadth of experience of roughly 250,000 Irish American servicemen across the wartime United States, what becomes apparent is that there were few sharp edges that marked Irish American service apart. Instead, what is evident is the extent to which their individual military experience was in many aspects comparable to that of other ordinary white men under arms. But there were also points of divergence and differentiation. While often subtle, they sometimes could be more marked. One of the means by which contrast and similarity can be explored is through the rite of passage that was common to almost everyone who volunteered for the Union—the challenge of adapting to military life.

ADAPTING TO MILITARY LIFE

Although the voices of ordinary Irish Americans are largely absent from scholarly works on the Civil War soldier, historians who have studied Union correspondence would recognize much of what the Irish had to say about military life. They filled their letters with descriptions of their camps and drill, outlined their military movements, and sometimes shared their experience of combat. They ruminated on the weather, on their lack of access to good food and tobacco, or on the cost of it where it was available. They grumbled about military life and its hardships. Some took to the military like ducks to water; others regretted their enlistment almost immediately. The experience of each man was different, and their views, morale, and outlook ebbed and flowed through the course of the war.

Like all other servicemen, following enlistment Irish Americans had to adapt to their new routines, a topic that dominated their early letters, as it did those of all new volunteer soldiers. Cork-born shoemaker John Toomey's description of his day in late 1861 was typical. The 15th Massachusetts Infantry soldier wrote home:

> we get up at sunrise, and wash and clean up our quarters then we have to drill from 7 to 8 Oclock with our knapsacks on then we come in and get our breakfast we go out again at 10 Oclock and drill to 11 ½ Oclock we have dinner at 12 ½ Oclock we go out to drill at 1 ½ Oclock in the afternoon and come in at 2 ½ Oclock we go out to Batalion drill at 3 Oclock and come in at 4 ½ Oclock then we have to go out on dress parade and when we get in it is About dark so you see we dont have much time to loaf.[3]

Many adapted well, particularly during their first weeks of service, when life in uniform remained a novelty. With large numbers already used to the long hours and the punishing physical toll of working-class life, it might be expected that Irish Americans acclimatized better than most. This was the case for some, who welcomed the downtime that life in camp and barracks afforded, not to mention the regular rations. John Riley, who entered the military as a laborer, was thrilled with his decision to join the U.S. Marine Corps in 1861. He informed his parents that he was "well satisfied with the life of a Marine I never had work since I was able to work that I like as well as this we only have three hours drill a day."[4] Former factory worker Charles O'Donnell, who also became a Marine, was equally pleased at the contrast between his old life in an overcrowded Philadelphia tenement and his new surroundings in barracks. "i get plenty to eat," he informed those at home, adding that "every one hase a bed to himself"—a luxury his family did not enjoy. The ready availability of necessities was also a new experience for Charles: "i dont want any thing the canteen opens twist a day and i kin get any thing i want."[5] Such enthusiasm was not always restricted to early war enlistees. Former mason James Finigan was not long in the 4th New York Heavy Artillery in 1864 before he was confiding to his parents that "I Would sooner be out heare than home sodiering is a nice Life."[6]

Irish Americans who were used to cramped and variable living conditions often reported an initial improvement in their health and physique. James Leahey, a Limerick-born upholsterer living in Charlestown, Massachusetts, told his wife three months after enlistment: "my health is very good and my eyes is as well as ever in fact i am stouter and stronger now than you ever see me."[7] John Deegan, a former coal weigher serving with the 19th Maine Infantry, revealed to his sister after his first winter in camp: "I am in the best of health and in fact have been ever since I come out here I never was so fat in my life before."[8] Another who felt soldiering compared well to his lot in civilian life was Offaly native William Delaney: "you ask me how i like it Down South i like it," he told those at home. "As for my Health i never Got better although i sleep On the ground but i Cannot Complain for my bed was not much better the last few weeks that i was i East Albany."[9]

Nonetheless, a working-class background was no guarantee of an easy adaptation to a life of soldiering. As with other groups, plenty of Irish Americans struggled greatly with the transition. A few days after his enlistment in the summer of 1862, Canadian-born Irish American carpenter Michael Martin poured out his misery to his wife. "you cant tink ho I suffer here I have to Sleep on the bare ground wet al. day last week I had to sleep on the ground and it poured raining all nit."[10] Martin had not signed up for ideological reasons, and he regretted joining the army. In the context of both early and late war recruits, early dissatisfaction was more readily expressed by those who had been less enthusiastic about their enlistment. "i dont belive i can stand soldiering," William Flaherty from Co. Galway told his mother shortly after signing up as a reluctant substitute in late 1863. Three weeks later he was "commenceing to think that Soldiering wont agree with me but i will try to Stick it out i am in hopes this war will be over before next winter."[11]

As Irish Americans transitioned from new volunteers and recruits into veterans, they fully embraced the age-old military tradition of grumbling about their lot. This was a common theme for all American Civil War soldiers.[12] It was especially true of those who had experienced hard marches and taxing campaigns. Christopher McGiff, a New York City moulder, told his mother in 1863 that "we eren our money hard in the first plase in laing out in the street and the rain beats on us a soldres life is hard thay say a sallors life is hard but it caint coame up to our life."[13] Co. Louth sailor John Buckley might have disagreed. He was distinctly unimpressed when he was transferred to the ironclad USS *Weehawken* in 1863, venting to his sister: "I assure you it is not very pleasant to be on one of these Monitors I have not had A dry foot since I came here when ever I do any work on deck the sea wets me from my head to my foot . . . the sea is always one or two foot deep over her deck in fact they are not fit for men to live on."[14] The men were just as quick to grumble about their officers. Just as good officers inspired them, little disillusioned the Irish American serviceman as much as when they perceived their commanders to be corrupt, incompetent, or overly disciplinary. As was so often the case with Civil War correspondents, Irish Americans were wont to discuss the bad far more than the good. What reverberates through their commentary is a clear belief that they felt very much the equal of anyone in shoulder straps, another feature they shared with their nonethnic comrades.[15] In 1862, Thomas Keating of the 9th New York State Militia was despondent with his company's lot, feeling that "us Poor solders are Rob of our food and gold and the Capt Pocket the Money and if We say anything about it We are Put in the guard house and a round iron ball Put around you foot."[16] Matthew

Eagan had a similarly negative view of some of his Excelsior Brigade captains. He considered that if defeat came, it would "not be the Private soldiers fault" but "the fault of Officers." He continued: "there are Capts getting pay from Government that Knows no more about Commanding Comp^{ys} no more than the Child that was never Born all they want is to make money and rob the poor soldier of what is thare due."[17] When Kilkenny native Jeremiah Keenan heard that his despised former first lieutenant and another ex-comrade were seeking to recruit a new company back in Rochester, he could not contain his anger. He wrote to his brother: "I tell you what I would do sooner to enlist in that company I would drown myself first sooner then to enlist with that scoundrel." He advised his sibling that if either officer approached him he was to respond with "a kick in the ass and spit in his face . . . I would rather have any one belonging to me shot to death sooner than to enlist with any of them two fellows."[18]

Difficulties with officers were not restricted to nonethnic regiments. Many men in Irish units were forced to look on as often bitter struggles developed among Irish officers for control within ethnic units, sometimes jeopardizing the stability of the entire formation. Just such a dispute erupted in the nascent Irish Brigade, bringing the colonel of the 63rd New York and the line officers to "dagger points." During the argument, the 63rd's officers were persuaded to sign a memorial against Thomas Francis Meagher in the belief he was about to break up the regiment.[19] These disputes had the potential to drag in the men in the ranks, and even their home communities. They could also be long lasting. As the 9th Massachusetts was looking toward its discharge and return home in 1864, bitter factions within the regiment threatened to turn what was supposed to be a momentous occasion into a violent debacle. James Healy warned his family off attending their march through Boston, cautioning them to make sure to "not at any time keep close by them." He explained that "there is two or three different parties in the Regt. some for and the most against the Colonel and it is expected there will be hot work if we go through places where some of the parties reside most especially through North End."[20]

As well as navigating their line officers and the internal politics of their units, like everyone else Irish Americans were ultimately at the mercy of the decisions of their commanding generals. Here they proved just as quick to offer assessments on competence. Following the infamous Mud March of January 1863, which had seen the Army of the Potomac become bogged down in an ultimately futile attempt to flank Confederate positions in Fredericksburg,

Virginia, William McIntyre expressed his pleasure at the removal of Ambrose Burnside from the head of the army. He was a general who William felt had turned his "Brigade into jack-asses or some other kind of animal." Still, he thought his replacement, Joe Hooker, was not the "right man" for command, instead advocating William Franklin or Edwin Sumner for the position, "as they are better engineer's."[21] There is no question that George B. McClellan, who had commanded the Army of the Potomac through much of 1861 and 1862, enjoyed an unassailable position as the war's most revered army commander among Irish Americans, but there was also room for the appreciation of others, such as Ulysses S. Grant. In 1864, John O'Connor of the 151st New York Infantry voiced his delight with Grant's appointment to command. He was confident that "old Lee will have to look sharp," as they finally had "A good General at our head . . . that Lee can not out general."[22]

Sooner or later, most Irish Americans came face to face with the realities of war. The shock of first seeing dead bodies and witnessing the destructive force of projectiles on the human form prompted many to share those experiences on paper. This is unsurprising, as initial encounters with mortality left a deep impression on most Civil War soldiers.[23] Patrick Carney, a Co. Tyrone carpenter in the 69th Pennsylvania, walked onto his first major battlefield at Fair Oaks, Virginia, in June 1862. "i never Saw in my life time the sight i saw," he admitted, as he sought to convey the scale of death he had witnessed. "our Company was sent out yesterday afternoon to berry the Dead and and we ware ought 2 hours and we berried 46 Rebles."[24] Thomas Hagan spared his mother few of the gory details when he reported back on his initial impressions of death on the battlefield. "what you hear about the dead soldiers is true thare is some with their legs and arms and heads stuck up out of thair graves thare is a bird that we call the turkey hawk that caries them off som times thay take a whole bodey off with them at a time."[25] Cork laborer Edmund Ford had his first taste of battle at Perryville, Kentucky, in October 1862. The experience remained seared into his mind when he wrote of it a month later: "in every diriction the ded bodys lein all around us . . . Some with there heds Cut of some there legs and arms it tuck them two days to pick them up."[26] Another Corkman, former day laborer Daniel Driscoll, was equally affected by what he saw at Fort Hindman in the aftermath of the January 1863 Battle of Arkansas Post, Arkansas. "it was horable to see the work that our shells had don," the USS *Cincinnati* sailor wrote, "there was horses and men Piled upon one Another compleetley torn to Peaces."[27]

As men grew used to the sights of the battlefield, they remarked on them less frequently. What emerged instead—as with Barney Carr—were indications of war weariness and battle fatigue.[28] The ordeal of the Peninsula in 1862 had certainly taken its toll on James Dowd of the Irish Brigade. Following their withdrawal, he confided to his wife: "we are out of the State of Virginia at last thank God safe I hope we will never get back to it again."[29] After their harrowing experience at Fredericksburg, another Irish Brigade soldier, William Dwyer from Co. Tipperary, responded negatively to rumors that they might have to renew the fight. He admitted, "I don't want to see any more for to see all the men that fell there on the 13th of decr last it was a heart rending sight to see them falling all around me."[30] These sentiments were not static. They ebbed and flowed with the coming and going of severe battles and campaigns. Former day laborer John Dougherty, a patriotic soldier who in early September 1862 described the good spirits of the Irish Brigade in which he served as the "envy of the rest of the army," had written just six weeks earlier of his hope that "none of the boys will take it in to their head to list for soldiering is not what it is cracked up to be."[31] His July letter was penned during a period of low morale in the army, which had recently endured the Seven Days' Battles in Virginia.

Some of those who enlisted later in the war provided the most candid combat accounts, shorn of all sentimentality. Thomas Reiley sent his mother a particularly visceral description of the panic and terror he felt when his 139th New York went into action at Bermuda Hundred in May 1864:

> thare was a battery a little on our right, i heared a nuf of thare nose you can bet for them and the Rebs was blazing a way most afful . . . i can tell you i was most affule hot about an half houre i do not wish to be in such a place a gain i never thought i would git of that feald a live you must tink it was kind of cloce [close] when the man alongside of me got it right in the arme next to me when he got hit i thought shure i was hit to for he let a yel out of him and turnd around to git of the feald when he ran right bang aganst me and over i when i wen i thought shure i was gon in but i found out thay was nothing the matter with me.[32]

Irish Americans varied greatly in how much they were prepared to divulge with respect to their experiences in action. This is unsurprising, given that many men were writing to their sisters, wives, and mothers, and naturally sought to shield them from the realities of the dangers they faced. Those who did discuss battle almost never portrayed their experiences through a filter of heroism and sentimentality; the overriding tendency for these working-class men was either to relay events in a descriptive matter-of-fact fashion, or to lay bare some of what they felt and experienced with a sense of realism. This is a feature that has previously been identified in the writings of semiliterate, working-class servicemen, no matter their ethnicity.[33] It remained true for Irish Americans regardless of whether or not they served in a green flag unit. When they were writing within their communities and out of the overtly public gaze, there was less need to cloak themselves in the mantle of the "Fighting Irish." However, the working-class Irish American tendency to present their experiences of combat in an unvarnished, unsentimental fashion can conceal the fact that they carried with them into action a set of societal and personal expectations that centered around the moral courage of themselves, their comrades, and their officers.[34] As a result, any individual who did not meet these expectations, or failed a test that the majority of their comrades passed, exposed themselves to censure. These attitudes conformed in almost every respect to the norms prevalent within wider American service.[35] While Irish American troops are often regarded as having had less exposure to the public shaming within home communities that others faced, this does not appear to have been the case when it came to combat.[36] On the contrary, they proved just as ready to name and shame those who exhibited these perceived deficiencies as were their nonethnic comrades, indicating that they—and many in their communities—expected men to perform bravely and honorably under fire.

Doubts about a comrade's moral strength were not just confined to performance on the field of battle. Writing to his family in Philadelphia in early 1862, William McIntyre of the 95th Pennsylvania Infantry shared his views on another Irish American comrade: "James Carroll was left at the Hospital . . . I dont know what is the matter with him unless it is weakness I think it is for he don't look sick."[37] Those serving in nonethnic units were more than willing to cast aspersions on the character of their countrymen if they didn't meet the mark. Cavan native James Fitzpatrick was serving with the 96th New York Infantry at Bermuda Hundred, Virginia, in 1864 when he heard that fellow Irish immigrant John Maguire—serving in a different regiment on a different front—had shot himself in the hand to avoid battle. "I understand that John

Maguire Maimed him Selfe in place of the Rebles he was not in the fight at Cold Harbour," he reported to his mother and sister, "and all the 98 [98th New York] knows it."[38] After the July 1862 Battle of Malvern Hill, Patrick Dooley of the 40th New York Infantry struggled with reports that emerged about his friend Mike Sexton. He had been within three yards of him when Confederate artillery began to take a toll on the unit, but Mike had soon disappeared. Dooley concluded that the bombardment must have "made poor Mike a little discouraged and induce him to crawll away to a more comfortable quarter." It was three days before he was next heard from, when he reported wounded. Despite their friendship, Patrick clearly harbored suspicions, and was willing to share them with the community at home. "all the men in the Company, and especially the Captain think that he Shot himself in the hand in order to get home" he explained, though he remained reluctant to believe that his friend "would act So barbarous towards himself."[39]

The instances related above took place in nonethnic regiments, but in each case involved one Irish American commenting on the actions of another. All of the soldiers they were referring to were members of their home communities, which were intrinsically Irish American in their makeup. By drawing attention to these perceived failings, these men were articulating their belief that their comrades had failed not only a test of manhood, but had failed in their duty to the community from which they were drawn. At the core of that expected duty was performance in combat.

Irish American writings on facing the enemy comprehensively demonstrate that tropes such as those that view the Irish as possessed of an "ardor for war" and "a sheer love of combat" are far wide of the mark.[40] There was no material difference between how Irish Americans reacted to battle in comparison to any other group. They shared the same fears and failings, the same capacity for courage. The majority also shared the same expectations that the man standing beside them would do their duty by their uniform, their regiment, their company, and their community—expectations that the dictates of nineteenth-century manhood demanded of almost everyone in Federal service, regardless of ethnicity. It was this that influenced their performance under fire, not some in-built predilection for violent confrontation.[41] As with their non-Irish comrades, those who wrote of a burning desire for battle generally found such sentiments did not survive first contact with armed Confederates.

A continuation of these trends can be seen in the development of esprit de corps during the war and how Irish American men referenced battlefield performance. The evolution of esprit de corps was a particularly important factor for Irish Americans in mixed units, as it could serve to ease ethnic, religious, and political differences.[42] In their writings, they consistently preferenced describing the exploits of their company, regiment, or brigade over personal or individual courage. James Hayes from Co. Cork offered a relatively rare exception in late 1862 when he proclaimed to his brother from Middle Tennessee: "I embrace danger."[43] Significantly, James was writing to a male relative, whereas many of his comrades were penning letters to female family members. More typical was Limerick immigrant Michael Daly, who put down a Confederate retreat from his regiment's front in Tennessee to the fact that "they heard that they were in action with the 7th Illinois Cavlry."[44] After overcoming some Confederates in northern Virginia during the early months of the war, Michael Foran of the 5th Pennsylvania Reserves reported to his cousin: "thay giv us a new name this morning Those rebels Was cald the Tigers and our Curnell Cold us the lines of Pinnsyliania and a Terer To the Vergnins Tigers."[45] As with most Civil War soldiers, Irish Americans' pride in their unit—ethnic or not—tended to strengthen as the regimental esprit de corps grew and the men endured hardships and battle together. Illiterate Irish-born laborer Joseph McConaghy of the mixed 73rd Pennsylvania Infantry spoke for many when he wrote in late 1863 that "i had rather be with my regtment than to be a way from it i did not like to leave the boys for i have ben with them too yers and half."[46]

As the war progressed, many old soldiers like Joseph McConaghy who had shown a consistent commitment to the war effort had to contend with an influx of new men who had not been there in 1861 and 1862. This was the case for many veterans, who often looked upon those who had sat out the conflict's early years with a sense of scorn.[47] When the draft loomed, some commented on their delight at the prospect that these men would now have to fight. Following the passage of the Militia Act in the summer of 1862, regular James McHugh from Co. Tyrone sarcastically asked his mother to "give my respects to the drafted men and tell them i wished they would all have to go girls and all."[48] Mathew McCourt was in similarly caustic mood when he told his mother and sister, "i guess i we will Soon see a good many more of the nice young men of Ann Arbor out here when they commence drafting but when they get here they wont think there is much fun in Souldering."[49] Some commentary, such as that from McCourt, suggests that they held particular resentment toward those from more well-to-do backgrounds who had heretofore avoided service. By the time the Enrollment Act was in full swing in late 1863, Timothy Toomey expressed his disgust at the antics of those seeking to avoid enlistment. He was glad he was in the army rather than "to be waiting the draft at home and getting up some dam lie about myself in order to get exempt why it seems that there is not a dozen sound men in Bloomfield every man that was drafted had something the matter of him."[50]

Some veterans' views on those sitting out the war were borne from contempt for a perceived lack of courage and patriotism. But for many of these working-class men there was also a heavy dose of emotional and economic resentment that these new recruits had avoided so much of the fighting, and were now able to join on better economic terms. Garrett Barry was already lamenting the improving terms of later enlistees by April 1863. Writing to family after meeting an acquaintance from home in a nine-month unit, he grumbled: "I for one if I new as mutch as I do now I should not have come when I did I should wait until this big Bounty would be given & thin come it would pay to get kiled then & not have to stay but nine mounths at that."[51] John Madden was of similar mind. By August 1863, wearied by the "awful carnage" and "fruitlessness of war," he gave voice to his feelings about the new draftees: "Wait Till some of them are in it going in 3 years since the bloody rebellion broke out and I left my fire to fight for the Country. Send them down into this hot climate and some of them will curse the hour they were born."[52] Some hoped that the draft would snare specific individuals from their community who they particularly disliked. William Carroll of the 7th Connecticut Infantry wrote to his mother: "i suppose the have a great time drafting up in Connecticut let me Know if the have Stephen Hall yet i hope the will."[53]

Irish Americans had the most to say about drafted men around the times when the draft lotteries were taking place. Outside of those periods, they expressed relatively little opinion on the matter. They had almost nothing to say about the still greater numbers who were coming to the war as substitutes and bounty volunteers, despite the large Irish contingent among them. This can be partly explained by the fact that these new men were overwhelmingly drawn from the same class and financial background as they were. Much as these veterans may have resented the financial inducements that brought the fresh recruits into service, the majority of Irish American servicemen did not have an expectation that every man of military age from their communities should be in uniform. They realized and accepted that this was an impractical commitment for men of their societal position, and in any event, most of them felt that their communities had already sent their fair share to the front.

Far and away the overriding sentiment prevalent among Irish Americans was not anger at who was not in the service, or when they had joined, but their hopes for who they wanted to avoid the uniform. Again and again, soldiers and sailors expressed a desire that their friends and family members avoid the dangers of a military life. This is another trait that the Irish shared with other Federal servicemen, though Irish Americans seem to have articulated it to an extremely high degree.[54] Many vocalized such hopes in almost the same breadth as condemning others who stayed at home. Just a few weeks before articulating his disgust at the antics of Bloomfield men seeking to avoid the draft, Timothy Toomey voiced his regret that his friend Daniel Sheehan's name had been drawn.[55] When it came to a desire for those closest to them to avoid the military life, there was little distinction between early or late war recruits. As men who were used to living an often precarious financial existence, they were all too familiar with the economic motivators that attracted substitutes to the military. This acknowledgment seems to have served to temper many Irish American veterans' reactions toward these financial recruits—as long as they did their duty.

The significant numbers of Irish Americans who entered the fray after 1861 and 1862—many of them substitutes or bounty volunteers—experienced the conflict from the perspective of the much-maligned late war recruit. This complex, important, and neglected group was vital to securing Union victory, particularly as the majority of early war volunteers chose not to reenlist at the close of their terms of service.[56] Certainly, not all substitutes and late war bounty enlistees were created equal, and there was undeniably extreme variability as to their quality.[57] Bounty jumpers in particular had a dramatic contemporary impact on perceptions of late war recruits, who often came to be seen as the antithesis of the volunteer ideals of 1861 and 1862. This led to the adoption of a more draconian approach in how these men were treated. That was something experienced by Co. Laois substitute Edward Fitzpatrick, who found himself virtually imprisoned in a Trenton camp in order to prevent his abscondment before he was assigned to his unit in November 1864: "this is not Just the place that you mite think it was we cant git out . . . wear pend rit up her lik Beef cretrs we cant luck over the fence it self and if i had to go a gane i wold not go as a sub for we Dont git the choise of regment thay send us war thay se fit to put us thare is all sorts hear thare is sum swaren and sum praing and sum dancn and sum singen."[58]

Within the ranks, the degree of opprobrium substitutes and bounty men received from early war enlistees often depended on when the new men entered their units and what they subsequently endured together. In the Eastern Theater, where most Irish Americans served, many of those who joined the army prior to the 1864 campaigning season integrated well, developed their own sense of esprit de corps, and came to be generally accepted by the bulk of their regiments. One of them was Irish immigrant John Hall, who joined the Irish Brigade in January 1864. When he reflected in 1865 on the hardships he had experienced over the previous year, he did so with the sorrow and pride of a veteran, lamenting "theres only 8 of us that left Hart Island n.y here at present out of our fine Company."[59] There was a marked distinction in perception between those—like Hall—who had endured the brutal summer of 1864 and those who had not. This was evident in the aftermath of a mass capture of 165 men of the famed 69th New York Infantry while on picket on 30 October 1864. The fallout from this incident was immediate and severe, and an investigation was launched into the events surrounding it. In seeking to explain the catastrophe, the 69th's Lieutenant Robert Milliken reported that 190 of his soldiers that night were "new men," and only forty were "old soldiers." Detailed analysis of the service history of the 120 captured men confirms what Milliken meant; he regarded someone as a "new man" if he had arrived in the late summer or fall of 1864, while anyone who had experienced the Overland Campaign—substitute or not—was regarded by him to be an "old soldier."[60]

Regardless of whether he was a volunteer or a substitute, any man who joined the military after the first year of war did so in the full knowledge of what he might face. As the war progressed, many throughout the service saw the army as little more than a death sentence. If you had to serve, most agreed, there was only one branch to consider. Cavan immigrant James Fitzpatrick of the 96th New York Infantry articulated this when he heard that one of his family had joined up. "I fill Sorry to think that he w going into the Cavelry I Rather he would go in to the Navy but I am glad he did not go into the Infantry."[61] The navy was considered the safer option, something that Irish American bluejackets freely admitted.[62] There is little doubt that this influenced many when they were deciding where to serve. Watching soldiers being transferred to the navy in early 1864, sailor Daniel O'Neil remarked how "the

Poor Fellows are glad to get rid of the Army."[63] Dublin sailor Thomas Hynes encountered one of these transferred men and found that he had previously known him in the East India Company. In conversation, he learned that the new tar had endured "one Brother shot down by his side," had been wounded himself, and had just received news that another brother had been killed. Hynes told his wife: "we often tallk of what difference there is between the Army & the Navy and of how small a chance I should have stood of ever returning alive if I had have been foolish enough to gone there . . . my old acquantance thanks his stars that he is out of it all right."[64] In the face of the frequent risks these servicemen faced with respect to their well-being and welfare, it is no surprise that many of them sought solace and protection in one the main constants of their lives—their religion.

FAITH

Whether a soldier or sailor, the majority of Irish Americans shared similar experiences to their non-Irish comrades when adjusting to life in camp and coming to terms with the shock of action. But one area that did set them apart was their religion. The Catholic faith was far and away the predominant creed among Irish Americans in the Union military. While much work has been done on how men of other denominations interacted with their religion, prior to the gathering of this corpus, the lack of letters from ordinary Irish soldiers has proved a major impediment for those seeking to understand the lives of nonelite Catholics.[65] Despite their numbers, throughout the conflict these men had to contend with a profound lack of access to their clergy. Only fifty-three Catholic chaplains are known to have served between 1861 and 1865, a modest presence that was supplemented by the hundreds of nuns who volunteered in wartime hospitals.[66] Soldiers and sailors outside ethnic regiments had particularly scant interaction with Catholic clerics. Their correspondence demonstrates that in their absence they had to develop alternative ways to interact with their faith.

The dominance of Catholicism has often led to the disappearance from the narrative of the many thousands of Presbyterian and Anglican Irish Americans in U.S. uniform. Yet they were there, often fighting shoulder to shoulder with their Catholic counterparts in ethnic Irish formations. Perhaps the best-known example is William McCarter of the Irish Brigade, a Protestant who after the conflict recorded his experiences with the 116th Pennsylvania Infantry.[67] As McCarter's reminiscences indicate, there seems to have been remarkably little in the way of sectarian tension between Anglican, Presbyterian, and Catholic Irishmen in these units.[68] Instead the bonds of shared military participation appear to have united them. A case in point is that of Co. Armagh Presbyterian Lieutenant Robert Boyle of Corcoran's Irish Legion, mortally wounded in June 1864 at Cold Harbor. When he was shot down, he fell beside Co. Tipperary Catholic James Hickey. In what proved to be his final letter to his wife from Libby Prison, Boyle took care to reveal Hickey's fate, stating that he "died beside me on the field." Boyle's widow, Agnes, subsequently donated this precious piece of correspondence to Hickey's widow, Alice, in order that she might receive a pension.[69] This absence of sectarian rancor among the military Irish also appears to have been broadly true outside the ethnic units, though there were contrary voices. One was offered by John Corcoran of the 2nd Massachusetts Infantry, who in 1862 accused "orange men" of being the "mean Irishmen" then seeking draft exemptions as foreign nationals in St. Louis. Corcoran felt sure that "a true Son of Earin" would attempt no such thing.[70]

Regardless of whether they were Catholic, Anglican, or Presbyterian, many Irish Americans were believers in the role of God's providence, and in God's potential to directly influence their lives. This was something they held in common with the majority of Civil War soldiers and sailors. William Finn certainly thought God was with him when his vessel, the USS *Shawsheen*, was captured and destroyed shortly after he left her, an incident that led him to "feel that gods Providence is on my side."[71] As the war dragged on, the seemingly random hand fate took in determining who lived and died forced veterans to adapt their notions of providence. Increasingly, it became something they hoped was playing a role even in the moment of death. Some of them joined their comrades in embracing what Peter Carmichael has termed "providential pragmatism," which allowed them to adapt to circumstance and maintain their belief in God in the face of such tumult.[72] When Irish immigrant and veteran volunteer Smith Davis was killed in action at Spotsylvania, his fellow Irish American veteran James Grogan wrote of his hope that "Providence in its mercy put some thought of the terrible danger his soul was in and as there is no limit to Gods mercy, let us hope his soul is at rest."[73] The pair also appear to offer another example of shared background outweighing religious difference; Smith Davis was a Presbyterian, while it is likely that James Grogan was a Catholic.

The mortal danger and strain of combat that these men consistently faced caused many to look to God in hopes of survival. Dennis Larkin from Co. Galway, a late war enlistee, invoked God again and again in the many letters he wrote home through 1864 and 1865. His hope that God would "protect" and "spare" him became a mantra that sometimes bordered on a desperate plea. For him and many like him, his religion and faith were fundamental in enabling him to endure. Typical were the sentiments he expressed when rumors circulated that his 6th New York Heavy Artillery was bound for the hard fighting around Petersburg: "some sayes that we are gone to PeatersBurg . . . i hoPe that we wont go to PeatersBurg i hoPe that we wont go thare fore that Place is a Bad if the regment go thare thay wont maney come out of thare But you must not feeal Bad aBout it if we go thare for I hoP that the great god will Bring me safe out of it and every other Poor man."[74] Dennis Larkin repeatedly hoped that God would enable him to see home again. For him, as it was for a lot of working-class Irish Americans, religion was completely intertwined with thoughts and manifestations of community and home—yet another similarity they shared with their non-Irish comrades.[75] Traditionally, Sundays had represented the day when working-class men had the opportunity to spend the most time with friends and family. When Thomas Keating of the 9th New York State Militia heard church bells while on guard duty in Maryland, it immediately conjured images of home: "i Stood and Listen and it Made me Cry it Put me in mined of father moony bells" [Father Mooney presided over his home parish in New York City].[76] Writing in 1862, Thomas Diver of the Irish 69th Pennsylvania told his mother, "this is Sunday and it is the day that I think the most of home I was at Mass this morning."[77] A rare chance to attend a church caused the thoughts of Thomas Doyle of the 4th Maine Infantry to turn to his wife: "I was glad to think bouth you and me herd the word of god to geather on the same Sunday all though far a part."[78]

Not all Irish American soldiers had such connections to the Church, or felt the need to practice their faith at the front. Asked if there was access to Catholic clergy in the 1st New York Cavalry, John Kelly replied, "there *is* But Prayers are all forgotten Cheif Devotion is Cleaning the horse + Sadle."[79] Nicholas Mahar noted how fleeting devotion could be among the men as he recalled a Sunday when "a man sing and praid for us Solgers but i gest tha forgot it befor tha got to camp."[80] Captain John Lynch of the Irish Brigade, in recounting how the men under his charge spent their leisure time, remarked that they "sit by the Camp fire & talk or go to their tents and say their Prayers (card playing)."[81] But even for those with little faith, access to a Catholic chaplain brought its benefits, as the interconnectivity between religion and community meant that, aside from spiritual succor, priests were regularly called upon to act as a link with home.

The most common manifestation of this association between chaplain and community involved the remittance of money. This was a benefit particularly enjoyed by men in ethnic units. "I will this day through the hands of the priest send you 50 Dollars," Michael Connerty of the Irish Brigade informed his mother in early 1862.[82] Even where Catholic soldiers had restricted access to the clergy, they often sought them out to perform this role. To this end Canadian-born Irish American Patrick Collins of the 6th Maine Infantry turned to Father Francis McAtee of the 31st New York Infantry, who served in the same division. He informed his family that the priest was "a Splended man i will send my money home by exepress . . . he will express it for me."[83] While the preference in such matters was to utilize chaplains of their own denomination, if unavailable Irish Americans were willing to turn to those of other faiths. When Catholic John Sheehan of the 94th New York Infantry failed to get to the express office himself, he asked his regiment's Presbyterian chaplain to go for him, as he "has always done it for the men and it always went safe."[84]

Regardless of the ancillary functions performed by Catholic chaplains, their primary purpose was to provide spiritual support and access to the sacraments. But the vast majority of Irish American Catholics did not encounter them with anything approaching regularity during the war. Instead, these men had to take any opportunities that arose to attend mass and, more importantly for men facing their mortality, to confess and receive absolution. Most commonly, this came when a priest passed through their brigade, division, or corps, or for sailors when they were in port. Outside of such occasions, many looked to the religious of other denominations for spiritual comfort. Joseph Hopkins Twichell, the Congregationalist chaplain of the 71st New York Infantry, found that while some of the many Irish under his charge sought out Catholic mass or avoided his services altogether, up to two-thirds of his attendees could be Irish Catholics.[85] Those reluctant to take such steps had to look to themselves and their families for their spiritual welfare. One of the methods they employed to this end was to have masses offered in their name. Before leaving for the front, Cavan native Thomas Doyle and his friend went to confession, received the Holy Sacrament, and "left 5 dollars apiece for Masses while we are away."[86] In 1863, Thomas Monaghan of the 95th Pennsylvania Infantry wrote to thank his mother for "the Mass you have got Said for me."[87] In the absence of direct contact with ministers of the Church, these actions helped provide some spiritual solace, particularly in the eyes of concerned relatives at home. But in order to feel a direct link with God at the front, Irish Americans turned instead to physical objects of their religion—objects that they could carry about their person.

For Irish American Catholics in the Union military, the most common expression of their faith came in the form of physical sacramentals. The regular use of such objects was a major plank of the "devotional revolution" that the Catholic Church had been engaged in, and Irish American servicemen eagerly and wholeheartedly embraced it. The comfort they provided allowed many to cope in the absence of the spiritual support that most of their comrades enjoyed.[88] Overwhelmingly, the devotional objects of choice were those that could be worn about the neck, especially scapulars and Agnus Dei.[89] Together with items such as religious medals, rosary beads, small crosses, and prayerbooks, these made up the religious toolkit of the Catholic Irish in the field. This was poignantly demonstrated with the 1988 discovery of the partial remains of Irish Brigade soldiers buried on the field at Antietam, where among the artifacts recovered was a miraculous medal, a crucifix, and rosary beads.[90] Such items were important for the devout, but they also took on the function of protective talismans for thousands of men of more moderate faith. One such man was sailor John Sullivan, who in 1863 described for his mother the measures he took to strengthen his resolve: "i have this agnus Die Next to my Hearth Mother and a pitchures of you and my Dear litel Brothers Witch Will give Me Courage through Every battll."[91] John Dougherty of the Irish Brigade confided that the "small articles" he wore "gave me a feeling of safty in the time of danger when the shells was busting over us and the bullets flying thick around I felt perfectly safe."[92]

Active servicemen obtained devotional objects through a variety of means, and arduous conditions necessitated their constant replacement. Catholic chaplains sought to distribute them to the faithful whenever they had an opportunity to do so. John O'Connell of the 2nd Massachusetts related that when "a priest came among the catholics of this regiment he . . . gave most of us Medals and Agnus Deis."[93] The scapular William Dwyer of the Irish Brigade had been given by his chaplain, Father James Dillon, had seen him safely through the 1862 bloodbaths of Antietam and Fredericksburg, but by January 1863 he was in need of a replacement, as it was "all wore and I lost the part that goes down my back."[94] Most obtained these items from home. Telling his mother he had not forgotten his "duty to God and the Blessed Virgin," Marine Peter Campbell requested she send "a scapular to wear . . . get it Blessed before you send the scapular."[95] James Healy of the 9th Massachusetts Infantry was pleased to receive a religious habit from his parents in August 1862, remarking that "it resembles the one Father Skully [Father Scully, the regimental chaplain] gave me."[96] Some men sought to augment their sacramentals, and it is probable they occasionally even did so with holy material from Ireland. In 1861, Patrick Dooley wrote of the "Blessed Clay" he had recently received. "I will Sew it to night to my Agnesdei," he determined, hoping that the addition would add to the power of his sacramental. It is possible that the clay he procured had originated from a holy site near his native Clonmel in Co. Tipperary.[97]

While most Irish Americans were stoic about their lack of access to Catholic ministration, the occasion when it could and did bring distress for them and their families came when they were approaching death. There can be little doubt that a fear of dying without the performance of last rites contributed toward unit selection for some of the more devout.[98] In the main, hospital staff and chaplains of other faiths made every effort to provide spiritual comfort and, where possible, to procure Catholic priests for dying Irish Americans, but often there was none to be had. In writing to the family of Dubliner Patrick

MRS. SAYERS
HAS FOR SALE CATHOLIC Books, Crucifixes, Rosaries, Holy Water Fonts, Biscuit Figures and Scapulars, stamped and worked in the neatest style. Habits made to order. No. 60 Prince st., two doors from Mulberry. 285

FIG. 3. An advertisement from the *New York Irish American* of 6 September 1862 offering the sale of religious items. (*New York Irish American Weekly.*)

Connely following his death in South Carolina, the Episcopal chaplain of the 6th Connecticut Infantry lamented that the soldier "could not have been buried by his own Priest. But there is *none* in all this Department. It is very wrong, I think, because I know it would be a great comfort to the boys to have some Father confessor where they could have his services."[99]

For many Catholics, the absence of a priest denied them a "good death" in the eyes of their loved ones.[100] Aware of the impact this could have on those at home, mortally wounded men occasionally sought to provide them with advance consolation, while undoubtedly some comrades were willing to put words into their mouths to achieve the same end. When Irish immigrant Marine Mathew Droney of the USS *Miami* was mortally wounded in August 1864, his sergeant informed his widow that Mathew requested the following words be passed on to her: "I die in full faith of our Blessed and Holy Religion, and am confident that the blood of Jesus has washed away my sins and that the blessed virgin is now interceding for me."[101] When seaman Thomas Hynes died while on service at Acapulco, Mexico, his wife asked if he had received Catholic rites. The response would have brought her little comfort. She was told that Thomas "had not the rights of the church but he had his senses to the last and Jesus the great high priest to hear."[102] In response to a like query, the widow of Kearn Phalen of the 11th Connecticut Infantry was informed by another Irish soldier: "About the Priest—he did not have one for I Can Assure you that they are not Very Plenty in the army I don't know that there is one in the 18th Corps + as for Being Prepared for death I Can not Say I hope that he was."[103]

Religion and faith may have helped many Irish Americans to better endure the trials of the American Civil War, but it rarely did so in isolation. Indeed, for many it paled in significance beside interactions of a more earthly nature, most especially those they maintained with home and family.

INTERACTIONS WITH HOME AND FAMILY

While their faith in God was important, for many Irish Americans the relationship of primary significance during their service was with the home front.[104] That was certainly the case for Irish immigrant Pat McConnell, who had left his widowed mother and four young siblings behind in Brooklyn to answer the call in November 1861. Within a few months, he had squirreled away $110 in the Williamsburgh Savings Bank, allowing him to boast of "what I have been doing since I have been sojering." He had big plans for his family's economic future. At the top of his list was his determination "to have a head Stone on my Fathers Grave" even if he had to go "hungry and bare legget" in order to achieve it.[105] Then, just as Pat's war was set to begin in earnest, a letter arrived from home and the bottom fell out of his world. June 1862 was the month Pat's 4th New York Infantry finally moved into Virginia. But he would have remembered it as the month that he learned—out of the blue—that all of his siblings had been placed in charitable care. While comrades were turning their minds toward facing the Confederates, he was frantically seeking to assist his family. His mother, Ann, believing Pat to have "trouble enough," had not informed him of the extent of her financial travails, and the semiliterate woman had been slow to pass on the address of their new, smaller accommodations.[106] "I hope to God you will bring them back again as soon as you receive this letter," he pleaded, firing off $20 to help secure his siblings' return. "my only request is that you get the childern back again and if you dont I donot want to hear from you again except it is impossible to do so." As a last resort, he offered to pay his siblings' board as soon as he next mustered for pay, suggesting the Catholic Half Orphans Asylum for them, where "besides being brought up to there Religion they would get a good education."[107]

In that summer of 1862, it was not military maneuvers that preoccupied Pat McConnell's mind, or army life that dictated his morale. It was the situation at home. Interactions with home—or a lack thereof—did as much to shape the Irish American experience of war as the trials at the front. For Pat McConnell and thousands of others, it was the most consequential relationship of their service. A preoccupation with the welfare and goings-on of those at home was something Irish Americans shared with the great majority of their comrades, Federal and Confederate, and its importance has been demonstrated by numerous scholars.[108] Already unused to long separations from family and community, many Irishmen also had to reckon with the additional stress created by the financially precarious environment in which their families lived. Though such circumstances were far from unique to their ethnicity, the socioeconomic position of the predominantly urban working-class Irish left them more vulnerable than a great number of their military peers. The Irish American reliance on often inconstant employment and rented accommodations created especially pronounced issues for those soldiers and sailors who harbored concerns for home. Such practical domestic issues far outstripped abstract ideological ones as the greatest challenge to their commitment to the Union, and uniformed Irish Americans spent infinitely more time fretting over the financial well-being of their families than they did contemplating the political futures of the United States, the Confederacy, or Ireland.

With those at home particularly susceptible to the vagaries of the wartime economy, thousands of men were forced to steer a course that allowed their duty as a Federal soldier to coexist with their duties and responsibilities to family. It is little surprise therefore that an enormous amount of their interactions with the home front revolved around living conditions and money. For men with families on the margins, a harsher than expected winter could warrant as much attention as the movements of the rebel army. It was the increased costs that accompanied the colder months that were playing on James McGaffigan's mind when he wrote to his wife from the camp of the Irish Brigade in February 1862. He wanted to make sure that she and the children had enough money to combat the "cold and stormy" weather he had heard was lashing the northern states.[109] Similarly, Martin Flanagan, serving with his brother in the Excelsior Brigade, felt the need to explain why the money he had sent home in early 1862 had gone astray, a failure that had left his mother and sister "in neide of Coal and Clothes."[110]

Though military wages offered a guaranteed income in uncertain economic times, the failure of the Federal government to meet the challenge of regularly paying hundreds of thousands of men proved enormously problematic for working-class Irish American troops. Gallons of ink were spilled as men sought to break the news to expectant family members that there was still no sign of the long-looked for paymaster. Union soldiers were supposed to be mustered for pay every two months, but there were frequent and often long delays. "the Cry is money money money," wrote Excelsior Brigade soldier Michael Carroll in January 1862, a sentiment many others frequently echoed.[111] Once these failings became common knowledge, it would have undoubtedly impacted working-class enlistments. The erratic nature of the pay also contributed toward a broader acceptance that some men had to stay at home in order to broaden the economic base upon which family groups could draw.

The ramifications of erratic army pay had the potential to be disastrous for those on the home front, and Irish American servicemen did not have to look far for cautionary tales. John Hayes was serving in the 105th New York

Infantry in 1862 when his wife, Hanora, died in Rochester shortly after giving birth to twin girls. At the time of the delivery she had been weakened by "utter want," owing to the fact that John "did not earn five dollors all winter he had got no pay yet for his soldiering." Hanora had been forced to move to cheaper accommodations just prior to the delivery, and had only avoided the poorhouse due to the intercession of an aunt. At the front, the newly widowed John learned of his wife's fate at the same time he discovered that five of his children had been placed in institutions and orphan asylums.[112]

The inevitable consequence of such unforgivingly harsh realities was that, unlike some of their comrades, Irish American troops were extremely reluctant to advocate patriotism as a balm for their family's wartime hardships. Patriotism lay at the core of being regarded a "good citizen" on the northern home front, and patriotic women were expected to accept any hardship they faced.[113] But taking solace from high-minded ideals was the privilege of those in more secure economic circumstances; lofty sentiments of shared national suffering carried little water for those facing potential destitution. As a result—and in contrast to many of their middle- and upper-class comrades—encouraging patriotic stoicism among their families was something the working-class Irish rarely did.[114]

Instead, they expended their energies in helping their families garner aid from relief committees and in seeking out every possible means of providing for their dependents. When Terrence McFarland's mother lost her relief ticket, the Co. Down native had to work out a way of securing another one in the absence of his colonel. He assured her he would "look after it and as soon as I get It I will send it to you."[115] The frequent difficulties families had in securing relief weighed heavily on men's minds. John Madden was angered when he learned that geography prevented his mother from accessing relief with the ticket he had sent. He was serving in a New York City regiment, but his mother lived in Troy. "i think it is all a humbug for there is no one outside of the city of New York gets any money from the city of New York," he seethed.[116] James McGee of the 69th New York Infantry was equally disgusted when he heard of his family's failure to secure relief: "I hardly know what to think of the manner in which the Relief Commitee are humbugging the relations of Volunteers that are at home depending on them for support."[117]

For their part, those at home were not shy in letting servicemen know of their struggles. In early 1864, Kearn Fitzpatrick of the 11th Connecticut

Infantry received a letter from his wife, Elizabeth, that could not have failed to shake him. In a demonstration of how word spread fast among the Irish American community as well as everywhere else, Elizabeth had become aware that "the men all got paid down thear for all the women around hear got thear money" but she was yet to receive anything herself. Elizabeth was desperate; their son Willy was dying of the "lung fever," and she had been forced to keep burning their limited fuel through the night. "I aint got as much wood as will do me a nother week," she told her husband. Angered at Kearn's apparent neglect, she raged: "how do you suppose that I can get along or do you care for three little children and a woman left to the waves of the world." To reinforce the seriousness of their plight and pile pressure on her husband to act, she added, "what ill do I dont know if you dont send me some money very soon" and "write quick."[118] Similar implications of failing in financial duty to family apparently lay behind correspondence James Corcoran received from his wife, which made the 5th New York Infantryman feel like "a Convicted felon."[119] John Kennedy of the 10th Ohio Infantry had to face the ignominy of the physical arrival of his mother in camp, where she proceeded to unsuccessfully plead with his captain for his discharge, on the basis that he was her "sole support."[120]

A feeling of having left family in the lurch by enlisting and putting their lives at risk came close to overpowering some men, especially during low points in their service. Patrick Carraher from Co. Armagh was utterly consumed by regret immediately prior to the July 1861 Battle of First Bull Run. He pleaded for his wife's forgiveness for enlisting, proclaiming it to be "the worst thing I ever done since I was born." Chastising himself for being a bad husband and father by risking death, he closed by stating: "I deserve all I am getting I might just as well shoot my self where you was and then I should die happy."[121] Similarly, the enlistment of an Irish American friend whom he had thought too "steady" to join up caused John Slattery of the 40th Massachusetts Infantry to reflect on the "wrong" he had done to his parents by going to war. He felt his actions deserved a fate worse than death in battle, vowing that "if heaven should spare my life to return home I shall devote the remainder of my life to their comfort hopping they have forgave me."[122]

Though self-doubt and fear probably played a role in forming such sentiments, these men held very genuine feelings of economic responsibility. These economic burdens were something that had to be borne by the young as well as the old, as the realities of life in Irish American communities forced financial responsibilities on teenagers and adults alike. While such strains were felt by men throughout the Union military, Irish Americans were particularly susceptible to them.[123] Beyond pure economics, their societal position exposed their families to increased mortality rates, which often impacted the major earner, while social issues such as alcoholism and abandonment also contributed toward an increased financial pressure on younger men. In consequence, for the responsible majority, successfully fulfilling their duty to those at home constituted a core element of their sense of manhood. This sense of responsibility was demonstrated by Christopher McGiff of the 119th New York Infantry, who had assumed the position of the primary breadwinner due to his father's drinking. "you must not think i wount Send my money i will Send it while i have tow hands i will work fore you like a man," he vowed to his mother.[124]

One of the ways this feeling of economic responsibility manifested itself among Irish American servicemen was in consistent exhortations for friends and family to stay at home, and not to enlist. Such pronouncements were born from two concerns centered around the economic and physical well-being of their family and community. At a personal level, to varying degrees the men at the front were putting their lives on the line at least in part to secure a steady income, and they were loath to see others from their immediate family have to do the same. They also understood that the financial realities facing them meant that while some men served, others had to stay behind. This created a sense of ethnic and class solidarity that mitigated some of the alienation with those at home that manifested itself elsewhere in the military.[125] Daniel O'Neil, who had enlisted in the Marine Corps in the war's first summer, was one who recognized the disproportionate impact the conflict could have on working-class families. He wrote of his hope in early 1862 that "the War will be at an end before that time [the summer] as I believe the Poor folks of the Country are suffering from by it."[126] Timothy Toomey, a dutiful soldier, urged his mother in early 1863 to avoid seeking money from "those fellows that stay at home and advise poor men to go ought to See to their families."[127] Added to such sentiments was the fact that these soldiers and sailors were well aware of the scale of commitment their communities had already given to the war effort in terms of numbers in service. As with their non-Irish comrades, they saw themselves as representatives of that community at the front, often felt pride in being such, and wanted their sacrifice to enable those they cared about most to stay beyond danger's reach.[128]

While the pressure of financial responsibilities toward those at home could depress morale, it also had the capacity to provide servicemen with a sense of self-worth, pride, and achievement. Successfully performing the dual duties of fighting for the nation at the front and supporting dependents at home could be empowering. This pride in the sacrifice they were making also left little tolerance for any actors at home who were deemed to be unsupportive, ungrateful, or exploitative. This was articulated by Richard Sheridan. After he left for the front, he continued to pay all the bills, but he was quick to show his disdain when he felt he was being treated poorly by his father's creditors. "I suppose your landlord and grocer think I am very good as long as I send the Greenbacks," he vented, "if I was home to morrow I do not think I would remain a customer of either of them long."[129] In a further demonstration of the very real precarity many in the Irish American community faced, Richard's death at the July 1863 Battle of Gettysburg ended his support, and his father would ultimately be admitted to Blackwell's Island Alms House.

Despite the significant financial pressure placed on Irish American troops, many nonetheless retained a positive outlook about the potential long-term benefits of service for their families. Although the character of written interactions tended to accentuate negative economic events, those who could weather the erratic nature of pay musters often managed to save substantial sums. These monies could then contribute toward an improvement in the living conditions of those at home, further boosting a soldier's or sailor's sense of achievement. Despite fretting over the delays with his pay, Co. Kerry native John Sullivan of the 99th New York Infantry adopted just such an outlook as he and his family worked toward increased financial security. Pleased that his mother had been offered a position that would allow her to "live rent free" (presumably as a domestic), he looked forward to putting his future pay toward buying furniture for them all so that they could "have a nice home when I return and commence a new life."[130] Thomas Hagan wanted to use his money to "try and by you [his mother] a plase to live instead of pain rent," while John Kennedy sought to placate his distraught parent by telling her "they would have a nice little farm" as a result of his service.[131] Having deposited another $100 for his father in the express office, John Sheehan, whose brother was in the naval service, told his father: "I think I have done as well for you the past year as I ever done." When he sent home more money a few months later he added, "now this makes $225 I have sent you I think the place must be pretty near payed for it is time you was building A house."[132]

Maintaining their central role in the financial management of the home also allowed Irish American servicemen to preserve their relevance and importance, despite their distance. Fear of losing their status while they were away at war, or of being "forgotten" by friends and family, weighed on the minds of Irish American servicemen, just as it did many of their comrades.[133] As was the case with so many Civil War soldiers and sailors, they moaned continuously about the perceived failure of their families to correspond with them as regularly as they should. Timothy Toomey's sentiments, written during a bout of homesickness while on campaign in Louisiana, were typical. "I have not received any letter from you since my last," he wrote his mother: ". . . I would like to hear from home as often as the other boys there is nothing makes a fellow feel worse than to see all the other men get letters and none for him I have seen some fellows feel so bad that they would cry but I am not so chicken hearted as that I would not cry if I never had one but still I would like to hear from home often as well as the next one."[134] The impatient appeals of American Civil War servicemen for letters from home, on some occasions articulated as heartfelt pleas, at others as angry demands, are ubiquitous.[135] Left with little to occupy their thoughts during long periods in camp, anxieties about home could fester—as could disagreements conducted at long distance. While in the midst of an argument with his wife in February 1862, Matthew Eagan petulantly advised her that she "need not think about me day nor night," suggesting she instead "begin to do for yourself the same as you were before you met with me and then by the time I am shot I will be out of your mind."[136] But these were words written in the heat of the moment. Being forgotten was the very last thing he wanted. Soon afterward he was signing off a letter with a poem that entreated her to "Remember Me":

Remember me! How sadly falls
That sound upon the ear
It fills the heart with memories s[weet]
And starts the bitter tear[137]

One strategy Irish American servicemen adopted in an effort to maintain their role within the home was to attempt to remotely direct family decisions and to dispense advice and instructions. This was particularly the case for married men. Former laborer Timothy Harrington of the USS *Cumberland* was concerned that in his absence his wife would be dragged down by undesirables among their Irish American community. He issued instructions that there were a number of people she was to "have no truck with." This was a directive that particularly applied to the Sullivans, a family he regarded as having "lost there shame long agoe." To emphasize the consequences of defiance, he warned her that "if you do you are done with me."[138] Many men sought to provide more practical and less threatening guidance. In offering his mother and sister "a little simple advice," Kerry native William Harnett of the 4th U.S. Infantry encouraged them to turn "to some industry that will be likely to support ye independent of me." He explained that in "such exciting times as these no one but God can tell what solemn cricis might set in next."[139] Pennsylvania Irishman Felix Burns had similar hopes of boosting his mother's earning power. Having committed to sending along money for her rent, he suggested she put the remainder toward the purchase of a sewing machine.[140] As well as ostensibly preparing their families for the worst possible outcome, these men were eager to maintain a direct connection and influence in their loved ones' lives—an act that helped them cope with both their protracted absence and the hardships they faced at the front. At a practical level, maintaining these interactions with home required engagement with the written word. Examining just how enlisted Irish Americans dealt with the physical act of writing and interfaced with the world of wartime newspapers reveals much about not only their interpersonal interactions but also their wider interests and perspectives on the United States.

STAYING IN TOUCH: NEWSPAPERS AND LETTERS

Irish Americans relied heavily on the newspapers they were able to access and the correspondence they were able to send and receive. Both helped to influence their thoughts and actions, and could profoundly impact their morale. This was true even for men who were unable to read or write, a disadvantage that was all too common among Irish American troops. For them, developing methods by which they could successfully navigate such impediments was an essential aspect of their service.

Much of the information Irish Americans garnered about the home front and the wider war effort came via the newspapers that they read and shared. The two most significant ethnic publications during the war were the *New York Irish American* and Boston-based *The Pilot,* both of which were read by many Irish American troops. In September 1861, American-born Francis Cullen of the 24th New York Infantry sent his thanks to Mick Conley "for the [Boston] pilot for it is the first one that i Seen Sence i Left home."[141] In early 1862, Kerry immigrant William Harnett of the 4th U.S. Infantry sent home a dollar for "my subscription for the [New York] Irish American News paper for 8 months." His Irish American news had been following him across the continent during his professional service. He asked his mother to go to the newspaper's premises and "Inform the proprietor that I received the first copy of his paper on the 3rd Jany. inst for the last six months since I left Ft Hoskins Ogn. [Oregon] in July last."[142]

Heretofore, the absence of evidence for the newspaper preferences of Irish American servicemen has forced historians to rely heavily on ethnic publications such as the *Irish American* and *Pilot* as a gauge for Irish opinion. Yet, despite their popularity, the correspondence of ordinary Irish American soldiers and sailors demonstrates that they were substantially more likely to request nonethnic newspapers that originated in their home localities, or which offered speciality content. Complaining about the lack of access to papers on the Virginia Peninsula, William Shea of the 23rd Pennsylvania Infantry told those at home to "send me the [Philadelphia] inqiurer onse in a while."[143] When William Martin of Corcoran's Irish Legion sought news following the New York City draft riots, he requested the *New York Sunday Mercury,* which was particularly popular among Irish Americans, and which became known for publishing soldiers' correspondence.[144] The following month, his comrade in the Brigade, James Hand, requested both "the Sundy mercuray And the police gazete."[145] Henry Burns of the 59th New York was searching for escapism when he requested the entertainment-focused *New York Clipper,* while William Cody of the 3rd Rhode Island Heavy Artillery was eager to see how his posting was depicted when he asked for "any of the Pictorials with the battle of Hilton Head pictured in it."[146]

When it came to Irish American newspaper consumption, one publication stood supreme, particularly for the New York Irish, and it was not ethnically focused. James Gordon Bennett's *New York Herald* was requested and referenced consistently by the Irish in uniform.[147] During the war, it provided the best of both worlds for the Empire State Irish, combining local coverage of New York with extensive reporting on the conflict. "send Me the New york heareld," "get the new york herald," and "you might have seen in the herald" were lines that reverberated through the correspondence of Irish Americans.[148] Accessibility to this paper was sometimes difficult, not least because of its Democratic leanings. This was especially true immediately after the Emancipation Proclamation, but no matter its availability, it was always in high demand.[149] In May 1863, Michael McCormick of the 65th New York Infantry reported that "We get the Herald every day and that is a great favour I suppose Joe Hooker thought that we were kept long enough without it so he granted us a great favour."[150] By November the supply had dried up again, and he complained that while it was always hard to get any papers on the march, "the Herald is very hard to get at pretty near any time."[151] When William Dolan wanted political news in 1863, it was to the *Herald* and the *Mercury* that he turned, in order "to here what the democrats are going to do this spring for they say that the democrats are going to End this war by May."[152]

The popularity and dominance of nonethnic papers like the *Herald* in the reading lists of wartime Irish Americans challenges the widespread representativeness of Ireland-centric viewpoints expressed by publications like the *Irish American* and *Pilot.* For the majority, keeping up to speed with what was happening in their American homes and in their American world was their first priority. To be sure, many were also interested in staying abreast of goings-on in their old communities across the Atlantic, but at least insofar as their newspaper choices would suggest, this was very much subordinated to the events and occurrences of most direct consequence to their daily lives.

While newspapers were important, it was the letters they sent and received that were the most crucial of these men's communications with home. In this, Irish American servicemen faced more pronounced practical challenges than any of their white comrades in arms. One of the most basic revolved around where they were to direct their correspondence. Most Irish Americans made their homes in rented accommodations, and while they tended to stay in the same neighborhoods, their precise address could change frequently. In addition, many of the female members of Irish servicemen's families were domestics, some of them moving from one live-in position to the next. As a consequence, many men encountered the problem faced by the 4th New York's

Patrick McConnell, who was forced to delay contact with home as he "did not know where to write."[153]

By far the most significant obstacle to communication faced by Irish American servicemen stemmed from the unenviable position they held as the least literate major white ethnic group in the United States. In 1860 the Mid-Atlantic illiteracy rate was 4.4 percent among males and 6.5 percent among females, while in New England the respective figures were 3.9 percent and 5.4 percent.[154] The picture among Irish immigrants was markedly different. Analysis of New York City indicates that almost 20 percent of individuals in the heavily Irish Sixth Ward were illiterate in 1855. In 1860 the same city recorded 8 percent of Irishmen and 14 percent of Irishwomen over the age of twenty as illiterate.[155] The actual rates of Irish illiteracy were almost certainly higher, as some immigrants chose not to divulge to census enumerators that they were unable to read and write, a fact demonstrated by comparison of census returns with information in the widows' and dependents' pension files. As a result, for thousands of Irish Americans in uniform, successfully communicating with loved ones required not only a consideration of how they would commit their words to paper, but how those words would then be comprehended when they reached home.

Even Irish-born officers could find this a torturous and laborious process. Francis McLaughlin from Co. Donegal was a prewar engineer who served as the first lieutenant of Battery D, 1st Pennsylvania Light Artillery. Such was his reticence to take up his pen that he appears to have had his early letters written for him.[156] However, his position as an officer demanded more, and he was soon doing his best to share his thoughts directly with his wife in Philadelphia. His struggles with sentence construction and spelling demonstrate the great effort he had to pour into each missive. On 5 February 1862 he opened his letter with "Deare whife i take this faverable opturtuiny of writhing those few linse to you to let you know that i am well at preastant thanks bee to god," while that of 19 May 1862 began, "Deare whife i receved your ltter Wich give me great plesher heare of you being well."[157]

The formulaic language used by Francis McLaughlin to initiate his correspondence is typical of Civil War letters, which tended to be highly structured in nature. They usually employed stock opening and closing elements, with the body given over to inquiries and statements as to the health and well-being of individuals, a general outline of news, inquiries about goings on at home, and requests to be remembered to family and friends.[158] The widespread utilization of formulaic elements has served to mask the numbers of Irish Americans who possessed no literacy skills whatsoever. Many of the Irish who "took their pen in hand" were in fact not doing so at all, but rather were relying on a scribe or amanuensis to convey their thoughts on their behalf. The lack of distinguishing features between letters mediated through a scribe and those directly authored by a soldier or sailor makes it extremely difficult to determine the literacy levels of many Irish American troops. Letter content rarely betrays any outward signs of this mediated literacy, as invariably the soldier or sailor was presented in the first person as the "writer" of the correspondence. In instances where an illiterate or partially literate serviceman changed scribe, and where examples of both letters survive, this mediation becomes apparent. John Brennan from Co. Kildare is a case in point. The Massachusetts soldier wrote at least three letters to his wife in February 1862; while the first and last were composed in the same hand, the one sent in the middle of the month was clearly set to paper by a different writer.[159]

There is little in the three surviving letters of James McGee written between May and November 1863 to betray his illiteracy. It was only after he lost his life to a torpedo explosion in 1864 that his comrade, fellow Irishman Andrew Mooney, provided an affidavit to the effect that he had "always endorsed the envelopes as deceased could not write, that he always wrote his letters."[160] Tellingly, where the identity of scribes is revealed, they were usually fellow Irish Americans. At the end of a letter home from Daniel Driscoll to his parents following his 1861 naval enlistment, the scribe added a note: "the

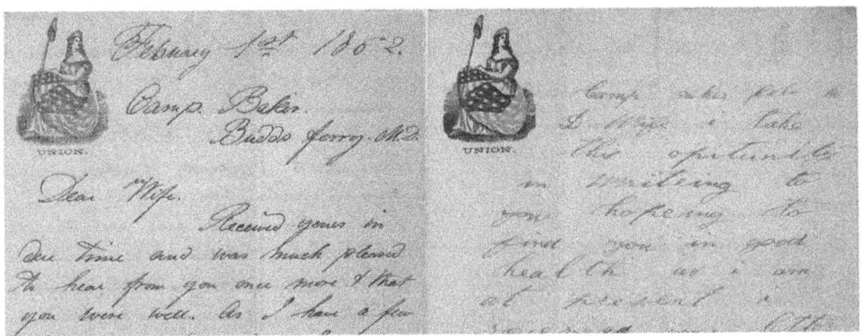
UNION.
February 1st 1862.
Camp Baker.
Budds ferry Md.
Dear Wife.
Received yours in due time and was much pleased to hear from you once more & that you were well. As I have a few

UNION.
Camp Baker Feb
D Wife I take this opertunity in writeing to you hoping to find you in good health as i am at present

FIG. 4. Comparison of handwriting in two letters "written" by John Brennan of the 11th Massachusetts Infantry. (U.S. National Archives and Records Administration.)

Scribler of this Note is your old friend Peter Murphy you Give my Respects to Jery Taylor and Wife and family Cousin Daniel Driskel & Wif father tirney and Jery Holland Desires to Be Remember to you."[161] The preference for friends and fellow community members to act as scribes was driven by the level of trust required in what was a fundamentally unequal relationship. The letters produced through mediation were generally not dictated transcripts, but rather were the product of a collaborative process between an individual and their scribe.[162] For those Irish American servicemen who were unable to read, scribes had the capacity to tamper with their messages home. As well as writing his letters, Scotsman Peter Campbell acted as something of an older brother to Laois native John Delaney in the ranks of the 18th Connecticut Infantry. There were some six years between them, John having been at most eighteen on his enlistment, Peter around twenty-four.[163] There is no evidence that either knew each other prior to service. Though they were from the same general area, they occupied different worlds; John was a paper mill worker who lived with his family in the Norwich suburb of Greenville, while Peter was a farmer's son from rural Preston. Nonetheless, John entrusted Peter with mediating his communications with home. He explained a lack of correspondence in April 1863 by stating that "I would wrote sooner but Peter being away I though I would wait till he come back."[164] Yet Peter still felt he had the authority to undermine John's correspondence. John had enclosed a cheque for $20 with his April letter, but wrote five days afterward saying he was out of money and asking his mother to send him back $1.50. Having duly written the message, Peter took it upon himself to add a postscript: "Mr [*sic*] Delaney Dear friend I told John when I come back that he wasent to send fore any money by any ones letter after this one if he did he wouldent get it because I wanted know what he wanted it fore he has be bouthering me this 2 days to write fore him because he knew."[165] Such examples demonstrate both the stigma and pitfalls attached to illiteracy, which contemporary society connected with both poverty and criminality.[166] Even in relatively close relationships, illiterate Irish American servicemen often had to deal with the presumptions of superiority that their literate comrades held over them. In such circumstances, their preference was to turn first to those who understood the workings of literacy that were specific to their own community.

As well as serving as a catalyst for increasing their correspondence, the long hours of inactivity that were a staple of military life could present Irish

American servicemen with opportunities for improving their literacy.[167] Nicholas Mahar, who struggled to find topics with which to fill his letters, wrote his sister in June 1864 that "the Capten told me tha was goin to hav a writing [s]Chool then i will try to rite ever[y] time." Regardless of the writing school, it is evident that Nicholas was already working hard to improve. At the end of the same letter, he proudly added a postscript: "this is the best leter i rot yet if i ever do i ges I will no how to rite when i Com home."[168] Martin Tiernan from Co. Roscommon was able to write home to his mother in the Five Points to tell her "I am improving in writing if I knew all the capital Letters I could Do first Rate." As if to emphasize the point, Martin practiced the capital "B" (for Company B) a total of twenty-one times at the end of his letter.[169]

Even those Irish American troops who were fully literate had to contend with the fact that many of the older generations—often the very individuals they were writing to—were not. The realities of differential intergenerational literacy meant that it regularly fell on younger generations to act as scribes and intermediaries within their own families, both for correspondence back to Ireland and with those at the front. While servicemen frequently addressed multiple family members in a single letter, it was often founded on an understanding that their siblings were acting as intermediaries. Though Thomas McCready began a letter of 30 November 1861 with "Dear Mother," he was aware that it was his sister who was reading it to her. Within a few lines he had slipped into referencing his mother in the third person: "I think it is better fore Mother . . . ," "it will seave Mother . . . ," "tell Mother . . . ," despite the fact he was purportedly directing the correspondence to her.[170] Knowledge of a parent's illiteracy also allowed servicemen to deliver information intended solely for their siblings in letters to the entire family. Jeremiah Keenan had started his 17 April 1863 letter by addressing his mother, before following it with a section specifically for his brother Richard, knowing she could not read it. Outlining the harsh realities of military life, he confided: "I did not want to let mother know about my hardship here I did not [want] her fretting about me I used to send her good letters to keep her from fretting."[171]

Those who had no access to a sufficiently literate individual within their immediate family group relied on more distant relatives, friends, and neighbors to perform that function. Such relationships not only engendered trust between the parties involved, it made them participants in the emotional lives of the family. During this period of variant intergenerational literacy, it allowed correspondence to play a significant role in ethnic community cohesion. This played out on both sides of the Atlantic. In Co. Kerry, Charles Greaney's parents took his letters to their next-door neighbor, who read them aloud for them.[172] Similarly, in College Point, Queens, Ann Dougherty relied on Patrick Curtin and Thomas Smyth, who lived nearby, to read her son's correspondence when it arrived from the Irish Brigade.[173] Over time, soldiers could come to recognize the style of a scribe, as was the case when Martin Noonan from Co. Clare received a letter from his mother and sister in late 1863: "I noticed some of James Smith writing at the latter end of your letter why dont Jimmy ever write to me any more I always thought a gread deal of him & always wished him well & do still."[174]

Written correspondence in such a partially literate society was by its very nature less private. Civil War soldiers and sailors were accustomed to their letters home being shared among family, friends, and acquaintances. Having developed against the backdrop of mass immigration, the ordinary writings of antebellum Irish Americans had already taken on a particularly public aspect, serving as vital communal links between communities in Ireland and the United States.[175] Irish American servicemen could expect their correspondence to be read aloud, normally multiple times, in a shared living space.[176] Though they could often predict who would read and hear their words, they could never be certain, particularly if the number of literate individuals in their immediate family group was small. This undoubtedly affected what they were willing to commit to paper, an important consideration when analyzing their correspondence.[177] Even so, not all Irish Americans were happy to learn that their private business had the potential to become public back home. Christopher McGiff was horrified to learn that information he had sent to his illiterate mother had become common knowledge. He had met a woman from their Irish American community who "coud tell me evey thing that i Sent home in a letter and hade a laughy over it." "Dear mother you must keep your mind to your self not tell every one whate i send home," he cautioned.[178] Peter Finegan sent a similar warning to his parents. "whoever writes letters for you I dont want such talking about affairs as was in the other I know wright from wrong."[179]

Demonstrably, literacy was not a requirement for engaging in the act of corresponding. Yet even with access to a scribe, illiterate and semiliterate Irish American troops attempted written communication with less frequency than their literate comrades.[180] The age profile of Civil War correspondents also indicates that the older an illiterate serviceman was, the lower the probability he would engage with the written word, even when an amanuensis was available. Many of these older soldiers and sailors had reached adulthood in a society dominated by the oral tradition, often with the Irish language as their native tongue. The majority of available scribes were also their juniors, and they may have been reluctant to enter into a vulnerable, unequal relationship that necessitated the unmasking of their feelings. Despite their own literary shortcomings, younger illiterates had grown up in a different epistolary landscape, one which made them more familiar and comfortable with the processes of written communication than their older brethren.[181] As a result, it provided them with easier access to the written outlet that was so central to soldier and sailor morale during the Civil War. Accessing this outlet was more emotionally demanding for the older men, something that would have served to make their wartime experience all the more arduous.

The correspondence of Irish American servicemen makes evident that a great many of the experiences, expectations, and emotions that Irish Americans contended with during the American Civil War were directly comparable to those of their non-Irish comrades. They reacted in similar ways to camp life and combat, and held similar expectations regarding the performance of their comrades and officers. They shared the same thirst for news from home and the same worries about maintaining their place within their communities. Where the greatest variance lay in these areas was in the scale and severity of some of the challenges they faced. Some were due to their working-class status, some to their ethnic and cultural background. Just as others did, many Irish Americans relied on their faith to help them through their wartime experiences—but it was harder for them to access the comfort of their religion. Like almost everyone in uniform, they sought to safeguard and provide for those at home, but economic circumstance made it harder to reconcile duty to flag and duty to family. And in common with almost all, they longed for the comfort and succor that came with exchanging letters with loved ones, but they faced a steeper learning curve and more significant obstacles than most in doing so. As with much else about their service, their capacity to overcome these challenges was not uniform. It depended on many factors that were often highly individual, not the least of which were circumstance, resolve, age, and adaptability.

4

Reputation, Race, and Politics

On 26 June 1865, Patrick Griffin was dragged across the New Orleans camp of the 6th Independent Battery, Massachusetts Light Artillery, to face field punishment. Earlier that morning, despite protesting he was sick, the eighteen-year-old had been ordered to ride out to exercise the horses. When he was thrown from his mount and claimed to be too weak to ride or walk back to camp, he was reported absent and a guard was sent to fetch him. Now he faced his officer's wrath. As his comrades looked on, Patrick was tied to a post and strung up by the thumbs, forcing him into a position that required him to stand on his toes. Within a few minutes he started to cry, complaining of headaches and begging "for God's sake to let him down." To quiet him, his captain ordered him gagged. A piece of wood was jammed into his mouth so tightly that it left the stick covered in the young man's blood. Eventually Patrick collapsed, vomiting as he was led off for a brief reprieve. He was strung up again in short order. Before long he passed out once more, and within the hour he was dead. Officially, the cause of Patrick Griffin's demise was recorded as "apoplexy," but many of his outraged comrades held a different view. That very day they fired off an anonymous letter of condemnation to his mother and reported his "torturing to death" to the newspapers, and they eventually would give postwar affidavits about what they felt had occurred. Unsurprisingly, Patrick's officers put forward a significantly different version of events, and their actions escaped serious censure.[1]

Patrick Griffin had been thirteen years old when he had arrived in Massachusetts from Athlone in 1860. Working first in the Lowell mills and then as a laborer, he had lied about his age in order to become a bounty volunteer in late 1863, and even then had required his widowed mother's consent to enlist as a minor. Patrick was no model soldier. He had deserted from his unit in May 1864, a charge that was changed to one of being absent without leave following his apprehension and the forfeiture of a portion of his bounty. In the months before his death, his officers apparently had grown weary of him being "constantly drunk and running away from camp." Investigating the incident in its aftermath, the inspector general reported to General Sherman that Griffin "had refused to do duty" and that, although there were "no symptoms of liquor" on the day he died, the view of the surgeon was that his system had likely been weakened by his prior "debauchery."[2]

While Irish Americans shared many commonalities with their fellows, there are also a number of negative stereotypes that were ascribed to them and/or became particularly associated with them during and after the war. The brief records of Patrick Griffin's tragic military life read like a rap sheet of such stereotypes. He was a working-class "rough." He was motivated by money. He was a deserter. He was ill-disciplined. He abused alcohol. He was an immigrant. Just as they were seen as imbued with aggressiveness in combat, many in contemporary society—and in the officer class—viewed Irish American men as being possessed of a plethora of character flaws derived from their social and ethnic background. Harsh discipline was often seen as the only means of keeping these perceived flaws in check. By examining such issues from the perspective of the ordinary Irish American serviceman, it becomes possible to move beyond the caricatures and generalizations to gain a fuller understanding of the origins, veracity, and context of such perceptions. One of the most central to the difficulties they faced in uniform revolved around their social status and sense of manhood, which in the minds of many of their superiors marked them out as troublesome from the start.

IRISH AMERICAN MANHOOD AND MASCULINITY

Terms like "roughs" and "rowdies" were used during the Civil War to describe the unruly dregs of the North's lowest social classes, men who were generally considered to be the most undesirable set in the Union military. Whenever and wherever these roughs and rowdies are mentioned, it quickly becomes apparent that large numbers of those categorized in this manner were Irish American.[3] Lorien Foote has laid bare the extent of the class divide that often existed between these largely urban working-class men and the officer elites who sought to lead them. This divide was the cause of frequent friction in the military and, as has been touched upon, was a fissure line that was visible even within Irish American communities and ethnic Irish regiments.[4]

The differing concepts of manhood that scholars have identified within the Federal military have been identified as a fundamental contributor toward these frictions. The middle and upper classes—especially evangelical Protestants—tended to espouse ideals of calmness, restraint, soberness, moral behavior, and duty.[5] More common among the lower classes was a form of masculinity that, in the words of one historian, lauded "physical courage, independence, class pride, and American patriotism."[6] To this could be added a respect for hard drinking, hard living, and hard fighting. The majority of Irish Americans (and those who might be classed as roughs or rowdies) were regarded as falling somewhere toward the latter end of this spectrum.

Like everyone else in the 1860s United States, the Irish were products of a world dominated by masculine ideals.[7] As such, some of the manly characteristics they exhibited were also common among their brothers in arms. It has been demonstrated how closely Irish American concepts of duty in combat paralleled those of their comrades, and how important the performance of their duty to those at home was to their sense of self. Neither of these traits are attributes that have traditionally been associated with Irish American service. Ascertaining the extent to which they otherwise adhered to the concept of martial manhood is challenging, especially as they did not make a habit of regaling their wives, mothers, and sisters with frequent stories of drinking, fighting, and "whoring." Nevertheless, their writings make it apparent that Irish American masculinity was significantly more complex (and individual) than a simple binary between restrained and martial manhood.[8]

Within the broad ranks of the Irish American soldiery, there were certainly those who conformed closely to the image of the Irish rowdy. Some who did so may have struggled with the vices that surrounded the world of the working-class poor, and may have been less anchored within a family unit. A case in point was Co. Antrim native Samuel Boyd. The New Jersey soldier had married his wife, Ann, on a floating bethel the very day they landed in New York, only to later abandon her for "a bad woman, a prostitute."[9] After he joined the army he sought to repair their relationship by having Ann join him in camp. His captain had objected, telling Samuel "thear was pleanty of wimen hear in this pleas" and there was no need to send for her. The officer supposedly next threatened to reveal to Ann that Samuel had been sleeping around. During the heated exchange that followed, his superior apparently also charged that Ann herself was "nothing but a prostate [prostitute]." Confronted by such a series of assaults on his manhood, Samuel snapped. "i lifted my gun and i fired at him . . . my pashing was tou high and my love was tou Strong fore you to Let ane wan say that abot you." As Samuel told it, a sergeant's intervention at the point of firing sent his shot high, and after a night in the guardhouse he was released without charge, having received an apology from the officer.[10] While he claimed his actions were driven by a love for his wife, it seems more likely that Samuel's violent, unrestrained response was driven by a personal affront at the barbs and condescension flung at him by his officer—a hot-headed, unbridled reaction that would have been seen as typical of a rowdy when faced with such a challenge.

While Boyd's case is extreme, elements of his experience fit into a wider pattern common among Irish Americans. There were undoubtedly many hard men who entered the service from the Irish American community, but they were rarely the one-dimensional rowdies of popular perception. It is apparent from their writings that large numbers sincerely hoped that their time in the military would prove transformative, instilling through discipline and duty the capacity for self-improvement, both for themselves as individuals and for their families.[11] Such hopes were often revealed at low points during their military service, and frequently while also referencing their previous wayward existence. As with Boyd, the hardships of military life accentuated these men's feelings of regret, prompting them to seek absolution for past transgressions. In 1862, William Barry of the Irish 10th Ohio Infantry wrote to his sister expressing "remorse for my wild life of a few years ago, and sorrow to think of the grief I must have caused all my friends by my conduct."[12] John Sullivan from Tralee, Co. Kerry, also carried guilt about his previous habits and actions into his military service. "God only knows how often I suffer thinking of the past," he confessed to his mother, but he was "hopeing and wishing for the future to redeem the past and be a Comfort to you the remainder of your days."[13] He assured her that there was "not the Slightest danger" of his getting drunk—something he seems to have struggled with in civilian life—as he was now "to much respected and I also respect myself to much for that."[14] Hugh O'Donnell from Co. Derry was another who became convinced of the transformative potential of service, telling his mother: "A Soldern life is A hard life to sirve 3 years for A Solders life aint Shure for 5 minets at A time but I head not complane for for I am a better man to day then I was when I left home."[15] Michael Foran of the 5th Pennsylvania Reserves saw his time in the army as the best way to change the man he was, telling his wife: "Whin i get at libirtey again i will be a dfirint man in timpor for i hav fond the plais that it would not do S to ras the mistif as i ust to do."[16] When Galwegian James Finnerty sought to explain to his Liverpool-based family why he had left his painting job to join the 72nd Illinois Infantry in August 1862, he simply stated that he took the step "thinking that I can better myself."[17] For many of those who held with the positive redemptive potential of military service, its promise was derived from more than just the discipline and responsible manliness they hoped it could instil. Chapter 5 will detail how it also came from the self-sacrifice of fighting for a cause that large numbers of them sincerely believed in.

While improving themselves as men was a major goal for many Irish Americans in the service, some had not reckoned with the loss of freedom that went hand in hand with life in the ranks. Despite their social status, they were proud and often fiercely independent, and some struggled to adapt. This is despite, and perhaps partly because of, the constraints of the society they or their parents had left behind in Ireland. Once in the United States, they had begun to imbibe the republican ideals that caused many volunteers across the North to grapple with this loss of free will, particularly given their conviction that they were the equals of those who sought to command them.[18] With his reference to getting "libirtey again," Michael Foran touched on this restrictive aspect of military service. Those who articulated concerns about their loss of freedom in uniform generally did so by describing their treatment as comparable to that of "slaves" or "dogs."[19] Irish immigrant Cornelius Donahoe had rushed to war in the summer of 1861, but reports that his father was considering enlisting the following October prompted him to fire off a stark warning: "tell him if he wants to make a slave of him self to list he will starve to deth and be kicked around like a dog without a tail . . . it is Bad enough for one of us to go to divel."[20] Cornelius's ire had not dimmed by the following February, when he proclaimed: "if i was at home now the man that would ask me two List i would Shoot him."[21] James Sharkey enlisted despite the remonstrations of his brother John—then serving with the 140th New York Infantry—who had warned him that being in uniform was to "live the life of a dog."[22] The difficulties these men had in adapting to the rigid hierarchical system of the military occasionally led to altercations with officers, as had occurred with Samuel Boyd. However, despite their complaints, and their reputation, most Irish Americans ultimately adjusted and accepted their lot, going on to perform the duties expected of them during the war.

Although many Irish Americans were tarred with the same brush as some of the wilder elements within their class and ethnic group, in reality the majority were neither rowdies nor roughs. Instead they adhered to what might be regarded as a more moderate form of martial manhood. They respected physical courage and accepted occasional exuberance and excess as a part and parcel of life. They jealously guarded their independence and their sense of equality, which had come hard won in their new home. They rarely complained about the morality or general behavior of their comrades, and viewed pastimes such as alcohol consumption, gambling, and music as intrinsic elements of who they were. But they were not without restraint. They and their communities considered duty to family to be an integral part of manhood, and most men in uniform regarded doing their duty in service in the same light. If overindulgence had a consistently negative impact on the lives of themselves or others, it was seen as a failing. Indeed, many who had come up short in this regard came to see the military as offering a potential path toward a greater level of restraint, and through it a path to redemption.

ALCOHOL

Few ascribed traits contributed as greatly toward negative stereotypes of Irish Americans in the 1860s United States as their supposedly unrestrained relationship with alcohol. It was seen as a vice that was particularly prevalent among roughs and rowdies, and its known or even suspected abuse frequently lay at the root of harsh disciplinary measures. Long before the guns starting firing, alcohol had been an intrinsic element of both Irish and German immigrant culture, and their consumption of it had been repeatedly targeted by nativist reformers. Although every stratum of society in the mid-nineteenth century was awash with alcohol, its abuse was regarded as a particular failing of the lower classes, for whom it represented one of the few escapes from the hardships of everyday life. While Irish American troops earned an especial reputation for excess, alcohol use and abuse was a major issue across all classes, ranks, and armies during the American Civil War.[23]

There is no doubt that alcohol abuse was a major scourge within working-class Irish American communities. Indeed, the widespread impact of alcoholism on individual families is a recurring theme through many Civil War widows' and dependents' pension applications. This fact was widely recognized within Irish America, where abstinence societies played prominent roles in society and were highly visible during events such as St. Patrick's Day parades. Typical of the message they sought to convey was that emblazoned on the banner of the South Brooklyn Temperance Cadets of the Visitation of the Blessed Virgin Mary in 1864: "All's Right—Dad's Sober."[24] Some Irish American servicemen, particularly those of a more religious persuasion, were influenced by the temperance message and the opportunity the military provided for a new start. The encouragement and popularity of the temperance movement among Irish units was a direct response to the dangers of excess. Early in the conflict, such sentiments led seven hundred of the Irish Brigade to take the temperance pledge.[25] Yet for the great majority, abstinence was not something they were prepared to consider. Instead, thousands of Irish Americans held with the policy of recent immigrant Edward Fitzpatrick, who wrote to his wife from the Petersburg front in 1865: "I am a very temperate young man i dont drink Any thing only when i can Get it."[26]

For some, alcohol's grip brought dire consequences, in the process helping to contribute toward the Irish American reputation for ill-discipline in camp. When William Meehan lost his father, who had been serving with him, to disease, he informed his mother that it had given him a wake-up call: "I have made a resolution to be better now than when he was living I will avoid every bad practice."[27] Despite his intentions, a few weeks later he found himself before a court-martial for being "grossly intoxicated" while on guard. Found guilty, he was fined $10 and ordered to have a twenty-four-pound ball attached to his left leg for thirty days.[28] Waterford native Garrett Condon paid a much higher price for a similar infraction, being sentenced to twelve months' hard labor without pay on Ship Island off Mississippi. Condon's actions also saw him fail in his familial duty, forcing his wife to launch a desperate appeal directly to General Banks for clemency "to keep his wife and children from Starving."[29] John Costello of the 1st Massachusetts Heavy Artillery provided a cautionary tale relating to the excesses of his comrade William Sheehan. His fellow Irish American was "shot at by the guard in Alexandria and was wounded in the hand which I think he will lose. He was drunk at the time and that was the result."[30]

Alcohol abuse occasionally led to Irish American servicemen paying an even higher price. A letter arrived at Eleanor Hogg's door in Ireland in 1862 informing her not only that her husband had died in the Irish Brigade, but that her son Pat, a Union sailor, had "got thirste" after receiving his pay and "fell down one Of the Hatch weays of the vessel . . . and died soon After wars."[31] The combination of pay and ready access to alcohol often proved a disastrous mix, no matter a man's ethnicity. Michael McCormick of the 65th New York told his family that "When Pay day comes there is always a rush of our men down to the City to get drunk there is as many as fifty down at a time," part of a culture of drinking that led to a "shocking affair" when an intoxicated sentry shot and killed a corporal.[32] James McGee from Co. Louth made it clear that while many in the Irish Brigade may have taken the abstinence pledge, the rhetoric did not match reality. Some men's commitment had already waned by early 1862, when he wrote that "Ever since pay day we had to have a Double Guard on the camp for the purpose I am sorry to say of keeping the Gin Figs in camp."[33]

However much men may have wanted to drink, availability was always an issue. The more ready access of officers to alcohol was often remarked upon with envy. When Tyrone native Bernard Curry of Corcoran's Irish Legion saw that Thomas Francis Meagher had come on a visit to his officers in 1864, he speculated: "i Supose the did not Come out with dry lips."[34] James Harrigan of the 72nd Pennsylvania Infantry told his mother in 1862 that when it came to alcohol, "the poor private you know cant get any of it, it is for the Big men *the officers*."[35] Other Irish served under officers who were not afraid to take drastic measures to restrict the men's opportunities to obtain alcohol. In an effort to stem drunkenness in the 1st New York Infantry, as Archey Laverty informed his mother, "thay Had to break open the Sutler Stores and Spill the Barrells of licquor."[36] Thousands of Irish Americans tried to circumvent alcohol shortages using any means they could, often with the complicity of wives and parents at home, who hid drink in packages sent to the front. William Delaney asked his mother for "a small bottle of good brandy in a little box and cover it with tobacco . . . i hav not got a drop since i Left."[37] Servicemen congratulated those at home when the ruses they devised proved successful. Henry Burns was delighted with his mother and her tenement neighbor for successfully concealing gin and brandy in a box for him, stating that they had "done it well" and had given "Me and My Comrades that is in the tent with me A joley good Night."[38]

Certainly a great many sought out drink whenever the opportunity arose. The extremely limited free time most men had enjoyed due to their long working hours in civilian life had encouraged occasional opportunistic "sprees," a pattern of consumption that was replicated in the military. This in turn undoubtedly led to many disciplinary infractions. But whereas the image of the Irish rowdy was of one who consistently reveled in alcoholic excess, most Irish regarded incessant drinking as a weakness and failing, especially if it had a demonstrably negative impact on the lives of themselves or their dependents. John Joseph Casey of the 2nd U.S. Infantry typified such sentiments. Having run afoul of "our old friend John Barleycorn" [whiskey] once too often, he felt he had to "issue the edict of banishment," as "it came very near putting the veto on me this last time and if I give it another chance it will be my fault."[39] Even legendary figures like Thomas Francis Meagher were not exempt from disapproving commentary. The Irish Brigade's much-loved leader suffered badly from alcohol abuse during his service, something that the otherwise devoted William McCarter described as the general's "one besetting sin." McCarter was speaking from experience, given that he had saved Meagher from collapsing into a bonfire while in a drunken stupor in November 1862.[40] Writing home the previous July, John Dougherty had been wondering why their chaplain, Father Dillion—someone whom he felt was "a very good man"—had been placed under arrest. The only conclusion he could draw was that it had been "a drunken freak of Genel Meagher."[41] Meagher's drinking problem was well known within the Brigade, though the men rarely commented publicly on it. That they did not do so was borne from both a respect for their commander and an awareness of the scrutiny and ethnic responsibility that was their lot as the premier Irish formation in service.

Drinking was undeniably important to Irish American servicemen. It was something that they valued for its role as a social stimulant and lubricant, a welcome diversion from the realities of often-hard lives. As the conflict dragged on, some likely sought it out as an escape from the horrors of war. Alcohol was also valued for its perceived health benefits, particularly in combating ailments such as colds and chills. Kerry immigrant and 99th New York soldier John Sullivan's interaction with hard spirits was likely typical: "you want to Know if I get any Drink here. I have not tasted any Liquor or get any except what you sent that I was very glad to get it is used up long since, when we go over to Fort Munroe any of us we get an Occasional glass of Lager

Beer and that Inferior this is the first Cold Day we have had this Winter a nip of Brandy wold be very good twice a Day I can Assure you."[42] While the central role alcohol played in Irish cultural life meant that men like John Sullivan were often more visibly associated with drinking than other groups, its use in the military was almost ubiquitous. While some abused it, the majority were more moderate in their consumption, their service interspersed with only occasional binges, or "sprees" that were dictated by location, opportunity, and circumstance.[43] The reality was that, regardless of stereotype, for the bulk of these men's time in the military alcohol was largely inaccessible. "a little of the Cratars [whiskey]" was, as James Harrigan put it in 1862, "hard to be had."[44] Nevertheless, their ethnic and class reputation preceded them, often unjustly—sometimes leading to incidents such as the tragic case of Patrick Griffin, whose officers' presumptions and preconceptions caused them to mistake illness for drunkenness. While it can be argued that Irish Americans were unjustly targeted with negative traits, such as rowdiness and alcoholic excess, the balance of evidence currently available suggests there may be more merit to another of the negative charges sometimes leveled at them—an increased propensity to desert.

DESERTION

Just as they were associated with excessive alcohol consumption, Irish Americans were also regarded as being more likely to desert.[45] Particularly compelling evidence to support this assumption has been forwarded by Dora L. Costa and Matthew E. Kahn in their major statistical study of Union servicemen, which found that Irish- and British-born soldiers were 1.4 times as likely to desert when compared to their native-born comrades.[46] Yet this picture is more complex than it may first appear. Ryan Keating's in-depth analysis of the ethnic Irish 9th Connecticut, 17th Wisconsin, and 23rd Illinois regiments found that desertion rates in those units were lower than the average for mixed formations.[47] During the war itself, those who regularly dealt with desertion often felt immigrants were more likely to abandon their posts than the native-born. Provost Marshal General James Barnet Fry expressed precisely that view when he speculated that "a more minute examination" of the statistics of the army "would reveal the fact that desertion is a crime of foreign, rather than native birth, and that but a small proportion of the men who forsook their colors were Americans."[48] Such judgements may have been built on prejudicial foundations, but the available information does suggest that men who had been born in Ireland deserted the northern military at higher rates than many other identifiable groups. An examination of their thoughts, actions, and circumstances helps to reveal why that may have been the case.

Invariably, Irish American desertion has been framed primarily in ideological terms, regarded as an indicator that they were not as invested in the ideals of the United States as others in uniform. Particular note is made of the Irish American turn against the war in early 1863, when mounting losses and the changing war aims heralded by the Emancipation Proclamation led some to abandon the cause.[49] The period between October 1862 and February 1863 that followed the announcement of the Proclamation did witness the highest levels of desertion experienced by the United States during the war, and no doubt many Irish Americans were among those who chose to abandon the Stars and Stripes at that point.[50] Irish Americans were also prominent among late war desertions, when enlistment conditions had been created that proved especially tempting for working-class men, drawing them out of their home communities in search of opportunities further afield. As Judith Lee Hallock has demonstrated in her analysis of Brookhaven, New York, where financial inducements were used to draw nonresident Irish Americans to the locality for the purpose of enlisting, the severing of community connection often meant that men felt more ready to abandon their military obligations.[51] However, this is a fact that has to be weighed against the evidence that Irish Americans were also proportionately more willing to enlist during the later war period than native-born white Americans.

No matter when in the war Irish Americans deserted, the primacy of ideology as a driver in their decision is open to question. A detailed analysis of the Irish Brigade's 63rd New York Infantry found that a number of occasions during the war outstripped this October 1862–February 1863 period for desertion rates. One of them came during the campaign movements of August/September 1862, which presented the first real opportunity to depart since the Brigade had initially tasted action, while another was in September/October 1863, when the regiment was taking in a major influx of recruits in New York. All were dwarfed by the exodus experienced by the regiment in November 1861, immediately prior to its departure from New York.[52] While a lack or loss of conviction for the cause may have been a factor in some of

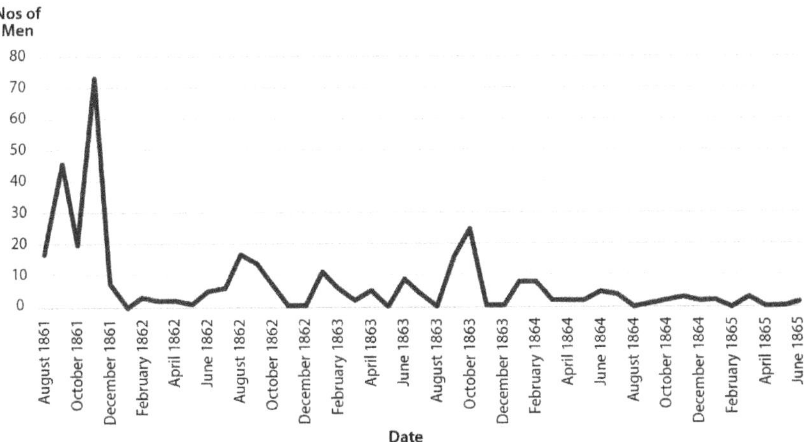

GRAPH 5. Desertion rates in the 63rd New York Infantry, Irish Brigade, through the Civil War. Drawn from individual soldier data within the Annual Report of the adjutant-general of the state of New York.

these cases, it was greatly overshadowed by more direct and personal concerns, such as coming face to face with the realities of military life, campaigning and battle, and the lack of financial security and stability that afflicted many men and their families.

The fact that the primary spark behind desertion was rarely ideological is supported by Irish American discussion of it in their correspondence. They were most likely to contemplate absconding when interactions with home had generated concern, particularly if those concerns were economic. If such worries coincided with a moment when their morale was already affected by micro factors within their unit or severe and/or unsuccessful campaigning, it greatly increased their willingness to consider departing. As it was for most Civil War servicemen, the role of family was an intrinsic element of the story of Irish American desertion. Peter Carmichael has identified that many of the men who deserted Union forces during the war did so as part of a "collaborative act" with those at home.[53] Irish Americans struggled the most when their sense of duty toward family came into direct conflict with their sense of duty to uniform. Many northern soldiers viewed duty to family and duty to Union as fundamentally linked, but this was based on the understanding that the military would not hinder their ability to provide for their support.[54]

Through failures such as those surrounding army pay, the military hampered that ability with such frequency that it seems remarkable Irish American working-class desertion was not significantly more commonplace. Men on the economic margins were less capable of enduring the financial peaks and troughs of wartime than were their more affluent fellows, and it is no surprise that Costa and Kahn's statistical study of the Union military demonstrated the poorest deserted more. Illiterate men were more than 1.5 times more likely to desert than literate; men with no personal property were more likely to desert than those whose family had $500 in personal property; and men who had been laborers—the bottom rung of the employment ladder—were more likely to desert than those from other occupations.[55] As the most readily identifiable working-class cohort of whites in northern service, Irish Americans were strongly represented in all of those categories.

Dan Sheehan was one of those Irish Americans who decided to illegally depart the fold. He deserted the army in April 1862, though he afterward enlisted in the naval service. While his justifications go unrecorded, circumstantial evidence suggests that difficulties at home were a major contributory factor. By 1863 he was advising his soldier brother John to follow him in abandoning his regiment. His reason was their father's worsening illness and financial situation; Dan argued that if John deserted he would be in a position to "go home and comfort" their failing parent. Facing an unenviable choice of competing duty to regiment and to family, John proposed a third way. He advised his father to "write to the president and explain your situation" in the hope that he might garner an honorable discharge.[56] John's refusal to follow his older brother's suggestion, despite the gravity of their father's position, was driven by a reluctance to tarnish his own character with the taint of desertion. In the main, this sense of duty toward uniform and comrades, together with concerns about potential disciplinary repercussions, stayed the hand of most Irish Americans in similar situations.

Even men who did decide to desert did not necessarily do so with the intention of permanently abandoning the military.[57] Those who followed through frequently returned of their own volition—or were caught. In such instances there was often a reluctance to attempt it again, particularly as punishments grew more severe from 1863 onward.[58] Daniel Reddy of the 16th Massachusetts Infantry was listed as a deserter when he failed to return from his veteran furlough in April 1864. When he eventually reappeared of his own accord nineteen days late, his captain preferred charges against him. In the end, his officer accepted the explanation that the absence had been due to the longer-than-anticipated time it had taken to settle the estate of his father, who had just died. However, that acceptance only came after the summer's fighting, when Daniel had repeatedly and consistently demonstrated his reliability and bravery.[59] Limerick immigrant Dan Dillon had already deserted once when he began to receive renewed pleas from family for his return home in 1863. The 10th Illinois cavalryman snapped back that he was "not gowing home until the war is over I have Deserted once and that ought to Be enough and not to do It again sow you need not expect me home untill I get to go home Deacent or dead."[60] Dillon was writing in early 1863, a period during which he voiced extreme anger about the changing nature of the war and his displeasure at the prospect of fighting with African Americans. But he did not consider those views to be sufficient reason to risk his "decency" by abandoning his post. When Thomas Diver's thoughts turned to desertion in 1862, he was contemplating only a short absence. The 69th Pennsylvania soldier began planning a return to see his mother in Philadelphia, who was "lonely at home." His strategy to take "French leave" in order to "cheer her up" went so far that he bought "a pair of Pants and an old Coat to go home with But on further consideration I changed my mind."[61] When James Harrigan and his colleagues were paid off in December 1861, "all had a merry time" and some decided to spend their wages—without permission—in Philadelphia, though doubtless many subsequently made their way back to the ranks.[62] As such incidents make clear, just as a lack of wages could lead to economic pressures at home, pay musters could also precipitate a rash of temporary and permanent desertions, something the military authorities had to constantly weigh up.

Regardless of whether a departure was intended to be temporary or permanent, men had to reflect on the potential repercussions they might face. When James Welsh of the 82nd Pennsylvania Infantry was asked by those at home to go AWOL if he was unable to procure a furlough, he responded: "as for desserting it hard to do where are are now and besid it is runing a greate risk of being brought back and punished by the military law."[63] Thomas Monaghan of the 95th Pennsylvania Infantry was forced to bear witness to the worst of those repercussions when he and his brigade comrades were compelled to watch the execution of a deserter in August 1863. "it was a hard sight to look at. to see a poor fellow dying as a deserter."[64] These executions were carried out to have precisely this impact, and they affected the men greatly, something evidenced in the often detailed accounts they provided for those at home. They proved effective as a military measure, as there tended to be a reduction in desertion rates in their immediate aftermath.[65]

Even among those men for whom financial hardship was not a primary consideration, it often remained interactions with home that stimulated thoughts of desertion. The recent death of James Hand's brother aboard the USS *Cincinnati* was likely the catalyst for his parents' appeal for him to wrangle a medical discharge from the 164th New York Infantry. Knowing such an approach would fail, he suggested an alternative. "I May be home Soon after Some Long March," he responded, referencing one of the occasions when soldiers found it easiest to desert. But when it came to it, the impulses that prompted thoughts of desertion tended to be fleeting, and often faded as circumstances changed. Within a few days James had given up on the idea, and he appears not to have contemplated it again through the remainder of his service.[66] Similar considerations likely led to the desertion of Robert Hanlon from the 42nd New York Infantry in September 1862; he disappeared from his unit just twelve days after his brother Edward had been killed in action with the 12th New York at the Battle of Second Bull Run.[67] In both cases, it appears that the emotional and economic consequences of their families potentially losing a second son to the war contributed toward these men's decisions.

Before the first major battle of the conflict, and despite his own fervor for the fight, Patrick Coffey of the 69th New York State Militia advised an acquaintance "to remain at home for there are many here who are sorry for coming out who would not go back as they have taken the oath and it is the last thing in this world that they would want to do to break it."[68] The men Coffey spoke of had many parallels among Irish Americans during the war: regardless of whether or not they wanted to be there, the oath they had taken and the sense of duty they felt came with it meant they would stay the course. The majority did so even when they were faced with economic pressures from home, and even when the changing political situation caused many of them to question their service. Even the hot-headed would-be rowdy Samuel Boyd bucked expectations in this regard. When his distress concerning his failing relationship with his wife combined with his growing vitriol toward his officers, he wrote of his plan to abscond when he next received his pay. He intended to arrive home "Like a thief in the night," before leaving to head "farther up in the Contrey and get work."[69] It was a plan he apparently never put into action.

There can be no denying that Irish Americans could and did abandon the colors for a wide variety of reasons—some because they were homesick, lonely, or weary, some because of the horrors they experienced, some because of their lack of investment in the cause, some because of their disillusionment with the war's direction. Still more did so because they felt their personal circumstances meant they could no longer afford to stay. But on the whole, it was economics and home front conditions that played by far the most significant role in Irish American desertion rates during the Civil War. Their greater-than-average exposure to financial precarity made them significantly less capable than others of enduring obstacles, such as erratic pay and economic fluctuations, while continuing to maintain their familial responsibilities. Fundamentally, it was circumstances related to these men's class background—not their ethnicity—that were the most crucial in determining whether or not they decided to forsake the Union cause. Where a potential exception is found is when enlisted men had the misfortune of enduring sustained encounters with the virulent discrimination that specifically focused on their ethnicity—the nativism that was an all too prevalent feature of 1860s America.

NATIVISM

Of the numerous factors that could negatively influence Irish American morale during the conflict—no doubt causing some to consider desertion—perhaps the most insidious and chronic was the nativist anti-immigrant and anti-Irish sentiment that was ever present during the Civil War. While nativism's severity varied regionally across the United States, it was most acutely felt by the working-class Irish poor of major urban centers in New York, Pennsylvania, and Massachusetts, from whence the great majority of Irish servicemen were drawn.[70] It is difficult to assess the degree to which this prejudice negatively impacted men in the service, but the strength of bigotry on display in the antebellum and postbellum periods suggests it was a major issue. It has also left a historical legacy, as it undoubtedly colored reporting and analyses of Irish American service during and immediately after the war, influencing many of the contemporary military appraisals and statistics on which historians now rely.[71]

Between 1861 and 1865, the most readily apparent anti-Irish sentiment came on the home front, visible in the aftermath of incidents like the 1863 New York City draft riots, and in the consistent targeting of the working-class Irish as war profiteers and members of the "shoddy aristocracy."[72] Within the military, some nativist soldiers and sailors wrote openly of their disdain for their Irish American comrades. In sharing his reasons for an intense dislike of a fellow soldier, John Westervelt of the 1st New York Engineers noted that, aside from being uneducated and ignorant, he was "sloven in his dress and manners," "immoderately fond of whiskey," and "always bullying his fellows but when home is bullyed by his wife." "To sum it up," Westervelt explained, "he is every inch an irish man."[73] Casualized forms of denigration and discrimination were a fact of life for many in the army and navy, particularly those in mixed units. Though harder to identify, the type of low-level prejudice that must have been familiar to many is occasionally glimpsed in the postwar memoirs of non-Irish servicemen. It was not unusual for Union veterans to write of Irish Americans in paternalistic and condescending tones, echoing the language often employed toward African Americans. An example can be seen in the recollections of the 20th Maine Infantry's Theodore Gerrish when describing his former comrade Tommy Welch. Though clearly fond of the Irish immigrant, an air of superiority permeates Gerrish's memories of Tommy's "most laughable blunders," his description of his slowness to obey commands, and his characterization of his "bewildered, serio-comic gravity of expression for which the Emerald Isle is so noted."[74]

Such representations serve as a reminder that discriminatory attitudes toward Irish Americans did not always take the form of aggressive and overt nativism, or manifest themselves in wanton brutality toward the Irish American rank and file. They could also be pernicious, subtle, and complex. Just how complex interactions between nativists and Irish Americans could be is evidenced by the case of Henry Livermore Abbott, an officer in the 20th Massachusetts Infantry. Although almost one in four of the men in his regiment were Irish-born, Abbott had no love for either the laboring classes or the Irish.[75] Abbott expressed the view that many New York and Pennsylvania units were filled with "half-clad savages," he described an ethnic officer as an "Irish pig," and he offered that a sergeant would have been ideal for promotion but for "his Irish characteristics."[76] Despite all this, Abbott also held the opinion that Irishmen could make very good soldiers with the proper discipline, noting in one letter how they and the English "suffer less" from their wounds than native-born Americans.[77] Perhaps more significantly, the bonds of shared service saw him develop a genuine affection for some of his Irish American charges. This is evident when he took up his pen to write to the families of those in his company who had died during the Fredericksburg street fighting of December 1862. He informed the immigrant mother of James Briody of the "great pang" that struck him when he saw her son lying dead, and how strongly he felt "the greatness of the loss."[78] To the sister of Cork native John Deasy he spoke of the Irishman's honesty and bravery, and his hope that "his orphan children will be properly cared for."[79] While Abbott never lost his feeling of superiority, or his broader nativist anti-Irish prejudice, the relationships he developed with his men likely moderated the degree to which he acted on them in uniform.

The types of direct military relationships that Irish Americans formed with officers like Abbott made it possible for them to serve in relative harmony under the majority of nativist and prejudiced leaders. Nevertheless, they walked a tightrope, and good relations were predicated on the acceptable performance of their duties. They could expect less leeway than others if they committed disciplinary infractions or played up to negative ethnic stereotypes. Despite such accommodations, the negative influence of constant, low-level prejudice undoubtedly had a corrosive effect on morale. Before the first major battle of the conflict, it had already had a life-changing impact on Armagh native Patrick Carraher, who went to war with the 2nd New York State Militia. Patrick had elected to serve under the alias of "John Carrier," a name he apparently purposely selected because of its un-Irishness. Specifically, he was seeking to avoid the abbreviation of his name into what had by then become a ubiquitous ethnic epithet. This had been a coping mechanism he first developed in civilian life, a relative later explained: "at the shop where he worked there was a large number of young men Americans and English who would keep calling him *Pat* and *Paddee* if he put his name in as Patrick, so he gave his name into the shop as John."[80] In an effort to limit the prejudice he faced, Patrick had adopted John as his professional name, carried it with him into the army, and died under it in July 1861 at First Bull Run. Patrick Kellegher had a similar tale to tell when explaining his service under the alias "John Kelly" in the Union navy. He apparently told friends that "he did not want to be called 'Pat' while in the service by his comrades."[81] In this case, the explanation was at least a partial falsehood; the name change was almost certainly a result of him having deserted the 88th New York Infantry following his wounding at the Battle of the Wilderness. Nevertheless, the offering up of the story demonstrates that it was sufficiently commonplace to be seen as a plausible argument.[82]

While the prejudice Irish Americans most commonly encountered was low level, some had to deal with more extreme discrimination. Regardless of where or with whom they served, the rank and file always had to reckon with the power of their officers to enforce harsh disciplinary measures upon them. Whether anti-Irish prejudice played a role in the fate of the unfortunate Patrick Griffin outlined at the beginning of the chapter remains unknowable, but ethnic bigotry certainly increased the susceptibility of men like him to severe punishment. Sentences such as hanging by the thumbs and "bucking and gagging" were disproportionately handed out to immigrant soldiers by Union officers.[83] This increased vulnerability is something of which Irish Americans would have been keenly aware, particularly in nonethnic units. Discipline became more harsh as attitudes toward Irish Americans in the military worsened from 1863 onward, driven largely by the influx of new immigrants into the army as substitutes and draftees, men who were seen as poor military material.[84] Many officers also regarded lower class and immigrant men as lacking the moral character and manly qualities required to make good soldiers.[85] If an Irish American was unlucky with his officer, preexisting biases around class, religion, or ethnicity could all grease the path toward censure and rebuke. In such circumstances, seemingly innocuous activities could cause friction. It was a clash of class and religious ideology that lay at the root of Irish sailor John Scanlan's ill-advised decision to damn his superior, an infraction that saw him clapped in double irons for a week. The reason for the dispute had been an order for him to "knock of[f] sewing on Sunday," a day that Scanlan and his middle-class superior viewed in very different terms.[86]

In the Union military, prejudice was something that impacted Irish American officers as well as those in the ranks. Immigrants were less likely to be appointed officers in the first place, and if they became one, they were less likely to advance through the officer corps.[87] Just as they did on the home front, these shared tribulations often served as a binding agent for those who shared ethnicity, no matter their social status. George D. Welles lumped the officers and men of the Irish 9th Massachusetts together in his disparaging account of the unit in 1862, claiming the officers were ignorant and vicious and the enlisted men drunkards in a confidential report to Governor Andrew.[88] Even those at the very top of Irish American military life were not immune. An April 1863 letter from Captain William Maroney of the 164th New York Infantry to his brother apparently confirms claims that prejudice played a role in the infamous 1863 incident that saw General Michael Corcoran shoot Lieutenant Colonel Edgar Kimball of the 9th New York Infantry for refusing to let him pass. According to Maroney, "the Gen toled the man who he was and what his buisness was and that he must go by but the man who was drunk toled him thad no damn Irish son of a bitch could pass him and drew a sword upon him the Gen drew his revelver and shot the man through the neck killing him almost instantly."[89]

For those serving in green flag formations like the 164th New York, perceptions of prejudice were heightened as a result of their status as the primary military representatives of Irish America. In the aftermath of the December 1862 Battle of Fredericksburg, the refusal to grant the Irish Brigade permission to return to New York and refit resulted in allegations of nativism. Most seriously for the authorities, they were sentiments that appear to have been held among the rank and file and their families. Private William Dwyer, a fifteen-month Irish Brigade veteran, captured something of the mood when he wrote to tell his family that he would not, after all, be returning to New York: "we thought surely that our brigade was going home to new york that time but we were Kept back and would not be let Go in account of we being Irish."[90] A few days later, in response to news that his family had traveled to the docks in expectation of seeing him, he implied the Brigade was being used as cannon fodder: "the will put us in to fight if their was only ten of us left in the Brigade all we have now is 250 men out of 3000 in the three old Regts."[91] The allegations that the Irish Brigade were being discriminated against have never been substantiated, but the perception was as damaging as any reality. The rumor that it was true spread into a working-class Irish American community that was already overrepresented among New York's rank and file, and which was being increasingly inundated with seemingly endless casualty notifications arriving from a multitude of different units. It added to a growing list of grievances that were gradually turning New York City into a powder keg ready for the match.

Despite the prevalence of anti-Irish sentiment in the 1860s United States,

Irish American servicemen tended not to discuss the discrimination they faced in their personal correspondence. This may be partially due to the fact that they had become inured to it, but it seems that in many instances the development of shared experiences and a shared esprit de corps allowed an accommodation to be reached between men whose backgrounds and outlook on life were often wildly disparate. While this was rarely sufficient to remove all trace of anti-Irish prejudice, it did mitigate it substantially. That situation evolved as the war continued, when the New York City draft riots and high Irish American representation within the late war recruits brought an increase in discrimination, and with it a time of particular vulnerability for Irish Americans in service. Facing prejudice over who they were was something most Irish American servicemen faced at one point or another during the conflict. Unfortunately, the evidence suggests that being on the receiving end of such negative experiences did not significantly mitigate their views when it came to the most underprivileged group in Civil War America, African Americans. If anything, it may have made them worse.

RACE

Just as Irish Americans faced discrimination, they in turn discriminated against African Americans. Even in a racist society, Irish Americans were noted for the virulence of their antipathy toward Blacks. It was Frederick Douglass's assertion that this animosity derived from the Irish being "instantly taught when they step upon our soil to hate and despise the Negro."[92] Irish Americans were undoubtedly profoundly influenced by their exposure to the racist divisions in U.S. society. However, their correspondence and actions on the issue of race suggest that their racial attitudes were built on a foundational belief in white supremacy—something that they shared with almost all other white groups, and something most had in all likelihood brought with them from Ireland.

The most infamous Irish American interaction with race during the Civil War came in July 1863, when African Americans were specifically targeted during the New York City draft riots. The months leading up to the riots had witnessed the lowest ebb of morale at the front and at home yet seen in the war, a depression that—at least as far as Irish America was concerned—was further exacerbated by the coming into force of the Emancipation Proclamation the preceding January. This was a measure that the majority of Irish Americans regarded as a fundamental alteration of the war's purpose, benefitting a group for whom they held little sympathy and who they regarded as a direct economic threat. *Harper's Weekly* had not been far wide of the mark with their August 1862 assessment that among Irish America's chief concerns was the fear that "the negro is to be exalted at the expense of the Irishman," a belief *Harper's* felt the Democratic Party were fomenting. In a piece entitled "A Word with Working Men," the journal assured anyone concerned about economic rivalry that emancipated people would not come North to compete with northern laborers, but would "stay where they were born, and where they prefer to live."[93] It was an argument that did not wash with the urban working class of places like New York City. It was into this powder keg that the match of the Enrollment Act was thrown. From the perspective of some of the New York Irish (and many other working-class New Yorkers), it was the final straw. They felt they had borne the brunt of the economic hardship of the war's early months, lost thousands to the service, and were now expected to sacrifice even more as wealthy natives continued to look on from the sidelines.[94] These grievances contributed—together with a multitude of other factors—toward the explosion of violence that erupted when the first effort to enforce the New York City draft occurred in July 1863.[95]

The riots were dominated by Irish Americans and have come to be seen as a barometer of Irish America's views on the war.[96] Nevertheless, it remained the case that the great majority of the New York Irish chose not to participate in them. Irish Americans in service had little to say with respect to the violence, and—at least initially—they did not regard the riots as a distinctly ethnic event. Part of the reason for their silence was the timing of the riots, which came in the midst of hard campaigning on multiple fronts; they had other things on their minds, and fewer opportunities to write. For Irish New Yorkers, their primary concern was the safety of those at home. Having heard reports that "Col Nugent was Killed By the mob and his Place was Burned Down," William Martin was eager to know "how things are going on in Brooklyn I hope there will Be no harm done around your Neighbourhood."[97] John McGillicuddy, serving in Louisiana, asked for a report on "how times are in New York," having heard "they were drafting in the city and had a great muss."[98] Within Irish American communities outside of New York, the riots occasioned even less comment.[99] While John Grimes of the 3rd Rhode Island

Heavy Artillery had seen an "account of the Riot in New York in one of the papers," he offered no opinion on it. Instead his thoughts and concerns lay with Irish friends such as James Murphy, Charley McElroy, and Arthur McSorley, whose names had been drawn in the Providence draft.[100]

Some Irish American servicemen expressed little sympathy for those who caused such unrest in their home communities. Though writing over a year after the riots, Irish-born Dennis Driscoll of USS *Metacomet* could just as easily have been referencing them when he commented that if the boys at home "wants to see shooting an smell pouder" they should come and fight for their country "instid of fighting Pollease officers."[101] For others, such turmoil was understandable, given the direction of the war. When tensions concerning the draft and the perceived threat posed by African Americans exploded in Detroit in March 1863, John Scanlan of the USS *Mystic* (and a veteran of the 2nd Michigan Infantry at First Bull Run) was a cheerleader of the racist violence that ensued. Writing from Hampton Roads, he expressed regret that the rioters "didnt burn every house where a n—r lives even if I was there old clarks would go shure I wouldnt care a pin for the shanties this side of it let them rip too."[102] Scanlan had little regard for African Americans, and he held the view that the neighborhood was being blighted by their presence. It was an outlook that many of his fellow Irish Americans shared.

Irish American prejudice and racism, such as that exhibited by John Scanlan, could be exacerbated by the tight-knit and insular nature of their communities, where those on the outside were often seen as "other." Thomas Hagan exemplified this attitude when writing home to discover his immigrant mother's new address in Troy, New York. Demonstrating the lack of solidarity he felt toward many of his ethnic neighbors, he expressed his hope that she would "find a better place to live then a mong the dutch," as he felt that "thay are not very plesent folks to live beside."[103] While Thomas Hagan was clearly no fan of the Germans, when Irish American servicemen negatively referenced others, invariably the people they were talking about were African Americans.

Regardless of whether they had lived all or most of their lives in the United States or were relatively recent arrivals, the great majority of Irish American servicemen regarded Black people, and particularly enslaved Black people, as their inferiors. When Edward Carroll signed off a letter to his Co. Monaghan parents back in Rhode Island from Virginia in 1861, the last news he shared with them was of how the "n—s ar just like dogs they will Com when you wisel they will run after you like adog."[104] It is apparent that encountering the enslaved was something completely beyond these Irish Americans' experience, a novelty that was newsworthy for those at home.[105] While seated beneath a beech tree on the Virginia Peninsula in 1862, John Toomey from Co. Cork sought to capture something of the strangeness and exoticism of the enslaved. He wrote of the "half dozen n—s sitting behind me gambling and they are Swearing So that I cannot think of anything but they talk So funny once in A while one calling the other A damned black n—r."[106] Both Carroll and Toomey would have encountered free Blacks in the North, but their accounts indicate there was little interaction between the two races. In addition to this, they appear to have subscribed to the commonly held view that slavery had further degraded those subjected to it, placing the enslaved at the very bottom of their conceived racial hierarchy.[107]

Adding to the culture shock for Irish Americans was the lack of whites they found in the South, particularly women. John Sherry of the 7th Pennsylvania Reserves remarked of his post outside Washington, D.C., that "there is No girls up heare but yellow Gals," and that they only saw white country girls when on picket.[108] John Sullivan of the USS *Underwriter* had much the same impression of North Carolina, observing that "there are Not Much White Women in Newberne there are nearly all N—s here."[109] Irish Americans held definite opinions on the appropriateness of forming any lasting interracial relationships with these women. In the wake of the Emancipation Proclamation it was apparently suggested to recent immigrant Michael Daly by his brother that he might secure a farm and marry an African American. He provided an unequivocal response: "about the farm and the n—r wife the farm would do very well without the n—r wife I go in to strong for my own colour give me one from the old sod."[110]

As the number of Blacks seeking freedom within Federal lines turned from a trickle to a flood, Irish Americans found themselves spending more and more time in their proximity. Increasing familiarity made encounters with the South's enslaved population less newsworthy, but some began to find their presence an annoyance, and grew suspicious of their motives. Reid Mitchell has argued that increased encounters with African Americans in the South did little to diminish the racism of northern whites, and in some cases led to its increase.[111] Such seems to have been the case among some Irish Americans. In June 1862, Edward Hanlin grumbled that "there is some of the awfulest looking n—s around here ever i seen we are Bothered with them the run away from their masters and Come to us for prot[ec]tion."[112] Landsman Owen McGowan of the USS *Keystone State* thought these "contrabands" could not be trusted. Writing from South Carolina, the Roscommon native was doubtful about their reliability in combat, commenting that some of the formerly enslaved men that General David Hunter had put into uniform "turned And fled or helped the south," though he admitted, "These are the rumors here I can't say how true they are." Regardless, he felt that "The Federal goverment can Never do any thing while they Permit n—s to enter and Leave thair camps for they find Out every thing and go back and Tell thair masters."[113] Others expressed views that demonstrated both more complexity and more pragmatism. Writing a few weeks after the 1862 fall of New Orleans, George Doherty of the USS *Horace Beals* managed to condemn both the city's Creoles and its slave owners in the same breadth. He informed his mother that it was a "pretty City" where the people were in some cases "Strong Union in Others as Strong Secesion as you can find," but noted that the latter were "of no account as they are mostly Créoles and N—r Drivers they have not got mutch lip now for it would not do as Generall Butler has Soldiers posted all Over the City where any feling is shown for Secesindom."[114] For his part, John Sullivan was pleased at the presence of Black refugees at Fort Calhoun in Hampton Roads, telling his mother: "there is n—rs who wash Our Clothes. we pay them five Cents a piece for every one they wash you Can fancy I am not much of a hand at washing."[115]

Yet even where Irish American opinions on enslaved African Americans were relatively neutral, their statements often betrayed feelings of superiority—echoing how they were themselves sometimes described by other white comrades. The way the enslaved tended to be treated by the military authorities did little to disabuse Irish Americans of the subservient status of those who had been held in bondage. While his regiment was on the march through Louisiana in 1863, John McGillicuddy recalled how "all the N—s used to come Along with us we mak Solders of Aall the men and the famileys are sent to N.O. [New Orleans]."[116] In Virginia a year earlier, Patrick Kinnane and his comrades of Corcoran's Irish Legion had "drove all the n—s from here except those hired by the government They have been sent to the Craney Island they had to leave there homes and many of their things as they were drove at the point of the bayonet."[117] When preconceived racial concepts were mixed with military callousness, some Irish Americans came to see Blacks as little more than unthinking workhorses. Timothy Toomey appears to have been one who held that view, expressing his delight when he received a new assignment in Thibodaux, Louisiana, as he had "nothing to do but work n—s there is no white person on the place but the OverSeer and myself."[118]

Not all Irish American utterances on the subject of Blacks were hostile, nor was every interaction negative. Charles Williams's exchanges with one elderly Black woman in Virginia demonstrates how cordial they could become. Having received a handsome new handkerchief from home, the Irish 69th Pennsylvania soldier related a story of their interaction over it: "an old Slave woman fell in love with it and she offered me 10 Dollars in Secesh money for it but i could not see it she said Before God she would she would have it but i don't think she will."[119] Middle-class Irish American John Lynch was one of the many officers who employed an African American servant. The Irish Brigade captain found the youth "a great comfort . . . he is a very intelligent lad and what is a rare thing in Negros a Roman Catholic." Lynch valued his service so much that he promised he would take him back to New York with him.[120] The scale of Irish American involvement in the Union military ensured that there were many who enjoyed good relationships with African Americans, and welcomed an opportunity to play a role in ending slavery. Perhaps the most notable example in this regard was Patrick Guiney, colonel of the Irish 9th Massachusetts Infantry, who held the view in 1861 that "slavery curses the land in which it is."[121] There was the occasional individual in the ranks who was of like mind; there was at least a proportion of Fenians in units like Corcoran's Irish Legion who were broadly supportive of emancipation as a war aim.[122] Unfortunately, though, these men's position was the minority one.

The weeks that followed the implementation of the Emancipation Proclamation in early 1863 heralded the most vocal period of Irish American commentary on the question of African American freedom and service. Large numbers viewed the Proclamation as a fundamental change in the war's purpose and were vehemently opposed to it.[123] "Who would'nt be a sodger to fight for Abolitionists," John Madden sarcastically mused from Baton Rouge that February. He was also seething at the temerity of the men of the new "n—r regiments," who had the "cheek to ask you if you have got a pass." His anger had reached a point where he now blamed African Americans for the war: "God damn the n—s the black buggars if it was not for them I would not be here."[124] When the Proclamation came into force, Limerick immigrant (and former deserter) Dan Dillon and the men of the 10th Illinois Cavalry were growing embittered about a delay in their pay. "the cry is amongh the troops down here that if the dont pay us more regular . . . the will lay there arms down and let the damned abelinesets and n—s fight them selves and see what the Can do." Dillon was confident that in his regiment "half of them wont fight to free negroes nor figh with them if ever the put a negro in the field with our armey every Black son of a Bich of them will get Killed."[125]

While Dan Dillion apparently left little room for ambiguity, as with all letters, his sentiments were of the moment. Despite his assertions, he stood to his post, and within weeks he was fighting alongside the Black soldiers he had so recently been threatening to murder. At the June 1863 Battle of Milliken's Bend, Louisiana, their performance against his ultimate enemy—the Confederates—greatly impressed him: "the rebles ran agreat many of them [the African Brigade] into the river and drowned them but the negroes Killed 75 of them and made them run back as quick as the could go and the blacks fought like hell . . . we made them run like cowerds and holer mercy and the got little of it from us and the negroes you may be sure."[126] As was the case with many of their other white comrades, actions like Milliken's Bend tempered the view of some Irish Americans on the question of Black service. It did not necessarily diminish their racism, and it remained the case that very few ever embraced emancipation to the extent often credited to their peers in the wider Union military.[127] While some could never be reconciled with the Emancipation Proclamation, many—perhaps most—eventually accepted the sentiments of the fictitious Irish American soldier Miles O'Reilly, who advocated sharing "the right to be kilt" with African Americans.[128] By the spring of 1864, men like John Deegan had accepted that these Black soldiers had a contribution to make. When news of the massacre of United States Colored Troops at Fort Pillow, Tennessee, in April 1864 reached his ears, he remarked: "if our fellows dont pay them [the Confederates] up for that I miss my guess."[129]

While there could be substantial variance and complexity in how Irish American servicemen viewed, interacted with, and responded to the issue of race, most of them cared little for the plight or fate of the enslaved. For that majority drawn from the urban working class, their own survival was of significantly more consequence to them than what they viewed as the high-minded ideals of anti-Irish abolitionists. Neither did these men regard themselves as being engaged in a struggle to prove their racial "whiteness" to others. They were extremely confident of their position in that hierarchy, and unstintingly believed in their racial superiority over African Americans. Although Frederick Douglass believed Irish American racism developed following arrival in the United States, analysis of the racial attitudes of these servicemen suggests that American conditions heightened a belief in white supremacy that had existed in many of these men before they left Ireland. The case of John O'Brien, one of Dan Dillon's comrades in the 10th Illinois Cavalry, is instructive. At Milliken's Bend in May 1863, O'Brien and a drunken comrade went on a rampage through the camp of the newly formed 1st Mississippi Volunteer Infantry (African Descent) and a nearby contraband settlement. Having first assaulted an African American soldier, they staggered on toward a shack, where they attempted to lead off a young girl with the intent of sexually assaulting her. As the girl's mother desperately held on to her child, one of the men—likely O'Brien—roared: "You damned n—s think you are free, and you are not as well off as you were with the Secesh! If you say a word I'll mash your damned mouth!" Almost too drunk to stand, the men turned on a young Black boy and beat him to a pulp, destroying one of his eyes in the process. They next fixed their attention on one of the women, ripping off her clothes and attempting to rape her before she managed to escape. Help was eventually raised, but John O'Brien, who was regarded as the chief perpetrator, escaped any serious repercussions for his actions.[130]

John O'Brien served through the war and went on to live a long life. The concept that his racism was a learned behavior in America is challenged by his backstory. His pension file reveals that he had only emigrated from East Cork in May 1859, when he was twenty years old. After a few months in New York, he spent a short time laboring in Richmond, Virginia, and Cairo, Illinois, before finally moving to Grenada, Mississippi. Following Mississippi's secession, he returned to Illinois, where he enlisted in 1861.[131] There can be little doubt that John O'Brien's shocking attitude toward African Americans was heavily informed by his time in the South (and southern Illinois). Nevertheless, the extremity of his behavior and the fact that he was a recent, adult arrival in America make it unlikely that he had landed in the United States as a racial blank slate. Rather, it seems far more probable that he had been confirmed in his views of white superiority before his departure from Cork, with all he encountered subsequently serving to heighten the self-perceptions of racial superiority and racial entitlement that allowed him to feel empowered to commit such an abhorrent assault.

As the case of John O'Brien and the writings of many of his comrades suggest, the paradigm for almost all Irish Americans was a fundamental, unshakable belief in their white supremacy, something that many had brought with them to their new home. When these convictions coalesced with their vulnerable financial position in the United States and the indignity of a perceived economic challenge from people they viewed as inferior, the perfect breeding ground for intense racism was created. There were very few active supporters of emancipation in Irish American ranks, although it seems probable that many Irish had—or developed—relatively neutral views with respect to the Blacks they encountered in bondage and in uniform. But many others held fast to their entrenched opinions and through the course of the war saw African Americans as an inferior people who posed a threat both to the future of the United States and to their own stability and advancement in American society. Many such opinions had been formed as a result of environmental and societal factors, but undoubtedly some had also been derived from politics. For in that sphere, the majority of the enlisted Irish marched through the war very much in lockstep with the Democratic Party.

IRISH AMERICAN POLITICS

While white supremacy and the threat of direct economic competition with Blacks fueled the racist position adopted by many Irish American servicemen, how they interacted with American politics also had a role to play. The support for the Democratic Party among the enlisted Irish in Union blue was all but universal.[132] Not a single letter examined within the corpus expressed support for the Republicans. This devotion to the Democrats was entirely understandable. Aside from having taken some former Know Nothings into the fold, the Republican Party was perceived by many Irish Americans as both anti-immigrant and anti-Catholic. In contrast, the Democrats had welcomed the potential of the Irish vote, offering a degree of political power and influence that the Irish had long been denied. The conservative outlook of the Democrats with respect to the Constitution also appealed to Irish Americans eager to maintain the integrity of a Republic that they and many others viewed as both essential and exceptional.[133] While the Democratic affiliation of Irish

Americans in uniform was seen as unremarkable early in the war, it became increasingly problematic as the conflict dragged on, particularly in the aftermath of the Emancipation Proclamation. Democrats who opposed government policy or were too vocal in their opinions were often painted as less loyal and less dedicated to Union victory than those who wholeheartedly supported Abraham Lincoln's administration. This was a perception that became crystallized in the minds of many in the United States following the president's 1865 assassination.[134] As such a readily identifiable block of Democratic supporters, that event proved particularly detrimental to Irish Americans.

William McIntyre, who was an apprentice printer before his enlistment in the 95th Pennsylvania Infantry, was one such ardent Irish American Democrat. He also fancied himself a political analyst. Following the Emancipation Proclamation, William expressed his views on the political situation to his immigrant parents. "I think the Radicals of the Northeast want this Gov't broken up and they think by so doing they will get the Middle States with them but they are mistaken Pennsylvania, New York and New Jersey will never take up with such a set of hypocrites and defamers of a country's Rights as the Abolition Party are." His own analysis of the "Question at Issue"—i.e., emancipation—was solidly in line with the Democrat position. "If a State has laws they ought to be respected and there is no Institution in any State that ought to be interfered with unless it is the wish of the majority of the inhabitants of that state."[135] While William McIntyre offered one of the most erudite explanations of his Democratic principles, his was one voice among many. James Welsh's concerns, expressed at the same time, were more blunt and succinct, but also more personal. January 1863 found him despairing at the actions of one of the women at home, who he hoped would "not be so foolish as to mary a Abe Lincoln Abolinsionist for I think it is the ruin of the country."[136]

In the war's early years, most Democratic Irish in mixed formations were able to engage openly with their political beliefs. During the 1862 New York elections, Irish immigrant Michael Higgins wrote from Camp Douglas, Illinois, to discover who had been elected from his home in Troy. "I hear that the Democrats carried the day bully for them if they did." For his own part, he had "quite an amuseing time" acting as one of the "inspecters of Election" for his company of the 125th New York Infantry as they voted on who should be governor of New York, a contest in which "The Republicans beat us by 9 majority."[137] In formations like the 125th New York, Higgins and his fellow Democratic Irish Americans served successfully in a unit that contained opposing political perspectives. This was something that would become progressively more difficult for them from 1863 onward, when the military began to discipline Democrats who were seen to be speaking against either emancipation or the administration.[138] By the time William McIntyre was sharing his thoughts on the topic, he was aware that expressing such sentiments was dangerous, even in private correspondence. "I have let myself too loose now," he confessed.[139] Theodore Lyman, who served on the staff of General George Meade, highlighted the differing perceptions of how Republicans and Democrats were handled during the late war period with reference to two Irish American officers who supported opposing candidates in the 1864 presidential election. Lyman observed that while Cork native Charles Henry Tucker Collis, a Republican, "sent letters and despatches . . . about the enthusiasm for Lincoln in the army . . . Nothing is said to him," but Martin McMahon, "a McClellan man" who "talks very openly and strongly about his side . . . is, without warning, mustered out of the service!"[140] After 1863, many Irish Americans—both officers and men—took the hint and became more circumspect about discussing their political affiliation.

Irish American Democrats in the Union military were undoubtedly impacted by the announcement of the Emancipation Proclamation in September 1862, and some were among those who abandoned the cause as a result.[141] However, the extent to which this was the case is overstated. The Preliminary Emancipation Proclamation occurred during one of the two major wartime waves of Irish American recruitment in the fall of 1862, and many even enlisted after Lincoln's announcement. Michael Corcoran's newly formed Irish Legion did not leave New York state for the front until early November. These late 1862 Irish American recruits did not turn on their heels the moment they had signed up. Like the great majority, they stuck to their task, even if it was only until the expiration of their term of service. Those that remained confined talk of politics to among those they felt able to trust. James Welsh, so horrified at the potential marriage of his female acquaintance to a Republican, contemplated desertion in January 1863 but chose to stay, and ultimately reenlisted as a veteran volunteer. Such commitment was not uncommon among Democratic Irish American servicemen, even with those who took issue with the Emancipation Proclamation. John O'Brien, the Cork immigrant who had so horrifically attacked African American refugees, likewise stayed to reenlist in 1864. His commitment to the Union seems to have been steadfast, given he had left the South following secession and had enlisted in the first summer of the war.[142] Another who stayed the course and reenlisted was former laborer Patrick McCaffrey. As the 1864 presidential election loomed, the Irish Brigade soldier was lying wounded in Washington, D.C.'s Lincoln Hospital. Furloughs were on offer for those who would go home to vote, but "they must promise to vote for lincln Be fore the Leave here." This widespread wartime practice of granting leave to those who would declare their intent to vote for the Republicans or Lincoln failed to tempt McCaffrey, despite the possibility that he would never get another chance to see home again. He stubbornly insisted it was something "Which I wont do if They never Give me a furlough."[143] Though he and the others remained, their personal political convictions had not changed. They had found a way to remain both committed Democrats and committed Union soldiers.

The 1864 presidential election in which McCaffrey was denied his franchise marked another upsurge in political discourse among Irish American troops. For those moved to comment on it, there was no mistaking where their allegiances lay. Writing from aboard the USS *Cyane* at Acapulco that August, Dubliner Thomas Hynes sarcastically pondered "if Old Abe will be reelected or will some other unknown broken down Lawyer take his place."[144] Charles Traynor, another veteran volunteer and member of the Irish Brigade, predicted on 1 November that the election would be a "hard Contest" but earnestly hoped "Little M[c] will be the Man."[145] The Democratic allegiance of Irish American servicemen was interwoven with a near adulation of "Little Mac"—George B. McClellan—particularly among those of the Army of the Potomac, which he had once commanded. Their admiration had begun early in the war, when Little Mac's reputation as a general who cared deeply for his men was reinforced by his personal magnetism. An awestruck Edward Hanlin captured something of the general's appeal when he described a June 1862 encounter with his hero: "General mc Clelland is one of the finest men i ever seen he is a real gentleman he does not put on one half of the airs that our Captain Does one Day last week he rode out to where we was on picket and he Came over to me and asked me to hold his horse and when he Came Back again thank you he says just as if i had Done some favour for him."[146] Writing to his family on patriotic paper that bore the image of McClellan shortly after the general had taken command in 1861, Francis Cullen informed them that "the picture on this papper is the man that Leads us to victory or death for he will counqure or die he good and to his men and Likes to See them in good health."[147] McClellan proved particularly adept at endearing himself to his Irish American men. When Abraham Lincoln visited the Army of the Potomac's Harrison's Landing camp in July 1862, the Irish Brigade gave the president "three Cheers" as he passed through. John Dougherty recalled that afterward "Genl mcClellan said boys give 3 more for the old green flag which was given in a style that must have astonished old Abe."[148] News of such public acknowledgment would have spread quickly throughout ethnic circles both at the front and at home.

Following McClellan's final removal from command in November 1862, John Sheehan spoke for many Irish Americans when he declared it would "be A happy day to the Army when he takes the command again Black abolitionsts make a great nois about McClellan but let them go out to the Army and hear what the soldiers say if they could have their say little mack would have command tomorrow."[149] The *New York Irish American* captured the mood at his departure, feeling it was "likely to prove more serious in its results than even his [Lincoln's] emancipation Proclamation."[150] With a keen eye to his future, following his dismissal McClellan was careful to maintain and cultivate his popularity among Irish Americans. One example came in his attendance at an April 1863 fundraiser in New York City for the relief of the poor of Ireland, a cause toward which many in uniform contributed. During his remarks, McClellan spoke of his sympathy for the relief efforts, of his feelings that he had "sprung . . . from a kindred race" and how in service he had "ever found the Irish heart warm and true."[151] It was a regard that many of his now veteran former charges reciprocated.

Much of this early war enthusiasm was maintained into McClellan's 1864 run for the presidency, with ethnic newspapers such as the *Irish American* and *Pilot* championing the Democratic ticket.[152] A large number of Irish American servicemen—men like Charles Traynor—shared those papers' sentiments and joined the approximately 20 percent of army voters in the field who cast their ballot for Little Mac.[153] Indeed, they appear to have been among the staunchest and most resolute of Democratic voters during that election, with many of the most heavily Irish units bucking what was an otherwise convincing Lincoln victory among Union troops.[154] Of the handful of Pennsylvania regiments that voted for McClellan, the Irish 69th Pennsylvania did so most overwhelmingly, with 95 percent going Democrat. In the West, almost 80 percent of the green flag 17th Wisconsin did likewise. Unsurprisingly, the New York units, whose state troops contained the highest number of Irish Americans, also provided McClellan with the greatest support. The surviving figures show that in the old Irish Brigade regiments, over 91 percent of the 63rd New York and 100 percent of the 88th New York voted for him. The 116th Pennsylvania, always the least ethnic of the Irish Brigade regiments, gave fifty-eight votes to the Democrats and fifty-four to Lincoln.[155] The men who gave their votes to McClellan did so with a conviction that they were being true to the Union and the Constitution.[156] But there were undoubtedly others who chose not to cast their ballot for McClellan. The Civil War had fractured the Democratic Party into War Democrats, who favored reunion through military victory, and Peace Democrats, who sought the cessation of hostilities. As Jonathan White has identified, by late 1864 many serving Democrats—particularly veterans—had become disillusioned by the actions of their party. The leadership had opposed the serving man's franchise, and went to the polls in 1864 with a Peace Democrat on the ticket in the shape of vice presidential candidate George H. Pendleton.[157] Although McClellan himself was regarded as a War Democrat, the power of the peace wing had forced his nomination on a peace platform.[158]

Any attractions the peace wing may have held were further undermined by the major Union military successes that arrived just as the election approached. As a result, some Irish American veterans opposed both candidates. James O'Neill of the 4th Delaware Infantry disliked Lincoln because he wanted the war to continue until "slavery is abolished," and McClellan because he "totely aposed the Interest of the Soldier."[159] In all probability, Democratic support in 1864 was likely weaker among the Irish American veterans of 1861 and 1862 than it was with their ethnic fellows who had come to the conflict from late 1863 onward. By then, the former's substantial physical and emotional investment in the conflict would have led many who had "re-upped" to become committed War Democrats, sharing in their comrades' determination to see the conflict through and reticent to support a platform that, although it had their idol at their head, had been compromised by the "Copperhead" Peace Democrats. McClellan's support would have been further suppressed by the fact that many Irish Americans were serving in units in which they were a minority, particularly outside of New York. In such circumstances the public nature of the vote must have dissuaded some from casting their ballot, particularly if in doing so they ran the risk of evoking the wrath of their comrades—or worse still, their officers. There were undoubtedly numerous Irish Americans among the roughly 20 percent of eligible serving soldiers in the field who chose not to vote at all.[160] Regardless of their degree of disillusionment with the Democratic ticket, the numbers who actually "lent" their vote to Lincoln were probably small, despite Republican efforts to attract Democratic votes by branding their national ticket the National Union Party.[161] Some may have been won over (or intimidated) into voting for Lincoln through the arguments advanced by their immediate superiors, something that Zachery Fry has identified as being particularly prominent in the Army of the Potomac.[162] However, any such efforts would not have been aided by what one historian has described as the "virulent anti-Irish animus" that was displayed by Abraham Lincoln's Union Party base in 1864.[163]

Irish American servicemen were overwhelmingly Democratic during the conflict, but like most of their fellow party supporters, the majority saw themselves as every bit as loyal and committed to the cause of the United States as any Republican.[164] They were, after all, putting their lives on the line to protect and preserve the Union. Within the Democratic tent, Irish Americans ran the gamut of political engagement, and circumstance and experience dictated the level of their commitment to placing a Democratic president in the White House in 1864. If newspapers reveal something of the opinions of their readers, then perhaps the dominant political view of Irish American servicemen is to be found within their paper of choice—the *New York Herald,* which by conflict's end was the leading daily newspaper in the United States. Politically, the paper had opposed Lincoln's election in 1860 and had initially called for compromise with the South. While it supported the war after Fort Sumter, it consistently maintained its disdain for abolitionist Republicans, opposing both the Emancipation Proclamation and, ultimately, Lincoln's reelection. Despite the fact that the newspaper shared the Irish adulation of George B. McClellan, by 1864 its gaze had shifted onto Ulysses S. Grant, whom it advocated for the presidency. By the time the election came around, they had moved from a lukewarm support of McClellan's candidacy to a position of neutrality, largely due to the *Herald*'s contempt for Copperheads.[165]

The assassination and martyrdom of Lincoln and Democratic opposition to emancipation have caused the Irish American wartime political stance to be increasingly marooned on the "wrong side of history" in popular perception. But an exploration of the reality of their lives and the society in which they lived makes their position, and even the virulent racism they all too often practiced, entirely comprehensible. In their view, the Republican Party, with its anti-immigrant and anti-Catholic component, was not their friend. Neither were "radical" abolitionists, many of whom were similarly anti-Catholic and anti-Irish. To the modern eye, there is an irony in the fact that a group of people that were so discriminated against could in turn exhibit such racism toward another even more downtrodden people. But as one of the poorest sections of northern society whose lives were often lived on the margins, they perceived themselves as having the most to lose through the emancipation of enslaved African Americans, people who—like nearly all whites of the day—they regarded as their inferiors in almost every respect. Most Irish American men carried these views with them into uniform, and many maintained them throughout the conflict. Others mitigated their outlook on the issues of race, emancipation, and even politics as the war progressed, albeit in a much less dramatic or profound way than other Union servicemen; they rarely went so far as to become advocates of either emancipation or Republicans.

All through their service these men continued to face the discrimination that they had endured in civilian life. It was often born of preconceptions about their class, their cultural norms, their character, and their commitment, but the stereotypical extremes rarely matched the reality. They were less wild, less violent, and less drunk—in essence less different—than they were often given credit for. Although many undoubtedly suffered increased hardship and violence at the hands of their officers due to such discrimination, most were able to carefully navigate their way through their military experience. Those in mixed units were greatly aided in this by the growing esprit de corps and unit pride that began to bond men together as the fighting progressed, and which served to mitigate some of the impulses of more nativist officers. In the end, despite the prejudice they faced, their political opposition to the administration, and their enmity toward African Americans, the number of Irish Americans in Federal uniform remained remarkably high throughout the four years of war. Given all these impediments, it begs the question: why did a quarter of a million of them choose to serve? The answer to that all-important question lies in an understanding of how these men identified themselves, and the factors that motivated them to enlist.

5

Identity and Motivations

John White's American journey began in the aftermath of his father's death during the Great Famine. In the wake of that loss, his mother took the decision to remove her young family across the Atlantic, and it was in the United States where John grew to manhood. As the years passed, he came to think of America, and especially the Massachusetts mill town of Easthampton, as home. Fifteen years old when the war came, John looked on as some of the local men went off to the front, helping to fill the ranks of regiments like the 27th Massachusetts Infantry. His turn came in August 1863, when he mustered into service in Company C of the 2nd Massachusetts Heavy Artillery and shipped out for North Carolina.[1]

John White held a deep and genuine affection for the laboring community around Nashawannuck Mills, where he and his family worked producing buttons.[2] He inquired after the welfare of both the "button shop boys and girls" and his employer, Hiram J. Bly. Perhaps this sense of place fostered in him a patriotism that led to his declaration that "if i be shot i will die in a good cause" and his hope—likely of doubtful comfort to his mother—that "you may be shure i will kill a few rebs before i go if i be spared."[3] Perhaps he sought to confirm his manhood, and to demonstrate his superiority to others, such as that "brave fellow" Charlie Smith, who preferred to "blow . . . about what he can do" but who ultimately would "rather stay at home with the girls." In uniform, John could look forward to a triumphant return, when Charlie would be forced to "hang his head the coward."[4] Perhaps John's motivations came down to money. The $13 a month he earned in the factory was exactly what he could expect in the army, but as everyone knew, in actuality there was much more on offer.[5] That figure was boosted by allowances and bonuses, such as the town, state, and federal bounties that by late 1863 were becoming increasingly attractive. During the course of the war, John's Easthampton home, which furnished some two hundred men for service, spent $40,000 on bounties.[6] Surely it was no coincidence that one of John's first pronouncements to his mother after enlisting was his desire for her to "build a house," promising he would send "all i can to help you along with it," for "i want a house that we can call our own when i go home so you might as well go about it as quick as you can."[7]

Why did Irish immigrants like John White enlist? In John's case, any one of the above quotes—or none—may have represented his primary reason for joining up.[8] Each individual's decision was shaped by a complex melting pot of influences, where factors such as timing, life experience, opportunity, misfortune, and circumstance competed and comingled with intangibles like identity, ideology, and patriotism to create a uniquely personal set of motivations. Those most frequently ascribed to Irish Americans include gaining military experience for a future revolution in Ireland, a desire to dispel negative stereotypes surrounding the Irish in the United States, the need for steady employment, and a desire to preserve the Union—not least so it could continue its role as a refuge for Irish emigrants.[9] This chapter uses the contextualized correspondence to discern these motivations, identify the major factors that drove enlistment, and challenge the relative importance that has historically been placed on others. But discerning that importance first requires an analysis of how these soldiers and sailors viewed themselves, viewed Ireland, and viewed the United States. Coming to grips with these aspects of identity are integral to understanding how they perceived their military service, enabling in turn a fuller comprehension of why so many enlisted.[10] Heretofore, scholars of the Irish American soldier have recognized in them often distinct and sometimes competing Irish and American identities, something Susannah Ural has termed "dual loyalties."[11] An assessment of how these "Irish" and "American" identities manifested and interacted in the common Irish soldier and sailor reveals a new perspective.

"IRISH" IDENTITY IN UNIFORM

Traditional perceptions of Irish American identity during the conflict revolve almost exclusively around their "Irishness," conjuring images of the green flags and boxwood-adorned caps of the Irish Brigade. This Irishness was intrinsic, but its visage has served to overwhelm all other facets of how these men perceived themselves. In reality, it was but one element of their personal, public, and cultural identities, which varied depending on both background and circumstance.

During the American Civil War, the best-known and most public celebration of Irish American identity came on St. Patrick's Day. As Sophie Cooper has demonstrated, nineteenth-century Irish Americans viewed the occasion as an opportunity to both celebrate their community internally and, importantly, to showcase and promote it externally.[12] For those in ethnic units, it held similar meaning and opportunity. Their patron saint's feast presented the chance to boost esprit de corps and to loudly trumpet Irish American cultural identity and Irish America's contribution to the war effort. Nothing surpassed the 1863 efforts of the Irish Brigade in this regard, with their legendary celebrations amounting to a public relations blitz on the Army of the Potomac. Irish American communities at home also used the day to highlight their contribution to the war effort, such as the major St. Patrick's Day event held in Philadelphia in 1864 to mark the return of the 69th Pennsylvania Infantry.[13] Like the Irish Brigade and the 69th Pennsylvania, the great majority of green flag regiments sought to make the day their own. David O'Keeffe, a former cabinetmaker from Co. Cork, recalled St. Patrick's Day 1863 in the Irish 9th Massachusetts Infantry as "quite a merry time," where officers and privates exchanged roles, a furlough was placed atop a greased pole, horse races were run, and a band entertained everyone with music.[14] A year later, fellow Corkman James Healy of the same regiment spoke of the "grand time" the men had, with "Horse races and match game of football hurdle sack races burlesque dress parade & c."[15] Nevertheless, for the majority of Irish Americans in mixed formations, where St. Patrick's Day was not an occasion of significance for their unit's identity, celebrations were necessarily more muted, confined to a small number of Irish American comrades. Indeed, it was rarely mentioned in the correspondence of Irishmen who served outside ethnic units. The 1865 St. Patrick's Day of Richard Barrington of the 1st Missouri Engineers was likely far more typical of how Irish Americans spent the occasion—thinking of home: "this is St padys day but we have no chance to drownd the old toad here. I hope that I will be home the next good old St day and drink his health a double time along with you and my friends."[16]

For the great bulk of soldiers and sailors, men like Richard Barrington, being Irish was but one element of their identity—and as a result it was not the primary driver behind their selection of who they marched to war with. This did not mean they were any less Irish American than those serving under green flags. In fact, when viewed in comparative perspective, it is apparent that little separated those who chose to represent distinctly ethnic units from those who served in mixed formations. As individuals, they were virtually indistinguishable, often sharing similar motivations, experiences, and pride in their Irish cultural heritage. The key difference came in their military identity. The men who marched to war in "Irish" companies and regiments had explicitly chosen to place themselves on the front lines as public representatives of Irish America. "Irishness" was the primary mark of identity within their units, just as for others it might be political affiliation, regional distinctiveness, or occupational status.[17] As such, those who served within them sought and were expected to proudly accentuate that Irishness. This was something that was understood by all Irish Americans, regardless of whether they served in ethnic or nonethnic units.

The explicit public trumpeting of Irishness by those who served in ethnic Irish American formations has sometimes been taken as evidence of divided loyalties, but when contextualized as part of the Irish American whole in the Union military, it takes on a different complexion. Despite their similar backgrounds, the majority of Irish Americans serving outside green flag regiments rarely vocalized an Irish identity to anything approaching the levels common within entities such as the Irish Brigade. Recognizing the relative exceptionalism of the culturally infused statements and actions of these ethnic Irish units suggests that their origins lay not in conflicted loyalties, but in an awareness of their position as the most public face of the Irish American war effort. This has most recently been demonstrated in Catherine Bateson's analysis of wartime Irish American songs, the lyrics of which overwhelmingly focus on a select number of ethnic formations. As Bateson demonstrates, this focus was because it was understood that units like the Irish Brigade "stood as representatives for the whole diaspora," and therefore were the symbolic standard bearers of Irish American participation.[18] One of the benefits this status brought for the men who served in ethnic units was greater opportunities to express their cultural identity—as with St. Patrick's Day—something their organizers and officers regarded as a necessity given their role in influencing popular opinion both within Irish America and across northern society. One of the burdens was that any failures or setbacks they encountered in service were just as bound up with their culture and ethnicity, something that the men themselves were all too aware of. A salutary example of the risks associated with ethnic identity being closely tied to military service was made fully evident in May 1863, when the significant German representation in the Federal XI Corps was used to scapegoat that immigrant group for the Army of Potomac's defeat at Chancellorsville.[19]

Given their choices, their position, and the burden they carried, it is no surprise then that those who went to war in ethnic units regarded "Irishness" as the core element of their military identity. In talking up the Irish Brigade's superior esprit de corps when compared to other units, John Dougherty of the 63rd New York referred to them explicitly as "the Irishmen."[20] When eager to get into the fray with the 69th New York State Militia in the first summer of the war, Patrick Coffey was disappointed that reports of a Confederate attack proved false, as the regiment "had no chance to fight or Show our Courage as we are waiting patiently for a chance to Show the Southerners what we Irishmen can do when we get a going."[21] Patrick Kelly, whose regiment had recently joined the Irish Brigade, was bursting with a sense of Irish pride as he looked forward to the 1862 advance on Fredericksburg: "Faugh a ballggh is the war cry and no turn back of course we will cross the river first but no mater trust to irelands bold Brigade to clear the road."[22] All these men were fully aware that the nonethnic units surrounding them were filled with Irish Americans, but they understood that only they represented their ethnicity to the extent that their entire regiment was seen both within and without as "Irish."[23] As evidenced in the introduction, men like Patrick Dooley—who gushed with pride about the performance of green flag regiments at Malvern Hill from the ranks of the mixed 40th New York—would have agreed with that assessment. Another who likely would have done so was American-born William Connell, who was serving with the nonethnic 7th Vermont Infantry on Ship Island, Mississippi, in early 1862. While there he informed his immigrant mother: "there is one irish regiment here is thi best on the island they is a priest with them" (referring to the 9th Connecticut Infantry).[24]

The exalted and exceptional position green flag regiments held as figureheads of the Irish American contribution to the war effort is further reinforced by the fact that Irish Americans serving in nonethnic units consistently looked for news of them and their officers. Any encounter with them in the field was deemed particularly newsworthy. Writing from the Virginia Peninsula in 1862, Matthew Eagan, a Kerry-born immigrant in the 72nd New York, added the titbit that "the Irish Brigade are making a road for our artilery to Come on and a telegraph line."[25] Thomas Keating, the American-born son of Irish immigrants, could have joined one of the New York Irish Brigade regiments when he enlisted in September 1861, but instead he went to war with the 83rd New York Infantry, perhaps because of prewar associations with the 9th New York State Militia. Nevertheless, he was keenly interested in the well-being of the Irish Brigade and its charismatic leader. He wrote to his mother that he was "sorry to heare that Tom Megher Was hurted at the battle of Antitam i Was Trying to find out if the battle Was Over but I couldint find out."[26] Irish American interest in these representatives extended across state lines and throughout Irish communities in the North. William Cody, another American-born son of Irish immigrants, wrote to his Providence-based family from the ranks of the 3rd Rhode Island Heavy Artillery in South Carolina: "I see by the papers you sent me that they are trying to get Colonel Corcoran released I hope they will succsed."[27]

The overt expressions of unit and, by extension, Irish identity seen within ethnic regiments had direct parallels in the wider development of esprit de corps witnessed in non-Irish formations. Just as Irish Americans serving under green flags lauded their military identity through their Irishness, those within mixed units were often equally keen to celebrate the pride, prowess, and military identity of their own regiments.[28] Excitement and ebullience about potential future feats was something many Irish Americans in nonethnic organizations expressed shortly after enlistment, and was manifest for many from the moment they got their uniforms. Irish-born Archey Laverty of the 1st New York Infantry was pleased to tell home "we have got our united states blue uniform and we look like sogers now."[29] Likewise, William Duff wrote back to Brooklyn in October 1861: "we have just received our new Zouave Uniform from the United States Quarter Master Department in New York so we look smart and neat."[30] New York Irish American John Slattery of the 40th Massachusetts remarked how their colonel was "a regular fighting man he means to fight, we have got a fine looking Regt."[31] Patrick Dooley—so proud of the Irish regiments—said of his own 40th New York Infantry in July 1861, "all our men are picked men we are sending all our delicate men home to New York so I expect what men we have will show a good fight, you shall not hear of the Mozart Regiment running away from the enemy."[32] John

Casey, born in America to Irish parents, reassured his mother that he hoped to come back with his "lorals unfaided," as his 45th Illinois was "the Pride of the West."[33] John Deegan, a late war recruit into the 19th Maine, listed the regiments in his brigade for those at home "so that if you should pick up a paper someday and see an account of their valiant deeds you will know that your humble servant is somewhere close at hand."[34]

While the overtness of their Irish identity tended to be reliant on the formation within which they served, there was one striking commonality that transcended all army regiments and naval vessels, be they ethnic or mixed. It demonstrates both the high levels of ethnic cohesiveness within Irish America and the importance of the cultural identity that all these men shared. The evidence is overwhelming that consistently and repeatedly within the armed forces, ethnic Irishmen sought out their coethnics to act as their closest confidants in the service. Invariably, they endeavored to coalesce in this way, irrespective of the degree of Irish American representation within a company or vessel. This translated itself into their writings, so that whenever an Irish American mentioned another serviceman by name, it was overwhelmingly to reference someone of the same ethnicity. To be sure, these were not the only bonds they had—it was but one in a series of interconnected and interrelated ties that also incorporated nonethnic men, their company, and their regiment. The level of bonding between Irish Americans and these other groups varied from unit to unit and individual to individual.[35] But it was ethnic and cultural identity that tended to drive the formation of the all-important microgroups that sustained them through their service. As James McPherson has identified, these "bands of brothers" proved especially vital for unit cohesion, representing as they did a small military community that could rely on each other for mutual dependence and support.[36]

Naturally, many Irish American comrades who coalesced in such a way had known each other prior to enlistment, having been drawn from the same northern communities. But the evidence reveals time and again that the ethnic Irish became close, tented, and messed together even where no previous relationship existed. These ethnic bonds were most frequently exposed when a soldier died and Irish Americans not known to family members communicated the news. When laborer James Conner of the 2nd Massachusetts Heavy Artillery succumbed, his family were told that his closest friend was "Denis Toomey of Lowell, who has been with him all the time since he came out."[37]

After John Gannon from Co. Tipperary was killed in action in August 1862 at Second Bull Run, his mother received a letter from fellow Irish American John Meehan stating, "I was to him Like a Brother and him to me the fact is we Both Slept and eate together since we first Enlisted."[38] Similarly, James Molony of the 31st New York Infantry stepped up when Stephen O'Shea lost his life in the June 1862 Battle of Gaines' Mill, telling O'Shea's wife he had been her "husbands comrade all the time he was in the armey and was at his side when he was Killed."[39]

Those who joined the navy also hoped to find ethnic Irish from home, or consciously enlisted with them. When he was assigned to the USS *Niagara* in late 1863, sixteen-year-old Dublin immigrant and First Class Boy Henry Clark was asked by his mother how he was settling in on his new vessel. His response demonstrated the importance of cultural affinity in adapting to military life: "I like this ship better than I thought I should, but as to being lonesome, I am getting over that feeling as there are a great many boys from your neighbahood in this ship so that it begins to be quite cheerful here."[40] James Burns asked his family from aboard the USS *Colorado* if they "knew if any the boys has joined the Navy if you do write and let me know what Ship they are in." That he was explicitly referencing fellow Irish is confirmed by the "boys" names: "Michael Fitz Jerald and Sly Bannon and Peter Matt Burns an Dan."[41] Daniel Driscoll told his father from the receiving ship USS *Ohio* in 1861 that his mother "must not freat abought me for I have a good time and plenty that nows me."[42] If an Irish American sailor was unfortunate enough to die, it was invariably coethnics among the crew who took the lead in dealing with his affairs. When Donegal native Patrick Dougherty passed away aboard the USS *South Carolina* off Tybee Island in 1864, fellow Irishmen Patrick Duffey and James Dunphey notified his family and made the headboard for his grave.[43] Similarly, when the aforementioned Henry Clark was killed, having had both his legs blown off on the USS *Hartford* during the August 1864 Battle of Mobile Bay, it was his shipmate William Lynam, likely also an Irish American, who broke the news to those at home, stating, "if he was my own Brother i cood not have felt worst."[44] Regardless of whether their service was in the army or navy, the importance of shared identity, culture, and community shone through for Irish Americans in the men they chose to most closely associate with while in uniform.

As has been outlined, it was ethnicity and cultural identity—not nativity—

that defined inclusion within Irish American micro-groups. When late war enlistee Patrick Galliven of the 10th New York sent his mother two photographs, one was of "a tent mate of mine name Dick Collins," a Canadian-born Irish American substitute.[45] Writing to his Irish-born wife back in Maine after the 1862 Battle of Fredericksburg, English-born Irish American Thomas Doyle lamented the fact that his closest friend, John Ward, was missing in action. Both men had been part of the Irish community in Searsport and were next-door neighbors.[46] Thomas confessed, "I feele lonsum with out him . . . for John and me allways tented to geather." Though he had enlisted from Belfast, Maine, rather than Searsport, the soldier who had taken care of Ward's possessions was also "a Irish man the name of michal butler."[47] These examples further demonstrate why nativity alone cannot be employed as a measure of ethnic Irish breakdown within the U.S. military. Foreign-born Irish Americans in the service regarded themselves as ethnically and culturally Irish, and actively sought to participate in the same ethnic Irish micro-groups as the Irish-born. They were also regarded as such by other groups in contemporary society. A good example of this can be seen in the 1861 autobiography of the formerly enslaved Harriet Jacobs, in which she described the racism faced by her son in Boston. Of those who leveled abuse against him, "some of the apprentices were Americans, others American-born Irish."[48] When the postwar historian of the 40th New York Infantry sought to describe the particularly Irish character of Company K, he remarked that it was "composed entirely of young men of Irish extraction, but principally born in America."[49] This ethnic identity was something articulated by John Slattery of the 40th Massachusetts Infantry. The son of immigrant parents from Co. Limerick, he had been born and raised in Utica, New York, but enlisted with the Bay Staters while away for work. It was a decision he initially regretted, or so he informed his sister, because: "I should like to be in the same Regt with the utica boys there is only two Irish fellows in this company besides my self," before adding, "our captain is a native."[50] When Irish Americans like Slattery discussed or asked after the "boys," they invariably meant Irish American boys. Slattery explicitly articulated this meaning and further underpinned his sense of cultural identity by differentiating his captain as "a native" despite the fact that both he and his officer had been born in the United States.

Beyond nurturing ethnic ties within companies and on board ships, Irish Americans also made efforts to maintain their community networks beyond their own units. They consistently sought out relatives and friends in the service, and made frequent excursions to meet with them when they were stationed nearby. This ethnic cohesiveness extended even into captivity. Statistical analysis of survival rates within the Andersonville prisoner of war camp indicate that an Irish-born soldier's chances of survival were greater if a fellow Irishman from his company was imprisoned with him.[51] Broader Irish American cohesion in camps like Andersonville can be qualitatively illustrated through cases like that of Arthur Mulholland, one of the unfortunate few of the Irish 69th Pennsylvania captured during Pickett's Charge at Gettysburg. Arthur did not survive, but those closest to him at the end shared his ethnicity, if not his regiment. John Doyle of the 183rd Pennsylvania Infantry later swore he had seen him alive in the notorious camp, while fellow Irish American Robert Torrey, a draftee in the 90th Pennsylvania Infantry, claimed to have "placed his name, Co and Regt on his breast" after Arthur had been lowered into the burial pit.[52]

"AMERICAN" IDENTITY IN UNIFORM

Taken at face value, the overt expressions of Irish identity by green flag units and the sometimes extraordinary degree of ethnic cohesion displayed by Irish American servicemen could be interpreted as evidence that they saw themselves as "others," set apart from American society. While this is what is often focused on, it is but one side of the story. The 1860s United States was characterized by diverse and often distinct groups—be they native-born or immigrant—who simultaneously perceived themselves as different from those around them and as part of the American project. These perceived differences were often based around religious belief, ethnic and/or social background, and race. While their relatively recent explosion in numbers meant that many Irish Americans were new additions to that project, they had quickly set about carving out a place for themselves within it. A close examination of what ordinary Irish American servicemen said and did reveals the more complex concepts of identity this produced. Increasingly, they came to see themselves not simply as "Irish" but as distinctly "American Irish."

While events like St. Patrick's Day were important to Irish American servicemen, their writings reveal that they were just as invested in celebrating and participating in traditional American holidays. Thomas McCarthy's immigrant mother was keen to mark Thanksgiving's relevance by sending the 12th Massachusetts Infantry soldier a gift, so he requested "a likeness of you and Becky you might get a Lozenger box."[53] Nothing—not even St. Patrick's Day—matched the Fourth of July as the holiday of most frequent reference among Irish Americans troops. The degree to which the Irish embraced America's Independence Day is an important indicator of the extent to which these immigrants sought to commit to their new nation. The postbellum effort that nineteenth-century ethnic groups such as the Irish and Germans went to in organizing public celebrations of American holidays has been characterized as an attempt to "interweave their story with America's" and demand their place in American culture as "ethnic Americans."[54] The private Civil War correspondence of working-class Irish Americans illustrates their early embrace of that ideal. During the Civil War, celebrating the Fourth of July and the nation's revolutionary heritage was viewed as the preeminent expression of what it meant to be an American by men both North and South.[55] The holiday also marked another time for gift giving. Limerick native Joseph Sheedy of the Irish 28th Massachusetts pledged in 1862 that he would "fulfil my promise, and will send him [his brother] some money for the fourth of July."[56] Tom Monaghan of the 95th Pennsylvania asked his mother to "give Charley for me a dollar to Spend for 4th of July."[57] Independence Day was invariably the date when Irish Americans hoped to be home from the war. Recent immigrant Thomas McCready from Donegal wrote in 1862, "i hope again the 4th of July that i will be shaking hands with you," while Felix Burns of the Irish-dominated 13th Pennsylvania Cavalry said a year later "you would Hear the boys talking they would say we will all be home for fourth of July."[58]

Just as telling as their embrace of the Fourth of July were the efforts Irish American servicemen went to in touring sites of historic importance to the United States. When in Charles Town, West Virginia, John Delaney from Co. Laois decided to visit the scene of John Brown's demise: "I was in the cell where he was confined and in the courthouse where he was tried and condemed and was where he was hung."[59] John Toomey from Co. Cork had the chance while on the Virginia Peninsula to see "the spot where Cornwallis delivered his sword to Washington."[60] John Boyle took time while stationed near Alexandria, Virginia, not only to see the church where George Washington worshiped but to make an excursion to Mount Vernon, where he saw "the grave of Washington and his wife the are Inside a Brick house having an Iron gate in front you can see the tomstone of himself & his wife beside him."[61] The significance of this history to many Irish Americans was demonstrated by Irish immigrant Daniel Collins of Corcoran's Irish Legion. When he took some booty at Fairfax Courthouse, Virginia, in 1863, the main prize he sent home was "the famous stamp that the Revolution was about."[62]

Such evidence makes it apparent that men from a wide variety of immigrant backgrounds deeply valued American culture and history and what it represented—a fact that has important ramifications when assessing the motivations that underpinned Irish American service. So, too, does their concept of community. The commitment and energy that Irish immigrants poured into their new communities during the immediate antebellum period had helped foster a sense of self that was not just Irish but concurrently and inseparably American *and* Irish.[63] Thousands of future servicemen had been born directly into these American Irish communities during the 1830s and 1840s, while thousands more had grown from children to adults within them. That this sense of community identity was well formed prior to the war is evidenced by the frequent allusions servicemen made to them. By the time young Cork immigrant Patrick Dugan entered Federal service, his "home" was indisputably the town of Wilmington, Illinois. He frequently communicated the welfare of "all the Wilmington Boys" and "all the boys from Wilmington Parish" to his mother, requesting in return information on "who from Wilmington got killed" following major battles.[64] In like fashion, Patrick Horan from Co. Galway, whose father had died in Ireland during the Famine, updated his mother on "all the Rochester boyes," Dubliner John Mahon wrote to tell of "all the Boys from Hudson," while Kilkenny immigrant Jeremiah Keenan transmitted news of "the Churchville boys."[65] Irish-born Daniel Reddy, in communicating the death of fellow immigrant John Murray to those at home in 1864, specifically referenced a number of his other Irish comrades and lamented the fact that "all the woburn boys are gone but Foley and me it makes me feel very lonesome when i think of it."[66] As Daniel's correspondence implies, these "boys" were most commonly ethnic Irish members of the community. The men John Mahon chose to name in his correspondence were civilian William Phillips—the American-born son of an Irish immigrant—and fellow soldiers John Barry, William Galbraith, and John Moore, all of whom were Irish-born.[67] The "Churchville boys" that Jeremiah Keenan identified, David O'Connell and George Weldon, had likewise been born in Ireland.[68]

Though less frequent, there are examples of Irish Americans including non-Irish among the "boys." American-born John Sullivan of the 102nd New York Infantry mentioned non-Irish Bill Hawley, Earnest Offerman, and John Hill-oves as some of "my own town boys" from Angelica who "are all very kind and Brotherlike to me."[69]

This sense of a distinctly American Irish regional identity had grown so much by the outbreak of the Civil War that it could even be a catalyst for disharmony within ethnic Irish units. Regional factionalization in itself was nothing new, and was something the Irish had carried with them to the United States—most famously in the form of the rival gangs of "Corkonians" and "Fardowners" who vied with each other for work on antebellum canals and railroads.[70] But by 1861, part of this sense of belonging had transferred onto specific American locales, causing some Irish to prefer to serve with others from their new towns and cities. Being unexpectedly denied this opportunity could lead to friction. An example of this can be seen with the reorganization that marked the early days of Corcoran's Irish Legion. When two Buffalo Irish companies were amalgamated with those from New York City, disaffection ensued. In protest at the move, the Buffalo Irish "threw off their knapsacks and would not mind their officers not even Corcoran." The men could only be placated by assurances of their value, and by being assigned duties to act as the Provost Guard.[71]

This growing embrace of an increasingly American Irish identity did not mean that all these men regarded themselves as the same as the non-Irish American soldiers they fought beside. In March 1865, late war recruit Dennis Larkin of the 6th New York Heavy Artillery wrote his parents to let them know that as "Jeff is gone up the Spout," the war would soon be drawing to a close. That outcome now seemed certain, despite the fact that Dennis's father and mother had "allways saidi that the south would get the Best of the yankes." In any event, Dennis clarified, "it is not the yankes that is doning the fighting it is the irish lads that is doning it."[72] Dennis Larkin viewed the native-born "Yankees" as other—and his parents certainly did. Yet despite his apparently overt rejection of "Yankees," Dennis's writings offer glimpses of the intergenerational development of a distinctly American Irish identity. The community he regarded as home, and that he felt was his own, was firmly embedded in the village of Canton, St. Lawrence County, New York. He peppered his correspondence consistently and repeatedly with references to it; his desire to see Canton once more, his inquiries after Canton friends and neighbors, and his pining for information on the Canton girls. Just because Dennis Larkin did not regard himself as a "Yankee" did not mean that he did not regard the United States as his home.

Analysis of Irish American service has largely failed to take into consideration the potential impact on identity of the experiential differences that marked out many of the young men who enlisted in the military from older generations within their community. This was particularly true for those who had arrived as children during the Famine migration. A boy who had arrived in the United States at the age of ten in 1851 could be significantly more pliable in terms of identity than a twenty-year-old who landed the same year. While both tend to be classified as "recent immigrants," only one had grown to adulthood in the streets and laneways of America, the country where most of the formative events that shaped them as men occurred. It could not fail to leave its imprint.[73] For soldiers like Dennis Larkin, it created a sense of self that was very Irish but also very centered on their local American community—in his case, Canton. Tens of thousands of the Irish Americans who served in the war shared a similar background.[74]

One of the consequences of the range and breadth of lived experiences within 1860s Irish America was that it opened the door for a number of men to exercise a degree of fluidity over their public identities. As was evident in the case of Patrick Carraher's name change discussed earlier, this may have been particularly attractive to those seeking to avoid or escape ethnic prejudice. For Irish Americans who had been born and grown up in the United States, or who had spent long enough in the country for their accents to pass as American, this may have enabled them to downplay their ethnicity as circumstances dictated. In a society where many viewed Irish cultural identity in a negative light, a degree of malleability in how they publicly presented themselves could prove useful. Though such activity is extremely difficult to identify, it is possible that some of the nativity discrepancies apparent in military records fossilize this fluidity. Cases abound of soldiers and sailors born in Ireland who were recorded as American-born on their enlistment, an "error" that is invariably unidirectional. Men like Michael Brady, James Carey, Dennis Driscoll, Owen McGowan, and James O'Neil were all recorded as Irish-born on the census, but as American when they enlisted.[75] Others, such as John Riley, an Irish American born in England, and John Scully, an Irish American born in Canada, were likewise said to have been native to the United States.[76] John Scanlan, who survived the war, was recorded as Canadian-born on his enlistment (under an alias), but as Irish-born on postwar censuses.[77] Neither was this restricted to men who had arrived in America as children. Patrick Finan and Denis Horgan were recent adult immigrants from Ireland who in the military were recorded as having been from the United States.[78] Barney Carr, the assisted immigrant from Co. Derry, had been taken from a New York institution to work on a farm out west; when he enlisted in Illinois, his birthplace was recorded as New York.[79] Though far less frequent, there are some for whom the opposite was the case. Jeremiah Dorgan, recorded as having been born in Maine while a child on the 1850 census, was listed as a Corkman when he joined the 2nd Louisiana Infantry.[80] James Healy had a birthplace of Massachusetts on the 1860 census, but when he entered the 9th Massachusetts Infantry—an ethnic Irish regiment—his nativity changed to Ireland.[81] Officers and local administrators undoubtedly played a role in misassigning nativity, but it seems that some Irish Americans may have made a conscious choice to misrepresent it themselves.[82]

The incidents of altered nativity appear to be particularly prevalent in naval records, and it is tempting to speculate that this may have been partially due to the reduced level of control Irish Americans had over where and with whom they served in that branch of service. That assertions of American birth were seen as advantageous where doubt existed is suggested by the cases of well-known figures such as General Phil Sheridan and Civil War photographer Timothy O'Sullivan. Both of these men contended that they had born in the United States, though question marks continue to surround those assertions. While Sheridan said he had been born in Albany, claims persist that he entered the world either in Co. Cavan or at sea during the family's crossing. Timothy O'Sullivan stated he was of American nativity on at least one job application, but following his premature death his father apparently listed him as having been born in Ireland.[83] Regardless of the actual location of their birth, both Sheridan and O'Sullivan were keenly aware that it was far more advantageous to be seen as American. On what was ostensibly his first visit to Ireland in 1871, Sheridan reinforced this by seeking to place considerable distance between himself and the home of his parents. He told a correspondent of the *New York Herald* that his "family emigrated so long ago that I am unable to say whether it belonged to the north or south [of Ireland]. It strikes me it came from Westmeath."[84] Given his background, it strains credulity that Sheridan would have been so ignorant of his Irish origins. It is quite possible that at least some of the altered nativity prevalent on enlisted men's military records was intended to achieve similar results. While in their private lives these men may well have been proud of their Irish cultural background, it was readily apparent that there was nothing but benefits to be had from presenting oneself in as American a fashion as possible.[85] The cases of men like James Healy and Jeremiah Dorgan suggest that, occasionally, this trend may have operated in reverse—perhaps among men who were keen to accentuate their Irishness within ethnic regiments, or with those who were particularly eager to overtly express their ethnic and cultural identity.

It is evident that, as the war loomed, American and Irish forms of identity and cultural association were increasingly grafting together. Further demonstration of the extent to which this was true was offered by Irish-born Sergeant James Livingston, who had enlisted in Corcoran's Irish Legion as a nineteen-year-old. When addressing a younger member of his family in an 1863 letter home from Suffolk, Virginia, he chose to use the quintessentially American sport of baseball as an analogy for the positions and movements of "miky Corcoran" and his Irishmen: "We are Plaing Ball here at Peresent i am hinder[?] and we have to Pitchers and Pleanty of Catcher the home Base is Suffolk or Richmond Fany and mat are Fielders and miky Corcoran holds the Bat Ben Conlin holds the Grub and Your uncle Nabs all Bad Playrs up in the Gaurd hous."[86] Though it was likely more frequent, becoming embedded in American society to the extent that James Livingston and others had was not the sole preserve of Irish Americans who had been born or grown to adulthood the United States. Day Laborer Thomas Carr was a married man when he immigrated with his wife and child in the late 1850s, settling in Cazenovia, Madison County, New York. When war came, he enlisted in the local regiment, the 35th New York Infantry, but he was later transferred to the 80th New York Infantry, formed largely of men from Ulster County. Within his new formation he struck up a friendship with Assistant Surgeon William Taylor. Taylor had no connections to Ireland. What the two men shared was an affection for Madison County.[87] Taylor later wrote that "Being from the same county (Madison) I had often conversed with him [Thomas] in relation to our local matters and always found him very much interested in anything pertaining to home affairs."[88]

There is perhaps no stronger evidence for how enmeshed these men's American and Irish identities had become than in the meaning they placed on the word "country." For when Irish Americans spoke of "country," they meant not Ireland but the United States. This was true even for recent immigrants. Writing to his father in Ireland from the USS *Wabash* in 1863, Patrick Finan was pleased that all the new arrivals from his native Sligo were "like to bee Drafted as Soone as the land" as "thear is a lot of young Fellows a round New York that Wont Fight For thear Country and the ought to Bee Made Fight or els clear out."[89] Finan's statement captures the belief held by many Irish that the United States became "thear Country" from the moment they decided to make a life there. William McCollister from Co. Antrim held a similar view. Facing battle on the Virginia Peninsula in the summer of 1862, he told his mother: "I am just as willing for to die for my Country as any white boy living."[90] Similarly, when Tyrone native James Kerr was greeted with troubling news from Philadelphia, he complained that he had "enough to perplex my mind without it the duties of a Soldier Battling for his Countrys rights."[91]

Irish Americans in the Union military were proud of their Irish ethnic and cultural identity. For those who served surrounded by fellow ethnics, that pride regularly manifested itself in overt displays of "Irishness." Such public manifestations of identity were necessarily more muted for the majority who served in mixed units, where energies were often channeled toward a pride in uniform and regiment. But no matter their surroundings, their cultural identity shone through in the company they kept—revealed in the ethnic background of the men they slept beside, ate beside, and died beside. Yet the public (and historiographical) dominance of the ethnic portion of these men's identities belies the fact that for many by 1861 being an American was also an intrinsically important part of who they were. Their Irish communities were in the United States, and by extension their home was in the United States. Thousands of them had bought into the history, culture, and ideals of that new home, and had come to regard it as their "country." This sense of commitment to the United States would prove highly significant once the guns started firing in 1861. But before examining how it influenced their enlistment, it is first appropriate to examine what is perhaps the most convincing form of evidence of their firm commitment to America—how they interacted with Ireland.

THE PLACE OF IRELAND IN IRISH AMERICAN IDENTITY

Coming to grips with Irish American identity is an important precursor to an examination of motivations for enlistment. So, too, is gaining a fuller understanding of how most Irish American servicemen viewed and interacted with Ireland during the mid-nineteenth century. The nineteenth-century Irish America of popular imagination is of an exiled people who longed for the opportunity to return to their true home. An image that was cultivated and promoted from within the Irish community through story and song, it has served to reinforce perceptions of the immigrant as victim, and the United States as a country that was subordinated to the interests of Ireland.[92] Doubtless, many felt that way. The evidence is compelling that most—particularly in the military—did not.

In the memory and historiography of the Civil War, analysis and discussion of the interaction of Irish American servicemen with Ireland has been utterly dominated by the role of the Fenian Brotherhood, the New York-based revolutionary organization formed in 1859 as an American branch of the Irish Republican Brotherhood, which had been founded in Dublin the previous year.[93] These Fenians, whose aim was to support the establishment of an Irish Republic, have long been regarded as one of the most substantial drivers of Irish enlistment in the Union military.[94] The support that the Fenians garnered for the "Cause of Ireland" has been seen as instigating a wave of recruitment into the U.S. armed forces, as men sought to gain the military experience the American Civil War offered so that they could apply it in a planned future confrontation with the British in Ireland. This in turn has lent credence to the argument that large numbers of the men in uniform were significantly more interested in the political future of Ireland than they were that of the United States. The wealth of source material written on and by some of the Fenian movement's major leaders and the consistent prominence of the organization in the pages of Irish nationalist publications have gone a long way to ensuring the continued focus on the Fenian role during the conflict. But while nationalist newspapers such as the *New York Irish American* and *Boston Pilot* consistently highlighted Fenian service and sacrifice during the conflict, when viewed in broader perspective, the evidence suggests that the practical influence and significance of Fenianism as a motivator for Irish enlistment was slight.

The Fenian Brotherhood was certainly extremely popular among Irish immigrants, and there were those Irish in Federal uniform for whom the interests of Ireland surpassed all else. It is also the case that many Fenians did join the Union military, while thousands more became paid up members during their service via the "Fenian Circles" that were dotted about the army and navy. At first glance, the figures seem impressive, as by 1865 the Brotherhood had as many as 50,000 members and up to 200,000 supporters in America.[95] However, while it was an undeniably important organization, the evidence suggests only a relatively few highly politicized hardliners enlisted to gain military experience in the hopes of a future war with Britain. Just a little more than one hundred Civil War veterans returned to Europe to participate in Fenian activities between 1865 and 1867—many of them former officers—while the Fenian force that launched its invasion of Canada from Buffalo in 1866 numbered in the region of one thousand men, only some of whom were former servicemen.[96] This is not to say that large numbers of Irish Americans in service did not support an independent Ireland—thousands of them did. But for the great bulk of the Irish, their political engagement with the national question was limited to a vocal support of the Irish independence struggle, a willingness to periodically dip into their pockets for the cause of Ireland, and, if they were so inclined, to publicly communicate that position through Fenian membership. As David Brundage has demonstrated, that membership was often about more than just Irish nationalism—it was also closely tied to the labor movement and the efforts of trade unionists to improve conditions for those who, like them, were on the lowest rungs of American society.[97] Simply put, while many ordinary Irish Americans viewed the survival of a strong United States as vital for both the future of Ireland and the Irish people, very few had any intention of a permanent return to the land of their birth. It was no accident that the Irish were among the least likely of all immigrants to return to Europe.[98]

When it came to it, even those Irish American servicemen who were apparently ardent Irish nationalists tended to subordinate that cause in favor of the immediate necessity of defeating secession. English-born John Corcoran offers one such example. When rumors abounded in the late summer of 1862 that Britain was on the cusp of recognizing the Confederacy, it caused him to fly into a rage: "if that damed England has any thing to do with us woe be to the Read Raskels you may thing strong of me for thes sentiments I use agаnst my Birth Place but if England was to intifere I wold neaver take a live English Soldgier I am down on that nation and willing to do anything to see that Nashion fall and Ireland the Home of the Brave free from Her Enemies Hands." Yet in the same breadth, John Corcoran demonstrated that he married this Irish nationalism with an unquestionable dedication to Union victory, a cause for which he was willing to give his life: "there is a place called Richmond it will fall and then the times will get first rate . . . we are willing to go there any minet and share in taking it we have got our minds made up neaver to surrender."[99] Patrick Finan, the USS *Wabash* crewman who felt his fellow Irishmen should be forced to "fight for their country" the moment they arrived in America, had immediately added: "But I Wish to God it Was For the Freedom of Ireland I Was Fighting for in the Place of What We are Fighting For."[100] These may seem contradictory or conflicting viewpoints, but it is apparent that Patrick Finan did not regard them as such. Notwithstanding his feelings toward the war at the time of writing (1863), or how much he may have perceived the freedom of Ireland as the purer or higher cause, he accepted Federal service as his primary duty.

Another whose letters could be interpreted as indicative of competing loyalties and allegiances is Sligo native James Henry. On the occasion of being promoted into the officer corps of the 37th New York "Irish Rifles," James wrote home of the speech he made before the regiment. "I used a great conglomeration of language about Ireland—native land—adopted country—free and religious liberty—dying for the cause—and all that kind of thing." These words in themselves are indicative of how the use of such imagery and phraseology about Ireland had an air of the performative about it, and were an expected flourish in public oration. Nevertheless, James did appear to believe them. He continued: "God Grant—and I hope it may not be far distant—that the time will come when I shall have the sacred task of leading on a band of my countrymen to free their native land. I think, if this war was now over, that I could raise 200 men, as good as ever stepped—out of this single regiment to follow me—that's something for only an acquaintance of 9 months."[101] Yet despite such rhetoric, James Henry was committed to the cause of the United States, and equally committed to his own future. An ambitious soldier, he had set himself the task of reaching the rank of colonel before war's end. When muster out came before he had accomplished that goal, he chose not to turn his full attention to the "sacred task" of Ireland. Instead, he opted to fight on for the Union, and to try his hand at forging a long-term military career in the regulars. He was mortally wounded at Spotsylvania Court House in 1864 as a sergeant in the 11th U.S. Infantry.[102]

Although John Corcoran, Patrick Finan, and James Henry each explicitly referenced the cause of Ireland, for them it was still the United States first.[103] Even then, what makes their sentiments regarding their ancestral home most notable is their rarity within written correspondence. The historiographical focus on Fenianism has served to almost entirely mask the reality of how the majority of Irish American servicemen viewed and interacted with Ireland. Like so much else in their service, these interactions were not dominated by the political, but by the practical and personal—not by the future of Ireland, but by their future lives in the United States.

Within ordinary Irish American correspondence, any occasional references to the political future of Ireland are entirely eclipsed by a very different form of interaction with the "Old Sod." These substantially more frequent exchanges provide further evidence of the extent to which Irish Americans had committed to their new country. Patrick Delanty of the USS *Carondelet* was one of those who held a deep and heartfelt affection for Ireland. Indeed, he hoped to return "on a visit" someday. As was the case with many other Irish Americans, he and his family members in the United States were expected to financially assist relatives who had not had the opportunity to emigrate.[104] By 1862, Patrick had grown particularly unimpressed with begging letters from his farmer uncle back in Laois, whom he felt "must live pretty high" if he was unable to survive on his income and produce. But Patrick also accepted that his uncle's situation was not what it had once been. The man's son and siblings had all emigrated, and the community had been transposed across the Atlantic to such an extent that there remained only "three or four persons he knowed" around his birthplace. The Union sailor admitted that it must now be "a gloomy looking place."[105] Patrick Delanty had a favored solution for his uncle's predicament. He hoped he would leave and join the rest of the family in America.[106]

The Irish American desire to bring as many of their family and friends as possible to the United States is demonstrated time and again in their correspondence. Writing from Chicago, future 23rd Illinois Infantry soldier Edmund Dwyer told his father in Co. Limerick that "we all would like to have you with us . . . it is bad for you to be separated from your children in your advanced age when you need them."[107] John Shea of the 1st Kansas Infantry felt the same, though in his case his first priority was his sister. He asked his mother in Co. Kerry whether she would "let my Sister come or not," adding "I donte want to be Sinding for her if you donte let her come."[108] Matthew Eagan of the 72nd New York Infantry was similarly keen to "send for John"—presumably a close relative—though he thought it best to wait until he was "free and done with the army."[109] For his part, Patrick Dougherty of the USS *South Carolina* did declare his intention "to go Home to Ireland" after being paid off, but rather than revolution, the purpose of his trip was "to bring his Mother out here."[110] From the South Carolina blockade, Patrick Finan of the USS *Wabash* wrote to Sligo town in order to let his father know he was "Willing to Pay your three Passiges in New York yours Mary Ann and Johnsey Mullroonys," though in the latter case it was on the precondition that "his Wife is Willing to let him Come hear."[111] Edward Fitzpatrick of the 10th New Jersey Infantry, who kept up a regular correspondence with the "Old Country," was pleased to hear the news while in the Petersburg trenches that "the old man paid the brothers pasage out to this country."[112] Michael Daly of the 7th Illinois Cavalry took the time to send money from Tennessee to his mother in New York, expressly in order to secure the passage of his sisters from Ireland. "it is about time that we should have them in this Country," he wrote.[113] His thoughts were also turning toward a family of his own. Michael wanted a wife from the "old sod" and was determined that if he could not find one "already to hand," he would "import one."[114]

There can be little doubt that throughout the four years of conflict vast sums of money earned in the ranks of the Union's armed forces was spent on realizing the permanent relocation of thousands of family and community members from Ireland to the United States. Far from seeking ways to return permanently to Ireland, what occupied the efforts of the great majority of Irish immigrants was ensuring they brought as much of Ireland as possible to them. In their unstinting efforts to assist large-scale immigration across the Atlantic these men signaled precisely where they conceived their futures. The future they wanted for themselves and their families was an American one, and accordingly their long-term commitments were to their new home, their transposed communities, and their new nation.

For these working-class men, the promise that America held often went beyond its capacity to offer a home for them and their extended families.

While politically they might not have shared much in common with Abraham Lincoln, many would have agreed with his assessment that the United States was the "last best hope of earth."[115] No matter the conditions they found themselves in, the American republic and its broad political franchise offered and promised far more immediate, practical, and personal benefit than the abstraction of physical sacrifice for Irish nationhood ever could. As a result, the immigrant embrace of the democratic republic and its ideals could be swift and immediate. Few expressed their ideological reasoning for committing themselves to their new home more forcefully than recent arrival Patrick O'Brien. Writing home to West Cork from the deck of the gunboat USS *Clifton,* he exhorted his mother to "make up your mind to come to this country," promising to send for her and the rest of the family. In offering one of the reasons why they should relocate, he launched a blistering attack on the Hungerfords, the landed family who had been his Irish landlords: "Tell Hungerford not to make a fool of himself, and that he could have a hungry hunt after my wages even to the day of judgement and then he would have no more of it than he has now and that is none, such men are no more thought of here then I am myself in fact a great deal less as him and his like would get well booted here."[116] For Patrick O'Brien, the United States was the great leveler, where the toxic relationship between landlord and tenant familiar to so many in Ireland could be overturned. Irish step-migrant and future Union sailor John Crowley was similarly impressed with the promise his new country held when he first arrived at the Emigrant Landing Depot in New York's Castle Garden. "The ship loads of people that are arriving here every day from all parts of Europe would astonish you but still there is plenty of room it is easy to get a job . . . there is no mistake about America it is finest Country in the world."[117] For Patrick O'Brien, John Crowley, and a multitude like them, the United States—no matter its faults—presented an opportunity to live in a society that did not have the social strictures that were placed on themselves and their families in Ireland. They would always be Irish and would always look to support Ireland and Irish people—but they were enthusiastic Americans now too.

When added to the evidence of their growing American Irish identity, the reality of the practical interactions these men had with Ireland adds significant complexity to our understanding of how they positioned themselves with respect to both Ireland and America. Their multilayered identity incorporated close ties to immigrants who hailed from their locality of origin within Ireland, and usually extended back across the Atlantic into those old regions. A sense of economic and moral obligation to those left behind—commonly manifested in efforts to procure passage for them, or to remit money—represented by far their most important duty to the "Old Country." This dwarfed any feelings of political obligation they felt to personally fight for Irish freedom. As a result, Fenian ideals motivated very few Irishmen to enter Union service. Though they were frequently willing to provide vocal and occasional financial support toward those aims, they saw their futures as American ones. The manifestation of this belief, which was broadly held throughout Irish America, is readily apparent in how these servicemen interacted with Ireland. It is in these interactions that the full extent of their relationship with the United States becomes evident. Understanding this identity and this relationship is of foundational importance when considering why some of them were motivated to follow the Stars and Stripes into battle.

MOTIVATIONS FOR SERVICE

The question of what motivated these men to enlist during the Civil War is one of the most discussed and analyzed aspects of Irish American service.[118] Such inquiry has normally set out from the negative stance of supposed Irish underrepresentation, but as this book has sought to demonstrate, this is something that must now be framed and approached from the inverse perspective. As demonstrated above, Fenianism had a relatively modest part to play in inspiring Irish American men to take up arms. Instead, the contextualized correspondence points clearly to the dominance of two factors in driving Irish American service—economics and patriotic duty.

Before examining the evidence for these dominant motivators in detail, it is worth recalling the story of John White, related at the outset of this chapter. We can never be sure of precisely what mix of motivations and factors came together to lead individual men to the recruiting officer's desk. While there were many commonalties, every Irish American serviceman was an individual, each with their own set of circumstances and life experiences.[119] The tipping point for Irish American John Slattery's enlistment came when his grandmother left him. In January 1862, the 12th Massachusetts Infantry soldier told her: "if you had stopt at home I would Not be out hear but when you left and all of my best fowl i though it was time for me to leave."[120] In late 1863, Galwegian William Flaherty left his Philadelphia home to travel to New Hampshire and enlist under an alias, having spent the previous year in the navy. William had chosen to serve under his mother's maiden name; apparently "he was ashamed to be known as related to his father," an abusive alcoholic who had neglected the family through "continual drunkenness" and who had brought "discredit" on the Flaherty name.[121] In a letter of 31 December 1863 breaking the news of his enlistment, William told his mother that "every time i went in to your home that i was insulted by him i call father i had no place to go . . . rather than hear my fathers tounge again i would go anywhere."[122]

Kilkenny laborer James Carroll supposedly spent a significant amount of time in 1861 searching for his wife and child, from whom he had been separated while working away. By the time he reestablished contact with them he had joined the army. He explained to his wife that in his sorrow he had "Got into Company" and drank his savings. "I despaired of ever seeing you and heart Broken I enlisted in this Regt."[123] Timing and the hand of fate played a similar role in Irish American Jeremiah Dorgan's path to the 2nd Louisiana Infantry in 1862. The sailor was originally bound for Liverpool when his vessel foundered halfway across the Atlantic. "we were picked up by a steamship and brought back to Boston," he explained to his mother. From there he shipped again, this time for New Orleans, where he enlisted.[124] Irish immigrant Edward Mooney's decision to enlist bears all the hallmarks of a Hobson's choice. The autumn of 1862 found him serving a twenty-five-year sentence in the Iowa State Penitentiary for second-degree murder. He was fortunate that his prison term had been commuted from the death penalty, the fate suffered by his co-accused.[125] On 14 August 1862, "the influence of his friends and his good conduct" won Edward a pardon, and apparently finding that his "patriotism would not allow him to be idle," he immediately enlisted in the 19th Iowa Infantry.[126] The fact that his pardon post-dated his enlistment by four days suggests that his ardor may have been substantially enhanced by a foreknowledge that a willingness to serve would help secure his release.[127]

As such examples illustrate, when dealing with a quarter of a million individuals, there were many different circumstances that could lead any one man into uniform during the American Civil War. Yet, while every story was different, the commonalties that played the most important role in bringing these men to their decisions repeatedly shine through. The first of them revolved around economics.

Writing in August 1861, two months after enlisting, John Fitzpatrick of the 19th Illinois Infantry expressed his concern "that times are very hard in the north now on account of trade being stopped."[128] Such descriptions of economic hardship, economic necessity, and economic opportunity are everywhere in the Civil War correspondence of Irish Americans. The former sentiments—those of hardship and want—were particularly prevalent during the war's first eighteen months. In September 1861, Thomas McCready of the 74th New York Infantry was informed that his brother-in-law "aint got his place to work" and that another Irish American acquaintance had suffered a "change" of circumstances.[129] January 1862 found fellow Excelsior Brigade soldier Michael Carroll telling his brother not to forsake New York for Washington in hopes of employment, as "Work is dull all over now."[130] That same month, Patrick Dooley of the 40th New York Infantry was informed "there is nothing doing in New York but peeling Potatoes for the Soldiers."[131] In February, John Mahon was being told of how "times are so dull" in Hudson.[132] Not much had improved by the following fall, when James Fitzgerald worried that his mother "Could not rent the house now to much advantage as times are so hard."[133] In Civil War historiography, a disproportionate reliance on the Civil War correspondence of the middle and upper classes has led to the belief that economics played little or no role in the decision-making process of the war's earliest volunteers, and that most of them made financial sacrifices to enlist.[134] Irish American correspondence demonstrates that this was not true for the lower classes, who formed the backbone of the Federal military. Regardless of their year of enlistment, economics almost always played a major role in the decision-making process of Irish Americans. It was one of the most significant drivers of their enlistment in the U.S. military, and doubtless for many it was the deciding factor.

From the first major engagement of the war to the last, there were Irishmen in uniform whose initial impulse to join up had been influenced by financial need, financial opportunity, or both. While this association with "mercenary" service has usually been regarded as evidence of diluted patriotism, it had significantly more to do with societal position and transnational tradition. Few groups were as susceptible to the vagaries of the wartime economy as the urban working class, where a lack of employment or rise in inflation was often enough to make consideration of a military career a necessity rather than a choice. The recession created by southern secession had a dramatic impact on employment early in the war, particularly in areas where the Irish predominated. The first calls for volunteers in 1861 came when the Massachusetts shoemaking trade was in the doldrums, Rhode Island textile works were struggling to stay open, and thousands of Philadelphia and New York factory employees had been laid off.[135] In January 1861, the *New York Herald* had been reporting how "the hard times have thrown at least fifteen thousand workingmen out of employment," while that month found the Home Missionary Society in Pennsylvania appealing in the pages of the *Philadelphia Inquirer* for breakfast subscriptions for the poor, whose suffering was "caused in part by so many persons being thrown out of employment, owing to the political crisis."[136] At the same time the *Pilot* in Boston was sharing news with its readers that "the workmen in the shoe towns are generally without employment, and there seems for them a gloomy prospect for the remainder of the winter."[137] In designating 4 January 1861 as a day for humiliation, fasting, and prayer throughout the Union due to the terrible crisis the country faced, President Buchanan specifically made reference to the fact that "our laboring population are without employment and consequently deprived of the means of earning their bread."[138] While some of the more sensational reporting was driven by political motive, there was no doubt that large swathes of Irish America struggled greatly during this period. In announcing the commencement of a relief fund for the families of volunteers less than two weeks after Fort Sumter, the *New York Irish American* remarked on these financial straits that applied "with the greatest force" to the "Irish-American portion of the volunteer army": "Many of them are laboring men and mechanics, upon whose pecuniary condition the dullness of the past six months has operated with the most disastrous effect, leaving them, in too many instances, totally without resources to sustain their families during their absence."[139] Accustomed to economic hard times, many Irish Americans were predisposed to look toward what was, by 1861, a longstanding traditional response to such a predicament: military service. Since the 1840s, enlistment in the U.S. Army had become an acceptable remedy to economic difficulty, just as service in the British Army had been since the 1790s.[140] As a result, the soldiering life did not carry the level of opprobrium for Irish Americans that had been attached to it in the immediate antebellum period by many of the native-born. One practical consequence was that when it came to financial crunches such as that of 1860 Irish Americans were less hesitant to see military service as a potential solution to their problems. This was a fact they openly admitted to in their correspondence.

Outlining for his parents why he had joined up in July 1861, shoemaker James O'Herrin explained that he had originally left his home in Waltham, Massachusetts, "in search of work," but as he "could not get any" he had decided to enlist "rather than be a burden on you."[141] Thomas Doyle told a similar story. During a low moment in 1863 he confided to his wife that his decision to join up in the war's first summer had come when "the times began to look very glumy and dul" and he had not wanted to be "dependen upon anny one for a support."[142] Writing to Ireland in April 1862, Edmund Dwyer believed that "it was nothing but want of employment" that had "compeled" his friend John Hayes to enlist, elaborating that "He has a helpless family and must provide for it in some manner."[143] With unfortunate timing, Irish immigrant John O'Brien landed in America just a few months before the war broke out. It was the summer of 1862 before he finally communicated with his wife and child back in Listowel, Co. Kerry, offering the explanation that when he had first "Come to this Country there was no employment . . . so I was obliged to join the Navy." Now a U.S. Marine, he explained that his silence was due to the fact he was "after a Cruise of long twelve months."[144] It was want of employment that had forced Antrim immigrant James Sheren to leave his wife and children in Baltimore and go west in search of opportunities. The stonecutter eventually found a job in Woodford County, Kentucky, "a good place for Work." Writing from there in May 1861, he described being "very onhappy" at not being with his loved ones, but told his wife that he looked forward to his pay, "then I Will see you and the children never agaien to part." But it seems the work dried up, as precisely a month later, and with his family still in Baltimore, James enlisted in the 2nd Kentucky Infantry at Pendleton, Ohio.[145] James McGinness from Co. Cavan did not reveal his motivations for enlisting in the 90th New York Infantry, but in exhorting his brother not to follow him into the army in August 1862, he linked service to economic need: "if Tho[s] has not Enlisted yet I would advise him not to for he will be sory . . . if he knew as much about Soldiering as I do he would never want to Enlist if he had to go to the Poor House."[146]

Even when the war economy was in full flight, the rising tide did not always lift all Irish American boats, and many servicemen made consistent references to "hard times" during the course of the conflict. Difficulties in procuring employment persisted as a reason for enlistment, particularly in the West. When farm laborer Cornelius O'Brien enlisted in February 1864 from Oquawka, Illinois, he put it down to the fact that "there was nothing for me to do."[147] Similar concerns were expressed by Pat Scannell, who became a member of the 1st New Hampshire Cavalry in the dying days of the war. "I am not Sorry that I enlisted I dont See what else I could do," he told his mother in April 1865. "Pay off your debts get in Something for the Summer let my Sisters have some clothes money and what there is Left lay it by for a wet day," he advised her.[148]

The hardships that secession wrought on employment were not restricted to the Irish American working class. Its impact was also felt by those in better circumstances, giving them pause to consider the potential economic positives of service. When 1861 dawned, the decidedly middle-class John C. Lynch was a clerk at De Forest, Armstrong and Co., a New York dry goods house that dealt "exclusively in the Southern trade." When it went under at the end of January with liabilities in excess of $2 million, it threw Lynch's financial future into doubt.[149] One year later, John was a captain in the Irish Brigade and outlining for his mother why his decision to remain in the army was "for the best": "I did not think we had enough of money saved to enter into business which will not be the case in a Couple of Months from now when I will have 3 or 4 hundred dollars to add to the little pile."[150]

While the advent of significant bounties for service from 1863 onward are often regarded as heralding a sea change with respect to motivation, in reality there were many tempting financial inducements on offer for the hard-up working-class man of 1861 and 1862. Charles McKenna, whose family were pre-Famine immigrants from Tyrone, enlisted in the 2nd Rhode Island Cavalry on 20 October 1862. It was a decision that enabled him to pass a $375 lump sum to his father, the equivalent of fifteen months of the maximum pay he had earned at the Dunnell Print Works of Pawtucket.[151] One of the most attractive incentives offered in the early war period was the prospect of land. "they pay us 11 Dollars and keep the other two for to have a fund to give each of us when we are discharged besides 100 Dollars Bounty and a grant of 100 acres of land," the 17th Massachusetts Infantry's James O'Herrin informed his father in 1861.[152] James Carroll of the 42nd New York Infantry was also promised "100 Acres of land at the Close of the War," which he assured his wife she would receive should he die.[153] Similarly, John Kennedy of the 10th Ohio Infantry promised his mother that "when he came back from the Army, they would have a nice little farm."[154] These early war monetary opportunities proved more than sufficient to draw Irish immigrants into the United States from abroad. Finding that he had "difficulty . . . in securing steady and constant employment" in Montreal, eighteen-year-old Irish immigrant Frederick Nightingale crossed the border to join the ranks of the 118th New York Infantry in August 1862. There he hoped that his "Pay and other monies" might prove sufficient to support his family back in Canada.[155]

As the war dragged on and financial incentives grew, more and more men in Ireland were attracted by the opportunities on offer in the United States. While folk songs like *Paddy's Lamentation* and cinematic depictions such as those in Martin Scorsese's 2002 *Gangs of New York* have fueled a belief that hordes of Irish immigrants arrived in America only to be immediately duped into service, it appears that far more left Ireland with the specific intention of enlistment. The potentially life-altering amounts of money on offer had attracted many toward the emigrant boat, a fact reflected in increased emigration figures from Ireland during the war's latter years.[156] Most did so in the hope that in one fell swoop they would earn enough to stake out a future for themselves and their families in the United States. Some had departed even before the sums grew eye-watering, perhaps attracted by the prospect of adventure, or hoping service would provide them with a leg up in American life. In March 1863, a domestic in Tralee, Co. Kerry, wrote to her sister in New York lamenting the fact she had financed her son Jimmy's passage, only "to be the manes of sending him to the war."[157] Nineteen-year-old Dubliner Alexander Scarff landed in New York on 6 November 1862, apparently with the express intention of joining the army. Just twenty-four hours after his arrival in the United States he joined the 174th New York Infantry under the alias Arthur Shaw.[158] Thomas Bowler left his wife and daughter behind in Youghal, Co. Cork, in order to travel to Brooklyn, where he joined the 69th New York Infantry under an alias in early 1864. Writing from Brandy Station, Virginia, to let them know of the remittances he had dispatched, he spoke of the "great fighting" he soon expected to participate in. "I have as good a chance to escape as any other man," he reassured them. He did not escape, and his wife and child remained in Ireland.[159]

In August 1863, James Ryan from Drogheda, Co. Louth, enlisted as a substitute for Christopher F. Douglas in Vermont. James had been working in Quebec, where he had been trying to gather together enough money to send to Ireland for his mother, who was then a pauper reliant on the support of her parish. The financial boon of becoming a substitute put him over the top, and he sent directly for her. She landed in Canada that December.[160] Even as men died on the battlefield or succumbed to fatal illness, the monies they earned in service continued to bring new family members across to America. Michael Ryan had left Co. Tipperary for the United States during the war, and on being drafted into the 95th New York Infantry he quickly sent his mother in Ireland $147. When he died in January 1864, that sum together with his remaining bounty and arrears funded her journey to the United States.[161] As has been noted, late war recruits like Thomas Bowler, James Ryan, and Michael Ryan remain one of the most understudied and denigrated bodies of men to see service during the conflict. Often dismissed as unscrupulous and unreliable mercenaries, close examination of their motives for enlistment indicates that many bear comparison to early war working-class volunteers, in so much as they hoped their service would help to secure the economic future of themselves and their families. Though they may have lacked the same ideological commitment, many of them had very compelling reasons for taking the decision to enlist, and the majority of them did their duty.

The ever-present theme that runs through all of these examples, no matter when these men joined up, was economics. While the overwhelming majority of Irish Americans who ended up in uniform due to financial reasons did so of their own volition, the prospect of monetary reward also caused some to be forced into service. Young Limerick immigrant Con Garvin was one such economically exploited recruit. Con suffered from an intellectual disability that in the parlance of the time had seen him branded an "idiot." Impressionable and easily led, his mother had ultimately been forced to have him placed in the Rensselaer House of Industry in Troy, New York. When there, the superintendent and an officer of the 52nd New York Infantry colluded to steal Con away and enlist him in the regiment under a pseudonym. The incident sparked a long and high-profile saga that reached as high as Abraham Lincoln, as Con's mother, Catharine, embarked on an ultimately fruitless mission to retrieve her abducted boy.[162] Dubliner Thomas Burke was another of those forced into the army through the machinations of an unscrupulous bounty broker. He had been signed up in Ireland by a Patrick Finney, ostensibly to work on American railroads, but on arrival in Portland, Maine, he was one of a number who were imprisoned until they consented to enlist. Before his release could be secured, Thomas was killed in the ranks of the 20th Maine Infantry at the Wilderness.[163] Alcohol was often a common denominator in ploys to dupe or cheat these men, and invariably the perpetrator, or at least the victim's initial contact, was a fellow Irishman. John Daly had been among those who left Ireland in late 1863 or early 1864 in the hope that the American wartime economy would provide himself and his family with the means for a new start. He may well have left with the express intention of joining the army. Either way, soon after landing he ran afoul of his unscrupulous host, Thomas Donnellan. As a private in the 51st New York Infantry, John later explained to his wife how Donnellan and his son had "drugged me day and night with the worst of spirits and other mixtures and then he thought to rob me of 100 dollars and more" before causing him to have to serve under an alias, as "that Robber Donnellan gave in my name as Ryan."[164]

It is no surprise that financial and economic considerations were a vital element in bringing so many working-class men into Federal uniform. But while the motivations of specific men can sometimes appear glaringly obvious, appearances can be deceptive. In truth, there was rarely a simplistic, single reason behind why men donned Union blue. In most instances, a cocktail of contributary elements came together to form the basis for their ultimate decision. Patrick Delanty serves as a case in point. There were few Irish Americans who appear to so readily fit the mold of the economically motivated early war volunteer than the USS *Carondelet* sailor. The Laois native had been working in Cairo, Illinois, during the conflict's early months, until a dispute with his employer over working hours and poor wages left him searching for a new position. To compound his problems, Patrick's remaining money was then stolen from his carpet bag, leaving him "without a cent." He "waited three days for a situation" in Cairo—a town he regarded as a "Mean Hole"—before deciding to join the navy. It was in the service that he finally found something he enjoyed. It provided him with "a good time," "not much to do," and "a good table to Sit at." Though his mother wanted him back in Chicago, he was reluctant to return to a place where he "would have to lay around and couldnt get a situation."[165] In any case, he felt his rewards would quickly come. "my opinin is that we have done all our fighting," Patrick wrote in the summer of 1862, as he looked forward to an honorable discharge, his bounty of $100, and the prize money he was due from vessels recently captured at Island No. 10 on the Mississippi River.[166]

Patrick Delanty's own words demonstrate how centrally important economics had been in his decision to enlist. But despite appearances, it was not all that moved him. Like many other Irish Americans, he appears to have been possessed of a sincere hope that his time in uniform would improve him as a man, and, just as importantly, improve how others perceived him as a man. Rather than being reflexive reactions to nativism and a desire to be accepted by American society, in many instances these sentiments seem to have been intimately and intensely personal. These men wanted to see themselves—and to be seen—as individuals of good character, as men who provided for their families, as men who did their duty. Military service seemed to offer these potential rewards in a way that working-class civilian life sometimes could not. It could also offer societal empowerment to men like Patrick Delanty, often for the first time in their lives. "I am glad the are drafting now," he wrote in August 1862, "now the loafers will have to Come and tri their hand at Soldering or Sailoring." He could now look down on those who had seen themselves as his betters, those men who "puts on So many airs around town with their good Cloaths" and who had looked at "a defender of their Country with Contempt."[167]

Along with all the other reasons that lay behind his enlistment, once Patrick Delanty became a Union sailor he came to view himself as a defender of his country. Even though he had been born in Laois, his personal ambition, his sense of identity, and his sense of allegiance were intrinsically tied to his future as an Irishman in the United States. In such sentiments are found the only motivators that compete with economics for prominence in the Civil War writings of working-class Irish Americans—a sense of duty and patriotism toward America.

It is apparent that thousands of Irish Americans donned Federal uniform because they felt a profound sense of responsibility toward the United States of America, and they took pride in the fact that they were in uniform fighting for its survival. Typical of them was Tommy Welch, the 20th Maine Infantry soldier who would later be recalled for his "most laughable blunders" and "bewildered, serio-comic gravity of expression" by former comrade Theodore Gerrish.[168] "Uncle Tommy" was in his late thirties when he went off to war with the 20th Maine in August 1862. Prior to joining up he had been supporting his elderly parents in Bangor, Maine, through seasonal log rafting on New Brunswick's Nashwaak River. He hoped his steady army wage would help toward that burden, but, as with Patrick Delanty, economics were not his only consideration. In an understated letter to his brother penned after his first full engagement at Fredericksburg in December 1862, Tommy admitted there had been "trouble and trials," but continued: "I bear them willingly and more Because the Flag that has given protection to persecuted Country men."[169] As Tommy Welch saw it, the United States had given him and his family a home, and in exchange, he was willing to lay down his life for it.

Many Irish Americans provided glimpses of their patriotic inclinations in more subtle fashion. When young Irish American John Sullivan lied about his age in January 1862 to enlist in the 102nd New York Infantry, he ostensibly did so to help his mother, as the wages were "much better than I could do at home."[170] But when she immediately asked him to leave the military, John refused. In his response John returned to his economic argument, but also hinted at the pride and duty he felt on having now committed to the army, something he was unwilling to forgo: "in regard to my coming home I never can as I have been sworn in and received my uniform."[171] Kerry immigrant William Harnett of the 4th U.S. Infantry told his family that "if the worst should come I will only share the fate of many better men."[172] Such understated determination to see the war settled in favor of the Union is also apparent in the correspondence of Irish American Michael McCormick. Serving during the 1862 Peninsula Campaign, the 65th New York Infantryman expressed his confidence in nearing victory, but quickly added that he was in no hurry to go home. "I do not want to go home until this war is over then I would be satisfied but not before."[173] Clare immigrant Martin Noonan of the 64th New York Infantry was more outspoken. For his part, he looked forward to the day when "we will be planting the poles for the glorious Stars and Stripes to wave over the Continant from the Atlantic to the Pacific Ocean."[174]

Among those who had been carried off to war on the early wave of patriotic sentiment was John Lane, whose mother had taken him to Boston following his father's death in Kildorrery, Co. Cork, during "Black '47." The journeyman stonecutter enlisted in June 1861, in circumstances that demonstrate just how enmeshed and inseparable economics and patriotism could be when it came to individual decisions. The twenty-six-year-old's mother later recalled how "for a week or so just before he enlisted, the 'war fever' prevailed, and he became unsteady and did not work (business being very dull) and at last he enlisted."[175] John's patriotic sentiments had been stoked at the very moment he was unable to find employment, removing a major potential impediment in his deliberations. Rather than having to carefully weigh and consider differing options, he found his choices aligned—he could both indulge his "war fever" and make the soundest economic decision. This coexistence of economic and patriotic motivators is one that repeats itself through much Irish American correspondence, and can be interpreted as a further indication of the adoption of an increasingly American identity. It was, after all, the American way to be patriotic *and* to prosper economically.[176] Michael Carroll is another whose correspondence indicates how economic, patriotic, and personal motivators coexisted as pull factors for Irish American men. The Excelsior Brigade soldier made frequent economic references in his letters, but also demonstrated his martial enthusiasm, such as when he announced the arrival of the regiment's new rifles, which he claimed could "Kill a Secesion a mile and a Half off."[177] Michael saw his service for the Union as something to be proud of, and it provided him with an enhanced sense of manhood. He signed off a January 1862 letter with "From your Afection Son Micheal carrol or the Bold Soldier Boy," a reference to a popular Irish American working-class ballad that boasted of manly prowess and Irish soldierly pride.[178]

Those Irish Americans who were motivated by support for the cause of the United States were often equally ready to express their desire to defeat Secession. When sending home a Rebel $10 note as a keepsake in early 1862, John Costello remarked on the currency's visual aspects: "the rebel flag is flying on it in all its glory. but it is short lived and will surely die."[179] Writing excitedly to his mother in late 1861, John Kelly from Tipperary opined: "there is no chance for secession now . . . we have now them hemd in on all quarters . . . the next news will be that we throw then in to the Potomac & winter in Richmond."[180] Tyrone native Charles Devlin was communicating with his wife and children back in Ireland when he remarked how the European powers would be disappointed if they recognized the "so called southeran Confederacy," as when "thay come here thay will be no such thing as the southern confederacy."[181] Some even turned toward lyrical expression. Each of the nine verses that Louth immigrant John Buckley of the USS *Flag* sent his sister in 1863 concluded with the refrain "To conquer the confederacy, And cause its overthrow."[182] Irish immigrant Timothy Dougherty of the 3rd Wisconsin Cavalry had been fated to go west and face Native Americans rather than Confederates, but he left no doubt as to how brightly his convictions burned, and how willing he was to test those convictions on those whom he deemed rebel sympathizers: "we are expecting to go home this Winter the Coperhead might as well be in hell as to abuse the Soldiers whin will they go home this Winter for I am going cary A pair of Revovers home with me this Winter."[183] Neither was an ideological investment in the outcome of the conflict the preserve of the early war volunteer. Late 1863 recruit John Deegan of the 19th Maine Infantry informed his sister in 1864 that while he expected hard times after the war, they were "nothing to what they will be should this war be settled unsatisfactory to our government."[184] Nicholas Mahar, another late war enlistee, left no doubt as to the extent to which he regarded the Confederates as both an enemy and as "other." In the summer of 1864 he sent his sister a macabre war trophy: "i sent kate a ring the 12 it is as niCe one i will send you one in ths letter tha ar maid out of rebs bons i mad them."[185]

Further demonstration of the significance Irish Americans placed on fighting for the Union can be gleaned from the words they chose when communicating a comrade's death to the bereaved. In his letter to the wife of fallen Irish Brigade soldier Patrick Dunnigan, recent Waterford immigrant Captain Patrick Clooney referenced "his last noble efforts beside the flags of his native and adopted fatherland."[186] After another Irish Brigade soldier's death at Antietam in September 1862, Sergeant William Loughran informed the man's widow that he fell "fighting in Defence of the Constution and Laws." Loughran would die for the same cause just over two months later at Fredericksburg.[187] After John Feeney fell in the ranks of Corcoran's Irish Legion, Captain Edward Byrne offered his mother the consolation that "he done his duty twards god and his Country."[188]

The patriotic motivation of Irish American servicemen could be particularly strong among those tens of thousands who, though technically "recent immigrants," had grown to adulthood in the United States. One of them was twenty-one-year-old Cavan immigrant Mike Brady, who by August 1862 had been selected to carry the 75th Ohio Infantry's national colors. Mike had left Ireland as a boy, departing with his father following his mother's death in the midst of the Great Famine. He had earned his right to carry the Stars and Stripes at the May 1862 Battle of McDowell, Virginia, leaping from cover in order to save the banner as it tumbled toward the Confederate line. Mortally wounded a few weeks later as he defiantly waved the flag at rebels decimating his regiment during Second Bull Run, he reportedly pronounced on his deathbed: "welcome be the will of God I couldnot loose my life in a better cause."[189] Throughout his brief service, his devotion to the United States had been absolute.

It is evident that the factors that drew most Irish Americans into uniform were economic necessity and opportunity, and a sense of patriotism and duty toward the United States. These far outstripped any other major motivators. Despite the connotations often associated with men who joined the military primarily for money, the fact was they were ever-present in Union uniform, from First Bull Run to Appomattox. The realities of working-class life in America, particularly for the urban poor, made such service a necessity for thousands. Many of them, both early and late war recruits, were motivated by concerns every bit as laudable as the ideological volunteer—a desire to provide for their families. Nonetheless, economics rarely acted as a sole pull factor, especially early in the war. There were undoubtedly some who hoped service might finally overcome native prejudice and see the Irish become more accepted in the United States. There were others who may have seen their service primarily as a means of advancing a distinctly Irish nationalist agenda. But of all, the degree to which ordinary working-class Irish Americans were motivated to fight for the preservation of the Union of the United States has been the most underestimated.

The often understated and matter-of-fact way in which Irish Americans expressed their determination to do their duty by their country suggests that it was not something they regarded as requiring regular overt pronouncement; it was a job—a duty—that needed to be done. Working-class Irish American men tended to view war and combat in such practical terms, and were not as quick to articulate the more idealized perspectives of conflict common among the upper classes. That did not mean they did not appreciate the stakes. For those who were more recent immigrants, and regardless of their personal circumstances, it was readily apparent that the voice, power, and favor the democratic institutions of the United States could bestow upon them were a world away from what they could hope for in Ireland. If they were to maintain their hopes of continuing the process of transposing their loved ones to new communities across the Atlantic, the ongoing strength and integrity of their new country was vital. For the thousands who had spent all or most of their formative years in America, those communities had already become their personal embodiment of what it meant to be American Irish in the United States.

All these were things that the Confederacy threatened. As a result, multitudes entered the fray with a deep and sustained commitment to the cause.

One of the most important aspects of these men's contextualized correspondence is the extent to which it reveals the pronounced sense of American community identity that many brought with them into uniform. They were the Rochester Boys, the Pittsburgh Boys, the Salem Boys, albeit most often the Rochester (Irish) Boys, Pittsburgh (Irish) Boys, or Salem (Irish) Boys. But most of them did not regard that ethnic tribalism as being any different from that exhibited by their fellow immigrants, by the privileged Boston Brahmins, by the descendants of the New England Puritans, or by the rural Ohio farmboys. Like those others, they tended to stick with people they knew best, and who best knew them. Like them, they felt they had a right to their own place within the great and varied milieu that was the American Republic. They were among the latest arrivals, but they felt they had already carved out their position and demonstrated their commitment. Rather than something that they viewed as facilitating their efforts to become American, it is apparent that tens of thousands of these men entered into the conflict in the fervent belief that they already were. For such men, enlistment during the Civil War was less of an attempt to prove their worth to the United States, and more of a duty they felt morally obliged to perform. They felt this while realizing that many others did not regard them in the same light, and likely while recognizing that a long struggle for acceptance lay ahead. Despite all that, many of the 250,000 ethnic Irish who fought for the United States did so in the belief that they were fighting for their country—every bit as much as their native comrades who touched elbows with them on the battlefield.

Conclusion

The American Irish

This book opened with the story of Patrick Dooley, the 40th New York Infantry private who on 1 July 1862 had taken such pride in the performance of the ethnic Irish regiments at the Battle of Malvern Hill, Virginia. The summer of 1862 found his fifty-six-year-old Irish immigrant mother, Mary Dooley, making her home in a small tenement apartment at 129 East 11th Street, New York City. She had come to the United States in 1854, leaving her husband and four of her eight children buried in the soil of "the Old Country." Her son had been working as a stonemason on one of New York's major new creations, Central Park, when he had first marched off to war in 1861. Although Mary was illiterate, Patrick had made sure to send her regular money and letters—letters read to her by her tenement neighbor, fellow Irish immigrant Mary Kearney. In August of 1862, it was also the task of an intermediary to impart the terrible news that Patrick was dead, taken by typhoid fever on 10 August, 1862.[1] Soon after, Mary visited the offices of Nettleton, Gilbert & Camp on 111 Broadway, answering an advertisement that had run under the banner "PENSIONS AND BOUNTIES" and promised to procure and collect monies "for soldiers, sailors and the relatives of such as are deceased."[2] Over the weeks that followed, Mary recounted to them the story of her and her son's journey from Tipperary to America, of their life in New York City, and of Patrick's time in the service. Finally, she also handed over the small collection of eleven wartime letters her son had sent to her from the front.

The identification of hundreds of letters like those of Patrick Dooley has allowed us to move beyond the words and opinions of the "great men" of Irish America to recover the thoughts, concerns, and considerations of the ordinary men and boys who made up the Irish American rank and file. *Green and Blue* is the first book do so at scale, and the first to reach beyond the ethnic regiments to seek out the experience of Irish American service throughout the Federal military. This has brought confirmation of some existing conceptions, and challenges to others, but its primary contribution is in the new detail and new insights it has unlocked. It has revealed that while they were highly ethnically cohesive, "Irish American" servicemen were not just natives of Ireland, but were also the American-, British-, and Canadian-born children of Irish immigrants. Together they numbered not 150,000, or even 180,000, but in the region of 250,000 men—an enormous figure that dispels the long-held belief that Irish Americans were underrepresented in the Union military. As a group, they have frequently been considered solely from the perspective of their ethnicity, but it is now apparent that their overwhelming working-class makeup was every bit as important in influencing their lives and decisions, and perhaps even more so. Both their ethnic and class backgrounds profoundly affected their war. In many respects their experiences were similar to those of other white men in uniform, but the contrast lay in the scale of impediments the average Irish American faced when seeking to successfully navigate the military arena. One of the most notable related to the precarity of their economic position, which has heretofore lain largely unexplored beyond reference to its important role as a motivator for enlistment. But for men in the ranks, economic influences consistently outweighed ideological factors in impacting morale and decisions, such as whether to stay or to leave the military. These enlisted men were ordinary individuals, who counted among their number the good, the bad, and the somewhere in between. Most were not the wild "rowdies" and ne'er-do-wells of their detractors' imaginations, but nevertheless the prejudice they faced caused them to endure varying degrees of discrimination based on their origins and religion. In their turn, they were more than capable of doing the same to others, exhibiting sometimes appalling racism toward African Americans—an intolerance borne of a conviction in their own racial superiority and a perceived economic and social threat.

The view many Irish held toward African Americans was just one of an apparent litany of rationales these men had for avoiding military service. Aside from being relative newcomers to America, most were staunch Democrats, opposed the Emancipation Proclamation, disliked the draft, and often felt they were being exploited by those who held power over them. That they were instead overrepresented among the rank and file is an incongruity explained by how they perceived themselves and, in turn, what drove them to enlist. It is now evident that a sense of patriotism and duty toward the United States, together with economic considerations, were the motivators that outstripped all others in influencing their service. Whereas most previous analyses have stressed their conflicting loyalties to Ireland and the United States, or viewed the conflict as one that precipitated their passage from "Irish" to "American," in fact many had developed a distinctly American identity prior to the Civil War.[3] The grafting together of American and Irish identities that characterized the period led them to closely connect their identity with the American towns and cities where they lived, hybrid communities that created a hybrid identity, concurrently American *and* Irish.[4] As recent Sligo immigrant and USS *Wabash* sailor Patrick Finan put it, when they were fighting for the United States, they were now fighting "for their country."[5] Thousands shared his belief that they owed America and the Union their primary fealty and that it was a patriotic duty to enlist—and to stay the course once they had.[6] In large measure, the Union Irish saw themselves as "American Irish."

Given how these American Irish viewed their Civil War service, it is perhaps little surprise that their legacy in the generations since the conflict has been a markedly American one. In Ireland, memory of the scale of Irish involvement and the impact it had on Irish people quickly dimmed. This is irrespective of the fact that in modern Irish history the American Civil War is only matched by World War I for the number of Irish men who marched off to the front. For those Irish counties worst hit by nineteenth-century emigration, it likely stands alone.[7] But while large numbers of the Union Irish had maintained financial and familial ties to Ireland before, during, and after their service, few ever went back—or had any real desire to do so. The sincerity of their long-term commitment to the United States is evidenced today by the countless Americans who cherish the story of their Irish ancestor's service, a direct connection to the Civil War that is vanishingly rare in Ireland. Within the popular memory of modern America, the Union Irish have now come to occupy a reverential, if sometimes uncomplicated, position. There are few more pronounced examples of this than their treatment in addresses delivered before the Irish Parliament, *Dáil Éireann,* by presidents of the United States.[8] It is a mark of the status they have attained that Irish American president John F. Kennedy chose to commence the first ever such address in 1963 with the story of the battlefield actions and sacrifices of the Irish Brigade. As they had done many times before, and many times since, the Brigade were being called upon to act as the universally recognizable representatives for Irish participation. Kennedy acknowledged as much. Presenting a flag of the Brigade as a gift to the Irish people, he did so "in recognition of what these gallant Irishmen and what millions of other Irish have done for my country."[9] President Bill Clinton followed in Kennedy's footsteps in 1995. In his address, he described the service of "nearly 200,000 Irishmen" as "the first of countless contributions to our nation." Clinton even went so far as to draw a direct line between that contribution and ongoing U.S. efforts to assist the brokering of peace in Northern Ireland, characterizing the Union Irish as men who "enabled us to remain a nation and to be here with you today in partnership for peace for your nation and for the peoples who live on this island."[10] On 13 April 2023, President Joe Biden became the fourth U.S. President to deliver an address before the Irish Parliament, and the third to specifically draw on the Union Irish as leading exemplars of Ireland's influence on the United States. Biden identified them as men who had "signed up in a new land to stand for old values, to defend freedom and the dignity of all people."[11] While clearly an oversimplification of Irish American service, imbuing them with a set of principles and a purity of purpose that was often unmatched by reality, such remarks aptly demonstrate the lofty place in American memory that Union Irish service ultimately won. It is a position many of them would have undoubtedly been proud to achieve.

President Biden continued his 2023 Dublin speech by remarking that "one or two" of his own Irish ancestors had themselves enlisted in the Union army. Among them was his great-granduncle, Co. Louth native Michael Finnegan.[12] Along with his brother, he had marched off to war with hundreds of other Irish Americans in the ranks of the 164th New York Infantry, Corcoran's Irish Legion. On 3 June 1864, Michael and his comrades participated in the ill-fated assault against Confederate works at Cold Harbor, Virginia. The ferocious fighting ended in their bloody repulse. In recalling the carnage, one of the Confederates who faced the Irish Americans remembered corpses in front of his position being "so thickly strewn that one could have walked on their bodies its whole extent."[13] Lying in their midst was Michael Finnegan, a working-class, enlisted immigrant, fallen in defense of a Union his great-grandnephew would one day rise to lead. A few yards away lay Robert Boyle, the Presbyterian emigrant from Armagh, mortally wounded in the thigh. He would soon write from his prison deathbed to tell of how Tipperary Catholic James Hickey had "died beside me on the field," a message that would secure for Hickey's widow a pension. Another who lay fatally wounded nearby was William Maroney, the glassmaker from Fethard, who had once related to his brother how General Corcoran shot down an officer that had purportedly shouted "no damn Irish son of a bitch could pass him." Staggering past the dead and dying was James Hand, a New Jersey son of Irish immigrants, who enjoyed reading "the Sundy mercuray And the police gazete," and whose parents had appealed for him to return home to them when his brother had died aboard the USS *Cincinnati.* By June 1864 at Cold Harbor, months had passed since he had told them "I May be home Soon after Some Long March," yet he was still with his comrades. Eight months later he met his own end in a Confederate prison.

The words of Michael Finnegan's Cold Harbor comrades have come to us only because they died premature deaths. The personal legacies they have left behind are sorrowful but revelatory ones. They have enabled us to move backward, beyond the eulogies and the memory, to the contemporary voices and experiences of the ordinary Irish Americans who filled the ranks of the Federal armies and navies. Along the way, they have revealed more than ever before about themselves and their comrades, men who together played such a vital role in securing U.S. victory in the American Civil War.

APPENDIX

Military Biographies

The brief biographies below, arranged alphabetically by surname, provide some of the established facts regarding men who are mentioned in the text. The majority formed part of the project corpus or are men referenced in correspondence. The information includes details such as their rank at enlistment, unit of service, and fate. The data was compiled from a combination of sources, including their widows' and dependents' pension files, military, ship, and regimental records, and census returns.

ABBREVIATIONS

KIA	Killed in Action
MIA	Missing in Action
MWIA	Mortally Wounded in Action
POW	Prisoner of War

BARRINGTON RICHARD

Artificer, 1st Missouri Engineers. Enlisted 21 January 1864. A farmer when he emigrated from Co. Wexford. Church of Ireland. Died 24 May 1865, inflammation of the pericardium, Alexandria, Virginia.

BARRY, GARRETT

Privatc, 3rd Massachusetts Cavalry. Enlisted 31 December 1861. Single. Farm laborer. Born in Massachusetts to Irish immigrant parents. Promoted to sergeant. KIA near Mansfield, Louisiana, 8 April 1864.

BARRY, JOHN

Private, 91st New York Infantry. Enlisted 17 November 1861. Laborer. Born in Ireland. Veteran volunteer. Promoted to corporal. Survived service.

BARRY, WILLIAM

Private, 88th New York Infantry. Enlisted 13 October 1861. Single. Born in the United States to Irish immigrant parents. Family step migrated through Canada. Discharged for disability due to tuberculosis, 29 April 1862. Died 2 May 1862.

BOWLER, THOMAS

Private, 69th New York Infantry. Enlisted 26 February 1864 under alias Thomas Murphy. Married. Laborer. From Youghal, Co. Cork, family remained in Ireland. MIA, the Wilderness, Virginia, 7 May 1864.

BOYD, SAMUEL

Private, 14th New Jersey Infantry. Enlisted 13 August 1862. Married on day of arrival in the United States in 1851. Born Co. Antrim. KIA, Cold Harbor, Virginia, 1 June 1864.

BOYLE, JOHN

Private, 38th New York Infantry. Enlisted 15 June 1861. Single. Likely born in Maine, parents Irish immigrants. KIA, Chantilly, Virginia, 1 September 1862.

BOYLE, ROBERT

First Lieutenant, 164th New York Infantry. Enlisted 18 September 1862. Married. Cooper. From Co. Armagh. Presbyterian. MWIA, Cold Harbor, Virginia, 3 June 1864. Died in Libby Prison, Virginia, 1 July 1864.

BRADY, MICHAEL

Private, 75th Ohio Infantry. Enlisted 30 December 1861. Single. Blacksmith. Born in Co. Cavan. MWIA, Second Bull Run, Virginia, 30 August 1862. Died 9 September 1862, Alexandria, Virginia.

BRENNAN, JOHN

Private, 11th Massachusetts Infantry. Enlisted 27 December 1861 under alias John Burns. Married. Laborer. From Monasterevin, Co. Kildare. Former British Army soldier. KIA, Williamsburg, Virginia, 5 May 1862.

BRIODY, JAMES

Private, 20th Massachusetts Infantry. Enlisted 11 August 1862. Single. Stonecutter, but different occupations listed. Born in the United States to Irish parents from Castlerahan, Co. Meath. KIA, Fredericksburg, Virginia, 11 December 1862.

BUCKLEY, JOHN

Seaman, USS *Weehawken.* Assigned New York. Enlisted 1 June 1862. Single. Comb-maker. From Co. Louth. Living in New York City's 21st Ward in 1860. Drowned when USS *Weehawken* sank at anchor off Morris Island, South Carolina, 6 December 1863.

BURKE, THOMAS

Private, 20th Maine Infantry. Enlisted 10 March 1864. Married. A native of Dublin. Recruited in Ireland ostensibly to undertake nonmilitary employment, forced to join the military on arrival in America. The British consulate was in the process of attempting his extraction from service at his death. KIA, the Wilderness, Virginia, 8 May 1864.

BURNS, FELIX

Private, 13th Pennsylvania Cavalry. Enlisted 16 January 1862. Single. Glassworker. Born in the United States to Irish parents. Died Falmouth, Virginia, on 28 May 1864 as a result of a wound received in the abdomen while serving as a sergeant.

BURNS, HENRY

Private, 59th New York Infantry. Enlisted 19 August 1861. Single. Laborer. Born in Ireland. MWIA, Petersburg, Virginia, 22 June 1864. Died in Washington, D.C., 6 July 1864.

BURNS, JAMES

Seaman, USS *Colorado.* Assigned Maine. Enlisted 22 September 1864 under alias George Lacey. Single. Seaman. Born in Ireland. Family step-migrated through Canada. Died of consumption, U.S. Naval Hospital, New York, 15 August 1865.

BUTLER, MICHAEL

Private, 4th Maine Infantry. Enlisted 3 December 1861. Born in Ireland. Transferred to 19th Maine Infantry. Mustered out 19 July 1864. Survived service.

CAMPBELL, PETER

Marine, U.S. Marine Corps. Assigned Pennsylvania. Enlisted 25 July 1862. Single. Employed as a boy in a type foundry. Born in United States to Irish parents. Recorded as Sweeny in 1860 census (Philadelphia Ward 1) due to mother's remarriage. Served aboard USS *Alabama.* Died of fever at sea, 29 July 1863.

CAREY, JAMES

Ordinary Seaman, USS *Carondelet.* Assigned Pennsylvania. Enlisted 13 August 1861. Single. Worked as an Oysterman. Born in Ireland on 1860 census (Philadelphia Ward 3), born in United States on naval enlistment. Killed following the explosion of a mine near Vicksburg, Mississippi, 1 October 1863.

CAREY PATRICK

Private, 5th New York Heavy Artillery. Enlisted 18 January 1864. Single. Born in Vermont, almost certainly to Irish parents. Likely underage at enlistment. KIA, Halltown, Virginia, 26 August 1864.

CARNEY, PATRICK

Corporal, 69th Pennsylvania Infantry. Enlisted 23 August 1861. Single. Carpenter. From Fintona, Co. Tyrone. MWIA, Gettysburg, Pennsylvania. Died of wounds, 29 July 1863.

CARR, BARNEY

Private, 79th Illinois Infantry. Enlisted 19 July 1862. Single. Farm laborer. From Co. Derry. Family were assisted emigrants. Recorded as New York-born on enlistment. Lived in Salem, Ohio, in 1860. KIA, Kennesaw Mountain, Georgia, 27 June 1864.

CARR, THOMAS

Private, 6th New York Cavalry. Enlisted 16 December 1863. Married. Printer. Born in Ireland. KIA, Todd's Tavern, Virginia, 7 May 1864.

CARRAHER, PATRICK

Private, 2nd New York State Militia (82nd New York Infantry). Enlisted 3 July 1861 under alias John Carrier. Married. Gas fitter. From Co. Armagh. KIA, First Bull Run, Virginia, 21 July 1861.

CARROLL, EDWARD

Private, 1st Rhode Island Light Artillery. Enlisted 4 September 1861. Possibly a printer by occupation. Born in Rhode Island to Irish parents. KIA, Antietam, Maryland, 17 September 1862.

CARROLL, JAMES

Private, 42nd New York Infantry. Enlisted 28 June 1861. Married. Laborer. Born in Co. Kilkenny. Died of bronchitis, Washington, D.C., 24 April 1862.

CARROLL, MICHAEL

Private, 72nd New York Infantry. Enlisted 21 July 1861. Single. Printer. Born in Ireland. KIA, Williamsburg, Virginia, 5 May 1862.

CARROLL, WILLIAM (1)

Private, 61st New York Infantry, Company D/Seaman, USS *Mound City*. Enlisted 2 October 1861. Single. Born in New York to parents from Dingle, Co. Kerry. Plumber and gas fitter. Transferred to Western Gunboat Flotilla, 17 February 1862. KIA, St. Charles, White River, Arkansas, 17 June 1862.

CARROLL, WILLIAM (2)

Private, 7th Connecticut Infantry. Enlisted 1 September 1861. Single. No occupation. Born in Ireland. Lived in Middletown, Connecticut, in 1860, recorded as thirteen years old. Veteran volunteer. Mother was a blind pauper. Captured, Drewry's Bluff, Virginia, 16 May 1864. Died a POW, Camp Lawton, Georgia, circa 19 November 1864.

CASEY, JOHN

Private, 45th Illinois Infantry. Enlisted 2 October 1861. Single. Born in the United States to Irish parents. KIA, Shiloh, Tennessee, 7 April 1862.

CASEY, JOHN JOSEPH

Private, 2nd U.S. Infantry. Assigned Washington, D.C. Enlisted 12 September 1863 under alias John Walker. Married. Tailor. Born in Ireland. Died of Cholera, Louisville, Kentucky, 18 August 1866.

CLARK, HENRY

First Class Boy, USS *Hartford.* Assigned New York. Enlisted 9 April 1863. Single. No occupation. Born in Co. Dublin. Birthplace recorded as Ireland on naval enlistment, New York on 1860 census. Father had served in 9th New York State Militia. Church of Ireland. KIA, Mobile Bay, Alabama, 5 August 1864.

CODY, WILLIAM

Corporal, 3rd Rhode Island Heavy Artillery. Enlisted 5 October 1861. Single. Born in Massachusetts to Irish parents from Cork City. KIA, Secessionville, James Island, South Carolina, 16 June 1862.

COFFEY, PATRICK

Private, 69th New York State Militia. Enlisted 9 May 1861. Married. Laborer. From Ireland. Step migrant through England. Wounded and captured at First Bull Run, 21 July 1861. Died a POW, Libby Prison, Richmond, Virginia, 17 August 1861.

COLLINS, DANIEL

Private, 155th New York Infantry. Enlisted 9 October 1862. Single. Recorded as a laborer and as a messenger. Born in Ireland. Died of typhoid fever contracted following wounding, Washington, D.C., 7 July 1864.

COLLINS, DICK

Private, 10th New York Infantry. Enlisted 25 August 1864. Substitute. Boatman. Born in Kingston, Canada, most probably into an Irish family. Survived service.

COLLINS, PATRICK

Private, 6th Maine Infantry. Enlisted 8 August 1862. Single. Born in New Brunswick, Canada, to Irish parents from Co. Donegal. MWIA, Spotsylvania Court House, Virginia, 10 May 1864. Died of wounds, Washington, D.C., 2 June 1864.

CONDON, GARRETT

Private, 3rd Massachusetts Cavalry. Enlisted 13 August 1862. Married. Laborer. From Co. Waterford. Captured in the Shenandoah Valley, Virginia, on 16 August 1864. Died a POW, Salisbury, North Carolina, 24 December 1864.

CONNELL, WILLIAM

Private, 7th Vermont Infantry. Enlisted 17 December 1861. Single. Farmer. Born in Vermont to Irish parents. Died of fever, New Orleans, Louisiana, 10 August 1862.

CONNELY, PATRICK

Private, 6th Connecticut Infantry. Enlisted 4 September 1861. Single. Mechanic. Born in Co. Dublin. Died of disease of the heart, Beaufort, South Carolina, 20 August 1862.

CONNER, JAMES

Private, 2nd Massachusetts Heavy Artillery. Enlisted 19 August 1863. Married. Laborer. Born in Ireland. Veteran, previous service in 6th Massachusetts Infantry from 31 August 1862. Died of heart disease, New Bern, North Carolina, 24 June 1865.

CONNERTY, MICHAEL

Corporal, 88th New York Infantry. Enlisted 20 September 1861. Single. Occupation unknown. Born in Ireland. A sergeant at the time of his death. MWIA, Fair Oaks, Virginia, 1 June 1862. Died of wounds, Savage Station, Virginia, 4 June 1862.

CONWAY, JOHN

First Lieutenant, 69th New York Infantry. Enlisted 25 October 1861. Married.

Gardener. A native of Tullamore, Co. Offaly. KIA, Antietam, Maryland, 17 September 1862.

CORCORAN, JAMES

Private, 5th New York Infantry. Enlisted 12 July 1864. Married. Unknown occupation. Born in Ireland. KIA, Hatcher's Run, Virginia, 5 February 1865.

CORCORAN, JOHN

Private, 2nd Massachusetts Infantry. Enlisted 25 May 1861. Single. Seaman. Born in Yorkshire, England, to Irish parents. KIA, Cedar Mountain, Virginia, 9 August 1862.

COSTELLO, JOHN

Private, 1st Massachusetts Heavy Artillery. Enlisted 5 July 1861. Single. Shoemaker. Born in Massachusetts, almost certainly to Irish parents. MWIA, Petersburg, Virginia, 16 June 1864. Died at City Point, Virginia, 26 June 1864.

CROWLEY, JOHN (1)

Second Class Fireman, USS *Santiago de Cuba.* Assigned Massachusetts. Enlisted 19 February 1864. Married. Laborer. Born in Ireland. Wounded at Fort Fisher, North Carolina. Survived service.

CROWLEY, JOHN (2)

Private, 3rd New Hampshire Infantry. Enlisted 26 September 1863. Single. Tinman's apprentice. Born in Ireland. Killed by explosion of magazine, Fort Fisher, North Carolina, 16 January 1865.

CULLEN, FRANCIS

Private, 24th New York Infantry. Enlisted 17 May 1861. Single. Laborer. Born in New York to Irish parents. MWIA, Antietam, Maryland, 17 September 1862. Died at Frederick, Maryland, 14 October 1862.

CURRY, BERNARD

Private, 182nd New York Infantry/6th U.S. Cavalry. Enlisted 28 September 1862. Single. Blacksmith. From Co. Tyrone. Recorded as a painter when he enlisted in the regulars in 1866. Shot and killed when entering a house to search for a murderer, Austin, Texas, 23 August 1868.

DALY, JOHN

Private, 51st New York Infantry. Enlisted 23 August 1864 under alias John Ryan. Married. Laborer. From Celbridge, Co. Kildare. Family remained in Ireland. Captured at Poplar Grove Church, Virginia, 30 September 1864. Died a POW, Salisbury, North Carolina, date unknown.

DALY, MICHAEL

Private, 7th Illinois Cavalry. Enlisted 10 August 1861. Single. Farm laborer. From Galbally, Co. Limerick. Father died in Ireland in 1848. Military record states he was born in Delaware, despite being a recent Irish immigrant. Died of dysentery, Port Hudson, Louisiana, 20 July 1863.

DAVIS, SMITH

Private, 65th New York Infantry. Enlisted 24 September 1861. Married. Laborer. From Ireland. Presbyterian. KIA, Spotsylvania Court House, Virginia, 12 May 1864.

DEASY, JOHN

Private, 20th Massachusetts Infantry. Enlisted 18 July 1861. Married. Operative. From Co. Cork. MWIA, Fredericksburg, Virginia, 11 December 1862. Died of wounds, 12 December 1862.

DEEGAN, JOHN

Private, 19th Maine Infantry. Enlisted 10 August 1863 under alias John Dixon. Single. Coal weigher. Born in Massachusetts to Irish parents from Co. Laois. KIA, Spotsylvania Court House, Virginia, 10 May 1864.

DELANEY, JOHN

Private, 18th Connecticut Infantry. Enlisted 17 July 1862. Single. Paper mill worker. From Co. Laois. Recorded as sixteen years old in 1860. KIA, Cool Spring, Virginia, 18 July 1864.

DELANEY, WILLIAM

Private, 43rd New York Infantry. Enlisted 16 September 1861. Single. Unknown occupation. A native of Philipstown, Co. Offaly. Died of diarrhea, West Philadelphia, Pennsylvania, 22 August 1862.

DELANTY, PATRICK

Landsman? USS *Carondelet*/Marine, U.S. Marine Corps. Assigned Illinois. Enlisted 1861. Single. Painter. From Co. Laois. Father died in Ireland. Emigrated 1851. U.S. Marine Corps records list as American born. Died of heart disease, Union Barracks, Philadelphia, Pennsylvania, 5 April 1871.

DEVLIN, CHARLES

Sergeant, 35th Indiana Infantry. Enlisted 12 December 1861. Married. Emigrated from Gortin, Co. Tyrone, in 1840s, where wife and children still resided at time of the Civil War. Mexican-American War veteran with 2nd Dragoons. Captured at Chickamauga, Georgia, 19 September 1863. Died a POW, Andersonville, Georgia, 26 July 1864.

DILLON, DAN

Private, 10th Illinois Cavalry. Enlisted 24 September 1861. Single. Laborer. From Ballyegran, Co. Limerick. KIA, Bayou Meto, Louisiana, 27 August 1863.

DIVER, THOMAS

Private, 69th Pennsylvania Infantry. Enlisted 19 August 1861. Single. Printer. Born in Ireland. Mother worked in U.S. arsenal. KIA, Gettysburg, Pennsylvania, 3 July 1863.

DOHERTY, GEORGE

Landsman, USS *Horace Beals*. Assigned New York. Enlisted 31 January 1862 under alias George Robinson. Single. Bookbinder. Born in Ireland. Promoted to seaman. Died of yellow fever, Pensacola, Florida, 6 October 1863.

DONAHOE, CORNELIUS

Private, 16th Massachusetts Infantry. Enlisted 12 July 1861. Single. Painter. Born in Ireland. KIA, Second Bull Run, Virginia, 29 August 1862.

DOOLEY, PATRICK

Private, 40th New York Infantry. Enlisted 14 June 1861. Single. Stonecutter. From Clonmel, Co. Tipperary. Died of typhoid fever, Philadelphia, Pennsylvania, 10 August 1862.

DORGAN, JEREMIAH

Private, 2nd Louisiana Infantry. Enlisted 19 October 1862. Single. Sailor. Born in Maine to Irish parents. Marked as American born on 1850 census, Irish-born on military record. Died of chronic diarrhea near Baton Rouge, Louisiana, 20 August 1863.

DOUGHERTY, JOHN

Private, 63rd New York Infantry. Enlisted 20 February 1862. Single. Day laborer. Born in Ireland. KIA, Antietam, Maryland, 17 September 1862.

DOUGHERTY, PATRICK

Coal Heaver, USS *South Carolina.* Assigned Massachusetts. Enlisted 12 June 1862. Single. Laborer. From Co. Donegal. Died of typhoid fever on board near Tybee Island, Georgia, 25 July 1864.

DOWD, JAMES

Private, 63rd New York Infantry. Enlisted 14 August 1861. Married. Tailor. Born in Ireland. KIA, Antietam, Maryland, 17 September 1862.

DOYLE, THOMAS (1)

Private, 1st Massachusetts Cavalry. Enlisted 5 August 1862. Single. Farmer (possibly farm laborer). From Borris, Co. Carlow. Father died in Ireland. Died on 7 September 1863, Hartwood, Virginia, from inflammation of the peritoneum caused by the kick of his horse.

DOYLE, THOMAS (2)

Private, 4th Maine Infantry. Enlisted 15 June 1861. Full name Martin Thomas Doyle. Married. Carpenter. Born in England into an Irish family. Wife Irish-born, married in London. MWIA, Gettysburg, Pennsylvania, 2 July 1863. Died 6 July 1863.

DRISCOLL, DANIEL

Landsman, USS *Cincinnati.* Assigned Massachusetts. Enlisted 11 December 1861. Single. Day laborer. From Castletownbere, Co. Cork (recorded as a seaman on naval enlistment). Died 21 August 1863 in Memphis, Tennessee from a disease of the throat contracted after he spent time in the water following the sinking of the USS *Cincinnati.*

DRISCOLL, DENNIS

Seaman, USS *Metacomet.* Assigned New York. Enlisted 19 December 1863. Single. Laborer. Born in Ireland. Recorded as born in Erie on naval enlistment, in Ireland on 1860 census. Survived service but died from disease of the bowels and stomach contracted in the navy on 12 June 1871.

DRONEY, MATHEW

Marine, USS *Miami.* Assigned Pennsylvania. Enlisted 20 October 1862 under alias Matthew Callahan. Married. Unknown occupation. Born in Ireland. Mortally wounded following the explosion of a shell from a rebel battery at Wilcox's Landing, James River, Virginia, 3 August 1864.

DUFF, WILLIAM

Corporal, 10th New York Infantry. Enlisted 2 May 1861. Single. Born in America, almost certainly to Irish parents. Promoted to color sergeant. MWIA, Second Bull Run, Virginia, 30 August 1862. Died 8 September 1862 on board steamer *Knickerbocker.*

DUFFEY, PATRICK

Second Class Fireman, USS *South Carolina.* Assigned Massachusetts. Enlisted 13 June 1862. Borne as Duffy. Born in Ireland. No previous employment recorded. Discharged 29 April 1865. Survived service.

DUGAN, PATRICK

Private, 39th Illinois Infantry. Enlisted 11 October 1861. Single. Farmer. From Co. Cork. KIA, Darbytown Road, Virginia, 13 October 1864.

DUNNICAN, PATRICK

Private, 32nd Massachusetts Infantry. Enlisted 7 September 1863. Single. Blacksmith. From Co. Roscommon. KIA, Laurel Hill, Virginia, 8 May 1864.

DUNNIGAN, PATRICK

Private, 88th New York Infantry. Enlisted 15 October 1861. Married. Unknown occupation. Almost certain Irish nativity. Promoted to corporal. MWIA, Fair Oaks, Virginia, 1 June 1862. Died 2 June 1862.

DUNPHEY, JAMES

First Class Fireman, USS *South Carolina.* Assigned Massachusetts. Enlisted 3 June 1862. Borne as Dumphy and Dumphry. Born in Ireland. Discharged 4 May 1865. Survived service.

DWYER, EDMUND

Private, 23rd Illinois Infantry. Enlisted 1 August 1862. Single. Laborer. From Boher, Co. Limerick. KIA, Fort Gregg, Petersburg, Virginia, 2 April 1865.

DWYER, WILLIAM

Private, 63rd New York Infantry. Enlisted 28 October 1861. Single. Coffee roaster. From Co. Tipperary, recorded as a laborer on muster roll. Veteran volunteer. Died of chronic diarrhea, City Point, Virginia, 12 July 1864.

EAGAN, MATTHEW

Private, 72nd New York Infantry. Enlisted 21 July 1861. Married. Occupation unknown. A native of Tralee, Co. Kerry. Step migrant through Wales. KIA, Williamsburg, Virginia, 5 May 1862.

FEENEY, JOHN

Private, 170th New York Infantry. Enlisted 10 September 1862. Single. Shoemaker. Born in New York to Irish parents. KIA in a skirmish between Carsville and Suffolk, Virginia, 20 May 1863.

FINAN, PATRICK

Coal Heaver, USS *Wabash.* Assigned New York. Enlisted 29 April 1861. Single. No occupation listed. A native of Sligo, Co. Sligo. Recent immigrant, but recorded as born in Brooklyn on naval records. Accidentally scalded by boilers aboard the *Wabash* off Port Royal, South Carolina, on 21 March 1864 while serving as a second class fireman. Died following an effusion of the brain, 6 April 1864.

FINEGAN, PETER

Private, 116th Pennsylvania Infantry. Enlisted 29 August 1862. Single. Wagon driver. Born in Ireland. KIA, Fredericksburg, Virginia, 13 December 1862.

FINIGAN, JAMES

Private, 4th New York Heavy Artillery. Enlisted 16 January 1864. Single. Mason. Born in Massachusetts. Parents almost certainly Irish immigrants. Wounded and MIA, Ream's Station, Virginia, 25 August 1864.

FINNEGAN, MICHAEL

Private, 164th New York Infantry. Enlisted 23 August 1862. Born in Co. Louth. Laborer. Brother served in same regiment. Ancestor of President Joe Biden. MIA, Cold Harbor, Virginia, 3 June 1864.

FINNERTY, JAMES

Private, 72nd Illinois Infantry. Enlisted 15 August 1862. Single. Painter. From Co. Galway. Step migrant through England, also lived in Canada. KIA, Vicksburg, Mississippi, 22 May 1863.

FITZGERALD, JAMES

Private, 53rd Pennsylvania Infantry. Enlisted 23 October 1861. Single. Laborer. Born in Ireland. Died of typhoid fever, Washington, D.C., 11 March 1862.

FITZPATRICK, EDWARD

Private, 10th New Jersey Infantry. Enlisted 4 November 1864 under alias Edward Honors. Married. Factory worker. From Co. Laois. Died of typhoid fever, Alexandria, Virginia, 1 July 1865.

FITZPATRICK, JAMES

Corporal, 8th Illinois Infantry. Enlisted 25 July 1861. Single. Carpenter. Born in New York to Irish parents. KIA, 26 June 1863, Vicksburg, Mississippi.

FITZPATRICK, JOHN

Private, 19th Illinois Infantry. Enlisted 4 June 1861. Single. Farm laborer. Born in England to Irish parents from Co. Waterford. Died of congestion of the brain, Nashville, Tennessee, 4 September 1862.

FLAHERTY, WILLIAM

Private, 6th New Hampshire Infantry. Enlisted 30 December 1863 under alias William State. Single. Hatter. From Co. Galway. Wounded and MIA, the Wilderness, Virginia, 6 May 1864.

FLANAGAN, MARTIN

Private, 74th New York Infantry. Enlisted 20 June 1861. Single. Gardener. Born in New York to Irish parents. Brother also served in regiment, and also died. Promoted to sergeant. KIA, Second Bull Run, Virginia, 29 August 1862.

FLYNN, RICHARD

Private, 117th New York Infantry. Enlisted 6 August 1862. Single. Farm laborer. Born in New York to Irish parents. Died 10 July 1864 in Petersburg, Virginia, of wounds received in action.

FORAN, MICHAEL

Private, 5th Pennsylvania Reserves. Enlisted 5 May 1861 under alias Miles Ford. Married. Almost certainly of Irish nativity, wife also Irish-born. KIA, White Oak Swamp, Virginia, 30 June 1862.

FORD, EDMUND

Private, 8th Kansas Infantry. Enlisted 24 October 1861. Single. Laborer from Co. Cork. Paid passage of parents to America. KIA, Chickamauga, Georgia, 19 September 1863.

GALBRAITH, WILLIAM

Private, 91st New York Infantry. Enlisted 15 October 1861. Married. Laborer. From Ireland. Died of dysentery, Pensacola, Florida, 27 September 1862.

GALLIVEN, PATRICK

Private, 10th New York Infantry. Enlisted 5 March 1864. Single. Printer. Born in Ireland. Accidentally shot and killed near Appomattox Court House, Virginia, 12 April 1865.

GANNON, JOHN

Private, 26th New York Infantry. Enlisted 4 June 1861. Single. Unknown occupation. A native of Co. Tipperary. Father died in Ireland in 1849. KIA, Second Bull Run, Virginia, 30 August 1862.

GARVIN, CON

Private, 52nd New York Infantry. Single. A native of Grange, Co. Limerick. Disabled, abducted from the Troy County House and sold into service, apparently under the alias Charles Becker. Likely MWIA at Spotsylvania Court House, Virginia, 18 May 1864.

GREANEY, CHARLES

Private, 9th Massachusetts Infantry. Enlisted 11 June 1861. Single. Bootmaker. From Castleisland, Co. Kerry. KIA, Gaines' Mill, Virginia, 27 June 1862.

GRIFFIN, PATRICK

Private, 6th Independent Battery, Massachusetts Light Artillery. Enlisted 23 December 1863 (15th Independent Battery, Massachusetts Light Artillery). Single. Laborer. From Athlone, Co. Roscommon. Died in New Orleans, Louisiana, on 26 June 1865 following field punishment by officers.

GRIMES, JOHN

Private, 3rd Rhode Island Heavy Artillery. Enlisted 14 December 1861. Single. Unknown occupation. Born in Rhode Island to Irish parents. Died of diphtheria, Fort Pulaski, Georgia, 5 March 1864.

GROGAN, JAMES

Private, 65th New York Infantry. Enlisted 1 September 1861. Upholster. Born in Ireland. Veteran volunteer. Promoted to sergeant. Mustered out as first sergeant in 1865. Survived service.

HAGAN, THOMAS

Private, 15th New York Cavalry. Enlisted 15 August 1863. Single. Carpenter. Born in New York to Irish parents, pre-Famine emigrants. KIA, Romney, West Virginia, 10 May 1864.

HALL, JOHN

Private, 63rd New York Infantry. Enlisted 20 January 1864. Likely single. Cooper. Born in Ireland. Wounded at Petersburg, Virginia, 16 June 1864. Mustered out June 1865. Survived service.

HAND, JAMES

Private, 164th New York Infantry. Enlisted 31 October 1862. Single. Born in New Jersey to Irish parents. Brother died serving aboard USS *Cincinnati.* Captured at Ream's Station, Virginia, 25 August 1864. Died a POW, Salisbury, North Carolina, 1 February 1865.

HANLIN, EDWARD

Private, 12th New York Infantry. Enlisted 17 December 1861. Single. Shop assistant. Almost certainly Irish American. KIA, Second Bull Run, Virginia, 30 August 1862.

HARRIGAN, JAMES

Private, 72nd Pennsylvania Infantry. Enlisted 10 August 1861. Single. Unknown occupation. Born in Pennsylvania to Irish parents. KIA, Antietam, Maryland, 17 September 1862.

HARRINGTON, TIMOTHY

Ordinary Seaman, USS *Cumberland.* Assigned Massachusetts. Enlisted 11 July 1861 under alias Thomas Harrington. Married. Laborer. Born in Ireland. KIA during the engagement with the CSS *Virginia* off Newport News, Virginia, 8 March 1862.

HARNETT, WILLIAM

Private, 4th U.S. Infantry. Enlisted 16 August 1859. Single. Laborer. From Co. Kerry. KIA, Antietam, Maryland, 17 September 1862.

HAYES, JAMES

Corporal, 38th Illinois Infantry. Enlisted 4 August 1861. Single. Laborer. From Bandon, Co. Cork. Paid for his mother's passage from Ireland. KIA, Chickamauga, Georgia, 19 or 20 September 1863.

HAYES, JOHN

Private, 105th New York Infantry. Enlisted 10 November 1861. Married. Unknown occupation. Promoted to sergeant March 1862, to second lieutenant November 1862. Discharged April 1863. Entered the 22nd New York Cavalry as a private on 6 November 1863. Deserted at Rochester, New York, 23 December 1863. Survived service.

HEALY, JAMES

Private, 9th Massachusetts Infantry. Enlisted 21 August 1862. Single. Carpenter. Born in Co. Cork. Nativity given as Massachusetts on census, Ireland on enlistment. At most seventeen years old at the time he joined up. MWIA, the Wilderness, Virginia, 5 May 1864. Died 6 May 1864.

HENNESSEY, JOHN

Private, 7th New York Heavy Artillery. Enlisted 30 December 1863 under alias John Quinn. Single. Bartender. Recorded as a clerk on census. Born in New York to Irish parents. MWIA, Petersburg, Virginia, 17 June 1864. Died Philadelphia, Pennsylvania, 18 December 1864.

HENRY, JAMES

First Sergeant, 37th New York Infantry. Enlisted 7 June 1861. Promoted to second lieutenant. Single. Carpenter. From Co. Sligo. Following muster out enlisted in the 11th U.S. Infantry. KIA while a sergeant, Spotsylvania Court House, Virginia, 12 May 1864.

HICKEY, JAMES

Private, 164th New York Infantry. Enlisted 9 August 1862. Married. Cooper. Born in Ireland. KIA, Cold Harbor, Virginia, 3 June 1864.

HIGGINS, MICHAEL

Private, 125th New York Infantry. Enlisted 7 August 1862. Single. Moulder. Born in Ireland. Recorded as a book agent on census. MWIA, Gettysburg, Pennsylvania, 3 July 1863. Died 6 July 1863.

HOGG, FARRELL

Private, 88th New York Infantry. Enlisted 22 October 1861. Married. Occupation unknown. A native of Co. Sligo. His wife remained in Ireland. Son died due to accident while in naval service. Wounded and captured at Savage Station, Virginia, 29 June 1862. Died following exchange, 16 August 1862.

HORAN, PATRICK

Private, 67th New York Infantry. Enlisted 24 June 1861. Single. Day laborer. From Co. Galway. Father died in Ireland in 1847. MWIA, Seven Pines, Virginia, 31 May 1862. Died at David's Island, New York, 25 June 1862.

HORGAN, DENIS

Ordinary Seaman, USS *Sachem.* Assigned Massachusetts. Enlisted 23 May 1862. Single. Cooper and whaler. From Shandon, Co. Cork. Recorded as born in New York on enlistment despite having immigrated in 1857. Serving as acting master-at-arms when he contracted malaria during operations on the Atchafalaya and Mississippi Rivers. Died at Brashear City, Louisiana, around 18 August 1863.

HYNES, THOMAS

Seaman, USS *Cyane.* Assigned Pennsylvania. Enlisted 2 May 1864. Married. Seaman. From Co. Dublin. Previous service in East India Company. Died at Acapulco, Mexico, of hemorrhage of the lungs, 6 October 1864.

KEATING, THOMAS

Private, 9th New York State Militia (83rd New York Infantry). Enlisted 13 September 1861. Single. Bookbinder. Born in New York to Irish parents. Captured on the march, May 1864. Died a POW, Andersonville, Georgia, 1 August 1864.

KEENAN, JEREMIAH

Private, 140th New York Infantry. Enlisted 30 August 1862. Single. Laborer. From Co. Kilkenny. KIA, Gettysburg, Pennsylvania, 2 July 1863.

KELLEGHER, PATRICK

Private, 88th New York Infantry/Landsman, USS *Frolic.* Assigned New York. Enlisted in army on 25 February 1864. Married. Blacksmith. Born in Ireland. Promoted to sergeant. Wounded at the Wilderness, 5 May 1864. Deserted from hospital, Washington, D.C., 3 June 1864. Enlisted in navy, undisclosed date in 1864, under alias John Kelly. Discharged 4 February 1871 due to consumption contracted during postwar naval service. Died four years later, 11 May 1875.

KELLY, PATRICK

Private, 28th Massachusetts Infantry. Enlisted 16 November 1861. Single. Shoemaker. From Ballinasloe, Co. Galway. Also recorded as a laborer. Promoted to corporal. KIA on picket duty at Kelly's Ford, Virginia, 3 December 1863.

KELLY, JOHN (1)

Private, 1st New York Cavalry. Enlisted 16 August 1861. Single. Weaver. From Co. Tipperary. Wounded in a skirmish at Hagerstown, Maryland. Died following amputation in Frederick, Maryland, 18 August 1863.

KELLY, JOHN (2)

Private, 16th U.S. Infantry. Enlisted 26 June 1862. Single. Farmer (likely farm laborer). Born in England to Irish parents. Captured at Chickamauga, Georgia, 19 September 1863. Died a POW, Andersonville, Georgia, 5 May 1864.

KENNEDY, JOHN

Sergeant, 10th Ohio Infantry. Enlisted 4 June 1861. Single. Tobacconist. From Dunkerrin, Co. Offaly. KIA, Carnifex Ferry, (West) Virginia, 10 September 1861.

KERR, JAMES

Private, 26th Pennsylvania Infantry. Enlisted 5 May 1861. Married. Laborer. From Co. Tyrone. KIA, Chancellorsville, Virginia, 2 May 1863.

KINNANE, PATRICK

Private, 155th New York Infantry. Enlisted 6 September 1862. Single. Finisher. Born in New York to Irish parents. Recorded as a varnisher on census. Responsible for sister's support after parents' death. Taken prisoner at Ream's Station, Virginia, 25 August 1864. Died a POW, Salisbury, North Carolina, 15 December 1864.

LANE, JOHN

Private, 12th Massachusetts Infantry. Enlisted 26 June 1861. Single. Journeyman stonecutter. A native of Kildorrery, Co. Cork. Father died in Ireland, 1847. MIA, Second Bull Run, Virginia, 30 August 1862.

LARKIN, DENNIS

Private, 6th New York Heavy Artillery. Enlisted 13 September 1864 under alias William Collins. Single. Laborer. From Co. Galway. Also recorded as a butcher. Drowned while on picket duty, Appomattox, Virginia, 19 May 1865.

LAVERTY, ARCHEY

Private, 1st New York Infantry. Enlisted 3 May 1861. Single. Upholsterer. Born in Ireland. Recorded as a waiter on census. An illegitimate child. KIA, Chancellorsville, Virginia, 2 May 1863.

LEAHEY, JAMES

Private, 99th New York Infantry. Enlisted 15 July 1861. Married. Upholsterer. From Co. Limerick. KIA aboard the USS *Congress* during the engagement with the CSS *Virginia* off Newport News, Virginia, 8 March 1862.

LIVINGSTON, JAMES

Sergeant, 155th New York Infantry. Enlisted 19 September 1862. Single. Bookbinder. Born in Ireland. Recorded as a clerk on military enlistment. Father died in Canada. Wounded, Cold Harbor, Virginia, 3 June 1863. Died of gangrene, Washington, D.C., 17 June 1864.

LOUGHRAN, WILLIAM

Sergeant, 88th New York Infantry. Enlisted 17 September 1861. Married. Policeman. Of Irish nativity. KIA, Fredericksburg, Virginia, 13 December 1862.

LYNAM, WILLIAM

Seaman, USS *Hartford.* Assigned Massachusetts. Enlisted 9 December 1861. Also borne as Lyman and Lynan. Born in Massachusetts, likely Irish American. Mustered out 20 December 1864. Survived service.

LYNCH, JOHN (1)

Private, 10th Illinois Infantry. Enlisted 19 August 1861. Single. Laborer. Born in Co. Limerick. Railroad laborer in 1850s Ohio, worked on Erie Railroad. Died in New Madrid, Missouri, of typhoid pneumonia, 5 April 1861.

LYNCH, JOHN (2)

Captain, 63rd New York Infantry. Enlisted 21 August 1861. Single. Clerk. Born in Co. Dublin. KIA, Chancellorsville, Virginia, 3 May 1863.

MADDEN, JOHN

Private, 162nd New York Infantry. Enlisted 13 October 1862 under alias John Martin. Single. Employed as a matchmaker, match peddler, and copper and tinsmith. Died off the coast of Florida while en route to Bermuda Hundred, 10 July 1864.

MAHAR, NICHOLAS

Private, 16th New York Heavy Artillery. Enlisted 21 December 1863. Single. Farmer. Born in New York to Irish parents. Died of disease, City Point, Virginia, 29 April 1865.

MAHON, JOHN

Private, 91st New York Infantry. Enlisted 6 December 1861. Single. Laborer. From Co. Dublin. Died of typhoid fever, Key West, Florida, 14 June 1862.

MARONEY, WILLIAM

Captain, 164th New York Infantry. Enlisted 18 September 1862. Single. Glassworker. From Fethard, Co. Tipperary. MWIA, Cold Harbor, Virginia, 3 June 1864. Died a POW, Richmond, Virginia, 20 June 1864.

MARTIN, MICHAEL

Private, 2nd Massachusetts Infantry. Enlisted 1 July 1862 under alias John Martin. Married. Carpenter. Born in New Brunswick into an Irish family. Married an Irish immigrant. KIA, Chancellorsville, Virginia, 3 May 1863.

MARTIN, WILLIAM

Corporal, 182nd New York Infantry (69th New York State National Guard

Artillery). Enlisted 28 September 1862. Single. Carriage blacksmith. Born in Co. Cavan. Father died in Ireland in 1840. Promoted to sergeant. MIWA, Cold Harbor, Virginia, 3 June 1864. Died at Divisional Hospital, 4 June 1864.

McCAFFREY, PATRICK

Private, 69th New York Infantry. Enlisted 3 February 1864. Married. Laborer. Born in Ireland. Wounded at Ream's Station, Virginia, 25 August 1864, and discharged. Died of wounds, New York, 11 May 1865.

McCARTHY, THOMAS

Private, 12th Massachusetts Infantry. Enlisted 26 June 1861. Single. Born in Massachusetts to parents from Shanbally, Co. Cork. KIA, Antietam, Maryland, 17 September 1862.

McCOLLISTER, WILLIAM

Private, 4th Pennsylvania Cavalry. Enlisted 4 September 1861. Single. Driver. From Co. Antrim. Wounded at Gaines' Mill, Virginia, 27 June 1862. Transferred to Veteran Reserves Corps. Died from his injuries, Fortress Monroe, Virginia, 4 March 1864.

McCONAGHY, JOSEPH

Private, 73rd Pennsylvania Infantry. Enlisted 20 February 1862 under alias Joseph May. Single. Laborer. Born in Ireland. Father had abandoned the family in Ireland and remarried in America. Veteran volunteer. KIA, Peachtree Creek, Georgia, 20 July 1864.

McCONNELL, PATRICK

Private, 4th New York Infantry. Enlisted 9 November 1861. Single. Unknown occupation. Born in Ireland. Wounded at Antietam, Maryland, 17 September 1862. Died following amputation of arm in Baltimore, Maryland, 12 October 1862.

McCORMICK, MICHAEL

Private, 65th New York Infantry. Enlisted 12 September 1861. Single. Brassfounder. Born in New York to Irish parents. KIA, the Wilderness, Virginia, 6 May 1864.

McCOURT, MATHEW

Private, 1st Michigan Infantry. Enlisted 15 July 1861. Single. Mason. Born in New York to parents from Co. Waterford. Older sister born in Ireland. Wounded and MIA, Second Bull Run, Virginia, 30 August 1862.

McCREADY, THOMAS

Wagoner, 74th New York Infantry. Enlisted 1 June 1861. Single. Gardener. From Co. Donegal. Step migrant through Scotland. KIA, Williamsburg, Virginia, 5 May 1862.

McFARLAND, TERRENCE

Private, 182nd New York Infantry. Enlisted 17 October 1862. Single. Stonecutter. From Newry, Co. Down. KIA, Petersburg, Virginia, 16 June 1864.

McGAFFIGAN, JAMES

Private, 63rd New York Infantry. Enlisted 7 August 1861. Married. Unknown occupation. A native of Co. Derry. In his forties at enlistment. KIA, Antietam, Maryland, 17 September 1862.

McGEE, JAMES (1)

Private, 132nd New York Infantry. Enlisted 27 August 1862. Single. Stage driver. Born in Ireland. Affidavits claim he was a laborer in a soda water manufactory. Killed by accidental explosion of torpedoes, Bachelor's Creek, North Carolina, 26 May 1864.

McGEE, JAMES (2)

Private, 69th New York Infantry. Enlisted 22 September 1861. Single. Baker. From Co. Louth. KIA, Antietam, Maryland, 17 September 1862.

McGIFF, CHRISTOPHER

Private, 119th New York Infantry. Enlisted 31 July 1862. Single. Moulder. Born in New York, almost certainly to Irish parents. KIA, Gettysburg, Pennsylvania, 1 July 1863.

McGILLICUDDY, JOHN

Private, 173rd New York Infantry. Enlisted 25 September 1862 under alias John

McCarty. Married. Laborer. Born in Ireland. Step migrant through England, married his second wife in Luton. Died of typhoid fever, Sandy Hook, Maryland, 7 October 1864.

McGINNESS, JAMES
Private, 90th New York Infantry. Enlisted 5 November 1861. Single. Laborer. From Co. Cavan. His mother had lost seven children, and came to America in advance of her husband. Died of yellow fever, Key West, Florida, 1 October 1862.

McGOWAN, OWEN
Landsman, USS *Keystone State.* Assigned Massachusetts. Enlisted 1 August 1862. Single. Porter. From Co. Roscommon. Naval record listed birthplace as Massachusetts. Scalded to death during an action off Charleston, South Carolina, 31 January 1863.

McHUGH, JAMES
Private, 19th U.S. Infantry. Enlisted 8 April 1862. Single. Shoemaker. From Co. Tyrone. KIA, Gettysburg, Pennsylvania, 2 July 1863.

McINTYRE, WILLIAM
Private, 95th Pennsylvania Infantry. Enlisted 9 October 1861. Single. Apprentice printer. Born in Pennsylvania to Irish parents. Promoted to corporal. KIA, Salem Church, Virginia, 3 May 1863.

McLAUGHLIN, FRANCIS
First Lieutenant, 1st Pennsylvania Light Artillery. Enlisted 5 August 1861. Married. Engineer. From Co. Donegal. Died of typhoid fever, Fair Oaks, Virginia, 4 June 1862.

MEEHAN, JOHN
Private, 26th New York Infantry. Enlisted 2 May 1861. Tailor. Born in Ireland. Captured at Second Bull Run, Virginia, 30 August 1862. Mustered out 28 May 1863. Enlisted as a private, 14th New York Heavy Artillery, 19 July 1863. Promoted to sergeant, reduced. Deserted at Bedloes Island, New York, 9 October 1864. Survived service.

MEEHAN, WILLIAM

Private, 47th New York Infantry. Enlisted 15 August 1861. Single. Mason. Born in New York to Irish parents. His father Michael, a forty-year-old laborer, served and died in the same company. Discharged 15 August 1864. Survived service.

MOLONY, JAMES

Private, 31st New York Infantry. Enlisted 2 May 1861. Born in Ireland. Captured at White Oak Swamp, Virginia, 30 June 1862. Promoted to corporal, reduced to ranks. Mustered out 4 June 1863. Survived service.

MONAGHAN, THOMAS

Private, 95th Pennsylvania Infantry. Enlisted 9 September 1861. Single. Plumber and gas fitter. Born in Pennsylvania to Irish parents. Promoted to corporal. MWIA, Spotsylvania Court House, Virginia, 12 May 1864. Died in Washington, D.C., 29 May 1864.

MOONEY, EDWARD

Private, 19th Iowa Infantry. Enlisted 14 August 1862. Single. Laborer. Born in Ireland, serving a twenty-five-year sentence for murder in Iowa State Penitentiary. KIA, Prairie Grove, Arkansas, 7 December 1862.

MOORE, JOHN

Private, 91st New York Infantry. Enlisted 15 October 1861. Single. Laborer. Recorded as New York-born on muster, but as Irish-born on 1860 census. Veteran volunteer. Mustered out with company, 3 July 1865. Survived service.

NIGHTINGALE, FREDERICK

Corporal, 118th New York Infantry. Enlisted 12 August 1862. Single. Printer. Born in Ireland. Family resident in Canada. MIA, Fair Oaks, Virginia, 27 October 1864.

NOONAN, MARTIN

Private, 64th New York Infantry. Enlisted 21 September 1861. Single. Unknown occupation. A native of Co. Clare. MWIA, Spotsylvania Court House, Virginia, 12 May 1864. Died near Fredericksburg, Virginia, circa 18 May 1864.

O'BRIEN, CORNELIUS

Private, 16th Illinois Infantry. Enlisted 19 February 1864. Single. Farm laborer. Born in England to Irish parents. Died of typhoid fever, Graysville, Georgia, 12 April 1864.

O'BRIEN, JOHN (1)

Private, 10th Illinois Cavalry. Enlisted 21 September 1861. Farm laborer. From Ladysbridge, Co. Cork. Emigrated 1859. Veteran volunteer. Mustered out 22 November 1865. Survived service.

O'BRIEN, JOHN (2)

Marine, U.S. Marine Corps. Assigned New York. Enlisted 24 May 1861. Married. Cooper. From Listowel, Co. Kerry. Survived service. Post war pension claimed by wife in Listowel, Co. Kerry.

O'BRIEN, PATRICK

Fireman, USS *Clifton*. Assigned Massachusetts. Enlisted 27 April 1862. Single. Laborer. From Rosscarbery, Co. Cork. Captured at Sabine Pass, Texas, 8 September 1863. Died a POW, 3 March 1864.

O'CONNELL, DAVID

Private, 140th New York Infantry. Enlisted 29 August 1862. Married. Master blacksmith. Born in Ireland. Deserted, no date given. Survived service.

O'CONNELL, JOHN

Private, 2nd Massachusetts Infantry. Enlisted 25 May 1861. Single. Weaver. From Co. Kerry. KIA, Winchester, Virginia, 25 May 1862.

O'CONNOR, JOHN

Private, 151st New York Infantry. Enlisted 27 August 1862. Laborer. Born in New York to Irish parents. Promoted to corporal. Brother was wounded in the same action in which he was killed. Mother went to a poorhouse. KIA, Spotsylvania Court House, Virginia, 10 May 1864.

O'DONNELL, CHARLES

Marine, U.S. Marine Corps. Assigned Pennsylvania. Enlisted 22 July 1862.

Single. Wool carder. From Co. Donegal. Died of typhoid fever, Washington, D.C., 9 September 1862.

O'DONNELL, HUGH

Private, 29th Pennsylvania Infantry. Enlisted 8 December 1863. Single. Laborer. From Co. Derry. Wounded at Atlanta, Georgia, 20 July 1864. Died of wounds, Philadelphia, Pennsylvania, 30 August 1865.

O'HERRIN, JAMES

Private, 17th Massachusetts Infantry. Enlisted 21 July 1861 under alias Francis Welsh. Single. Shoemaker. From Co. Cork. Veteran volunteer. Captured at Bachelor's Creek, North Carolina, 1 February 1864. Died a POW, Andersonville, Georgia, 13 May 1864.

O'KEEFFE, DAVID

Private, 9th Massachusetts Infantry. Enlisted 12 August 1862. Married. Cabinetmaker. From Co. Cork. Died from overexertion on campaign, Fairfax Seminary, Virginia, 23 June 1863.

O'NEIL, DANIEL

Marine, U.S. Marine Corps. Assigned Massachusetts. Enlisted 4 June 1861. Single. Bootmaker. Born in Pennsylvania to Irish parents. MWIA, Fort Fisher, North Carolina, 15 January 1865. Died aboard USS *Minnesota,* 15 January 1865.

O'NEIL, JAMES

Private, 2nd New York Mounted Rifles. Enlisted 28 September 1863. Single. Boatman. Born in Ireland. Nativity of Ireland on census, America on muster. KIA, Petersburg, Virginia, 30 July 1864.

O'NEILL, JAMES

Private, 4th Delaware Infantry. Enlisted 22 August 1862. Single. Unknown occupation. Born in Ireland. Served with his brother Daniel. Promoted to corporal and sergeant. Survived service.

PHALEN, KEARN

Private, 11th Connecticut Infantry, Company E. Enlisted 19 September 1862 under alias Kearn Fitzpatrick. Married. Wool carder. Born in Ireland. Died of chronic diarrhea, Point of Rocks, Virginia, 6 September 1864.

REDDY, DANIEL

Private, 16th Massachusetts Infantry. Enlisted 2 July 1861. Single. Jappaner. Born in Ireland. Veteran volunteer. Promoted to corporal. Transferred to 11th Massachusetts Infantry in July 1864. Survived service.

REILEY, THOMAS

Private, 139th New York Infantry. Enlisted 9 January 1864 under alias Thomas McGory. Single. Laborer. Born in New York to Irish parents. Recorded as Irish-born on enlistment. KIA, Cold Harbor, Virginia, 2 June 1864.

RILEY, JOHN

Marine, U.S. Marine Corps. Assigned Pennsylvania. Enlisted 22 June 1861. Single. Laborer. Son of Irish immigrants. Parents married in Leeds, England. Recorded as both Irish-born and American-born. KIA, First Bull Run, Virginia, 21 July 1861.

RYAN, JAMES

Private, 3rd Vermont Infantry. Single. Laborer. From Drogheda, Co. Louth. Enlisted 19 August 1863. Substitute. Mother in Ireland at time of enlistment. KIA, Spotsylvania Court House, Virginia, 12 May 1864.

RYAN, MICHAEL (1)

Private, 3rd Ohio Infantry. Enlisted 13 June 1861. Married. Unknown occupation. Native of Co. Cork. Died of chronic diarrhea, Nashville, Tennessee, 20 January 1863.

RYAN, MICHAEL (2)

Private, 95th New York Infantry. Enlisted 2 September 1863. Single. A native of Co. Tipperary. Father died in Ireland. Left Ireland in April 1862, employed as a helper in a blacksmith shop before enlistment. Died of typhoid fever, Washington, D.C., 4 January 1864.

SCARFF, ALEXANDER

Private, 174th New York Infantry. Enlisted 6 November 1862 under alias Arthur Shaw. Single. An Irish-born clerk from Co. Dublin. Joined up the day after landing in New York. KIA, Kock's Plantation, Louisiana, 13 July 1863.

SCANLAN, JOHN

Private, 2nd Michigan Infantry/Landsman, USS *Mystic*. Enlisted 22 May 1861. Married. Clerk. Either born in Canada to Irish parents or in Ireland. Listed as being of Canadian birth on naval records, Irish birth on census. Following service in the 2nd Michigan was enlisted into naval service on 11 September 1862. Served under alias Charles Stanley in the navy. Survived service.

SCANNELL, PAT

Private, 1st New Hampshire Cavalry. Enlisted 3 April 1865. Single. Porter. Born in Ireland. Died of typhoid fever, Darnestown, Maryland, 18 April 1865.

SCULLY, JOHN

Private, 9th Massachusetts Infantry. Enlisted 28 July 1862. Single. Shoemaker. Born in Nova Scotia to Irish parents. Recorded as Nova Scotian birth on census, Massachusetts birth on military record. Captured at Spotsylvania Court House, Virginia, 8 May 1864. Died a POW, Richmond, Virginia, 15 July 1864.

SHARKEY, JAMES

Private, 21st New York Cavalry. Enlisted 11 August 1863. Single. Nurseryman. Born in New York to Irish parents. Brother served in 140th New York Infantry. Died of typhoid fever, Washington, D.C., 26 October 1863.

SHEA, JOHN

Private, 1st Kansas Infantry. Enlisted 3 June 1861. Single. Unknown occupation. A native of Co. Kerry. Mother in Ireland during service. Died of chronic diarrhea, Natchez, Mississippi, 3 September 1863.

SHEA, WILLIAM

Private, 23rd Pennsylvania Infantry. Enlisted 14 August 1861. Single. Laborer. Of Irish nativity. Died of wounds received at Cold Harbor, Virginia, 1 June 1864.

SHEEDY, JOSEPH

Private, 28th Massachusetts Infantry. Enlisted 9 December 1861. Single. Painter. From Co. Limerick. Recorded as a clerk on census. KIA, Gettysburg, Pennsylvania, 2 July 1863.

SHEEHAN, JOHN

Private, 105th New York Infantry/Private, 94th New York Infantry. Enlisted 6 March 1862. Single. Laborer. Born in Ontario, Canada, to Irish parents. Step migrants. Transferred to 94th New York on 10 March 1863. Promoted to corporal. Captured at the Weldon Railroad, Virginia, 19 August 1864. Died a POW, Salisbury, North Carolina, 19 November 1864.

SHEREN, JAMES

Private, 2nd Kentucky Infantry. Enlisted 6 June 1861. Married. Stonecutter. From Co. Antrim. Promoted to sergeant. KIA, Shiloh, Tennessee, 7 April 1862.

SHERIDAN, RICHARD

Private, 2nd New York State Militia (82nd New York Infantry). Enlisted 21 May 1861. Single. Bookbinder. Born in New York to Irish parents. Pension claimed in Blackwell's Island Alms House. Promoted to corporal. KIA, Gettysburg, Pennsylvania, 3 July 1863.

SHERRY, JOHN

Private, 7th Pennsylvania Reserves, Company K. Enlisted 27 July 1861. Single. Weaver. Born in Pennsylvania to Irish parents. KIA, White Oak Swamp, Virginia, 30 June 1862.

SLATTERY, JOHN (1)

Private, 12th Massachusetts Infantry. Enlisted 26 June 1861. Single. Laborer. Born in Massachusetts to Irish parents. KIA, Thoroughfare Gap, Virginia, 28 August 1862.

SLATTERY, JOHN (2)

Private, 40th Massachusetts Infantry. Enlisted 25 July 1862. Married. Operative. Born in New York to Irish parents. Captured at Drewry's Bluff, Virginia, 16 May 1864. Died a POW, Florence, South Carolina, 16 October 1864.

SULLIVAN, JOHN (1)

Landsman, USS *Underwriter.* Assigned Massachusetts. Enlisted in 1862. Single. Teamster. From Co. Cork. Also recorded as a laborer. Captured off New Bern, North Carolina, 2 February 1864. Died a POW, Andersonville, Georgia, 15 June 1864.

SULLIVAN, JOHN (2)

Corporal, 99th New York Infantry. Enlisted 28 September 1861. Single. Carpenter. From Tralee, Co. Kerry. Discharged for disability, 25 March 1862. Died of consumption and dropsy, New York City, 10 October 1862.

SULLIVAN, JOHN (3)

Private, 102nd New York Infantry. Enlisted 4 January 1862. Single. Unknown occupation. Born in Vermont to Irish parents. Lied about his age to enlist. Died of pneumonia, Washington, D.C., 18 March 1862.

TIERNAN, MARTIN

Private, 61st New York Infantry. Enlisted 10 October 1861. Single. Apprentice hatter. From Co. Roscommon. Promoted to corporal. KIA, Fair Oaks, Virginia, 1 June 1862.

TOOMEY, DENIS

Private, 2nd Massachusetts Heavy Artillery. Laborer. Born in Ireland. First enlisted in 6th Massachusetts Infantry, 31 August 1862. Veteran volunteer. Joined 2nd Massachusetts Heavy Artillery on 10 August 1863. Mustered out 3 September 1865. Survived service.

TOOMEY, JOHN

Private, 15th Massachusetts Infantry, Company E. Enlisted 12 July 1861. Single. Shoemaker. From Co. Cork. KIA, Fair Oaks, Virginia, 31 May 1862.

TOOMEY, TIMOTHY

Private, 160th New York Infantry. Enlisted 31 August 1862. Single. Farmer. Born in Ireland. MWIA, Winchester, Virginia, 19 September 1864. Died 26 September 1864.

TRAYNOR, CHARLES

Private, 69th New York Infantry. Enlisted 16 August 1862. Single. Bricklayer. Of Irish nativity. KIA on picket at Skinner's House, Petersburg, Virginia, 25 March 1865.

WARD, JOHN

Private, 4th Maine Infantry. Enlisted 15 June 1861. Born in Ireland. Recorded in 1860 living with a group of ship's carpenters. His occupation is not recorded. Captured at Fredericksburg, Virginia, 13 December 1862. Mustered out 19 July 1864. Survived service.

WELDON, GEORGE

Private, 140th New York Infantry. Enlisted 30 August 1862. Single. Farm laborer. Born in Ireland. Sixteen years old in 1860. Wounded at Laurel Hill, Virginia, 8 May 1864. Promoted to corporal. Mustered out with company on 3 June 1865. Survived service.

WELSH, JAMES

Private, 82nd Pennsylvania Infantry. Enlisted 24 August 1861. Single. Mason. Born in Ireland. Veteran volunteer. KIA, Cold Harbor, Virginia, 1 June 1864.

WHITE, JOHN

Private, 2nd Massachusetts Heavy Artillery. Enlisted 21 July 1863. Single. Mechanic. From Templemore, Co. Tipperary. Seventeen years old at enlistment. Died of yellow fever, New Bern, North Carolina, 23 October 1864.

WILLIAMS, CHARLES

Sergeant, 69th Pennsylvania Infantry. Enlisted 1 December 1861. Single. Carpenter. Born in Pennsylvania. Promoted to first sergeant. Died of wounds received at Petersburg, Virginia, 17 June 1864.

NOTES

ABBREVIATIONS

CMSR	Compiled Military Service Record
CWMRA	Civil War Muster Roll Abstracts
NARA	National Archives and Records Administration
NYSA	New York State Archives
OR	Official Records of the Union and Confederate Armies
PHMC	Pennsylvania Historical and Museum Commission
USSC	United States Sanitary Commission

INTRODUCTION

1. Patrick Dooley to "Dear Mother," 7 July 1862, in Widow's Certificate No. 6206, Approved Pension File of Mary Dooley, Mother of Patrick Dooley, Company C, 40th New York Infantry, Case Files of Approved Pension Applications of Widows and Other Dependents of the Army and Navy Who Served Mainly in the Civil War and the War with Spain, Records Group 15, Records of the Department of Veterans Affairs, NARA. Hereafter all pension files are referred to by WC number.

2. Patrick Dooley to "Dear Mother," 7 July 1862, WC6206.

3. Patrick Dooley to "Dear Mother," 15 July 1862, WC6206.

4. Significantly, these parallel the findings that emerged from Catherine Bateson's recent study of wartime music associated with the Irish. See Catherine Bateson, *Irish American Civil War Songs: Identity, Loyalty, and Nationhood* (Baton Rouge: Louisiana State Univ. Press, 2022), 219.

5. David Gleeson's work on the Confederate Irish suggests that around 20,000 Irish natives served in CSA forces during the war. See David T. Gleeson, *The Green and the Gray: The Irish in the Confederate States of America* (Chapel Hill: Univ. of North Carolina Press, 2013), 60. For the Union Irish numbers, see the detailed discussion in chapter 2.

6. *Daily Richmond (Va.) Examiner*, 19 May 1862. "Dutch," derived from "Deutsch," was a term frequently employed during this period to reference those of German ethnicity.

7. Estimates as to the number of native-born Germans in the army alone range between 187,000

and 216,000. See Christian B. Keller, *Chancellorsville and the Germans: Nativism, Ethnicity, and Civil War Memory* (New York: Fordham Univ. Press, 2007), 172n9.

8. For a discussion of German service in ethnic versus nonethnic regiments, see Keller, *Chancellorsville and the Germans,* 29.

9. For the best argument put forward for this Irish American downturn of support and its consequences, see Susannah Ural, *The Harp and the Eagle: Irish-American Volunteers and the Union Army, 1861–1865* (New York: New York Univ. Press, 2006).

10. David Power Conyngham, *The Irish Brigade and Its Campaigns* (New York: William McSorley, 1867), 3. A journalist by profession, Conyngham had attached himself to the Irish Brigade during the early part of the conflict.

11. See Michael H. MacNamara, *The Irish Ninth in Bivouac and Battle, or, Virginia and Maryland Campaigns* (Boston: Lee and Shepard, 1867); Daniel George MacNamara, *The History of the Ninth Regiment, Massachusetts Volunteer Infantry, Second Brigade, First Division, Fifth Army Corps, Army of the Potomac, June, 1861–June, 1864* (Boston: E. B. Stillings, 1899); Anthony W. McDermott, *A Brief History of the 69th Regiment Pennsylvania Veteran Volunteers: From Its Formation until Final Muster out of the United States Service* (Philadelphia: D. J. Gallagher, 1889); St. Clair A. Mulholland, *The Story of the 116th Regiment Pennsylvania Infantry* (Philadelphia: F. MacManus Jr., 1899); Thomas Hamilton Murray, *History of the Ninth Regiment, Connecticut Volunteer Infantry, "The Irish Regiment," in the War of the Rebellion, 1861–65: The Record of a Gallant Command on the March, in Battle and in Bivouac* (New Haven, Conn.: Price, Lee, and Adkins, 1903); William Corby, *Memoirs of Chaplain Life: Three Years Chaplain in the Famous Irish Brigade, "Army of the Potomac"* (Chicago: La Monte, O'Donnell, 1893); W. F. Lyons, *Brigadier-General Thomas Francis Meagher: His Political and Military Career* (New York: D. and J. Sadlier, 1870); Michael Cavanagh, *Memoirs of General Thomas Francis Meagher, Comprising the Leading Events of His Career* (Worcester, Mass.: Messenger Press, 1892).

12. From the account of Irish Brigade veteran Thomas McGrath, *San Francisco Chronicle,* 3 August 1913. When McGrath went to a veteran encampment in 1921, he was escorted across San Francisco Bay by the Knights of St. Patrick, an indication of the value they placed on his wartime service. See Damian Shiels "The Crashing Volleys and the Wild Irish 'Hurroos': An Irish Brigade Veteran Remembers Gettysburg, Fifty Years On," *Irish in the American Civil War* (2019), https://irishamericancivilwar.com/2019/02/16/the-crashing-of-the-volleys-and-the-wild-irish-hurroos-an-irish-brigade-veteran-remembers-gettysburg-fifty-years-on/ (accessed 28 June 2023). As Andrew Mach has demonstrated, between 1865 and 1925 Irish Catholics in particular made use of the American Civil War to "define and defend their understanding of the American nation." See Andrew Mach, "Claiming America: Irish-Catholic Memory and the Nation, 1865–1925" (PhD diss., University of Notre Dame, 2019), 186.

13. Lawrence Frederick Kohl, "The Harp and the Eagle: Irish-American Volunteers and the Union Army, 1861–1865 (Review)," *Civil War History* 54, no. 3 (2008): 314.

14. For a recognition of this deficit, see e.g. Ural, *The Harp and the Eagle,* xii, 3, 4; Ryan W. Keating, *Shades of Green: Irish Regiments, American Soldiers, and Local Communities in the Civil War Era* (New York: Fordham Univ. Press, 2017), 17.

15. For discussion of the Irish American press in the Civil War, see Cian T. McMahon, *The Global Dimension of Irish Identity: Race, Nation, and the Popular Press, 1840–1880* (Chapel Hill: Univ. of North Carolina Press, 2015), 111–144.

16. On the role of Ireland and Irish nationalism in the Irish American press, see Cian T.

McMahon, "Ireland and the Birth of the Irish-American Press, 1842–61," *American Periodicals: A Journal of History and Criticism* 19, no. 1 (2009): 5–20; William Leonard Joyce, *Editors and Ethnicity: A History of the Irish-American Press, 1848–1883* (New York: Arno Press, 1976), 74–100. For an analysis of the *Pilot* with a specific focus on its meanings with respect to Irish American identity, see Gamze Katı Gümüş, "'An Organ of the Irish Race on the Continent': The *Pilot,* Irish Immigration, and Irish-American Identity, 1851–66" (PhD diss., University of Kansas, 2018). Newspapers such as the *Pilot* and *Irish American* enjoyed a wide readership that extended well beyond their immediate catchment areas. Figures available for 1869 indicate in that year the *Pilot* had a circulation of 45,000 and the *Irish American Weekly* 35,000. See McMahon, *Global Dimension,* 155.

17. William L. Burton, *Melting Pot Soldiers: The Union's Ethnic Regiments* (New York: Fordham Univ. Press, 1998), 29, 152–154, 227, 233.

18. Ural, *The Harp and the Eagle,* 81, 134–135.

19. Christian G. Samito, *Becoming American Under Fire: Irish Americans, African Americans, and the Politics of Citizenship During the Civil War Era* (Ithaca, N.Y.: Cornell Univ. Press, 2009), 111–112, 119, 130, 133, 173.

20. The foundation of Keating's analysis was based on information compiled on 5,029 men from the 9th Connecticut Infantry, 17th Wisconsin Infantry, and 23rd Illinois Infantry. See Keating, *Shades of Green,* 16. In addition to Keating, Marion A. Truslow's 1994 PhD dissertation examined 280 pension files associated with the New York regiments of the Irish Brigade, while James Zibro's 2016 PhD dissertation also sought to take a bottom-up approach to the Irish, assessing 3,701 Irish soldiers using as a primary building block regimental descriptive books. See Marion A. Truslow, "Peasants into Patriots: The New York Irish Brigade Recruits and Their Families in the Civil War Era, 1850–1890" (PhD diss., New York University, 1994), xix–xx; also Marion A. Truslow, "The New York Irish Brigade Recruits and Their Families," in *Fighting Irish in the American Civil War and the Invasion of Mexico: Essays,* ed. Arthur H. Mitchell (Jefferson, N.C.: McFarland, 2017), 37–59; James Zibro, "The Life of Paddy Yank: The Common Irish-American Soldier in the Union Army" (PhD diss., Catholic University of America, 2016), 9–17, 233–243. For a further call to utilize service records in an effort to gain an insight into working-class Irish American soldiery, see Tyler Anbinder, "The Harp and the Eagle: Irish-American Volunteers and the Union Army, 1861–1865 (Review)," *Journal of Southern History* 75, no. 2 (2009): 164–165.

21. Keating, *Shades of Green,* 13, 15, 246n22, 157, 172–173.

22. Bateson, *Civil War Songs,* 20–21, 226–232. From a Confederate perspective, the leading examination of the Irish is Gleeson, *The Green and the Gray.* A comprehensive scholarly history of the Irish Brigade that takes their story beyond the Civil War is yet to be undertaken, but there are a number of useful studies. Perhaps the best military history of the Brigade currently available is Joseph G. Bilby, *Remember Fontenoy!: The 69th New York and the Irish Brigade in the Civil War* (Highstown, N.J.: Longstreet House, 1995). For a particularly fine example of an ethnic Irish regimental study, see James B. Swan, *Chicago's Irish Legion: The 90th Illinois Volunteers in the Civil War* (Carbondale: Southern Illinois Univ. Press, 2009). Thomas Francis Meagher continues to dominate works on individual Irish Americans from the conflict. Arguably the most useful is John M. Hearne and Rory T. Cornish, *Thomas Francis Meagher: The Making of an Irish American* (Dublin: Irish Academic Press, 2006). The standard for future studies of major Irish figures in northern service has now been set by Mark Dunkelman. See Mark H. Dunkelman, *Patrick Henry Jones: Irish American, Civil War General, and Gilded Age Politician* (Baton Rouge: Louisiana State Univ. Press, 2015).

23. The website was established in 2010 and now contains hundreds of referenced articles and resources exploring the Irish in the American Civil War. For some early discussions of issues such as ideological motivations, see e.g. Damian Shiels "Preserving the Union? The Irish and the Union War," *Irish in the American Civil War* (2011), https://irishamericancivilwar.com/2011/09/23/preserving-the-union-the-irish-and-the-union-war/ (accessed 11 July 2023); Damian Shiels "The Fight Was for the Union, Not for the Abolition of Slavery," *Irish in the American Civil War* (2013), https://irishamericancivilwar.com/2013/03/21/the-fight-was-for-the-union-not-for-the-abolition-of-slavery/ (accessed 11 July 2023). Since 2021 the website has been run in conjunction with Associate Editors Catherine Bateson and Brendan Hamilton.

24. Damian Shiels, *The Forgotten Irish: Irish Emigrant Experiences in America* (Dublin: The History Press Ireland, 2016).

25. The files form part of the Records of the Department of Veteran Affairs, Record Group 15. They are contained within the *Case Files of Approved Pension Applications of Widows and Other Dependents of the Army and Navy Who Served Mainly in the Civil War and the War with Spain, 1861–1934* and the *Case Files of Approved Pension Applications of Widows and Other Dependents of Navy Veterans, 1861–1910*. On the wider potential of this underutilized resource for the study of Irish America, see Damian Shiels, "Widows' and Dependent Parents' American Civil War Pension Files: A New Source for the Irish Emigrant Experience," in *The Famine Irish: Emigration and the Great Hunger*, ed. Ciarán Reilly (Dublin: The History Press Ireland, 2016), 85–97.

26. The letter identification and compilation phase of the project was primarily undertaken between 2010 and 2018. The digitized files were accessed via https://www.fold3.com/ (formerly called Footnote).

27. The 1,135 letters written by the 395 soldiers and sailors was designated the "Correspondents Only" Database. These letters when combined with the 297 other pieces of identified contemporaneous correspondence (within files linked to 173 additional Irish American men) were designated the "Full Corpus" Database, which captured the details of all 568 men who were associated with wartime correspondence in the files.

28. The methodological process of identifying Irish American correspondence among the digitized files was significantly complicated by the lack of any outward indicators of either a file's contents or the serviceman's ethnic affiliation. As a result, the primary determinant for investigating a file was based on surname analysis. The effectiveness of surname analysis as an approach for identifying nineteenth-century Irish immigrants has previously been demonstrated. See e.g. Malcolm Smith and Donald M. MacRaild "The Origins of the Irish in Northern England: An Isonymic Analysis of Data from the 1881 Census," *Immigrants and Minorities* 27, no. 2/3 (July/November 2009). When a file was deemed to be potentially Irish American, it was digitally "opened" to review the documents within and to determine if original correspondence was included. With army files this procedure was undertaken systematically by state, unit, and company; for navy files, alphabetically by surname. Where letters were located, an extensive analysis of the full pension file, available military and service records, published rosters, and census returns followed to confirm Irish American ethnicity. Once established, an individual was entered into the database.

29. Library of Congress, Statutes at Large, 37th Congress, vol. 12, chapter 166, "An Act to grant Pensions," https://www.loc.gov/law/help/statutes-at-large/37th-congress/session-2/c37s2ch166.pdf (accessed 29 October 2020).

30. William H. Glasson, *Federal Military Pensions in the United States* (New York: Oxford Univ. Press, American Branch, 1918), 125.

31. Keating, *Shades of Green,* 13, 15.

1. THE UNION IRISH ON THE EVE OF WAR

1. Affidavit of Mary Horgan, 28 December 1871, affidavit of Owen Sullivan, 3 May 1869, affidavit of John Duggan, 29 April 1869, affidavit of Cornelius Cunniff, 27 December 1877, affidavit of William Conlon, 1 January 1878, all in Navy WC2318.

2. Denis Horgan to "Dear grand mother and uncle," 21 March 1857, Navy WC2318.

3. Affidavit of Mary Horgan, 28 December 1871, affidavit of Owen Sullivan, 3 May 1869, affidavit of John Duggan, 29 April 1869, affidavit of Cornelius Cunniff, 27 December 1877, affidavit of William Conlon, 1 January 1878, all in Navy WC2318; Weekly Returns of Enlistments at Naval Rendezvous ("Enlistment Rendezvous"), January 6–August 8, 1891, NARA. Hereafter "Naval Rendezvous."

4. Kerby A. Miller, *Emigrants and Exiles: Ireland and the Irish Exodus to North America* (New York: Oxford Univ. Press, 1985), 193.

5. Miller, *Emigrants and Exiles,* 291.

6. Kerby A. Miller, "'Revenge for Skibbereen': Irish Emigration and the Meaning of the Great Famine," in *The Great Famine and the Irish Diaspora in America,* ed. Arthur Gribben (Amherst: Univ. of Massachusetts Press, 1999), 183. W. L. D. O'Grady, "88th Regiment Infantry," in New York Monuments Commission, *Final Report on the Battlefield of Gettysburg,* vol. 2 (New York: J. B. Lyon, 1902), 510–516. For a discussion of evidence for the Irish language in the Civil War, see Damian Shiels, "A Few Spoke Nothing But Gaelic: In Search of the Irish Language in the American Civil War," *Irish in the American Civil War* (2016), https://irishamericancivilwar.com/2016/04/03/a-few-spoke-nothing-but-gaelic-in-search-of-the-irish-language-in-the-american-civil-war/ (accessed 8 July 2023).

7. Miller, *Emigrants and Exiles,* 291.

8. David Noel Doyle, "The Remaking of Irish-America, 1845–80," in *A New History of Ireland VI: Ireland under the Union: 1870–1921,* ed. W. E. Vaughan (Oxford: Oxford Univ. Press, 2010), 730.

9. Miller, *Emigrants and Exiles,* 347.

10. Miller, *Emigrants and Exiles,* 347.

11. Miller, *Emigrants and Exiles,* 347.

12. Kevin Kenny, *The American Irish: A History* (London: Routledge, 2000), 48, 50, 99; Miller, *Emigrants and Exiles,* 195–201.

13. There were also around 50,000 "assisted emigrants" who crossed the Atlantic during this period. See Miller, "Revenge for Skibbereen," 182.

14. Kenny, *American Irish,* 99.

15. David Noel Doyle, "The Irish as Urban Pioneers in the United States, 1850–1870," *Journal of American Ethnic History* 10, no. 1/2 (1990): 36–59.

16. Doyle's precise figure is 705,218 (43.77 percent of Irish-born in 1860) who lived in one of the forty-three largest cities. See Doyle, "The Irish as Urban Pioneers," 41–42, 48.

17. Paul A. Gilje, "The Development of an Irish American Community in New York City

before the Great Migration," in *The New York Irish,* ed. Ronald H. Bayor and Timothy J. Meagher (Baltimore: John Hopkins Univ. Press, 1996), 75–76.

18. Joseph Camp Griffith Kennedy, *Population of the United States in 1860; Compiled from the Original Returns of the Eighth Census, under the Direction of the Secretary of the Interior* (Washington, D.C.: Government Printing Office, 1864), xxxi–xxxii.

19. The cities with the largest 1860 Irish-born populations were New York with 203,740; Philadelphia with 95,548; Brooklyn with 56,710; Boston with 45,991, and St. Louis with 29,926. See table 1.

20. Hasia R. Diner, "'The Most Irish City in the Union': The Era of the Great Migration, 1844–1877," in *The New York Irish,* ed. Ronald H. Bayor and Timothy J. Meagher (Baltimore: John Hopkins Univ. Press, 1996), 92.

21. Dennis Clark, *Hibernia America: The Irish and Regional Cultures* (New York: Greenwood Press, 1986), 119.

22. Doyle, "Irish as Urban Pioneers," 48.

23. In the mid-1850s, up to 90 percent of Irish-born women could expect to wed an Irish spouse. See Doyle, "The Remaking of Irish-America," 756.

24. Laurence A. Glasco, "The Life Cycles and Household Structure of American Ethnic Groups: Irish, Germans, and Native-Born Whites in Buffalo, New York, 1855," *Journal of Urban History* 1, no. 3 (1975): 348; Kevin Kenny, *Making Sense of the Molly Maguires* (New York: Oxford Univ. Press, 1998), 54–55.

25. Tyler Anbinder and Hope McCaffrey, "Which Irish Men and Women Immigrated to the United States During the Great Famine Migration of 1846–54?" *Irish Historical Studies* 39, no. 156 (2015): 632.

26. Tyler Anbinder, *Five Points: The 19th-Century New York City Neighborhood That Invented Tap Dance, Stole Elections, and Became the World's Most Notorious Slum* (New York: Free Press, 2001), 98. For a discussion of why many of these county- and region-based enclaves may not have left a greater mark on the historical record, see John T. Ridge, "Irish County Colonies in New York City, Part 2," *New York Irish History* 26 (2012): 47–55.

27. Ridge, "Irish County Colonies in New York City, Part 1" *New York Irish History* 25 (2011): 58.

28. Doyle, "The Remaking of Irish-America," 726.

29. These are the nineteenth-century monetary values. Kerby A. Miller, "Emigration to North America in the Era of the Great Famine, 1845–55," in *Atlas of the Great Irish Famine,* ed. John Crowley, William J. Smyth, and Mike Murphy (Cork: Cork Univ. Press, 2012), 215; Arnold Schrier, *Ireland and the American Emigration, 1850–1900* (Chester Springs, Pa.: Defour Editions, 1997), 167. Miller calculated his £1.2 million average based on Schrier's yearly totals. Schrier computed the 1850s pound to dollar ratio at £1 to $5.

30. Anbinder, *Five Points,* 91–97; Dennis Clark, *The Irish in Philadelphia: Ten Generations of Urban Experience* (Philadelphia: Temple Univ. Press, 1973), 41; Oscar Handlin, *Boston's Immigrants: A Study in Acculturation* (Cambridge, Mass.: Belknap Press of Harvard Univ. Press, 1979), 94.

31. Cormac Ó Gráda, "The New York Irish in the 1850s: Locked in by Poverty?," *New York Irish History* 19 (2005): 10; Alan M. Kraut, "Illness and Medical Care Among Irish Immigrants in Antebellum New York," in *The New York Irish,* ed. Ronald H. Bayor and Timothy J. Meagher (Baltimore: John Hopkins Univ. Press, 1996), 158–159; Doyle, "The Remaking of Irish-America," 747; Clark, *Irish in Philadelphia,* 49.

32. Glasco, "Life Cycles," 345–347.

33. For analysis of Irish upward (and downward) mobility in comparison to other contemporary immigrant groups, see Joseph P. Ferrie, "The Entry into the U.S. Labor Market of Antebellum European Immigrants, 1840–1860," *Explorations in Economic History* 34, no. 3 (1997): 295–330; Joseph P. Ferrie, *Yankeys Now: Immigrants in the Antebellum United States, 1840–1860* (New York: Oxford Univ. Press, 1999), 87–92.

34. Doyle, "The Remaking of Irish-America," 753.

35. Handlin, *Boston's Immigrants,* 57, table XV.

36. Clark, *Irish in Philadelphia,* 76.

37. This was demonstrated in Glasco's analysis of 1855 populations in Buffalo. See Doyle, "The Remaking of Irish-America," 756.

38. Analysis of the Irish in Buffalo in 1855 found that Irish boys tended to start work at seventeen, a year later than native-born boys, but that a third of Irish men still listed occupations into their seventies, compared with 14 percent of native-born men. Glasco, "Life Cycles," 348. The widows' and dependents' pension files suggest that seventeen was late, and that at least part-time employment from the early teens onward was commonplace.

39. For the figures from the Panic of 1857, see Joseph Glatthaar, "A Tale of Two Armies: The Confederate Army of Northern Virginia and the Union Army of the Potomac and Their Cultures," *Journal of the Civil War Era* 6, no. 3 (2016): 330.

40. Kenny, *American Irish,* 113.

41. For some of the latest work on how the Catholic faith interacted with Irish identity, see Sophie Cooper, *Forging Identities in the Irish World: Melbourne and Chicago, c. 1830–1922* (Edinburgh: Edinburgh Univ. Press, 2022).

42. Doyle, "The Remaking of Irish-America," 725–726.

43. Larkin, "Devotional Revolution," 644–645, 649.

44. For the most comprehensive analysis of the Catholic Church during the American Civil War, see William B. Kurtz, *Excommunicated from the Union: How the Civil War Created a Separate Catholic America* (New York: Oxford Univ. Press, 2015).

45. For a discussion of how native-born white Americans viewed the Irish in the antebellum United States, see Dale T. Knobel, *Paddy and the Republic: Ethnicity and Nationality in Antebellum America* (Middletown, Conn.: Wesleyan Univ. Press, 1986).

46. Kenny, *American Irish,* 115.

47. Tyler Anbinder, *Nativism and Slavery: The Northern Know Nothings and the Politics of the 1850s* (New York: Oxford Univ. Press, 1992), xiii–xiv.

48. Anbinder, *Nativism and Slavery,* ix.

49. On the movement of nativist support to the Republicans, see e.g. Eric Foner, *Free Soil, Free Labor, Free Men: The Ideology of the Republican Party before the Civil War* (New York: Oxford Univ. Press, 1970), 258; Anbinder, *Nativism and Slavery,* xii.

50. As David Noel Doyle points out, Irish Catholic efforts to create denominational schools in antebellum New York City was one factor "in drawing them [the Irish] to the Democrats. Whigs, and later Republicans, tended to be more sympathetic to the popular feeling that believed a broadly evangelical curriculum to be American without being a formal establishment of religion." See David Noel Doyle, "The Irish in North America, 1776–1845," in *Making the Irish American: History*

and Heritage of the Irish in the United States, ed. J. J. Lee and Marion R. Casey (New York: New York Univ. Press, 2006), 199. In his analysis of why Irish Americans were drawn to the Democratic Party, Kevin Kenny has noted that the "Whig party was closely associated with Protestantism and nativism" and how "Irish opposition to reform movements, especially abolitionism, found a natural home in the Democratic Party." See Kenny, *American Irish,* 82–83.

51. Amy Bridges, *A City in the Republic: Antebellum New York and the Origins of Machine Politics* (New York: Cambridge Univ. Press, 2008), 99–101.

52. Though some Irish had advanced in the Democratic leadership of organizations like Tammany Hall by the outbreak of the war, for the most part their heyday was still to come, and the majority of Irish served as "foot soldiers." See Timothy J. Meagher, *The Columbia Guide to Irish American History,* Columbia Guides to American History and Cultures (New York: Columbia Univ. Press, 2005), 88–89; Tyler Anbinder, "'We Will Dirk Every Mother's Son of You': Five Points and the Irish Conquest of New York Politics," in *New Directions in Irish-American History,* ed. Kevin Kenny (Madison: Univ. of Wisconsin Press, 2003), 106–108. For a discussion of the history of Tammany Hall, see Terry Golway, *Machine Made: Tammany Hall and the Creation of Modern American Politics* (New York: Liveright Publishing, 2014).

53. Diner, "'The Most Irish City in the Union,'" 101–102.

54. Noel Ignatiev, *How the Irish Became White* (New York: Routledge, 1995), 2–3.

55. For some scholarship that critically examines Ignatiev's argument, see e.g. Patrick R. O'Malley, "Irish Whiteness and the Nineteenth-Century Construction of Race," *Victorian Literature and Culture* 51, no. 2 (2023): 167–198; Shahmima Akhtar, "Learning 'The Customs of Their Fathers': Irish Villages in Chicago's Columbian Exposition, 1893," *Journal of Victorian Culture* 20, no. 20 (2023): 1–25; Eric Arneson, "Whiteness and the Historians' Imagination," *International Labor and Working-Class History* 60 (2001): 3–32.

56. See David R. Roediger, *The Wages of Whiteness: Race and the Making of the American Working Class,* rev. ed. (London: Verso, 2007), 133–163.

57. For a discussion of the history behind the anti-abolitionism of many Irish American nationalist leaders and their influence on ordinary Irish people, see Ian Delahanty, "The Transatlantic Roots of Irish American Anti-Abolitionism, 1843–1859," *Journal of the Civil War Era* 6, no. 2 (2016): 164–192. On Irish attitudes toward abolitionism both at home and abroad, see David T. Gleeson, "Failing to 'Unite with Abolitionists': The Irish Nationalist Press and U.S. Emancipation," *Slavery and Abolition* 37, no. 3 (2016): 622–637. For the perspective and history of the abolitionist movement, see e.g. Manisha Sinha, *The Slave's Cause: A History of Abolition* (New Haven, Conn.: Yale Univ. Press, 2016).

58. Kenny, *American Irish,* 119.

59. Ural, *The Harp and the Eagle,* 43.

60. Graham Hodges, "'Desirable Companions and Lovers': Irish and African Americans in the Sixth Ward, 1830–1870," in *The New York Irish,* ed. Ronald H. Bayor and Timothy J. Meagher (Baltimore: John Hopkins Univ. Press, 1996),108. This could work both ways. It was the Irish who had initially supplanted the traditional labor opportunities of African Americans in New York City as the former's numbers increased. See Kenny, *American Irish,* 62–63.

61. For a discussion, see Bateson, *Civil War Songs,* 14–15.

62. See Patrick Fitzgerald, "Mapping the Ulster Diaspora: 1607–1960," *Familia* 22 (2006): 16.

63. "Second generation" in this context meaning the foreign-born children of Irish parents. The need to adopt a multigenerational approach to the Irish in the Civil War has been highlighted by scholars such as Catherine Bateson. See e.g. Bateson, *Civil War Songs,* 14.

64. An example can be seen in James McPherson's analysis as part of the seminal *Battle Cry of Freedom,* where he uses the U.S. Sanitary Commission nativity-based figure to argue for underrepresentation of Irish Americans in service, but in *For Cause and Comrades* uses the letters of Canadian-born Peter Welsh in order to discuss the Irish American experience—a soldier not counted as "Irish" in the Sanitary Commission's analysis. See James M. McPherson, *Battle Cry of Freedom: The Civil War Era* (New York: Oxford Univ. Press, 1988), 606; James M. McPherson, *For Cause and Comrades: Why Men Fought in the Civil War* (New York: Oxford Univ. Press, 1997), 113. Welsh is frequently described as "Irish" and "Irish-born" in Civil War historiography despite his Canadian nativity. Among the other non-Irish-born men who are regularly utilized to describe the ethnic Irish experience are James Mulligan of the 23rd Illinois and Thomas Cahill of the 9th Connecticut, both of whom were born in America. See for example Keating, *Shades of Green,* 41, 178; Burton, *Melting Pot Soldiers,* 53.

65. The precise figure recorded for Irish-born in 1860 was 1,611,304. Kennedy, *Population of the United States in 1860,* xxviii.

66. Much work remains to be done on long-term Irish step-migration from Britain to the United States in this period. One example is the analysis of Irish movement through South Wales en route to America. See David Morris, "'Gone to Work to America': Irish Step-Migration through South Wales in the 1860s and 1870s," *Immigrants and Minorities* 34, no. 3 (2016): 297–313.

67. Graham Davis, "The Irish in Britain, 1815–1939," in *The Irish Diaspora,* ed. Andy Bielenberg (Essex: Longman, 2000), 20.

68. Richard B. McCready, "Revising the Irish in Scotland: The Irish in Nineteenth- and Early Twentieth-Century Scotland," in *The Irish Diaspora,* ed. Andy Bielenberg (Essex: Longman, 2000), 39.

69. The 1860 Federal census records 431,692 people as born in England, 108,518 born in Scotland, and 45,763 as born in Wales. See Kennedy, *Population of the United States in 1860,* xxviii.

70. See e.g. Damian Shiels, "The Forgotten County: Exploring the American Civil War Service of Britain's Irish Communities," *Irish in the American Civil War* (2015), https://irishamericancivilwar.com/2015/09/03/the-forgotten-county-exploring-the-american-civil-war-service-of-britains-irish-communities/ (accessed 12 December 2019).

71. Figures derived from Kennedy, *Population of the United States in 1860,* xxviii.

72. Donald H. Akenson, "Irish Migration to North America, 1800–1920," in *The Irish Diaspora,* ed. Andy Bielenberg (Essex: Longman, 2000), 125–126.

73. Doyle, "The Irish as Urban Pioneers," 41–42. As Doyle notes, if true this would increase the 1860 Irish population in the leading forty-three U.S. cities from 705,218 Irish-born to an ethnic Irish total of 1,057,827.

2. IN SEARCH OF THE IRISH AMERICAN SERVICEMAN, 1861–1865

1. *New York Irish American,* 10 December 1859.

2. Damian Shiels, *The Irish in the American Civil War* (Dublin: The History Press Ireland, 2013), 27–29.

3. Shiels, *Irish in the American Civil War,* 34–35.

4. *Cork Examiner,* 31 May 1861.

5. National Park Service, "Fort Sumter's Garrison by Nationality," https://www.nps.gov/fosu/learn/historyculture/upload/FOSU-Garrison-by-Nationality.pdf (accessed 19 September 2012). These are figures for the military detachment only. They do not include civilian workers and servants who were present at Fort Sumter.

6. Mark W. Johnson, "'Where Are the Regulars?' An Analysis of Regular Army Recruiting and Enlistees, 1851–1865" (PhD diss., State University of New York at Albany, 2012), 150, 295.

7. Johnson, "Where Are the Regulars?" 39–41, 207.

8. The Irish-born constituted some 32.2 percent of the total number in the British Army at that date. See Edward M. Spiers, "Army Organisation and Society in the Nineteenth Century," in *A Military History of Ireland,* ed. Thomas Bartlett and Keith Jeffery (Cambridge: Cambridge Univ. Press, 1996), 335–336.

9. Spiers, "Army Organisation," 337.

10. Johnson, "Where Are the Regulars?" 2, 150, 295, 306.

11. For detailed analysis, see Damian Shiels, "More Irish than the Irish: The Forgotten Irishmen of Gettysburg's Wheatfield," *Irish in the American Civil War* (2018), https://irishamericancivilwar.com/2018/04/02/more-irish-than-the-irish-the-forgotten-irishmen-of-gettysburgs-wheatfield (accessed 2 April 2018). Irish American casualties were also high in Colonel Hannibal Day's 1st Brigade of regulars.

12. The most prominent among them was Dubliner Stephen Rowan, commander of the USS *Pawnee* during the Fort Sumter operation. For more on Rowan, see S. C. Ayres, *Sketch of the Life and Services of Vice Admiral Stephen C. Rowan, U.S. Navy, Read before the Ohio Commandery of the Loyal Legion, April 6, 1910* (Ohio: Ohio Commandery of the Loyal Legion, 1910).

13. Michael J. Bennett, *Union Jacks: Yankee Sailors in the Civil War* (Chapel Hill: Univ. of North Carolina Press, 2004), 5, 9.

14. Bennett, *Union Jacks,* 8–9.

15. Bennett, *Union Jacks,* 15–17.

16. Bennett, *Union Jacks,* 17–19.

17. The histories of the 69th New York State Militia and 69th New York National Guard Artillery are often confused with that of the 69th New York Volunteer Infantry, which was a separate unit. Recent research suggests that relatively few of the 69th New York State Militia chose to enter three years of service with the 69th New York Volunteers of Irish Brigade fame. See Christopher M. Garcia, "The Forgotten Sixty-Ninth: The Sixty-Ninth New York National Guard Artillery Regiment in the American Civil War" (Master's thesis, Old Dominion University, 2012).

18. Christian G. Samito, "Introduction," in Daniel George MacNamara, *The History of the Ninth Regiment Massachusetts Volunteer Infantry,* ed. Christian G. Samito (1899; reprint, New York: Fordham Univ. Press, 2000), xv–xvi.

19. Don Ernsberger, *At the Wall: The 69th Pennsylvania "Irish Volunteers" at Gettysburg* (Bloomington, Ind.: Xlibris, 2006), 11–12; McDermott, *A Brief History of the 69th Regiment Pennsylvania Veteran Volunteers,* 5–6. The titles selected by the companies honored the names of significant Irish American leaders, in this case former Young Irelander Thomas Francis Meagher from Co. Waterford, who would go on to form the Irish Brigade, James Shields, a Mexican War hero and Illinois politician from Co. Tyrone who would serve as a general during the Civil War, and United Irish-

man Robert Emmet, who had been executed in Dublin for launching a rising against the British administration in 1803.

20. However, it should be noted that record sets such as the widows' and dependents' pension files and the compiled military service records do not seem to reflect this supposed underrepresentation, as both give the impression of large-scale Irish American service from Massachusetts. Massachusetts is also the only major outlier when comparing the relative percentages of identified correspondents with the Sanitary Commission figures. While 16.71 percent of the letter group were from men in Massachusetts service, only 6.94 percent of the Irish-born in the commission's report were credited to there.

21. For discussion of the contemporary focus on the Irish Brigade as evidenced through the music being produced, see e.g. Bateson, *Civil War Songs,* 15–17.

22. David Power Conyngham, *The Irish Brigade and Its Campaigns,* reprint, ed. Lawrence Frederick Kohl (New York: Fordham Univ. Press, 1994), 50.

23. The 29th Massachusetts Infantry, a non-Irish unit, was also briefly brigaded with the New York regiments, and fought with them at Antietam.

24. Lawrence Frederick Kohl, "Introduction," in David Power Conyngham, *The Irish Brigade and Its Campaigns,* reprint, ed. Lawrence Frederick Kohl (New York: Fordham Univ. Press, 1994), x.

25. For discussion, see e.g. Ural, *The Harp and the Eagle,* 81–82.

26. Ural, *The Harp and the Eagle,* 134.

27. For the importance of Fredericksburg in Irish memory of the war, see Craig A. Warren, "'Oh, God, What a Pity!': The Irish Brigade at Fredericksburg and the Creation of Myth," *Civil War History* 47, no. 3 (2001): 193–221.

28. For the most detailed discussion of the Legion, see Garcia, "The Forgotten Sixty-Ninth." The relative "forgetting" of Michael Corcoran in Irish American memory of the war as compared with Thomas Francis Meagher is discussed in Bateson, *Civil War Songs,* 222–224.

29. Dunkelman, *Patrick Henry Jones,* 22–29.

30. Ryan Keating's work on the 9th Connecticut, 17th Wisconsin, and 23rd Illinois in particular has served to highlight this. See Keating, *Shades of Green.*

31. David W. Judd, *The Story of the Thirty-Third N.Y.S. Vols, or Two Years Campaigning in Virginia and Maryland* (Rochester, N.Y.: Benton and Andrews, 1864), 28–29.

32. Ralph Orson Sturtevant, *Pictorial History Thirteenth Regiment Vermont Volunteers: War of 1861–1865* (N.p.: n.p, 1910), 425.

33. Richard F. Miller, *Harvard's Civil War: A History of the Twentieth Massachusetts Volunteer Infantry* (Hanover, N.H.: Univ. Press of New England, 2005), 22.

34. For a history of the 42nd New York, see Fred C. Wexler, *The Tammany Regiment: A History of the Forty-Second New York Volunteer Infantry, 1861–1864* (Bloomington, Ind.: iUniverse, 2016). For a discussion of the service of New York's firemen in the Civil War, see Augustine E. Costello, *Our Firemen: A History of the New York Fire Departments, Volunteer and Paid* (1887; reprint, New York: Knickerbocker Press, 1997), 717–736.

35. Reverend Frederic Denison, *Shot and Shell: The Third Rhode Island Heavy Artillery Regiment in the Rebellion, 1861–1865* (Providence, R.I.: J. A. and R. A. Reid, 1879), 25, 27.

36. Orson Blair Curtis, *History of the Twenty-Fourth Michigan of the Iron Brigade, Known as the Detroit and Wayne County Regiment* (Detroit, Mich.: Winn and Hammond, 1891), 34, 42, 331–333. The lieutenant colonel of the 24th Michigan was Mark Flanigan, from Co. Antrim.

37. Fred C. Floyd, *History of the Fortieth (Mozart) Regiment New York Volunteers* (Boston: F. H. Gilson Company, 1909), 35. Many of the Massachusetts Irishmen in the 40th New York were Fenians. See Patrick Steward and Bryan P. McGovern, *The Fenians: Irish Rebellion in the North Atlantic World, 1858–1876* (Knoxville: Univ. of Tennessee Press, 2013), 32.

38. Though beyond the scope of this book, there is a need for a broad-range analysis of northern regiments at a company level to determine the nature and extent of "Irish" companies in nonethnic units, which would add to the discussion on Irish ethnic cohesiveness in the Federal military.

39. William Carroll to "dear parants," 6[?] December 1861, Navy WC2901.

40. The historiographical pattern of concentrating analysis on early war volunteers is something that has also been noted in the study of Confederate servicemen. See Kenneth W. Noe, *Reluctant Rebels: The Confederates Who Joined the Army after 1861* (Chapel Hill: Univ. of North Carolina Press, 2010), 7.

41. Eugene C. Murdock, *One Million Men: The Civil War Draft in the North* (Madison: State Historical Society of Wisconsin, 1971), 6; Eugene C. Murdock, *Patriotism Limited, 1862–1865: The Civil War Draft and the Bounty System* (Kent, Ohio: Kent State Univ. Press, 1967), 6–7.

42. Murdock, *Patriotism Limited,* 7–10.

43. Murdock, *One Million Men,* 6–7. For the best study of the murky and fraudulent world of substitute broking, see Brian P. Luskey, *Men Is Cheap: Exposing the Frauds of Free Labor in Civil War America* (Chapel Hill: Univ. of North Carolina Press, 2020).

44. These were summer 1863, spring 1864, fall 1864, and spring 1865. See Murdock, *Patriotism Limited,* 13.

45. *Harper's Weekly,* 23 August 1862.

46. For an analysis of the New York City draft riots, see Iver Bernstein, *The New York City Draft Riots: Their Significance for American Society and Politics in the Age of the Civil War* (New York: Oxford Univ. Press, 1991). For Irish opposition in Pennsylvania's anthracite coal region, see Kenny, *Making Sense of the Molly Maguires,* 86–96. On the impact that the riots had on perceptions of Irish Americans, see e.g. Ural, *The Harp and the Eagle,* 188–189; Samito, *Becoming American,* 132.

47. The Irish in the South employed similar tactics to escape Confederate conscription. See Gleeson, *The Green and the Gray,* 60–62.

48. Tyler Anbinder, "Which Poor Man's Fight? Immigrants and the Federal Conscription of 1863," *Civil War History* 52, no. 4 (2006): 346.

49. Murdock, *One Million Men,* 356.

50. Murdock, *One Million Men,* 356.

51. On the 1863 loss of support, see e.g. Ural, *The Harp and the Eagle,* 4; Kohl, "Introduction," in Conyngham, *Irish Brigade,* xvi. For an assessment that sees continued support for the war among Irish American communities outside the large eastern cities, see Keating, *Shades of Green,* 95, 111, 133, 177.

52. Anbinder, "Which Poor Man's Fight?," 369. Among the records that Anbinder analyzed, he found that about half of the soldiers who were recruited as a result of the 1863 draft were immigrants, the vast majority having enlisted as substitutes. Anbinder, "Which Poor Man's Fight?," 372.

53. Thomas R. Kemp, "Community and War: The Civil War Experience of Two New Hampshire Towns," in *Toward a Social History of the American Civil War: Exploratory Essays,* ed. Maris A. Vinovskis (Cambridge: Cambridge Univ. Press, 1990), 67–68.

54. *New York Herald,* 5 June 1864.

55. For figures, see Miller, *Emigrants and Exiles,* 347.

56. Miller, *Emigrants and Exiles,* 347. For a discussion of the appeals to American consuls in Ireland and consular activities during the war, see Bernadette Whelan, *American Government in Ireland, 1790–1913: A History of the US Consular Service* (Manchester: Manchester Univ. Press, 2010), 105–156.

57. Murdock, *One Million Men,* 226.

58. OR, series 3, vol. 5, 668–669. For more on public attitudes toward the war, and differing perceptions on whether natives or immigrants were more likely to jump, see Michael Thomas Smith, "The Most Desperate Scoundrels Unhung: Bounty Jumpers and Recruitment Fraud in the Civil War North," *American Nineteenth Century History* 6, no. 2 (June 2003): 149–172.

59. See e.g. McPherson, *For Cause and Comrades,* ix.

60. For these figures, see J. Matthew Gallman, *Defining Duty in the Civil War: Personal Choice, Popular Culture, and the Union Home Front* (Chapel Hill: Univ. of North Carolina Press, 2015), 7–8.

61. For the use of this figure, see for example Shiels, *The Irish in the American Civil War,* 7; Ural, *The Harp and the Eagle,* 2; Keating, *Shades of Green,* 26.

62. See e.g. McPherson, *Battle Cry of Freedom,* 606; J. Matthew Gallman, *The North Fights the Civil War: The Home Front* (Chicago: Ivan R. Dee, 1994), 67. McPherson's assessment appears to be based on the volunteer figures devised for the U.S. Sanitary Commission. Gallman argues that immigrants made up 30 percent of the northern military-age population but composed only about a quarter of the men in the northern armies. This leads him to seek to ascertain why this apparent underrepresentation existed. McPherson's *Battle Cry of Freedom* has been particularly influential as a reference point for historians discussing immigrants in the Union military and is frequently cited as the source for statements regarding underrepresentation. For an example, see Paul A. Cimbala, *Soldiers North and South: The Everyday Experiences of the Men Who Fought America's Civil War* (New York: Fordham Univ. Press, 2010), 65.

63. Benjamin Apthorp Gould, *Investigations in the Military and Anthropological Statistics of American Soldiers* (New York: Hurd and Houghton for the U.S. Sanitary Commission, 1869), 27.

64. William F. Fox, *Regimental Losses in the American Civil War 1861–1865* (Albany: Albany Publishing Company, 1889), 62; Gould, *Investigations in the Military and Anthropological Statistics of American Soldiers,* 27.

65. Gould's precise phraseology was as follows: "We thus arrive at the following table of nativities for the volunteers from the several States, the colored troops being, of course, omitted, as also the navy, and the 92 000 volunteers from States and Territories not here considered. The word 'volunteers' is here used in the official signification, as denoting the citizen soldiery in distinction from regular soldiers, and not, as in a subsequent chapter, in distinction from recruits." Gould, *Investigations in the Military and Anthropological Statistics of American Soldiers,* 26.

66. The Irish-born population across the twenty-one states and Washington, D.C., was enumerated at 1,487,058 in 1860, with the total population across the same regions being 20,893,479. Of the 1,994,900 white volunteers, 143,671 were estimated to be Irish-born.

67. Ó Gráda, "The New York Irish in the 1850s: Locked in by Poverty?," 9. His analysis is based on the Integrated Public Use Microdata Series (IPUMS), made up of high-precision samples of the Federal census.

68. Don H. Doyle, *The Cause of All Nations: An International History of the American Civil War* (New York: Basic Books, 2015), 173.

69. Impacting this figure in relation to the widows' and dependents' files is the fact that the earlier a man enlisted and the longer he served, the greater his chances of dying.

70. Ultimately 91,816 men were furnished in answer to this call. See Frederick Phisterer, *Statistical Record of the Armies of the United States* (New York: Charles Scribner's Sons, 1883), 3. A proportion of the subsequent three-year Irish American enlistees in 1861 would have also been among the number who had given three months of service at the commencement of the war.

71. McPherson, *Battle Cry of Freedom,* 322.

72. Phisterer, *Statistical Record,* 4; OR, series 3, vol. 4, 1264. A total of 657,868 men who answered this call enlisted for three-year terms, and 30,950 for two years.

73. Phisterer, *Statistical Record,* 62.

74. Richard F. Miller, ed., *States at War,* vol. 4, *A Reference Guide for Delaware, Maryland, and New Jersey in the Civil War* (Hanover, N.H.: Univ. Press of New England, 2015), 113–115; McPherson, *Battle Cry of Freedom,* 491.

75. Phisterer, *Statistical Record,* 4–5; OR, series 3, vol. 4, 1265.

76. Phisterer, *Statistical Record,* 62.

77. Employment information was gathered from a range of sources, including pension files, census returns, compiled military service records, enlistment records, muster rolls, and regimental descriptive books. The percentages are based on the men for whom employment could be identified; it was not established for 93 of the 568 men in the full corpus, and for 58 of the 395 correspondents.

78. Research indicates that officers and their families received more money, more easily, than those associated with the enlisted ranks. See Russell L. Johnson, "'Great Injustice': Social Status and the Distribution of Military Pensions after the Civil War," *Journal of the Gilded Age and Progressive Era* 10, no. 2 (2011): 137–160.

79. CMSR of James Briody, Company I, 20th Massachusetts Infantry, NARA.

80. Affidavit of Mary Jane Briody and Maggie Briody, 6 March 1863, affidavit of Margaret Briody, 24 October 1863, both in WC9732.

81. CWMRA of James McGee, 132nd New York Infantry, NYSA; affidavit of Owen McGinn and Jane Satchwell, 24 June 1864, WC96027.

82. CMSR of Patrick Kelly, Company K, 28th Massachusetts Infantry, NARA; Massachusetts Adjutant General, *Massachusetts Soldiers, Sailors, and Marines in the Civil War,* vol. 3 (Norwood, Mass.: Norwood Press, 1932), 242.

83. Affidavit of Patrick Byrne and Morris Fitzgibbon, 15 February 1864, WC22521.

84. See Breandán Mac Suibhne, *The End of Outrage: Post-Famine Adjustment in Rural Ireland* (Oxford: Oxford Univ. Press, 2017), 216.

85. Illinois, Databases of Illinois Veterans Index, 1775–1995, Ancestry.com; WC100612, relating to Barnard Carr, Company C, 79th Illinois Infantry; 1860 U.S. Census, West Liberty, Salem, Champaign, Ohio, NARA; affidavit of Michael McCormick, 16 December 1869, WC143339; 1860 U.S. Census, Township 15 N Range 8 E, Douglas, Illinois, NARA; WC56115, relating to John Fitzpatrick, Company E, 19th Illinois Infantry; CWMRA of Richard Flynn, 117th New York Infantry, NYSA; 1860 U.S. Census, Kirkland, Oneida, New York, NARA; WC91465, relating to Richard Flynn, Company K, 117th New York Infantry.

86. 1860 U.S. Census, Bangor Ward 6, Penobscot, Maine, NARA; WC101875, relating to John Crowley, Company C, 3rd New Hampshire Infantry.

87. 1860 U.S. Census, Troy Ward 8, Rensselaer, New York, NARA; WC97970, relating to John Hennessey (alias John Quinn), Company H, 7th New York Heavy Artillery; CWMRA of John Hennessey, 7th New York Heavy Artillery, NYSA.

88. 1860 U.S. Census, Milton, Norfolk, Massachusetts, NARA; CMSR of Patrick Dunican, Company G, 32nd Massachusetts Infantry, NARA.

89. WC85252, relating to Mathew McCourt, Company A, 1st Michigan Infantry; 1860 U.S. Census, Ann Arbor Ward 3, Washtenaw, Michigan, NARA.

90. For comparison, Benjamin Apthorp Gould for the Sanitary Commission (USSC) credits 35.50 percent of the Irish volunteers to New York, compared to 40.51 percent in the correspondent sample (CS). The relative figures for other major states are as follows: Pennsylvania—USSC: 12.08 percent, CS: 16.46 percent; Massachusetts—USSC: 6.94 percent, CS:16.71 percent; Illinois—USSC: 8.35 percent, CS: 5.32 percent; Connecticut and Rhode Island—USSC: 5.31 percent, CS: 4.56 percent; Ohio—USSC: 5.64 percent, CS: 2.53 percent; New Jersey—USSC: 6.16 percent, CS: 2.03 percent. It is of note that the representation of Massachusetts among the letter writers is far closer to their proportion of the Irish American population than the Sanitary Commission estimates of Irish volunteer service from that state.

91. Only 219 U.S. military pensions are recorded as being claimed in Ireland in 1883, despite the scale of Irish service. See U.S. Senate, *List of Pensioners on the Roll, January 1, 1883,* vol. 5 (Washington, D.C.: Government Printing Office, 1883), 638–640; Damian Shiels, "The Long Arm of War: Exploring the 19th-Century Ulster Emigrant Experience through American Civil War Pension Files," in *Irish Hunger and Migration: Myth, Memory and Memorialization,* ed. Patrick Fitzgerald, Christine Kinealy, and Gerard Moran (West Haven, Conn.: Quinnipiac Univ. Press, 2015), 146.

92. The prevalence of Massachusetts correspondents is again noteworthy, particularly when compared to Pennsylvania, and given the low volunteer figures credited to the state by the Sanitary Commission.

93. WC100612, relating to Bernard Carr, Company C, 79th Illinois Infantry; WC143339, relating to Michael Daly, Company A, 7th Illinois Infantry; WC23216, relating to James C. Fitzgerald, Company F, 8th Illinois Infantry; WC56115, relating to John Fitzpatrick, Company E, 19th Illinois Infantry; WC54548, relating to John Lynch, Company A, 10th Illinois Infantry.

94. The men were distributed across units from twenty-one states and the District of Columbia. The total number of formations the men served in was greatly in excess of 270. Although 274 different units were represented by the files, the majority of naval personnel served on multiple naval vessels during their enlistment, and a number of those in the army spent time in different regiments.

95. Again, if these nativity proportions held true for Irish American Union service as a whole, it would indicate that between 240,000 and 250,000 Irish Americans served the North during the American Civil War.

96. Analysis of Irish immigration to New York between 1846 and 1854 indicates those from Cork were the most numerous. See Anbinder and McCaffrey, "Which Irish Men and Women Immigrated," 627.

97. Munster's dominance is in line with the position of that province as the greatest source of Irish American immigrants during this period. For a discussion, see e.g. Doyle, "The Remaking of Irish-America," 734–736.

98. Many of these Connacht immigrants originated in Galway, Ireland's second most populous

county in 1841. See Anbinder and McCaffrey, "Which Irish Men and Women Immigrated," 627. The relatively low number of men for whom provincial nativity could be established adds a note of caution to these figures.

99. Gould, *Investigations in the Military and Anthropological Statistics of American Soldiers,* 15.

100. WC92361, relating to William Carroll, Company I, 7th Connecticut Infantry. William was recorded as thirteen years old in the 1860 census. See 1860 U.S. Census, Middletown, Middlesex, Connecticut, NARA.

101. WC98996, relating to Felix Mooney, Company O, 61st New York Infantry; CWMRA of Felix Mooney, 61st New York Infantry, NYSA.

102. Gould, *Investigations in the Military and Anthropological Statistics of American Soldiers,* 35. The median age for white Union volunteers was 23.477. The average age of Irish American correspondents is based on the 336 for whom age data was identified.

103. Marriage information was retrieved for all 395 correspondents. 77.22 percent were single at the time of enlistment, while 22.78 percent were married.

104. Amy E. Holmes, "'Such Is the Price We Pay': American Widows and the Civil War Pension System," in *Toward a Social History of the American Civil War: Exploratory Essays,* ed. Maris A. Vinovskis (Cambridge: Cambridge Univ. Press, 1990), 174. Similarly, James McPherson found that 29 percent of the 647 Union letter writers he examined were married. See McPherson, *For Cause and Comrades,* viii.

105. While economic need is generally mentioned as one of a number of motivators, class often elicits little further consideration.

106. See e.g. Ural, *The Harp and the Eagle,* 3–4. While acknowledging their working-class status, Ural frames her argument primarily in terms of ethnicity, e.g. "the interest of Ireland and the Union," and "their interests as Irishmen." During the Civil War, class and ethnicity were frequently tied together. Mark A. Lause has identified contemporary efforts to directly equate working-class agitation with what were perceived to be the ethnically "dangerous classes." Lause argues that the form labor struggles took during the war resembled those of the antebellum period (though differing in composition and scale), but during the war employers sought to undermine them by framing them as riotous ethnic disruptions. This wartime characterization of labor agitation as distinctly ethnic is a measure of the prevalence and purchase of nativist sentiment during the conflict. See Mark A. Lause, *Free Labor: The Civil War and the Making of an American Working Class* (Urbana: Univ. of Illinois Press, 2015), 76, 80.

107. See Glatthaar, "A Tale of Two Armies," 329.

108. McPherson, *For Cause and Comrades,* ix.

109. See for example Christopher Hager, *I Remain Yours: Common Lives in Civil War Letters* (Cambridge, Mass.: Harvard Univ. Press, 2018); Peter S. Carmichael, *The War for the Common Soldier* (Chapel Hill: Univ. of North Carolina Press, 2018); and the University of Georgia's "Private Voices" website, run by project directors Michael Ellis, Michael Montgomery, and Stephen Berry, which examines ordinary Civil War letters: https://altchive.org/ (accessed 10 July 2023).

110. Analysis such as that recently conducted by scholars like William Marvel and Joseph T. Glatthaar is going some way toward beginning to redress this imbalance. See William Marvel, *Lincoln's Mercenaries: Economic Motivation Among Union Soldiers During the Civil War* (Baton Rouge: Louisiana State Univ. Press, 2018); Glatthaar, "A Tale of Two Armies."

111. Frederick S. Voss, "Adalbert Volck: The South's Answer to Thomas Nast," *Smithsonian Studies in American Art* 2, no. 3 (1988): 74.

112. Charles Brady to "Dear Sister," 5 October 1862, WC2415.

113. 1860 U.S. Census, Skaneateles, Onondaga, New York, NARA.

114. William V. Shannon, *The American Irish: A Political and Social Portrait,* 2nd ed. (Amherst: Univ. of Massachusetts Press, 1989), 142.

115. John C. Lynch to "My dear darling Mother," 17 December 1861, WC94532. Emphasis in original.

3. LIFE IN UNIFORM

1. Barney Carr to "Dear Parent," 20 June 1864, WC100612.

2. On the Carr story, see Shiels, *The Forgotten Irish,* 166–174.

3. John Toomey to "Dear Father And mother," 10 November 1861, WC5388.

4. John Riley to "Dear Father & Mother," 10 July 1861, Navy WC2821.

5. Charles O'Donnell to "my dear mother," 7 August 1862, Navy WC2479.

6. James Finigan to "My Deare father," 19 April 1864, WC110019.

7. James Leahey to "Dear wife," 25 October 1861, WC2537.

8. John Deegan to "Sister Kate," 28 April 1864, WC68309.

9. William Delaney to "Dear Mother," 6 November 1861, WC8306.

10. Michael Martin to "My dear wife," 21 July 1862, WC16416.

11. William Flaherty to "Dear Mother," 7 January 1864, and William Flaherty to "Dear Mother," 28 January 1864, WC117088.

12. See e.g. Joseph T. Glatthaar, *The March to the Sea and Beyond: Sherman's Troops in the Savannah and Carolinas Campaigns* (Baton Rouge: Louisiana State Univ. Press, 1995), 42–43; McPherson, *For Cause and Comrades,* 27.

13. Christopher McGiff to "My Dear mother," 25 April 1863, WC114360.

14. John Buckley to "Dear Sister," 29 November 1863, Navy WC4219.

15. On this feeling of equality, see Lorien Foote, *The Gentlemen and the Roughs: Manhood, Honor, and Violence in the Union Army* (New York: New York Univ. Press, 2010), 153.

16. Thomas Keating to "My Deare Mother," 24 January [no date, but 1862], WC88338.

17. Matthew Eagan to "Dear Wife," 10 November 1861, WC25637.

18. Jeremiah Keenan to "Dear Mother," 17 April [no date, but 1863], WC14441.

19. John C. Lynch to "My dear darling Mother," 21 January 1862, WC94532. The "memorial" in this context is akin to a petition.

20. James Healy to "Dear Parents," 7 April 1864, WC65439. For more on the background to these disputes, see Christian G. Samito, ed., *Commanding Boston's Irish Ninth: The Civil War Letters of Colonel Patrick R. Guiney, Ninth Massachusetts Volunteer Infantry* (New York: Fordham Univ. Press, 1998).

21. William McIntyre to "Dear Father & Mother," 30 January 1862 [but 1863], WC45770.

22. John O'Connor to "Dear mother," 18 March 1864, WC86354.

23. See Earl J. Hess, *The Union Soldier in Battle: Enduring the Ordeal of Combat* (Lawrence: Univ. Press of Kansas, 1997), 37.

24. Patrick Carney to "Dear mother & Brothers & Sister," 3 June 1862, WC18510.

25. Thomas Hagan to "Dear Mother & sisters," 27 September 1863, WC51663.

26. Edmund Ford to "Dear father and mother brothers and sisters," 16 November 1862, WC96716.

27. Daniel Driscoll to "Father & Mother," 15 February 1863, Navy WC3265.

28. As men's initial enthusiasm was replaced by growing pessimism, there was a knock-on effect on discipline. See Steven J. Ramold, *Baring the Iron Hand: Discipline in the Union Army* (DeKalb: Northern Illinois Univ. Press, 2010), 53–69. On the psychological impact of the war on soldiers, see e.g. Eric T. Dean, "'We Will All Be Lost and Destroyed': Post-Traumatic Stress Disorder and the Civil War" *Civil War History* 37, no. 2 (1991): 138–153. For a study of the mental impact of the Civil War, see Dillon J. Carroll, *Invisible Wounds: Mental Illness and Civil War Soldiers* (Baton Rouge: Louisiana State Univ. Press, 2021).

29. James Dowd to "Dear wife," 4 September 1862, WC47691.

30. William Dwyer to "Dear Mother," 23 January 1863, WC103233.

31. John Dougherty to "Dear Mother," 4 September 1862, and John Dougherty to "Dear Mother," 19 July 1862, both in WC93207.

32. Thomas Reiley to "Dear Mother," 26 May 1864, WC126607.

33. See Carmichael, *The War for the Common Soldier,* 121, 129–130.

34. For a detailed and wide-ranging discussion on concepts of courage during the Civil War, see Gerald F. Linderman, *Embattled Courage: The Experience of Combat in the American Civil War* (New York: Free Press, 1987), 7–110.

35. On the parallels with nonethnic service, see McPherson, *For Cause and Comrades,* 80. For a discussion on attitudes toward cowardice during the war, see Chris Walsh, "'Cowardice Weakness or Infirmity, Whichever It May Be Termed': A Shadow History of the Civil War," *Civil War History* 59, no. 4 (2013): 492–526.

36. This is largely due to a perceived lesser ideological commitment among Irish American communities to the war effort. The powerful influence that the perceptions and expectations of those at home could have on the conduct of Civil War soldiers has been noted by a number of scholars. See e.g. Reid Mitchell, *The Vacant Chair: The Northern Soldier Leaves Home* (New York: Oxford Univ. Press, 1993), 13, 24–25.

37. William McIntyre to "Dear Father & Mother," 20 April 1862, WC45770.

38. James Fitzpatrick to "Dear Mother & Sister," 10 September 1864, WC75056; CWMRA of James Fitzpatrick, 96th New York Infantry, NYSA. Maguire's Irish nativity and his wounding in the hand on 2 June 1864 are confirmed by his muster roll abstract. See CWMRA of John Maguire, 98th New York Infantry, NYSA.

39. Patrick Dooley to "Dear Mother," 15 July 1862, WC6206.

40. Ella Lonn, *Foreigners in the Union Army and Navy* (New York: Greenwood Press, 1969), 47; Bell Irvin Wiley, *The Life of Billy Yank: The Common Soldier of the Union* (Indianapolis, Ind.: Bobbs-Merrill, 1952), 138–139.

41. Long after any initial eagerness for combat had been extinguished, this sense of duty prevailed, and helped men return to face further trials under fire. See James M. McPherson, *This Mighty Scourge: Perspectives on the Civil War* (Oxford: Oxford Univ. Press, 2007), 160.

42. For a study on how esprit de corps developed within a regiment, see Mark H. Dunkelman,

Brothers One and All: Esprit de Corps in a Civil War Regiment (Baton Rouge: Louisiana State Univ. Press, 2004).

43. James Hayes to "my Dear brother," 9 December 1862, WC37552.

44. Michael Daly to "My Dear Mother," 14 March 1863, WC143339.

45. Michael Foran to "Dear Cusen," 29 October 1861, WC126742.

46. Joseph McConaghy to "Dear mother," 4 October 1863, WC84155.

47. On negative views of veterans toward late war enlistees, see e.g. McPherson, *For Cause and Comrades,* 116.

48. James McHugh to "Dear mother," 23 July 1862, WC80051.

49. Mathew McCourt to "Dear Mother and Sister," 7 August 1862, WC85252.

50. Timothy Toomey to "Dear Mother," 9 December 1863, WC46367.

51. Garrett Barry to "Dear farther," 8 April 1863, WC97336.

52. John Madden to "Dear Mother," 2 August 1863, WC86549.

53. William Carroll to "Dear mother," 4 September 1862, WC92361.

54. As Reid Mitchell has noted, most soldiers were eager to see shirkers drafted, but hoped that their own family members would escape. See Reid Mitchell, *Civil War Soldiers: Their Expectations and Experiences* (New York: Penguin, 1988), 84–85.

55. Timothy Toomey to "Dear Mother," 17 August 1863, WC46367.

56. There is much disagreement as to how many eligible Union soldiers chose to reenlist. Earl Hess estimates that 100,000 veterans chose not to do so in 1864, with around 136,000 deciding to sign on again and see the war through. See Hess, *The Union Soldier in Battle,* 89. Joseph Glatthaar estimates that only 6.5 percent of all Union soldiers re-upped, but places the reenlistment rate in Sherman's army at 48.53 percent. See Glatthaar, *The March to the Sea and Beyond,* 187. In contrast, Jonathan White estimated reenlistment in the Army of the Potomac at just 14.8 percent, though this is disputed by Zachery Fry, whose analysis suggests 33.1 percent of that army signed on for the duration. See Jonathan W. White, *Emancipation, the Union Army, and the Reelection of Abraham Lincoln* (Baton Rouge: Louisiana State Univ. Press, 2014), 167–169; Zachery A. Fry, *A Republic in the Ranks: Loyalty and Dissent in the Army of the Potomac* (Chapel Hill: Univ. of North Carolina Press, 2020), 197–199. Seventy-five percent of a unit had to reenlist for it to become a veteran volunteer regiment.

57. See Michael Thomas Smith, *The Enemy Within: Fears of Corruption in the Civil War North* (Charlottesville: Univ. of Virginia Press, 2011), 127–153.

58. Edward Fitzpatrick to "Dr Wife," 17 November 1864, WC142303. The measures put in place to keep new recruits in the army grew increasingly severe as 1864 progressed. By September of that year, Ulysses S. Grant was complaining about the extreme level of desertion among new men, claiming that only one effective soldier was being gained for every five reported as enlisted. See Smith, "The Most Desperate Scoundrels Unhung," 159.

59. John Hall to "Friend Patrick," 30 April 1865, WC77334.

60. For the detailed analysis of this incident, see Damian Shiels, "'Our Pickets Were Gobbled': Assessing the Mass Capture of the 69th New York, Petersburg, 1864," *Irish in the American Civil War* (2015), https://irishamericancivilwar.com/2015/12/10/our-pickets-were-gobbled-assessing-the-mass-capture-of-the-69th-new-york-petersburg-1864/ (accessed 4 May 2019). Of the 120 identifiable men captured, only twenty-six had been in the unit prior to the Overland. The bulk had arrived from August on, with 50 percent in September alone.

61. James Fitzpatrick to "Dear Mother & Sister," 10 September 1864, WC75056.

62. See Bennett, *Union Jacks,* 13.

63. Daniel O'Neil to "Dear Parents," 30 April 1864, Navy WC1994.

64. Thomas Hynes to "My Dear Wife," 28 August 1864, Navy WC4104.

65. Kurtz, *Excommunicated from the Union,* 5–6. Kurtz's work was a groundbreaking contribution to our understanding of the Catholic experience of the American Civil War. Another recent monograph to concentrate on Catholics and the conflict is Robert Emmett Curran, *American Catholics and the Quest for Equality in the Civil War Era* (Baton Rouge: Louisiana State Univ. Press, 2023).

66. Kurtz, *Excommunicated from the Union,* 4. As Randall M. Miller points out, one of the reasons there were so few Catholic chaplains was the refusal of Protestant officers to accept priests into the role. See Randall M. Miller "Catholic Religion, Irish Ethnicity, and the Civil War," in Randall M. Miller et. al., *Religion and the American Civil War* (Oxford: Oxford Univ. Press, 1998), 265. Analysis of the correspondence of Catholic chaplains has revealed that they often shared similar views to the enlisted men when it came to their support for both the Constitution and the Union. See David J. Endres, "'Three Cheers for the Union': Catholic Chaplains and Irish Loyalty During the American Civil War," *Catholic Historical Review* 108, no. 1 (winter 2022): 92–117.

67. William McCarter, *My Life in the Irish Brigade: The Civil War Memoirs of Private William McCarter, 116th Pennsylvania Infantry,* edited by Kevin E. O'Brien (El Dorado Hills, Calif.: Savas, 1996).

68. For a discussion of McCarter in this respect, see Kevin O'Neill, "The Star-Spangled Shamrock: Meaning and Memory in Irish America," in *History and Memory in Modern Ireland,* ed. Ian McBride (Cambridge: Cambridge Univ. Press, 2001), 128–129.

69. Robert Boyle to "my dear wife," 4 June 1864, WC82386; WC49639, relating to Robert Boyle, Company B, 164th New York Infantry.

70. John Corcoran to "Dear parents," 1 August 1862, WC10461. Though evidence for sectarian divisions among Irish Americans in uniform is sparse, it certainly existed in civilian life. Its most famous manifestation came in the so-called Orange Riots that broke out in New York City in 1870 and 1871. See Michael A. Gordon, *The Orange Riots: Irish Political Violence in New York City, 1870 and 1871* (Ithaca, N.Y.: Cornell Univ. Press, 1993).

71. William Finn to "My Dear Mother and Sister," 12 May 1864, Navy Survivor Pension Certificate No. 5517, NARA. For discussion of the role that a belief in God's providence played in the war, see e.g. Mark A. Noll, *The Civil War as a Theological Crisis* (Chapel Hill: Univ. of North Carolina Press, 2006); George C. Rable, *God's Almost Chosen Peoples: A Religious History of the American Civil War* (Chapel Hill: Univ. of North Carolina Press, 2010).

72. On providence and the concept of "providential pragmatism," see Carmichael, *The War for the Common Soldier,* 67.

73. James Grogan to "Mrs MJ Davis," 11 June 1864, WC76523.

74. Dennis Larkin [no salutation, but to parents], 27 December 1864, WC120669.

75. See Carmichael, *The War for the Common Soldier,* 92.

76. Thomas Keating to "My Dear Mother," 10 December 1861, WC88338.

77. Thomas Diver to "Dear Mother," 2 February 1862, WC38010.

78. Thomas Doyle to "My Dear Margaret," 8 October 1861, WC27522.

79. John Kelly to "Dear Mother," 22 November 1861, WC26080.

80. Nicholas Mahar to "Dear sister," 13 June 1864, WC107142.

81. John C. Lynch to "My dear darling Mother," 17 December 1861, WC94532.

82. Michael Connerty to "Dear Mother," 17 January 1862, WC8938.

83. Patrick Collins to "Dear Sister," 6 April 1863, WC94716.

84. John Sheehan to "Dear Father," 12 September 1863, WC93487. The 94th New York's chaplain was Reverend Philos G. Cook. See Benedict R. Maryniak and John Wesley Brinsfield Jr., *The Spirit Divided: Memoirs of Civil War Chaplains: The Union* (Macon, Ga.: Mercer Univ. Press, 2007), 251.

85. Rable, *God's Almost Chosen Peoples,* 125, 136.

86. Thomas Doyle to "Dear Mother," 7 August [1862], WC133177.

87. Thomas Monaghan to "Dear Mother," 14 August 1863, WC52908.

88. This was recognized by some senior Catholic Union officers, who occasionally requested objects such as scapulars and rosaries for the men. See Kurtz, *Excommunicated from the Union,* 71.

89. See Larkin, "Devotional Revolution," 644–645.

90. See Stephen R. Potter and Douglas W. Owsley, "An Irishman Dies at Antietam: An Archaeology of the Individual," in *Archaeological Perspectives on the American Civil War,* ed. Clarence R. Geier and Stephen R. Potter (Gainesville: Univ. Press of Florida, 2000), 56–72.

91. John Sullivan to "Dear Mother," 18 June 1863, Navy WC2254.

92. John Dougherty to "Dear Mother," 4 September 1862, WC93207.

93. John O'Connell to "My Dear Mother," 5 February 1862, WC27032.

94. William Dwyer to "My Dear Mother," 26 January 1863, WC103233.

95. Peter Campbell to "Dear Mother," 5 September 1862, Navy WC2023.

96. James Healy to "My Dear Parents," 10 August 1862, WC65439.

97. Patrick Dooley to "Dear Mother," 20 September 1861, WC6206.

98. The 9th Massachusetts Infantry specifically referenced their Catholic chaplain on one of their recruiting posters, noting that he would minister to the men's "spiritual wants and dispense the priceless blessings of religion." See Kurtz, *Excommunicated from the Union,* 54.

99. C. T. Woodruff to "Mrs Conroy," 13 September 1862, WC26932. Emphasis in original.

100. On concepts of a good death in the Civil War, see Drew Gilpin Faust, *This Republic of Suffering: Death and the American Civil War* (New York: Knopf, 2008).

101. William Stanly to "Respected Madam," 9 August 1864, Navy WC3230. Mathew Droney may well have spoken these lines. His very last words were supposedly "Comrades remember my wife and children," and his crewmates duly responded by gathering together a substantial sum for their future security.

102. William K. Nowles to "Dear Madam," 6 January 1865, Navy WC4104.

103. Michael O'Flaherty to "Mrs fitz Patrick," 25 September 1864, WC71372.

104. As Peter Carmichael notes, during the Civil War "There was no boundary between the home front and the army." See Carmichael, *The War for the Common Soldier,* 12.

105. Pat McConnell to "Dr. mother," 11 July 1862, WC109749.

106. Pat McConnell to "Dr. mother," 1 July 1862, WC109749. The 1855 New York census records that Ann was able to read, but not write. See 1855 New York State Census, Kings, Brooklyn City, Ward 17, Ancestry.com.

107. Pat McConnell to "Dr. mother," 1 July 1862, WC109749. The family fortunes appear to have worsened after Pat's mortal wounding at Antietam, as by 1866 they had moved from Williamsburgh

to Corlear's Hook in Manhattan, an area described as being filled with "malarious slums." See *New York Times,* 1 July 1870. By the time his mother came to claim a pension, one of the children appears to have died.

108. See e.g. Mitchell, *The Vacant Chair;* Lesley J. Gordon, *A Broken Regiment: The 16th Connecticut's Civil War* (Baton Rouge: Louisiana State Univ. Press, 2014). Home and family were also of central importance to Confederate soldiers. See e.g. James J. Broomall, *Private Confederacies: The Emotional Worlds of Southern Men as Citizens and Soldiers* (Chapel Hill: Univ. of North Carolina Press, 2019), 44. As Aaron Sheehan-Dean has noted, nearly all men in uniform maintained a sense of being both soldiers and civilians through the conflict. See Aaron Sheehan-Dean "The Blue and the Gray in Black and White: Assessing the Scholarship on Civil War Soldiers," in *The View from the Ground: Experiences of Civil War Soldiers,* ed. Aaron Sheehan-Dean (Lexington: Univ. Press of Kentucky, 2007), 12.

109. James McGaffigan to "My dear Wife," 4 February 1862, WC2177.

110. Martin Flanagan to "Dear Mother," 21 February 1862, WC61242.

111. Michael Carroll to "Dear mother Brothers and Sisters," 22 January 1862, WC40248.

112. Edmund Dwyer to "My Dear Father," 21 May 1862, WC132012. CWMRA of John Hayes, 105th New York Infantry, NYSA.

113. See Gallman, *Defining Duty,* 210, 220.

114. Scholars such as James McPherson have identified such sentiments as a feature of the letters of middle- and upper-class soldiers. See McPherson, *For Cause and Comrades,* 131–132, 135–136.

115. Terrence McFarland to "Dear Mother," 4 December 1862, WC127929.

116. John Madden to "Dear Mother," 20 October 1863, WC86549.

117. James McGee to "Dear Sisters," 27 December 1861, WC98814.

118. Elizabeth Fitzpatrick to "Dear husband," 4 April 1864, WC71372.

119. James Corcoran to "My Deir Wife," 24 January [1865], WC116032.

120. Shiels, *Forgotten Irish,* 44; affidavit of Stephen J. McGroarty, 23 July 1866, WC117744.

121. Patrick Carraher to "Dear Margaret," [no date but early July 1861], WC124533.

122. John Slattery to "My Dear Sister," 20 October 1862, WC145128.

123. As Reid Mitchell has pointed out, if a Civil War soldier's patriotism had to compete with issues at home, it could threaten his devotion to the military. See Mitchell, *The Vacant Chair,* 29.

124. Christopher McGiff to "My Dear Mother," 25 April 1863, WC114360.

125. Scholars of the northern soldier have identified the emergence of a growing distance between men at the front and those at home as the war progressed, as those in uniform felt increasingly neglected and began to view those outside the service with contempt. See e.g. Mitchell, *The Vacant Chair,* 32–33; and especially Steven J. Ramold, *Across the Divide: Union Soldiers View the Northern Home Front* (New York: New York Univ. Press, 2013).

126. Daniel O'Neil to "Dear Father and Mother," 12 January 1862, Navy WC1994.

127. Timothy Toomey to "My Dear Mother," 30 January 1863, WC46367.

128. On men seeing themselves as representatives of their families while in service, see Mitchell, *Civil War Soldiers,* 17.

129. Richard Sheridan to "Dear Father," 23 February 1863, WC117836.

130. John Sullivan to "My Dear Mother," 8 December 1861, WC8731.

131. Thomas Hagan to "Dear Mother + sisters," 27 September 1863, WC51663.

132. John Sheehan to "Dear Father," 28 March 1863, and John Sheehan to "Dear Father," 12 September 1863, WC93487.

133. Reid Mitchell argues that the men often felt neglected by those at home and could find "the spectacle of life going on without them . . . profoundly unsettling," something that could anger and depress them. See Mitchell, *The Vacant Chair*, 33.

134. Timothy Toomey to "Dear Mother," 13 October 1863, WC46367.

135. This is a feature of many conflicts. Studies of semiliterate correspondence from the First World War reveal a similarly insatiable desire for letters, and distress at delays in receiving them. See Martyn Lyons, "'Ordinary Writings' or How the 'Illiterate' Speak to Historians," in *Ordinary Writings, Personal Narratives: Writing Practices in 19th and Early 20th Century Europe*, ed. Martyn Lyons (Bern: Peter Lang, 2007), 18–19; Martyn Lyons, *The Writing Culture of Ordinary People in Europe, c. 1860–1920* (Cambridge: Cambridge Univ. Press, 2013), 35–37.

136. Matthew Eagan [no salutation, but to wife], 11 February 1862, WC25637.

137. Matthew Eagan to "Dear Wife," 14 April 1862, WC25637. The poem "Remember Me" was published in 1855 by Emma Garrison. See Emma Garrison, *A Collection of Brief Poems on Various Subjects* (Baltimore: Sherwood, 1855), 22–24. With thanks to Carly Silver for the identification.

138. Timothy Harrington to "My dear wife," 7 November 1861, Navy WC1580.

139. William Harnett to "Dear Mother," 23 January 1862, WC20688.

140. Felix Burns to "Dear Mother," 21 April [1863], WC123070.

141. Francis Cullen to "Deare mother," 17 September 1861, WC134902.

142. William Harnett to "Dear Mother," 23 January 1862, WC20688.

143. William Shea to "Dear Mother," 27 April 1862, WC64963.

144. William Martin to "My Dear Mother," 25 July 1863, WC79466.

145. James Hand to "Dear Farther And Mother Brothers And Sisters," 9 August 1863, WC114954.

146. Henry Burns to "My Dear Mother," 12 April 1863, WC103877; William Cody to "Dear Mother," 21 November 1861, WC10828.

147. For a history of the newspaper, see James Crouthamel, *Bennett's New York Herald and the Rise of the Popular Press* (New York: Syracuse Univ. Press, 1989).

148. Patrick Carey to "Dear Mother," 23 [no month] 1864, WC56206; Dennis Larkin to "dear father and mother," 12 March[?] 1865, WC120669; Edward Hanlin to "Dear mother," 27 April [no year, but 1862], WC88981.

149. On efforts to discourage criticism of Lincoln and emancipation within the army from 1863, which included limiting access to Democratic newspapers, see White, *Emancipation, the Union Army, and the Reelection of Abraham Lincoln*, 40–41.

150. Michael McCormick to "Dear Mother Sisters & Brothers," 24 May 1863, WC96255. Hooker was a Democrat, which was why McCormick thought he may have interceded to secure a supply.

151. Michael McCormick to "Dear Mother Sisters & Brothers," 17 November 1863, WC96255.

152. William Dolan to "Dear Mother & Sisters," 11 March 1863, WC25547.

153. Patrick McConnell to "Dr Mother," 11 July 1862, WC109749.

154. Harvey J. Graff, *The Legacies of Literacy: Continuities and Contradictions in Western Culture and Society* (Bloomington: Indiana Univ. Press, 1987), 344.

155. See Ó Gráda, "The New York Irish in the 1850s: Locked in by Poverty?," 9. Ó Gráda's analysis is based on the IPUMS 1860 census sample. He also demonstrates that the Irish were significantly more likely to "age-heap" than other groups—i.e., record their ages in years ending with a zero or five, another indicator of low literacy and numeracy rates.

156. McLaughlin's letters written in Camp Curtin in June and early July 1861 display markedly better spelling and sentence construction than those that came afterward. They also appear to be in a different hand. See Francis McLaughlin to "Dear wife," 21 June 1861, and Francis McLaughlin to "Dear wife," 12 July 1861, WC1056.

157. Francis McLaughlin to "Deare whife," 5 February 1862, and Francis McLaughlin to "Deare whife," 19 May 1862, both in WC1056.

158. For a discussion of the construction of letters by ordinary Civil War soldiers, see Hager, *I Remain Yours,* 17–53. Many soldiers and sailors were making use of manuals that offered the inexperienced correspondent guidance on how their letters should be formatted, and what they should contain. Among the most popular during the Civil War was *Beadle's Dime Letter-Writer,* first published in 1861.

159. John Brennan to "Dear Wife," 1 February 1862, John Brennan to "D Wife," 16 February 1862, John Brennan to "Dear Wife," 27 February 1862, all in WC27309.

160. James McGee to "Dear Mother," 13 May 1863, James McGee to "Dear Mother," 22 June 1863, James McGee to "Dear Mother," 20 November 1863, affidavit of Daniel Hammill and Andrew Mooney, 7 August 1865, all contained in WC96027; CWMRA of James McGee, 132nd New York Infantry, NYSA.

161. Daniel Driscoll to "Dear father & Mother," 1 December [1861], Navy WC3265.

162. Lyons, *The Writing Culture,* 48–49. Just such a collaborative process has been observed between scribes and their clients in Mexico City during the 1990s. See Judy Kalman, *Writing on the Plaza: Mediated Literacy Practice Among Scribes and Clients in Mexico City* (Creskill, N.J.: Hampton Press, 1999).

163. William C. Walker, *The Eighteenth Regiment Connecticut Volunteers in the War for the Union* (Norwich, Conn.: Gordon Wilcox for The Committee, 1885), 395; 1860 U.S. Census, Preston, New London, Connecticut, NARA; 1860 U.S. Census, Norwich, New London, Connecticut, NARA.

164. John Delaney to "Dear Mother," 15 April 1863, WC39990.

165. John Delaney to "Dear Mother," 20 April [1863], WC39990.

166. Graff, *Legacies of Literacy,* 343.

167. This was common throughout the military during the Civil War. As Hager notes, "The Civil War sparked ad hoc literacy education on a vast scale." See Hager, *I Remain Yours,* 12.

168. Nicholas Mahar to "Dear Sister," 13 June 1864, WC107142.

169. Martin Tiernan to "Dear Mother," 20 January 1862, WC4869.

170. Thomas McCready to "Dear Mother," 30 November 1861, WC70669.

171. Jeremiah Keenan to "Dear mother," 17 April [1863], WC14441.

172. Affidavit of James Graney and John Hearn, 16 April 1869, WC139152.

173. Affidavit of Patrick Curtin and Thomas Smyth, 9 March 1867, WC93207.

174. Martin Noonan to "Dear Sister & Mother," 16 August 1863, WC71872. Families and soldiers alike were quick to recognize different hands, a fact vividly portrayed in Walt Whitman's 1865 poem "Come Up from the Fields Father." For a discussion of the poem's use of an "alien hand" from

an epistolary perspective, see Rebecca Weir, "'An Oblique Place': Letters in the Civil War," in *The Edinburgh Companion to Nineteenth-Century American Letters and Letter-Writing,* ed. Celeste-Marie Bernier et al. (Edinburgh: Edinburgh Univ. Press, 2016), 281–282. Concerning family recognition of other hands, see Hager, *I Remain Yours,* 172.

175. For the importance of correspondence in sustaining an "imagined community" between those at home and members of the diaspora (even those born into that diaspora), see Lyons, "Ordinary Writings," 18. On the concept of the "imagined community" and the origin of the term, see Benedict Anderson, *Imagined Communities: Reflections on the Origins and Spread of Nationalism* (London: Verso, 1983).

176. This was an expectation that the majority of their contemporaries shared, no matter their ethnicity. See Hager, *I Remain Yours,* 42–43.

177. Hager's analysis of the writings of ordinary Civil War soldiers found that although there was no censorship in place, there were many constraints on what semiliterate people would commit to letters. Hager, *I Remain Yours,* 74. Similarly, Martyn Lyons has demonstrated that the expected public nature of ordinary correspondence in this period and the highly ritualized form of letters often limited what a correspondent might choose to say. See Lyons, *The Writing Culture,* 76–77, 89.

178. Christopher McGiff to "My Dear Mother," 26 May 1863, WC114360.

179. Peter Finegan to "Dear Father & Mother," 29 September 1862, WC138689.

180. Indications that those Irish who were less literate were less likely to participate in correspondence has also been identified in nineteenth-century communication networks in Australia, where female-written letters are rare. See David Fitzpatrick, *Oceans of Consolation: Personal Accounts of Irish Migration to Australia* (Ithaca, N.Y.: Cornell Univ. Press, 1994), 473–474.

181. The changes in postal communications during theses younger men's formative years had been revolutionary. Reduction and revisions to postal rates in 1845 and 1851 had opened up the service to the masses, helping spur an increase in the number of letters carried annually in the United States from 27 million in 1840 to 161 million by 1860. The system operated at its greatest efficiency in the major urban centers, where the Irish congregated. See David M. Henkin, *The Postal Age: The Emergence of Modern Communications in Nineteenth-Century America* (Chicago: Univ. of Chicago Press, 2006), 3, 22, 29, 31.

4. REPUTATION, RACE, AND POLITICS

1. Anonymous to "Mrs. Griffin," 26 June 1865, affidavit of Alfred Hackett, 19 September 1865, affidavit of Patrick Carey, 28 August 1866, affidavit of George Bagshaw, 28 August 1866, all in WC85142; *Cleveland Daily Leader,* 8 July 1865; *Lowell Daily Citizen and News,* 11 July 1865 and 16 August 1865; *Boston Traveler,* 4 August 1865.

2. Patrick Griffin CMSR, 15th Independent Battery, Massachusetts Light Artillery, and 6th Independent Battery, Massachusetts Light Artillery; *Cleveland Daily Leader,* 8 July 1865. Patrick had first seen service in the 15th Independent Battery, Massachusetts Light Artillery, transferring to the 6th in January 1865. For a more detailed discussion of the case, see Damian Shiels, "Killed by Torture? The Story of an 18-Year-Old Irishman's Death at the Hands of His Officers, New Orleans, 1865," *Irish in the American Civil War* (2016), https://irishamericancivilwar.com/2016/07/23

/killed-by-torture-the-story-of-an-18-year-old-irishmans-death-at-the-hands-of-his-officers-new-orleans-1865/ (accessed 8 September 2020). It should be noted that although severe punishments such as that meted out to Patrick Griffin had become an increasing feature of the Union military as the war progressed, it was unusual for them to lead to a soldier's death. It is also worth considering the potential impact his young age at enlistment may have had on the drinking problems he appears to have developed.

3. See Foote, *The Gentlemen and the Roughs,* 8, 120; Lorien Foote, "Rich Man's War, Rich Man's Fight: Class, Ideology, and Discipline in the Union Army," *Civil War History* 5, no. 3 (2005): 269–287. Foote's work is extremely important in exposing the extent of the class divide within the Union military. The surnames of many of the examples of "roughs" she cites throughout her work clearly indicate that they were Irish American.

4. Recognizing that class distinction could exist between Irish American officers and their men is particularly important, given the frequency with which the statements of the Irish American officer class are taken as representative of the entirety of the Irish American experience.

5. McPherson, *For Cause and Comrades,* 26; Gordon, *A Broken Regiment,* 43; Foote, *The Gentlemen and the Roughs,* 20; Carmichael, *The War for the Common Soldier,* 84.

6. Michael Kaplan, "New York City Tavern Violence and the Creation of a Working-Class Male Identity," *Journal of the Early Republic* 15, no. 4 (1995): 592. For more on Irish American masculinity, particularly of the middle classes, see Patricia Kelleher, "Class and Catholic Irish Masculinity in Antebellum America: Young Men on the Make in Chicago," *Journal of American Ethnic History* 28, no. 4 (summer 2009): 7–42.

7. On concepts of masculinity as it relates to Ireland see, Rebecca Anne Barr, Sean Brady, and Jane McGaughey, eds., *Ireland and Masculinities in History* (London: Palgrave MacMillan, 2019). For an overview of masculinities in the Civil War, see James J. Broomall, "Wartime Masculinities," in *The Cambridge History of the American Civil War,* vol. 3, *Affairs of the People,* ed. Aaron Sheehan-Dean (Cambridge: Cambridge Univ. Press, 2019), 3–24.

8. On the development of the concepts of "restrained" and "martial" manhood, see Amy S. Greenberg, *Manifest Manhood and the Antebellum American Empire* (Cambridge: Cambridge Univ. Press, 2005).

9. Statement of David Anderson, 18 July 1868; Special Agent Report, 24 April 1869, both in WC132926.

10. Samuel Boyd to "my Dear Ann," 2 December 1861, WC132926.

11. This was a common theme for many ordinary soldiers, who saw the conflict as an opportunity both to redeem themselves and to build character. See e.g. Carmichael, *The War for the Common Soldier,* 3, 12.

12. William Barry to "Dear Sister," 4 June 1862, WC138896.

13. John Sullivan to "Dearest Mother," 19 February 1862, WC8731.

14. John Sullivan to "Dear Mother," 12 December 1861, WC8731.

15. Hugh O'Donnell to "Dear Mother," 15 November 1863, WC74835.

16. John Foran to "Dear Wife," 6 October 1861, WC126742.

17. James Finnerty to "Dear Mother," 14 August 1862, WC31621.

18. On the topic of how ordinary soldiers viewed themselves as the equals of their officers, and as a result conformed to their own sense of duty, see Foote, *The Gentlemen and the Roughs,* 153. On Irish American resistance to authority in the military, see also Mitchell, *The Vacant Chair,* 42–43.

19. This was another feature that was common among many northern Civil War soldiers. See Mitchell, *Civil War Soldiers,* 58.

20. Cornelius Donahoe to "Dear f Mother," 10 October 1861, WC56405.

21. Cornelius Donahoe to "Dear father and Mother," 8 February 1862, WC56405.

22. James Sharkey to "Dear Mother," 20 September 1863, WC28175; Shiels, *Forgotten Irish,* 153–154.

23. For the latest work on alcohol consumption in the Civil War, see Megan L. Bever, *At War with King Alcohol: Debating Drinking and Masculinity in the Civil War* (Chapel Hill: Univ. of North Carolina Press, 2022). On the wide-ranging abuse of alcohol in the military, see also Scott C. Martin, "'A Soldier Intoxicated Is Far Worse Than No Soldier at All': Intoxication and the American Civil War," *Social History of Alcohol and Drugs* 25, no. 1–2 (2011): 67; Ramold, *Baring the Iron Hand,* 123–124. Ramold recounts how the supposed Irish love of alcohol was also used to diminish Irish performance in battle, through an oft-repeated tale that explained away an Irish soldier's heroic actions by revealing they were all so he could retrieve his whiskey flask. See Ramold, *Baring the Iron Hand,* 99.

24. *New York Irish American,* 26 March 1864.

25. John F. Quinn, "Father Mathew's Disciples: American Catholic Support for Temperance, 1840–1920," *Church History* 65, no. 4 (1996): 628.

26. Edward Fitzpatrick to "Dear Wife," 23 January 1865, WC142303.

27. William Meehan to "My dearly beloved Mother," 2 August 1863, WC31563.

28. Proceedings of a Trial Court which Convened at Hilton Head SC, 29 December 1863, CMSR of William Meehan, Company G, 47th New York Infantry, NARA.

29. Mary Condon to "Honourable General," 21 September 1863, CMSR of Garrett Condon, Company G, 3rd Massachusetts Cavalry, NARA.

30. John Costello to "Dear Sister," 21 April 1862, WC58007. Sheehan was sentenced to one year at hard labor, but he deserted shortly afterward. See CMSR of William Sheehan, Company A, 1st Massachusetts Heavy Artillery, NARA.

31. Patt Winn to "Dear Ant," 12 September 1862, WC98727.

32. Michael McCormick to "Dear Mother Sisters & Brother," 12 January 1862, WC96255.

33. James McGee to "Dear Sister," 29 January 1862, WC98814. This was a ubiquitous problem for regiments in camp, particularly early in the war. Irish American John Ryan of the 28th Massachusetts remembered after the conflict that in January 1862 "there was a little settlement back of the camp called Dublin and there was a good deal of trouble caused by the men running the guards, going to Dublin and getting intoxicated and then being put into the guard house. Of course, each man had his friends in the company and when one of his friends was on guard duty, he would allow his chum to slip out." Sandy Barnard, ed., *Campaigning with the Irish Brigade: Pvt. John Ryan, 28th Massachusetts* (Terre Haute, Ind.: AST Press, 2001), 23.

34. Bernard Curry to "Dear Mother," 12 August [no year, but 1864], WC137303.

35. James Harrigan to "My Dear Mother," 1 May 1862, WC3130. Emphasis in original.

36. Archey Laverty to "Dear Mother," 1 August 1861, WC100498.

37. William Delaney to "Dear Mother," 6 November 1861, WC8306.

38. Henry Burns to "Dear Mother," 2 April 1864, WC103877.

39. John Joseph Casey to "Dear Ben," 29 January 1865, WC98455.

40. McCarter, *My Life in the Irish Brigade,* 16, 70–71.

41. John Dougherty to "Dear Mother," 19 July 1862, WC93207.

42. John Sullivan to "Dear Mother," 12 December 1861, WC8731.

43. This was common across the Union military, with drinking increasing around special occasions. For example, see Gordon, *Broken Regiment,* 97. For a discussion of this in an Irish and German context, see Ramold, *Baring the Iron Hand,* 142–143.

44. James Harrigan to "My Dear Mother," 1 May 1862, WC3130.

45. In the region of one in every eleven Union soldiers deserted at some point during the war. All told, the Union army suffered 421,627 desertions, 260,339 from among the enlisted men and 161,286 in the form of absent draftees. See Ramold, *Baring the Iron Hand,* 220.

46. Dora L. Costa and Matthew E. Kahn, *Heroes and Cowards: The Social Face of War* (Princeton, N.J.: Princeton Univ. Press, 2008), 100. Costa and Kahn based their work on a sample of 40,000 enlisted white Union soldiers and 6,000 black Union soldiers. The Irish-born were also more likely to desert in the Confederate service. See Gleeson, *The Green and the Gray,* 221. Steven J. Ramold offers a particularly useful analysis of Union desertion, and its causes and consequences, in *Baring the Iron Hand,* 219–263.

47. Keating, *Shades of Green,* 126. Martin Öfele likewise argues that immigrants did not desert at higher rates than the native-born. See Martin Öfele, *True Sons of the Republic: European Immigrants in the Union Army* (Westport, Conn.: Praeger, 2008), 160.

48. This extract from Fry's report was reproduced in Gould's *Investigations in the Military and Anthropological Statistics of American Soldiers* (29), published for the U.S. Sanitary Commission.

49. See e.g. Ural, *The Harp and the Eagle,* 4, 81.

50. On this representing the period of highest desertion, see White, *Emancipation, the Union Army, and the Reelection of Abraham Lincoln,* 85.

51. Hallock's analysis demonstrated that from late 1862 the town supervisor from Brookhaven traveled outside the locality on the hunt for recruits. Of the 240 men he found between August and November 1862, 109 were foreign-born, and 74 of them were Irish. The vast majority were not from the area, and these men showed a greater propensity to desert. See Judith Lee Hallock, "The Role of the Community in Civil War Desertion," *Civil War History* 29, no. 2 (June 1983): 128–129.

52. See Damian Shiels, "Charting Desertion in the Irish Brigade, Part 1," *Irish in the American Civil War* (2016), https://irishamericancivilwar.com/2016/08/14/charting-desertion-in-the-irish-brigade-part-1/ (accessed 4 February 2020). Hallock's analysis likewise found that men were most likely to desert soon after entering the military; the majority of the deserters she identified left within a month of enlistment. Hallock, "The Role of the Community," 129.

53. See Carmichael, *The War for the Common Soldier,* 177.

54. Mitchell, *The Vacant Chair,* 30.

55. Costa and Kahn, *Heroes and Cowards,* 100–102.

56. Dan had originally served in Company I of the 105th New York Infantry with his younger brother, John. CWMRA for Dan Sheehan, 105th New York Infantry, NYSA; CWMRA for John Sheehan, 105th New York Infantry, NYSA; John Sheehan to "Dear Father," 18 March 1863, WC93487.

57. Once found to be missing, Union soldiers were reported AWOL (absent without leave). If they returned within ten days, they only faced the consequences of this lesser charge. After that period they were listed as deserters. See Ramold, *Baring the Iron Hand,* 224–225.

58. Discipline grew harsher as the influx of new men led to challenges in maintaining order. See Foote, *The Gentlemen and the Roughs,* 70, 128–129.

59. Captain R. F. Lombard to Adjutant of 16th Massachusetts Infantry, 1 July 1864, in CMSR of Daniel Reddy, Company F, 16th Massachusetts Infantry, NARA.

60. Dan Dillon to "Dear mother," 29 February 1862 [but actually 1863], WC88094.

61. Thomas Diver to "Dear Mother," 2 February 1862, WC38010.

62. James Harrigan to "My Dear Mother," 10 December 1861, WC3130.

63. James Welsh to "Dear Mother," 18 January 1863, WC85074.

64. Thomas Monaghan to "Dear Mother," 14 August 1863, WC52908.

65. Carmichael, *The War for the Common Soldier,* 224–225.

66. James Hand to "Dear father and Mother," 31 July 1863, and James Hand to "Dear Father And Mother And Brothers And Sisters," 9[?] August 1863, WC114954; CWMRA for James Hand, 164th New York Infantry, NYSA.

67. CWMRA for Robert Hanlon, 42nd New York Infantry, NYSA; WC88981, relating to Edward Hanlin, Company E, 12th New York Infantry.

68. Patrick Coffey to "My dear Wife," 10 May 1861, WC19650.

69. Samuel Boyd to "My Deare Ann," 2 December 1861, WC132926.

70. The degree to which Irish American service prompted a tempering in anti-Irish attitudes after the Civil War remains a topic of debate. Susannah Ural has convincingly argued that, at least in many of the major cities, their contribution had remarkably little impact on anti-Irish sentiment. See Ural, *The Harp and the Eagle,* 232. Christian Samito has highlighted how Irish American service led to increased calls for inclusion and equal treatment for Irish Americans, but also points to the fact that the New York City draft riots and opposition to emancipation were utilized in the postwar period by nativists seeking to demonstrate Irish American disloyalty. See Samito, *Becoming American,* 103, 132.

71. See for example the comments of the provost marshal general, James Barnet Fry, quoted elsewhere, which in turn impacted the Sanitary Commission statistics compiled by Benjamin Apthorp Gould. It also affected the recording of Irish Americans during the war, likely influencing decisions such as the commonplace activity of inputting a man's place of residence under the nativity section of the enlistment form, rather than his place of birth. See Gould, *Investigations in the Military and Anthropological Statistics of American Soldiers,* 15.

72. On Irish immigrants perceived to have "violated the accepted rules of class, ethnicity, and gender" and who were characterized as the "shoddy aristocracy," see Gallman, *Defining Duty,* 91–122. As Ryan Keating has noted, although the New York City draft riots came to "define broader issues of Irish American dissent" during the nineteenth century, the degree to which they led to a nativist backlash against the Irish varied considerably. Keating found that backlash to be much less pronounced in locations such as Connecticut, Illinois, and Wisconsin (his study areas), where a different dynamic often existed between Irish communities and their neighbors. See Keating, *Shades of Green,* 133.

73. Anita Palladino, ed., *Diary of a Yankee Engineer: The Civil War Story of John H. Westervelt, Engineer, 1st New York Volunteer Engineer Corps* (New York: Fordham Univ. Press, 1997), 204–205.

74. Theodore Gerrish, *Army Life: A Private's Reminiscences of the Civil War* (Portland, Maine: Hoyt, Fogg and Donham, 1882), 42–43.

75. Richard F. Miller, "The Trouble with Brahmins: Class and Ethnic Tensions in Massachusetts' 'Harvard Regiment,'" *New England Quarterly: A Historical Review of New England Life and*

Letters 76, no. 1 (2003): 40. Abbott's attitude was one shared by many of the senior officers in the regiment. At one point the colonel prevented Catholic mass attendance for fear that it would lead to whiskey drinking. See Kurtz, *Excommunicated from the Union,* 55.

76. Foote, *The Gentlemen and the Roughs,* 121; Henry Livermore Abbott, *Fallen Leaves: The Civil War Letters of Major Henry Livermore Abbott* (Kent, Ohio: Kent State Univ. Press, 1991), 50; Miller, "The Trouble with Brahmins," 49. Abbott appears to have despised all foreigners. See Richard F. Miller, *Harvard's Civil War,* 320–321.

77. Abbott, *Fallen Leaves,* 76.

78. Henry Livermore Abbott to "Mrs. Briody," 17 December 1862, WC9732.

79. Henry Livermore Abbott [no salutation, but to soldier's wife], 18 December 1862, WC11238.

80. Affidavit of Francis Carahar, 1 September 1868, WC124533.

81. Affidavit of Margaret Hill and Eliza Kelly, alias Eliza Keligher, 23 November 1875, Navy WC2196.

82. CWMRA for Patrick Kellegher, 88th New York Infantry, NYSA.

83. Ramold, *Baring the Iron Hand,* 37.

84. Foote, *The Gentlemen and the Roughs,* 128–131.

85. Carmichael, *The War for the Common Soldier,* 83–84.

86. John Scanlan to "My Dear Mother," no date [1863?], Navy WC18243.

87. See Kevin J. Weddle, "Ethnic Discrimination in Minnesota Volunteer Regiments During the Civil War," *Civil War History* 35, no. 3 (1989): 239–259. In some mixed units, while Irish Americans were accepted in the ranks, their presence among the officer corps was an entirely different matter. In 1861 a number of Irish officers were "purged" from the 6th Wisconsin Infantry by their fellows. Some of the purged Irish officers subsequently joined the ethnic 17th Wisconsin Infantry. See William J. K. Beaudot and Lance J. Herdegen, eds., *An Irishman in the Iron Brigade: The Civil War Memoirs of James P. Sullivan, Sergt., Company K, 6th Wisconsin Volunteers* (New York: Fordham Univ. Press, 1993), 34.

88. Thomas H. O'Connor, *Civil War Boston: Home Front and Battlefield* (Boston: Northeastern Univ. Press, 1997), 74.

89. William Maroney to "Dear James," 14 April 1863, WC87287. This description of events would be repeated in Corcoran's subsequent court-martial. See Phyllis Lane, "Corcoran and the Irish Legion: Colonel Michael Corcoran, Fighting Irishman of the Irish Brigade," in *The History of the Irish Brigade: A Collection of Historical Essays,* ed. Pia Seija Seagrave (Fredericksburg, Va.: Sergeant Kirkland's Museum, 1997), 30.

90. William Dwyer to "Dear Mother," 23 January 1863, WC103233.

91. William Dwyer to "My Dear Mother," 26 January 1863, WC103233.

92. Frederick Douglass, *Life and Times of Frederick Douglass* (Boston: De Wolfe and Fiske, 1892), 366.

93. *Harper's Weekly,* 16 August 1862.

94. The impact that massive Irish American losses at the front had on morale on the home front has previously been highlighted. See Ural, *The Harp and the Eagle,* 81.

95. In the most influential book on the topic, Iver Bernstein sees the riots as much more than an outpouring of Irish American racism. He argues that they were the result of a complex mix of social, cultural, and political factors that were impacting New York. See Bernstein, *The New York City Draft Riots,* 6.

96. Just as the New York City draft riots have come to be seen as the defining event of the war for Irish America, Mark A. Lause contends that they occupy a similar position for the working class more generally. He argues that the July 1863 events in New York City represent "the only brief cameo of the white working class into Civil War history." See Lause, *Free Labor,* 69.

97. William Martin to "My Dear mother," 25 July 1863, WC79466. Nugent was a senior officer in the 69th New York and the Irish Brigade, and would lead the latter toward the war's end. The report he had been killed was incorrect, though his home had been ransacked due to his association with the draft as acting assistant provost marshal for the Southern District of New York.

98. John McGillicuddy to "Dear wife," 27 July 1863, WC138484.

99. Ryan Keating has demonstrated the markedly different ways in which the riots were viewed by both Irish and native communities outside New York. See Keating, *Shades of Green,* 133–149.

100. John Grimes to "Dear Father & Mother," 5 August 1863, WC31685.

101. Dennis Driscoll to "Dear Father & Mothr," 30 October 1864, Navy WC2633.

102. John J. Scanlan to "Dear Sister," 21[?] March 1863, Navy WC18243. On the background and course of the Detroit attacks on African Americans, in which Irish Americans played a prominent role, see Paul Taylor, *"Old Slow Town": Detroit During the Civil War* (Detroit, Mich.: Wayne State Univ. Press, 2013), 78–118.

103. Thomas Hagan to "Dear Mother," 27 November 1863, WC51663.

104. Edward Carroll to "Dear mother," 11 November 1861, WC63799.

105. This was true for the majority of northern soldiers. See e.g. Glatthaar, *The March to the Sea and Beyond,* 52.

106. John Toomey to "Dear Father," 20 May 1862, WC5388.

107. The concept that slavery had degraded those subjected to it was widespread, even among abolitionists. See David Brion Davis, *Inhuman Bondage: The Rise and Fall of Slavery in the New World* (Oxford: Oxford Univ. Press, 2006), 250–267.

108. John Sherry to "Dear Father & Mother," 21 August 1861, WC93096.

109. John Sullivan to "Dear Mother," Navy WC2254.

110. Michael Daly to "Dear Brother," 5 March 1863, WC143339.

111. Mitchell, *Civil War Soldiers,* 121.

112. Edward Hanlin to "Dear mother," 23 June [no year, but 1862], WC88981.

113. Owen McGowan to "My Dear Brotherinlaw," 24 October [no date, 1862?], Navy WC2255.

114. George Doherty to "Dear Mother," 15 June 1862, Navy WC2390.

115. John Sullivan to "My Dear Mother," 8 December 1861, WC8731.

116. John McGillicuddy to "Dear wife," 27 July 1863, WC138484.

117. Patrick Kinnane to "Dear Sister," 27 [no month] 1862, WC75830.

118. Timothy L. Toomey to "Dear Mother," 17 August 1863, WC46367.

119. Charles Williams to "Dear Sister," 24 September [no date, but 1863], WC69603. The exchange also demonstrates the economic activity that went on between the formerly enslaved and Irish American troops.

120. John C. Lynch to "My Own darling Mother," [no date, but summer 1862], WC94532.

121. Samito, ed., *Commanding Boston's Irish Ninth,* xxvi.

122. Garcia, "The Forgotten Sixty-Ninth," 35–38. See also David Brundage, *Irish Nationalists in America: The Politics of Exile, 1798–1998* (Oxford: Oxford Univ. Press, 2016), 101.

123. Ural, *The Harp and the Eagle,* 81.

124. John Madden to "Dear Mother," 16 February 1863, WC86549.

125. Dan Dillon to "Dear mother," 19 February 1862 [1863], WC88094. When the Irish 90th Illinois Infantry was asked to offer three cheers for the policy to recruit African American soldiers, they refused. Reports disagreed as to whether they hissed or were largely silent, save for a few cries of "Never! Never!" See Swan, *Chicago's Irish Legion,* 59–63. At least one Union soldier charged that Irish troops in the 49th Pennsylvania were among those who fired on retreating United States Colored Troops during the disastrous Battle of the Crater in July 1864. See Ramold, *Across the Divide,* 84.

126. Dan Dillon to "Dear mother," 14 May 1863, WC88094.

127. For the most important argument for Union soldiers' embrace of emancipation, see Chandra Manning, *What This Cruel War Was Over: Soldiers, Slavery, and the Civil War* (New York: Knopf, 2007). Also see Chandra Manning, "A 'Vexed Question': White Soldiers on Slavery and Race," in *The View from the Ground: Experiences of Civil War Soldiers,* ed. Aaron Sheehan-Dean (Lexington: Univ. Press of Kentucky, 2007), 31–66. As Gary Gallagher notes, even those within the military who did eventually support emancipation chiefly did so "for what seem to be the wrong reasons," as they regarded it as a war aim that would help ensure the preservation of the Union. See Gary W. Gallagher, *The Enduring Civil War: Reflections on the Great American Crisis* (Baton Rouge: Louisiana State Univ. Press, 2020), 113.

128. Miles O'Reilly was the creation of Irish immigrant Charles Graham Halpine, who served during the war. Through his character he communicated the song "Sambo's Right to be Kilt," which, among other messages, put forth the argument that Irish Americans should accept Black service as it reduced the risk to themselves. For lyrics, see Charles Graham Halpine, *The Life and Adventures, Songs, Services, and Speeches of Private Miles O'Reilly* (New York: Carleton, 1864), 55–56. For a detailed discussion of the song, see Christian McWhirter, *Battle Hymns: The Power and Popularity of Music in the Civil War* (Chapel Hill: Univ. of North Carolina Press, 2014), 94, and Bateson, *Civil War Songs,* 181–183.

129. John Deegan to "Sister Kate," 28 April 1864, WC68309.

130. David Henson Slay, "New Masters on the Mississippi: The United States Colored Troops of the Middle Mississippi Valley" (PhD diss., Texas Christian University, 2009), 73–76; Linda Barnickel, *Milliken's Bend: A Civil War Battle in History and Memory* (Baton Rouge: Louisiana State Univ. Press, 2013), 71–72; Linda Barnickel, "10th Illinois Cavalry at War with Isaac Shepard," *Milliken's Bend: A Civil War Battle in History and Memory* (2013), http://millikensbend.com/10th_illinois_cavalry_at_war_with_isaac_shepard/ (accessed 1 February 2016).

131. Affidavit of John O'Brien, 17 July 1883, SC266425, NARA; Illinois, Databases of Illinois Veterans, Index, 1775–1995, Ancestry.com; Special Schedule of the Eleventh Census, 1890, Enumerating Union Veterans and Widows of Union Veterans of the Civil War, NARA. For more detail and analysis on the case of John O'Brien, see Damian Shiels, "'The Blacks Fought Like Hell': Racism and Racist Violence in the Words and Actions of Two Union Irish Cavalrymen," *Irish in the American Civil War* (2016), https://irishamericancivilwar.com/2016/02/05/the-blacks-fought-like-hell-exploring-racism-racist-violence-through-the-words-actions-of-two-union-irish-cavalrymen/ (accessed 6 June 2020).

132. For background on how the Democrats cultivated Irish American support, see e.g. Bridges, *A City in the Republic.*

133. Ryan Keating has pointed out how "democracy, republicanism, and citizenship were vital components of public rhetoric surrounding Irish service and the continued support of the Irish Americans at home." Keating, *Shades of Green,* 155.

134. For the best discussion of the negative consequences that adherence to the Democratic Party had for Irish Americans in mainstream American perception, see Ural, *The Harp and the Eagle,* 190–232, 263–264.

135. William McIntyre to "Dear Father & Mother," 30 January 1862 [1863], WC45770.

136. James Welsh to "Dear Mother," 13 January 1863, WC85074.

137. Michael Higgins to "Dear Mother," 10 November 1862, WC26768.

138. On the harsh policies initiated in the military to crack down on those expressing anti-emancipation views, something which caused Democrats to be more circumspect about sharing their opinions, see White, *Emancipation, the Union Army, and the Reelection of Abraham Lincoln,* 38–68. For a discussion of the political partisanship that grew more marked as the war progressed, see Mark E. Neely, *The Union Divided: Party Conflict in the Civil War North* (Cambridge, Mass.: Harvard Univ. Press, 2002), and especially Adam I. P. Smith, *No Party Now: Politics in the Civil War North* (New York: Oxford Univ. Press, 2006). For insight into how the slavery question impacted politics and nationalism among the wider northern populace, see Adam I. P. Smith, The Stormy Present: Conservatism and the Problem of Slavery in Northern Politics, 1846–1865 (Chapel Hill: Univ. of North Carolina Press, 2017).

139. William McIntyre to "Dear Father & Mother," 30 January 1862 [1863], WC45770.

140. George R. Agassiz, ed., *Meade's Headquarters, 1863–1865: Letters of Colonel Theodore Lyman from the Wilderness to Appomattox* (Boston: Atlantic Monthly Press, 1922), 247–248.

141. For a detailed discussion of negative Irish American reactions to the Emancipation Proclamation and of morale at this time, see Ural, *The Harp and the Eagle,* 136–189. For the perspective of the wider Union army, see Gary W. Gallagher, *The Union War* (Cambridge, Mass.: Harvard Univ. Press, 2012), 75–118.

142. Affidavit of John O'Brien, 17 July 1883, SC266425, NARA; Illinois, Databases of Illinois Veterans, Index, 1775–1995, Ancestry.com; Special Schedule of the Eleventh Census, 1890, Enumerating Union Veterans and Widows of Union Veterans of the Civil War, NARA.

143. Patrick McCaffrey to "Dear Margret," 2 September 1864, WC96706. On the practice of allowing men to go home to vote if they were Republican, see White, *Emancipation, the Union Army, and the Reelection of Abraham Lincoln,* 24, 32.

144. Thomas Hynes to "My Dear Wife," 28 August 1864, Navy WC4104.

145. Charles Traynor to "My Dear Mother," 1 November 1864, WC88894.

146. Edward Hanlin to "Dear mother," 23 June [no year, but 1862], WC88981.

147. Francis Cullen to "Deare mother," 17 September 1861, WC134902.

148. John Dougherty to "Dear Mother," 19 July 1862, WC93207. For an analysis of George McClellan's time in command that seeks to understand his political and social perspective, see Ethan S. Rafuse, *McClellan's War: The Failure of Moderation in the Struggle for the Union* (Bloomington: Indiana Univ. Press, 2005).

149. John Sheehan to "Dear Father," 18 March 1863, WC93487.

150. *New York Irish American,* 15 November 1862.

151. *New York Irish American,* 9 April 1863.

152. *New York Irish American,* 5 November 1864; Francis R Walsh, "The Boston Pilot Reports the Civil War," *Historical Journal of Massachusetts* 9, no. 2 (1981): 12.

153. White, *Emancipation, the Union Army, and the Reelection of Abraham Lincoln,* 1. By 1864, nineteen northern states had enacted legislation that allowed soldiers to vote in the field. See White, *Emancipation, the Union Army, and the Reelection of Abraham Lincoln,* 23.

154. Of the 164 surviving regimental voting returns, 130 gave majorities to Lincoln. See Fry, *Republic in the Ranks,* 178–180.

155. For the available figures showing how the Army of the Potomac regiments voted, see Fry, *Republic in the Ranks,* 210–225. For the available figures from Sherman's army, see Glatthaar, *The March to the Sea and Beyond,* 200–202.

156. Although the Copperhead and peace wing factions within the Democratic Party tend to be highlighted, many Democrats maintained a position of loyal opposition to the administration during the conflict. On this, see Mark E. Neely Jr., *Lincoln and the Democrats: The Politics of Opposition in the Civil War* (New York: Cambridge Univ. Press, 2017).

157. White notes that by this point the activities of the peace wing had caused most Democratic soldiers "to doubt their party's loyalty," with some showing no confidence in either party. See White, *Emancipation, the Union Army, and the Reelection of Abraham Lincoln,* 116.

158. McPherson, *Battle Cry of Freedom,* 771–772.

159. James O'Neill to "Mother and Father," 12 October 1864, in "Letters from Sergeant James O'Neill, 4th Delaware Volunteers, Army of the Potomac, 1863–1865," Petersburg National Battlefield, Five Forks Unit, Delaware Folder, Petersburg, Virginia, cited in "The 1864 Election—A View from the Trenches," National Park Service, Petersburg National Battlefield, https://www.nps.gov/pete/learn/historyculture/the-1864-election.htm#_ftn8 (accessed 18 September 2019).

160. For this figure, see White, *Emancipation, the Union Army, and the Reelection of Abraham Lincoln,* 112.

161. McPherson, *Battle Cry of Freedom,* 716.

162. Fry, *A Republic in the Ranks,* 1. Among the most notable Irish Americans to express support for Lincoln's reelection were Thomas Francis Meagher and Colonel Patrick Guiney of the 9th Massachusetts Infantry. It did neither man any favors within the Irish American community.

163. Smith, *No Party Now,* 147.

164. As Keith Altavilla puts it with reference to the 1864 presidential election, "Union soldiers who supported McClellan did so because they thought his election was the best path to winning the war and because of their long-standing loyalty to the party through traditional ideological and ethnic ties." See Keith Altavilla, "McClellan's Men: Union Army Democrats in 1864," in *Upon the Field of Battle: Essays on the Military History of America's Civil War,* ed. Andrew S. Bledsoe and Andrew F. Lang (Baton Rouge: Louisiana State Univ. Press, 2018), 228.

165. Crouthamel, *Bennett's New York Herald,* 112–151. The *Herald* had also defended the New York Irish when they were blamed for the draft riots.

5. IDENTITY AND MOTIVATIONS

1. Affidavit of Robert Ramsey, 21 January 1865, WC64111; CMSR of John White, Company C, 2nd Massachusetts Heavy Artillery, NARA; Payson W. Lyman, *History of Easthampton: Its Settle-*

ment and Growth: Its Material, Educational and Religious Interests, Together with a Genealogical Record of Its Original Families (Northampton, Mass.: Trumbull and Gere, 1866), 112–113.

2. Affidavit of George S. Clark and Hiram J. Bly, 20 January 1865, WC64111; 1860 U.S. Census, Easthampton, Hampshire, Massachusetts.

3. John White to "Dear mother," 8 December 1863, WC64111.

4. John White to "Dear Mother," 14 September 1863, WC64111.

5. Affidavit of George S. Clark and Hiram J. Bly, 20 January 1865, WC64111.

6. Lyman, *History of Easthampton,* 124.

7. John White to "Dear Mother," 14 September 1863, WC64111.

8. This in itself demonstrates why selective quotation from Civil War letters must be treated with caution, particularly with respect to uncontextualized correspondence.

9. See e.g. Ural, *The Harp and the Eagle,* 54; Keating, *Shades of Green,* 19.

10. Peter Carmichael has characterized identity as a "soft analytical category," noting that "too often historians invest ideology and identity with an all-encompassing explanatory power," creating an impression that soldiers acted in reflexive ways to things like nationalism and duty. See Carmichael, *The War for the Common Soldier,* 236, 10. While this needs to be acknowledged and recognized, tackling the issue of identity is nevertheless fundamental to gaining a fuller understanding of the Irish American experience of the Civil War.

11. See Ural, *The Harp and the Eagle,* 52–54, 60. Ryan Keating has used the term "dual patriotism." See Keating, *Shades of Green,* 43. While Susannah Ural sees the Irish portion of these men's identity as dominant, and increasingly so as the war went on, Ryan Keating argues that they also strongly identified with the ideals and opportunities offered by their American home. See e.g. Ural, *The Harp and the Eagle,* 52, 54, 134–135; Keating, *Shades of Green,* 19, 25, 110–111.

12. Cooper, *Forging Identities,* 186, 188. Cooper aptly titles her chapter on St. Patrick's Day celebrations "St Patrick's Day and the Public Performance of Identity." The public nature and motivational intent behind much of the championing of Irishness among the ethnic regiments is an important factor to consider when analyzing their actions and pronouncements.

13. J. Matthew Gallman, *Mastering Wartime: A Social History of Philadelphia During the Civil War* (Cambridge: Cambridge Univ. Press, 1990), 100.

14. David O'Keefe to "Dear Jane," 26 March 1863, WC32321.

15. James Healy to "Dear Parents," 30 March 1864, WC65439.

16. Richard Barrington to "My Dear Wife," 17 March 1865, WC116156.

17. For example, of units who highlighted their political affiliation or backgrounds, see e.g. the Democratically affiliated 40th "Mozart" and 42nd "Tammany" Regiments, or the 13th Pennsylvania Reserves, the "Bucktails," who were formed around a nucleus of woodsmen and hunters.

18. Bateson, *Civil War Songs,* 16–17.

19. Such was the degree of opprobrium heaped upon German troops as a result of Chancellorsville (and the XI Corps' experience of Gettysburg) that Christian Keller has argued it impacted the German population in the United States until well into the postwar period, and may even have slowed their American acculturation. See Keller, *Chancellorsville and the Germans,* 2–3, 164–165.

20. John Dougherty to "Dear Mother," 4 September 1862, WC93207.

21. Patrick Coffey to "My dear Wife," 10 May 1861, WC19650.

22. Patrick Kelly to "Dear Parents," 27 November 1862, WC22521.

23. Ryan Keating argues that while Irish Americans rarely viewed their service through an

ethnic lense, the public use of ethnicity was vital to the Americanization of green flag units, with their service reaffirming "individual conceptions of republicanism and the place of these men within their adopted nation." Keating, *Shades of Green,* 110–111.

24. William Connell to "Dear mother," 12 April [1862], WC4028.

25. Matthew Eagan to "Dear Wife," 4 April 1862, WC25637.

26. Thomas Keating to "My Deare Mother," 17 February 1863, WC88338.

27. William Cody to "Dear Mother," 7 February 1862, WC10828. As well as demonstrating the interest Irish Americans took in the leading lights of their ethnicity in the military, these examples, coming from American-born children of Irish immigrants, provide further evidence of the cohesiveness of Irish American communities and identity during this period.

28. The pride and accentuation of "Irishness" in units like the Irish Brigade should be viewed in comparative perspective with other like formations during the Civil War. For example, an accentuation of Texan origins was an intrinsic element in the identity of Hood's Texas Brigade, just as a "western" identity came to be seen as a fundamental component of the Iron Brigade's success. See Susannah J. Ural, *Hood's Texas Brigade: The Soldiers and Families of the Confederacy's Most Celebrated Unit* (Baton Rouge: Louisiana State Univ. Press, 2017); Alan T. Nolan, *The Iron Brigade: A Military History,* First Indiana Univ. Press edition (Bloomington: Indiana Univ. Press, 1994).

29. Archibald Laverty to "Dear Mother," 1 August 1861, WC100498.

30. William Duff to "Dear Mother," 4 October 1861, WC18836.

31. John Slattery to "My Dear Sister," 20 October 1862, WC145128.

32. Patrick Dooley to "Dear Mother," [illegible] July 1861, WC6206.

33. John Casey to "Dear Mother," 29 December 1861, WC45783.

34. John Deegan to "Sister Kate," 28 April 1864, WC68309.

35. For evidence of a positive bonding experience across the ethnic and class divide in the 5th New York Infantry, see Foote, *The Gentlemen and the Roughs,* 2. For a negative one in the 16th Connecticut Infantry, see Gordon, *Broken Regiment,* 87. There is substantial evidence for widespread friction between Irish Americans and natives across a number of units. For further examples, see e.g. Ramold, *Baring the Iron Hand,* 98–100.

36. McPherson, *For Cause and Comrades,* 85.

37. Alfred H. Pulcifer to "Mrs Elizabeth Connor," 25 June 1865, WC63536. Denis and James had previously served together in Company A of the 6th Massachusetts Infantry.

38. John Meehan to "Mrs Gannon," 27 April 1863, WC105102.

39. James Molony to "Mrs O Shea," 10 September 1862, WC62805; CWMRA of James Molony, 31st New York Infantry, NYSA.

40. Henry Clark to "Dear Mother and Father," 6 November 1863, Navy WC4180.

41. James Burns to "Dear father and Mother," 16 November 1864, Navy WC2286.

42. Daniel Driscoll to "Dear Farther," 28 November 1861, Navy WC3265.

43. Patrick Duffey to "Friend Mary Dougherty," 31 August 1864, Navy WC2947.

44. William Lynam to "My friend Mr Clark," 7 August 1864, Navy WC4180.

45. Patrick Galliven to "Dear mother," 10 March 1864, WC127032; CWMRA of Richard Collins, 10th New York Infantry, NYSA.

46. 1860 Census, Searsport, Waldo, Maine.

47. Thomas Doyle to "My Dear Margaret," 2 January 1863, WC27522.

48. Harriet Jacobs, *Incidents in the Life of a Slave Girl, Written by Herself* (Boston: Published for the Author, 1861), 279.

49. Floyd, *History of the Fortieth (Mozart) Regiment,* 56.

50. John Slattery to "My Dear Sister," 20 October 1862, WC145128.

51. Costa and Kahn, *Heroes and Cowards,* 152.

52. R. McCrummy to "Hon S.O. Randall," 15 February 1865, affidavit of Robert Torrey, 23 August 1866, both in WC86792. Torrey is confirmed as Irish American, as both of his parents were recorded as being from Ireland on his 1906 death certificate. See Robert H. Torrey Pension Index Card, NARA; Robert Henry Torrey death certificate, 6 February 1906, Pennsylvania Death Certificates, PHMC.

53. Thomas McCarthy to "Dear Mother and Sister," 16 October 1861, WC4642.

54. Ellen M. Litwicki, "'Our Hearts Burn with Ardent Love for Two Countries': Ethnicity and Assimilation at Chicago Holiday Celebrations, 1876–1918," *Journal of Ethnic American History* 19, no. 3 (spring 2000): 6. These celebrations were in large part organized by the middle classes, a similarity they shared with many St. Patrick's Day events. See also Ellen M. Litwicki, *America's Public Holidays, 1865–1920* (Washington, D.C.: Smithsonian Institution Press, 2003).

55. See Mitchell, *Civil War Soldiers,* 20–21. The significance of the Fourth of July during the American Civil War has been recognized by Civil War scholars who have established dedicated initiatives to explore it, such as the digital "Mapping the Fourth of July in the Civil War Era" project established at Virginia Tech. See https://civilwar.vt.edu/mapping-the-fourth-of-july-in-the-civil-war-era/ (accessed 23 November 2023).

56. Joseph Sheedy to "Dear Father & Mother," 22 May 1862, WC106040.

57. Tom Monaghan to "Dear Mother," 23 June 1862, WC52908.

58. Thomas McCready to "Dear Mother," 3 May 1862, WC70669; Felix Burns to "Dear Mother," 9 May 1863, WC123070.

59. John Delaney to "Dear Mother," [no date] December 1863, WC39990.

60. John Toomey to "Dear Father and Mother," 8 May 1862, WC5388.

61. John Boyle to "My Dear Mother," 11 February 1862, WC103714.

62. Daniel Collins to "Dear Mother," 25 July 1863, WC83617.

63. As has been noted, this is a sense of identity that Catherine Bateson has also discerned from analysis of Irish American Civil War songs. See Bateson, *Civil War Songs,* 18, 219.

64. Patrick Dugan to "Dear Mother," 3 August 1864, and Patrick Dugan to "Dear Mother," 19 January 1863, both in WC144840.

65. Patrick Horan to "Dear mother," 16 February 1862, WC47243; John Mahon to "Dear Mother," 26 February 1862, WC10604; Jeremiah Keenan to "Dear mother," 16 April 1863, WC14441.

66. Daniel Reddy to "Mrs Murry," 23 June 1864, WC91242.

67. John Mahon to "Dear Mother," 5 January 1862, and John Mahon to "Dear Mother," 26 February 1862, both in WC10604. For William Phillips's ethnicity, see 1850 U.S. Census, Hudson Ward 2, Columbia, New York, NARA. For John Barry, see CWMRA of John Barry, 91st New York Infantry, NYSA. For William Galbraith, see New York, State Census, 1855, Hudson Ward 4, Columbia, New York, Ancestry.com. For John Moore, see 1860 U.S. Census, Hudson Ward 4, Columbia, New York, NARA. John Moore appears to be another of the many Irish recorded as of Irish nativity on the Federal census, but entered as American-born on the muster rolls.

68. Jeremiah Keenan to "My fond and loving mother," 27 January [1863], and Jeremiah Keenan to "Dear mother," 16 April 1863, both in WC14441; CWMRA of David O'Connell and George Weldon, 140th New York Infantry, NYSA. O'Connell had enlisted from Churchville, while in 1860 Weldon had been working as a farm laborer in nearly Riga. See 1860 U.S. Census, Riga, Monroe, New York, NARA.

69. John Sullivan to "Dear Mother," 30 January 1862, WC12866. For Sullivan as for most of these men, groups such as these formed the "band of brothers" that McPherson has identified as so important for unit cohesion. See McPherson, *For Cause and Comrades,* 85.

70. Kenny, *American Irish,* 65; Kevin Kenny, "Labor and Labor Organisations," in *Making the Irish American: History and Heritage of the Irish in the United States,* ed. J. J. Lee and Marion R. Casey (New York: New York Univ. Press, 2006) 355.

71. Patrick Kinnane to "Dear Sister," 27 [November] 1862, WC75830.

72. Dennis Larkin to "Farther and mother," 23 March 1865, WC120669.

73. Susannah Ural has argued that because many Irish Americans were recent immigrants, they viewed the war first and foremost from the perspective of what it could provide them as Irishmen before doing so in terms of their American identity. See Ural, *The Harp and the Eagle,* 134–135.

74. The different views and perspectives that young men who grew up in the 1850s could have when compared to older generations has been examined with respect to other demographic groups in the Civil War. See e.g. Peter S. Carmichael, *The Last Generation: Young Virginians in Peace, War, and Reunion* (Chapel Hill: Univ. of North Carolina Press, 2005).

75. WC13603, relating to Michael Brady, Company F, 156th New York Infantry; 1860 U.S. Census, Saugerties, Ulster, New York, NARA; CWMRA of Michael Bradym 156th New York Infantry, NYSA; Navy WC2356, relating to James Carey, USS *Carondelet;* 1860 U.S. Census, Philadelphia Ward 3, Philadelphia, Pennsylvania, NARA; Naval Rendezvous, NARA; Navy WC2633, relating to Dennis Driscoll, USS *Metacomet;* 1860 U.S. Census, Erie, Erie, Pennsylvania, NARA; Naval Rendezvous, NARA; Navy WC2255, relating to Owen J. McGowan, USS *Keystone State;* 1860 U.S. Census, Boston Ward 7, Suffolk, Massachusetts, NARA; Naval Rendezvous, NARA; WC129489, relating to James O'Neil, Company I, 2nd New York Mounted Rifles; 1860 U.S. Census, Population Schedule, Lockport, Niagara, New York, NARA; CWMRA of James O'Neil, 2nd New York Mounted Rifles, NYSA.

76. Navy WC2821, relating to John Riley, U.S. Marine Corps; 1850 U.S. Census, Philadelphia Cedar Ward, Philadelphia, Pennsylvania, NARA; Military Enlistment of John Riley, U.S. Marine Corps, NARA; WC55575, relating to John Scully, Company F, 9th Massachusetts Infantry; 1860 U.S. Census, Salem Ward 5, Essex, Massachusetts, NARA; CMSR of John Scully, Company F, 9th Massachusetts Infantry, NARA.

77. Navy WC18243, relating to John J. Scanlan (alias Charles E. Stanley), USS *Mystic;* 1870 U.S. Census, Detroit Ward 9, Wayne, Michigan, NARA; 1880 U.S. Census, Detroit, Wayne, Michigan, NARA; Naval Rendezvous, NARA.

78. Shiels, *Forgotten Irish,* 126; Navy WC2318, relating to Denis Horgan, USS *Sachem.*

79. Shiels, *Forgotten Irish,* 67; Illinois, Databases of Illinois Veterans, Index, 1775–1995, Ancestry .com.

80. WC130737, relating to Jeremiah Dorgan, Company H, 2nd Louisiana Infantry; 1850 U.S. Census, Ellsworth, Hancock, Maine, NARA; CMSR of Jeremiah Dorgan, Company H, 2nd Louisiana Infantry, NARA.

81. WC65439, relating to James J. Healy, Company D, 9th Massachusetts Infantry; 1850 U.S. Census, Boston Ward 7, Suffolk, Massachusetts, NARA; CMSR of James Healy, Company D, 9th Massachusetts Infantry, NARA.

82. On the practice of substituting place of residence for place of nativity on enlistment forms, see Gould, *Investigations in the Military and Anthropological Statistics of American Soldiers,* 15. The number of incorrect nativities recorded for recent immigrants in the naval records may have been an effort by recruiters to downplay the enlistment of foreign sailors in the service, which for the first years of the war was technically prohibited by law. See Dennis J. Ringle, *Life in Mr. Lincoln's Navy* (Annapolis, Md.: Naval Institute Press, 1998), 16.

83. The question of Sheridan's birthplace seems unlikely to be resolved. For a forceful assertion that Sheridan was born in Co. Cavan, see Eric J. Wittenberg, *Little Phil: A Reassessment of the Civil War Leadership of Gen. Philip H. Sheridan* (Dulles, Va.: Brassey's, 2002), 142–143. On Timothy O'Sullivan, see Shiels, *The Irish in the American Civil War,* 246; James D. Horan, *Timothy O'Sullivan: America's Forgotten Photographer* (New York: Bonanza Books, 1966), 22–26.

84. *New York Herald,* 12 May 1871.

85. David Gleeson has identified a similar case in the form of noted southern author William Gilmore Simms. The son of an Irish father with whom he was estranged, Simms discarded his Irish heritage to accentuate his South Carolina identity, becoming the antebellum South's leading novelist. See Gleeson, *The Green and the Gray,* 6–7.

86. James Livingston to "Dear mother," [no date] April 1863, WC108486. During this period baseball was particularly popular among young men from major population centers, and players of immigrant descent—particularly Irish—would come to dominate the sport for much of the late nineteenth century. For a discussion of their role, see Jerrold I. Casway, *The Culture and Ethnicity of Nineteenth Century Baseball* (Jefferson, N.C.: McFarland, 2017), 7–31. On baseball during the Civil War, see George B. Kirsch, *Baseball in Blue and Gray: The National Pastime During the Civil War* (Princeton, N.J. Princeton Univ. Press, 2003). Kirsch notes that while most of those who played in the 1850s were native-born, hundreds of Irish names appeared on the rosters of major and minor clubs in places like Brooklyn, Newark, and Jersey City. See Kirsch, *Baseball in Blue and Gray,* 81.

87. William Taylor's parents hailed from Massachusetts. He appears in the 1860 census as a physician student in Nelson, Madison County. 1860 U.S. Census, Nelson, Madison, New York, NARA.

88. William Taylor to "Doctor Chamberlain," 22 November 1864, WC77208.

89. Patrick Finan to "Dear Father," 24 June 1863, Navy WC2867.

90. William McCollister to "Dear Mother," 19 June 1862, WC53297.

91. James Kerr to "Dear Friends," 28 March 1863, WC25992.

92. The majority of Irish immigrant ballads that Kerby Miller examined were melancholic in nature, with many characterizing the immigrant as a politicized exile from Ireland. The motif of the immigrant as involuntary exile was particularly strong in ballads that dramatized the immigrant's story, which often referenced a longed-for return to Ireland. See Miller, *Emigrants and Exiles,* 560–566. On the "culture of exile" in popular song during this period, see Phil Eva, "Home Sweet Home? The 'Culture of Exile' in Mid-Victorian Popular Song," *Popular Music* 16, no. 2 (1992): 131–150. In contrast, Catherine Bateson's examination of Irish American references to "home" in Civil War ballads led her to assess that this music demonstrates "one of the clearest contemporary popular and public articulations of the American Union being an Irish home nation." See Catherine V.

Bateson, "'Forward for Our Homes!': Lyrical Expressions of Home Heard in Irish American Civil War Songs," *Journal of History and Cultures* 9 (2019): 98.

93. On the formation of the Fenians, see Brundage, *Irish Nationalists in America,* 99–100. For a detailed discussion of the Fenians during the American Civil War, see Steward and McGovern, *The Fenians,* 29–47. On how Fenians in the United States attempted to influence the country's policy toward Britain and Irish independence, see David Sim, *A Union Forever: The Irish Question and U.S. Foreign Relations in the Victorian Age* (Ithaca, N.Y.: Cornell Univ. Press, 2013).

94. See e.g. Ural, *The Harp and the Eagle,* 41.

95. For these figures, see Brundage, *Irish Nationalists in America,* 89.

96. For a discussion on the backgrounds of Fenians who returned to Ireland for revolutionary purposes after having served in the U.S. military, see Michael H. Kane, "American Soldiers in Ireland, 1865–67," *The Irish Sword: The Journal of the Military History Society of Ireland* 23, no. 91 (2002): 103–140. Although the numbers who participated in such operations were impacted by divisions within the Fenian movement, the figures are still extremely low given the supposed primacy of Irish freedom in the minds of many Irish Americans. For an insight into some of the divisions and failures that accompanied efforts to support the postwar Fenian efforts in Ireland, see Lucy E. Sayler, *Under the Starry Flag: How a Band of Irish Americans Joined the Fenian Revolt and Sparked a Crisis over Citizenship* (Cambridge, Mass.: Belknap Press of Harvard Univ. Press, 2018), 75–88. For analyses of the incursions into Canada, see Peter Vronsky, *Ridgeway: The American Fenian Invasion and the 1866 Battle That Made Canada* (Toronto: Allen Lane Canada, 2011), and Christopher Klein, *When the Irish Invaded Canada: The Incredible True Story of the Civil War Veterans Who Fought for Ireland's Freedom* (New York: Doubleday, 2019).

97. Brundage, *Irish Nationalists in America,* 102.

98. Between 1852 and 1913, Irish return migration from America is estimated to have run at only about 6 percent of the outflow. See Timothy J. Hatton and Jeffrey G. Williamson, "After the Famine: Emigration from Ireland, 1850–1913," *Journal of Economic History* 53, no. 3 (1993): 575–576. Though figures are scant for the mid-nineteenth century, it is telling that, given the scale of Irish American service, only 219 Federal pensions were being claimed in Ireland in 1883. Figures for the turn of the twentieth century suggest the Irish had the lowest repatriation ratio of any major European country at that point, and that those Irish who did journey back to Ireland did so for only short periods before returning to the United States. For a discussion, see David Fitzpatrick, *The Americanisation of Ireland: Migration and Settlement, 1841–1925* (Cambridge: Cambridge Univ. Press, 2020), 6–18.

99. John Corcoran to "Dear Parents," 1 August 1862, WC10461. John Corcoran provides yet another example of the problem of equating nativity with ethnic identity in American Civil War servicemen.

100. Patrick Finan to "Dear Father," 24 June 1863, Navy WC2867.

101. James Henry to "My Dear Father," 10 January 1861 [1862], WC134153.

102. WC134153, relating to James Henry, Company E, 11th U.S. Infantry.

103. Patrick Steward and Bryan McGovern's analysis of Fenians during the war supports this conclusion. They found that many potential Fenian recruits appeared to be more ideologically attached to the United States than their homeland, and that Irish American Union servicemen often referenced Ireland's future independence as a means of creating an "imagined community" among their fellows. In their determination, "Irish American soldiers were more inclined to risk their lives

for the United States than for Ireland." Steward and McGovern, *The Fenians,* 38–40. Catherine Bateson has identified similar sentiments in her analysis of wartime music that referenced the Fenian and Irish nationalist struggle. See Bateson, *Civil War Songs,* 134–155. As William L. Burton characterized it, "most Irish-Americans were committed to America and to themselves, not to historic and Old World quarrels." See Burton, *Melting Pot Soldiers,* 154.

104. The correspondence of working-class Irish Americans makes it apparent that those who had immigrated to the United States were regarded as the fortunate ones, and they were expected to assist those less fortunate who had remained in Ireland. Old and new communities on both sides of the Atlantic remained umbilically linked across decades, with many immigrants feeling a profound sense of obligation to those left behind. For a telling example of this, see Shiels, *Forgotten Irish,* 83–88.

105. Patrick Delanty to "My Dear Mother & Sisters," 19 May 1862, Navy WC2163.

106. Patrick Delanty to "My Dear Mother & Sisters," 19 May 1862, Navy WC2163.

107. Edmund Dwyer to "my dear Father," 30 January 1859, WC132012.

108. John Shea to "Dear Mother," 6 October 1861, WC15721.

109. Matthew Eagan to "Dear Wife," 16 March 1862, WC25637.

110. Patrick Duffy to "Friend Mary Dougherty," 31 August 1864, Navy WC2947.

111. Patrick Finan to "Dear Father," 25 January 1863, Navy WC2867.

112. Edward Fitzpatrick to "My Dear Wife," 23 March [1865], WC142303.

113. Michael Daly to "My Dear Mother," 14 March 1863, WC143339.

114. Michael Daly to "Dear Brother," 5 March 1863, WC143339. The pension files indicate that it was commonplace for single Irish men in America to have matches made with young women from their locality of origin in Ireland, who would then follow them to the United States.

115. Lincoln referred to the United States as such in his Annual Message to Congress on 1 December 1862.

116. Patrick O'Brien to "Dear Mother," 15 October 1862[?], Navy WC2732.

117. John Crowley to "My Dear Tom," 12 May [no year], Navy WC2920.

118. This is true of all Civil War service, and it is a topic that continues to see much detailed analysis. See, for example, McPherson, *For Cause and Comrades;* Aaron Sheehan-Dean, *Why Confederates Fought: Family and Nation in Civil War Virginia* (Chapel Hill: Univ. of North Carolina Press, 2007).

119. An increasing acknowledgment of the individuality of American Civil War servicemen and the problems inherent in making broad generalizations regarding them has become a strong theme in Civil War soldier studies. As Peter Carmichael points out, "no one man can stand for all the experiences in the ranks and no single individual can possibly represent the approximately 2.7 million men who served in the Union forces. . . . There was no common soldier in the Civil War." Carmichael, *The War for the Common Soldier,* 12. This breadth of experience has been acknowledged by scholars of the Irish soldier, with Susannah Ural outlining that "the motivations of Irish-American volunteers and their families are as varied as their own communities." See Ural, *The Harp and the Eagle,* 2.

120. John Slattery to "My Dear Grandmother," 25 January 1862, WC130731.

121. Affidavit of Ann Leonard and Mary Leonard, 5 February 1868, WC117088.

122. William Flaherty to "Dear mother," 31 December 1863, WC117088.

123. James Carroll to "Dear Wife," 22 March 1862, WC10231.

124. Jeremiah Dorgan to "Dear Mother," 12 May 1863, WC130737.

125. Edward had been found guilty of murdering Charles Wood in Dubuque, Iowa, on 9 November 1859. He and his co-accused Kerry immigrant, Daniel Clifford, had supposedly killed Wood for his money, having first tried to obtain it from him by luring him to a "sink of corruption." Clifford was hanged on 19 October 1860. For details of the murder, trial, and sentencing, see *New Oregon (Iowa) Plaindealer,* 13 January 1860; *St. Charles City (Iowa) Republican Intelligencer,* 6 September 1860; *Muscatine (Iowa) Weekly Journal,* 26 October 1860; *Buchanan County (Iowa) Guardian,* 16 April 1861; *Iowa Transcript,* 18 April 1861.

126. James H. Reynolds, Deputy Warden Iowa Penitentiary, to "Mrs Mary Mooney," 11 January 1863, WC84797.

127. WC84797, relating to Edward Mooney, Company E, 19th Iowa Infantry.

128. John Fitzpatrick to "Dear Mother," 9 August 1861, WC56115.

129. Thomas McCready to "Dear mother," 24 September 1861, WC70669.

130. Michael Carroll to "Dear mother Brothers and Sisters," 22 January 1862, WC40248.

131. Patrick Dooley to "Dear Mother," 28 January 1862, WC6206.

132. John Mahon to "Dear Mother," 26 February 1862, WC10604.

133. James Fitzgerald to "Dear Mother," 28 September 1862, WC23216.

134. See, for example, McPherson, *For Cause and Comrades,* 5. McPherson asserts, "They did not fight for money. The pay was poor and unreliable; the large enlistment bounties received by some Union soldiers late in the war were exceptional; most volunteers and their families made economic sacrifices when they enlisted." For an important counterpoint to this narrative, see Marvel, *Lincoln's Mercenaries.*

135. Marvel, *Lincoln's Mercenaries,* 36, 56, 58–60. The reports of "hard-times," closures, and layoffs were everywhere in northern newspapers in the war's early months.

136. *New York Herald,* 16 January 1861; *Philadelphia Inquirer,* 19 January 1861.

137. *Boston Pilot,* 5 January 1861.

138. The president's proclamation was printed in numerous papers in January 1861. See e.g. *Evansville (Ind.) Daily Journal,* 4 January 1861, *New York Herald,* 4 January 1861, *Boston Pilot,* 5 January 1861.

139. *New York Irish American,* 27 April 1861. Writing more than three decades after the war, Andrew Byrne, a veteran of the prewar regulars who returned to America from Ireland to fight to preserve the Union, recalled the scene on his 1861 arrival in New York: "Business was very Bad in New York in consequence of the Breaking up of trade between the North and Southt thousands of men were idle yet thousands of emigrants were landing every week in the Castle Garden." Andrew J. Byrne, *Memoir of Andrew J. Byrne: Veteran of the American Civil War,* ed. Nicola Morris (Dublin: Original Writing Ltd., 2008), 97.

140. See Spiers, "Army Organisation," 335–340.

141. James O'Herrin to "dear Father," 10 October 1861, WC125192.

142. Thomas Doyle to "My Dearest Margaret," 12 March 1863, WC27522.

143. Edmund Dwyer to "My Dear Father," 6 April 1862, WC132012.

144. John O'Brien to "My Dr Wife," 4 June 1862, in Navy WC18084.

145. James Sheren to "Dear Wife," 6 May 1861, and affidavit of Maria Sherden, 15 October 1863,

both in WC11095. The file is recorded under the name "Sheriden," as it was one of the ways in which James's surname was recorded in the military.

146. James McGinness to "Dear Mother," 8 August 1862, WC1694.

147. Cornelius O'Brien to "Dear Mother," 19 February [no date, but 1864], WC84143.

148. Pat Scannell to "Dear mother," 10 April [1865], WC62659.

149. Affidavit of Charles L. Rabitte and Thomas Mullen, 13 September 1866, WC94532; *Hartford (Conn.) Daily Courant,* 31 January 1861.

150. John. C. Lynch to "My Own darling Mother," no date [but circa April 1862], WC94532.

151. Affidavit of Daniel McKenna and John McKenna, 1 October 1868, WC124498.

152. James O'Herrin to "dear Father," 10 October 1861, WC125192.

153. James Carroll to "Dear Wife," 22 March 1862, WC10231.

154. Affidavit of Stephen J. McGroarty, 23 July 1866, WC117744.

155. Affidavit of John Ballard, 24 December 1885, WC259125; CWMRA for Frederick Nightingale, 118th New York Infantry, NYSA.

156. Miller, *Emigrants and Exiles,* 347.

157. Unknown to "Dear Sister," 31 March 1863, WC116873. For more on the experience of this family, the Madigans, see Shiels, *Forgotten Irish,* 83–88.

158. Across the next seven years Alexander's family sought information on his fate, unaware that he had almost certainly been killed in action in Louisiana in 1863. *Boston Pilot,* 18 April 1863; *Irish American,* 2 April 1870; Ruth-Ann M. Harris, Donald Jacobs, and Emeer O'Keeffe, eds., *Searching for Missing Friends: Irish Immigrant Advertisements Placed in "The Boston Pilot" 1831–1920* (Boston: New England Historic Genealogical Society, 1989), 186; CWMRA for Arthur Shaw, 174th New York Infantry, NYSA. For more on the case, see Damian Shiels, "A 150 Year Old Missing Persons Case—In Search of a 19-Year-Old Irishman," *Irish in the American Civil War* (2014), https://irishamericancivilwar.com/2014/04/13/a-150-year-old-missing-persons-case-in-search-of-a-19-year-old-irishman/ (accessed 2 June 2020).

159. Thomas Bowler to "My Dear Ellen," 17 April 1864, WC115828; Shiels, *Forgotten Irish,* 79–83.

160. Affidavit of Mary Ryan, 9 December 1864, affidavit of John Hallawell, 9 December 1864, and affidavit of Margaret Smith, 9 December 1864, all in WC63566; *Lamoille (Vt.) Newsdealer,* 4 June 1863; *Burlington (Vt.) Daily Times,* 15 July 1863; Consolidated Lists of Civil War Draft Registrations, NARA; CMSR of James Ryan, Company I, 3rd Vermont Infantry, NARA; Damian Shiels, "In Defence of Substitutes: The Story of Mary and James Ryan of Drogheda, Canada and Vermont," *Irish in the American Civil War* (2020), https://irishamericancivilwar.com/2020/02/18/in-defence-of-substitutes-the-story-of-mary-james-ryan-of-drogheda-canada-vermont/ (accessed 3 June 2020).

161. Affidavit of Thomas Ryan and Bridget Howard, 1 October 1866, WC124030.

162. For a detailed accounting of the Con Garvin case, see Shiels, *Forgotten Irish,* 18–30; WC78263, relating to Cornelius Garvin (alias Charles Becker), Company I, 52nd New York Infantry.

163. WC57059, relating to Thomas Burke, Company D, 20th Maine Infantry. For an account of the incident and its aftermath, see Eugene H. Berwanger, *The British Foreign Service and the American Civil War* (Lexington: Univ. Press of Kentucky, 1994), 155–161. On Finney's actions in Ireland, see Damian Shiels, "'Watch the Man's Movements': Illegal Recruitment for the Union in Ireland, Part One," *Irish in the American Civil War* (2013), https://irishamericancivilwar.com/2013/04/03/watch-the-mans-movements-illegal-recruitment-for-the-union-in-ireland-part-one/ (accessed 21

June 2020). The topic of illegal and forced recruitment is touched on by a number of scholars. See, for example, Joseph M. Hernon, *Celts, Catholics and Copperheads: Ireland Views the American Civil War* (Columbus: Ohio State Univ. Press, 1968); Robert L. Peterson and John A. Hudson, "Foreign Recruitment for Union Forces," *Civil War History* 7, no. 2 (1961): 176–189. For a detailed examination of a number of specific cases in New York, see Brendan Hamilton and Damian Shiels, "Recruited Straight Off the Boat? On the Trail of Emigrant Soldiers From the Ship Great Western," *Irish in the American Civil War* (2015), https://irishamericancivilwar.com/2015/10/01/recruited-straight-off-the-boat-on-the-trail-of-emigrant-soldiers-from-the-ship-great-western/ (accessed 25 June 2020); Brendan Hamilton and Damian Shiels, "'It Was Not For To Be Soldiers We Came Out': Recruited Straight Off The Boat—Some New Evidence," 2019, *Irish in the American Civil War* (2019), https://irishamericancivilwar.com/2019/01/12/it-was-not-for-to-be-soldiers-we-came-out-recruited-straight-off-the-boat-some-new-evidence/ (accessed 25 June 2020).

164. John Daly to "My dear Wife," 23 September 1864, WC126148. For more on the Daly family story, see Shiels, *Forgotten Irish,* 93–98.

165. Patrick Delanty to "My Dear Mother & Sisters," 17 February 1862, Navy WC2163. Based on his letter, Patrick was likely working for English-born merchant Henry Winter in Cairo, Illinois. See 1860 U.S. Census, Cairo, Alexander, Illinois, NARA.

166. Patrick Delanty to "My Dear Mother & Sisters," 1 June 1862, Navy WC2163.

167. Patrick Delanty to "My Dear Mother and Sisters," 11 August 1862, Navy WC2163.

168. Gerrish, *Army Life,* 42–43.

169. Shiels, *Forgotten Irish,* 139–140. Thomas Welch to "Dear Brother," 26[?] January 1863, WC141783.

170. John Sullivan to "Dear Mother," 13 January 1862, WC12866.

171. John Sullivan to "Dear Mother," 30 January 1862, WC12866.

172. William Harnett to "Dear Mother," 3 May 1862, WC20688.

173. Michael McCormick to "Dear Mother," 19 June 1862, WC96255.

174. Martin Noonan to "My Dear Sister," 2 March 1862, WC71872.

175. Affidavit of Michael Holland and John Myres, 10 June 1867, and affidavit of Elizabeth "Alice" Lane, 10 June 1867, both in WC121011. CMSR of John Lane, Company A, 12th Massachusetts Infantry, NARA.

176. A good example of this ideal can be seen in the promotion of Union bonds. See e.g. David K. Thomson, "'Like a Cord through the Whole Country': Union Bonds and Financial Mobilization for Victory," *Journal of the Civil War Era* 6, no. 3 (September 2016): 347–375. However, as J. Matthew Gallman has demonstrated, much of northern society did not take kindly to Irish American efforts to share in the pursuit of patriotic profits. See Gallman, *Defining Duty.*

177. Michael Carroll to "Dear mother Brothers and Sisters," 15 December 1861, WC40248.

178. Michael Carroll to "Dear mother Brothers and Sisters," 28 January 1862, WC40248. For a detailed discussion of the "Bold Soldier Boy" and its place and meaning in Irish American culture and society, see Stephen Rohs, "'The Bold Soldier Boy': Performance and Irish Boldness in New York in 1855," *American Studies* 44, no. 1/2 (2003): 157–182. On the importance of song in Irish America, and particularly about what it can tell us regarding Irish American service, see Bateson, *Civil War Songs.* For a similar analysis that covers a century of Irish America, see Dan Milner, *The Unstoppable Irish: Songs and Integration of the New York Irish, 1783–1883* (Notre Dame: Univ. of Notre Dame Press, 2019).

179. John Costello to "Dear Sister," 21 April 1862, WC58007.

180. John Kelly to "Dear Mother," 22 November 1861, WC26080.

181. Charles Devlin to "Dear Wife and Children," 9 March 1862, WC161452. For more on the Devlin family story, see Shiels, *Forgotten Irish,* 174–186.

182. John Buckley, "Greeting Home," [no date] 1863, Navy WC4219.

183. Timothy Dougherty to "Dear Mother," 19 December 1864, WC115555.

184. John Deegan to "Sister Kate," 28 April 1864, WC68309. Perhaps the most notable example of an Irish American who was not among the first to rush to war but who was nonetheless strongly devoted to the Union was Peter Welsh of the 28th Massachusetts Infantry. His enlistment in September 1862 came after a drinking spree in which he had spent all his money. See Lawrence Frederick Kohl and Margaret Cossé Richard, eds., *Irish Green and Union Blue: The Civil War Letters of Peter Welsh* (New York: Fordham Univ. Press, 1986).

185. Nicholas Mahar to "Dear sister," 13 June 1864, WC107142.

186. Patrick Clooney to "Mrs Dunigan," 2 June 1862, WC954.

187. William Loughran to "Mrs Tye," 7 October 1862, WC51891; WC26018, relating to William Loughran, Company C, 88th New York Infantry.

188. Edward Byrne to "Mrs Feeney," 29 May 1863, WC23343.

189. Ohio Roster Commission, *Official Roster of the Soldiers of the State of Ohio in the War of the Rebellion 1861–1866,* vol. 6 (Akron, Ohio: General Assembly 1888), 210; affidavit of William Brogan and Michael Curran, 23 January 1868, WC107715; Whitelaw Reid, *Ohio in the War: Her Statesmen, Her Generals, and Soldiers,* vol. 2 (Cincinnati: Moore, Wilstach and Baldwin, 1868), 434–435; Scott C. Patchan, *Second Manassas: Longstreet's Attack and the Struggle for Chinn Ridge* (Washington, D.C.: Potomac Books, 2011), 67–68; John J. Hennessy, *Return to Bull Run: The Battle and Campaign of Second Manassas* (Norman: Univ. of Oklahoma Press, 1999), 381–396. C. R. Bigalow to "Mr. Brady," 24 September 1862, WC107715.

CONCLUSION

1. Affidavit of Mary Dooley, 24 September 1862, affidavit of Mary Kearney, 22 October 1862, certificate confirming death of Patrick Dooley, General Hospital, U.S. Army, Philadelphia, 16 April 1863, all in WC6206.

2. *New York Times,* 26 September 1862.

3. For analyses that discern conflicting loyalties, see e.g. Ural, *The Harp and the Eagle,* 52–54; Burton, *Melting Pot Soldiers,* 37; Keating, *Shades of Green,* 27. On the war speeding their passage toward becoming American, see especially Samito, *Becoming American,* 173, 221. As previously noted, the American identity reflected in these men's letters is one that has also been identified by Catherine Bateson in her analysis of their wartime music. See Bateson, *Civil War Songs,* 18, 219.

4. Ryan Keating also identified the importance of American community to these men, noting that when they volunteered "they did so as men not cast apart from mainstream American society, but as full economic participants in a vibrant Northern society." See Keating, *Shades of Green,* 19.

5. Patrick Finan to "Dear Father," 24 June 1863, Navy WC2867.

6. Irish Americans shared many of the same concepts of duty as their native comrades. As Peter Carmichael has identified, duty was the watchword of many Civil War veterans, as "it made the job

of soldiering sacred while also offering men a degree of latitude in dealing with the dilemmas of army life." See Carmichael, *The War for the Common Soldier,* 7.

7. For a discussion of this, see Damian Shiels, "Ireland's Forgotten 'Great War'?," *History Ireland* 24, no. 4 (July/August 2019): 30–33.

8. To date, four American presidents have addressed the Irish Parliament: John F. Kennedy (1963), Ronald Reagan (1984), Bill Clinton (1995), and Joe Biden (2023). Only Reagan did not make direct reference to Irish participation in the Civil War, but he did quote from Abraham Lincoln's first inaugural, speaking of the "mystic chords of memory" that had stirred in him since arriving in Ireland.

9. John F. Kennedy, "Address before the Irish Parliament in Dublin, 28 June 1963," John F. Kennedy Presidential Library and Museum, Historic Speeches, available at https://www.jfklibrary.org/learn/about-jfk/historic-speeches/address-before-the-irish-parliament (accessed 14 July 2023). The color Kennedy gifted was created for the 69th New York Infantry in late 1862. It remains in Dáil Éireann to this day. For more on the event, see Shiels, *The Irish in the American Civil War,* 226–229.

10. Bill Clinton, "Address of President Clinton, 1 December 1995," Houses of the Oireachtas Website, available at https://www.oireachtas.ie/en/debates/debate/dail/1995-12-01/2/ (accessed 16 July 2023). At the time of his address to the Irish Parliament, Clinton had just become the first American president to visit Northern Ireland, having done so on 30 November 1995.

11. Remarks by President Joe Biden to the Houses of the Oireachtas, Leinster House, Dublin, Republic of Ireland, 13 April 2023. Available at https://www.whitehouse.gov/briefing-room/speeches-remarks/2023/04/13/remarks-by-president-biden-to-the-houses-of-the-oireachtas/ (accessed 18 July 2023).

12. The Irish roots of Joe Biden, including his American Civil War links, were identified through the research of genealogist Megan Smolenyak. See Megan Smolenyak, "Joey from Scranton," *Irish America Magazine,* April/May 2013, 56–59.

13. Wilson G. Lamb, "Seventeenth Regiment," in *Histories of the Several Regiments and Battalions from North Carolina in the Great War 1861–'65,* vol. 2, ed. Walter Clark (Goldsboro, N.C.: Nash Brothers, 1901), 5. Originally quoted in Gordon C. Rhea, *Cold Harbor: Grant and Lee, May 26–June 3, 1864* (Baton Rouge: Louisiana State Univ. Press, 2002), 336.

BIBLIOGRAPHY

PENSION FILES

The pension files are held by the National Archives and Record Administration in Washington, D.C., where they form part of Record Group 15, Records of the Department of Veterans Affairs. Original scanned images of the pension files were consulted on https://fold3.com, with a small number of supplementary files examined in person at the National Archives.

Case Files of Approved Pension Applications of Widows and Other Dependents of the Army

Widow's Certificate No. 954, Widow of Patrick Dunnigan, Company E, 88th New York Infantry.

Widow's Certificate No. 1056, Widow of Francis McLaughlin, Battery D, 1st Pennsylvania Light Artillery.

Widow's Certificate No. 1694, Mother of James McGinness, Company G, 90th New York Infantry.

Widow's Certificate No. 2177, Widow of James McGaffifan, Company A, 63rd New York Infantry.

Widow's Certificate No. 2415, Widow of John Conway, Company K, 69th New York Infantry.

Widow's Certificate No. 2537, Widow of James Leahey, Company D, 99th New York Infantry.

Widow's Certificate No. 3130, Mother of James Harrigan, Company D, 72nd Pennsylvania Infantry.

Widow's Certificate No. 4028, Mother of William Connell, Company B, 7th Vermont Infantry.

Widow's Certificate No. 4642, Mother of Thomas McCarthy, Company A, 12th Massachusetts Infantry.

Widow's Certificate No. 4869, Mother of Martin Tiernan, Company B, 61st New York Infantry.

Widow's Certificate No. 5388, Mother of John Toomey, Company E, 15th Massachusetts Infantry.

Widow's Certificate No. 6206, Mother of Patrick Dooley, Company C, 40th New York Infantry.

Widow's Certificate No. 8306, Mother of William Delaney, Company F, 43rd New York Infantry.

Widow's Certificate No. 8731, Mother of John Sullivan, Company I, 99th New York Infantry.

Widow's Certificate No. 8938, Mother of Michael Connerty, Company C, 88th New York Infantry.

Widow's Certificate No. 9732, Mother of James Briody, Company I, 20th Massachusetts Infantry.

Widow's Certificate No. 10231, Widow of James Carroll, Company G, 42nd New York Infantry.

Widow's Certificate No. 10461, Mother of John Cochrane [Corcoran], Company C, 2nd Massachusetts Infantry.

Widow's Certificate No. 10604, Mother of John Mahon, Company I, 91st New York Infantry.

Widow's Certificate No. 10828, Mother of William Cody, Company K, 3rd Rhode Island Heavy Artillery.

Widow's Certificate No. 11095, Widow of James Sheriden [Sheren], Company E, 2nd Kentucky Infantry.

Widow's Certificate No. 11238, Minor Children of John Deasy, Company I, 20th Massachusetts Infantry.

Widow's Certificate No. 12866, Mother of John Sullivan, Company D, 102nd New York Infantry.

Widow's Certificate No. 13603, Widow of Michael Brady, Company F, 156th New York Infantry.

Widow's Certificate No. 14441, Mother of Jeremiah Keenan, Company G, 140th New York Infantry.

Widow's Certificate No. 15721, Mother of John Shea, Company B, 1st Kansas Infantry.

Widow's Certificate No. 16416, Widow of Michael Martin (alias John Martin), Company I, 2nd Massachusetts Infantry.

Widow's Certificate No. 18510, Mother of Patrick Carney, Company D, 69th Pennsylvania Infantry.

Widow's Certificate No. 18836, Mother of William Duff, Company I, 10th New York Infantry.
Widow's Certificate No. 19650, Widow of Patrick Coffey, Company D, 69th New York State Militia.
Widow's Certificate No. 20688, Mother of William J. Harnett, Company F, 4th U.S. Infantry.
Widow's Certificate No. 22521, Mother of Patrick Kelly, Company G, 28th Massachusetts Infantry.
Widow's Certificate No. 23216, Mother of James C. Fitzgerald, Company F, 8th Illinois Infantry.
Widow's Certificate No. 23343, Mother of John Feeny, Company D, 170th New York Infantry.
Widow's Certificate No. 25547, Mother of William Dolan, Company I, 174th New York Infantry.
Widow's Certificate No. 25637, Widow of Matthew Eagan, Company C, 72nd New York Infantry.
Widow's Certificate No. 25992, Minor Children of James Kerr (alias John Kerr), Company E, 26th Pennsylvania Infantry.
Widow's Certificate No. 26018, Widow of William Loughran, Company C, 88th New York Infantry.
Widow's Certificate No. 26080, Mother of John Kelly, Company F, 1st New York Cavalry.
Widow's Certificate No. 26768, Mother of Michael H. Higgins, Company B, 125th New York Infantry.
Widow's Certificate No. 26932, Mother of Patrick Connely, Company G, 6th Connecticut Infantry.
Widow's Certificate No. 27032, Mother of John G. O'Connell, Company H, 2nd Massachusetts Infantry.
Widow's Certificate No. 27309, Widow of John Brennan (alias John Burns), Company H, 11th Massachusetts Infantry.
Widow's Certificate No. 27522, Widow of Thomas Martin Doyle (alias Thomas Doyle), Company I, 4th Maine Infantry.
Widow's Certificate No. 28175, Mother of James Sharkey, Company C, 21st New York Cavalry.
Widow's Certificate No. 31563, Widow of Michael Meehan, Company G, 47th New York Infantry.
Widow's Certificate No. 31621, Mother of James Finnerty, Company B, 72nd Illinois Infantry.
Widow's Certificate No. 31685, Mother of John Grimes, Company K, 3rd Rhode Island Heavy Artillery.

Widow's Certificate No. 32321, Widow of David O'Keefe, Company A, 9th Massachusetts Infantry.

Widow's Certificate No. 37552, Mother of James Hayes, Company C, 38th Illinois Infantry.

Widow's Certificate No. 38010, Mother of Thomas C. Diver, Company I, 69th Pennsylvania Infantry.

Widow's Certificate No. 39990, Mother of John Delany [Delaney], Company A, 18th Connecticut Infantry.

Widow's Certificate No. 40248, Mother of Michael Carroll, Company C, 72nd New York Infantry.

Widow's Certificate No. 45770, Mother of William McIntyre, Company H, 95th Pennsylvania Infantry.

Widow's Certificate No. 45783, Mother of John Casey, Company C, 45th Illinois Infantry.

Widow's Certificate No. 46367, Mother of Timothy L. Toomey, Company E, 160th New York Infantry.

Widow's Certificate No. 47243, Mother of Patrick Horin [Horan], Company H, 67th New York Infantry.

Widow's Certificate No. 47691, Minor Children of James Dowd, Company B, 63rd New York Infantry.

Widow's Certificate No. 49639, Widow of Robert Boyle, Company B, 164th New York Infantry.

Widow's Certificate No. 51663, Mother of Thomas Hagan, Company E, 15th New York Cavalry.

Widow's Certificate No. 51891, Widow of Patrick McTeague, Company C, 88th New York Infantry.

Widow's Certificate No. 52908, Mother of Thomas J. Monaghan, Company A, 95th Pennsylvania Infantry.

Widow's Certificate No. 53297, Mother of William McCollinster, Company B, 4th Pennsylvania Infantry.

Widow's Certificate No. 54548, Mother of John Lynch, Company A, 10th Illinois Infantry.

Widow's Certificate No. 55575, Mother of John Scully, Company F, 9th Massachusetts Infantry.

Widow's Certificate No. 56115, Mother of John Fitzpatrick, Company E, 19th Illinois Infantry.

Widow's Certificate No. 56206, Mother of Patrick Carey, Company F, 5th New York Heavy Artillery.

Widow's Certificate No. 56405, Mother of Cornelius Donahoe, Company G, 16th Massachusetts Infantry.

Widow's Certificate No. 57059, Widow of Thomas Burke, Company D, 20th Maine Infantry.
Widow's Certificate No. 58007, Mother of John Costello, Company F, 1st Massachusetts Light Artillery.
Widow's Certificate No. 61242, Mother of Martin Flanagan, Company C, 74th New York Infantry.
Widow's Certificate No. 62659, Mother of Ambrose Patrick Scannell, Company I, 1st New Hampshire Cavalry.
Widow's Certificate No. 62805, Widow of Stephen O'Shea, Company A, 31st New York Infantry.
Widow's Certificate No. 63536, Mother of James Conner, Company D, 2nd Massachusetts Heavy Artillery.
Widow's Certificate No. 63566, Mother of James Ryan, Company I, 3rd Vermont Infantry.
Widow's Certificate No. 63799, Mother of Edward Carroll, Company D, 1st Rhode Island Light Artillery.
Widow's Certificate No. 64111, Mother of John White, Company C, 2nd Massachusetts Heavy Artillery.
Widow's Certificate No. 64963, Mother of William Shea, Company E, 23rd Pennsylvania Infantry.
Widow's Certificate No. 65439, Mother of James J. Healy, Company D, 9th Massachusetts Infantry.
Widow's Certificate No. 68309, Mother of John Deegan, Company I, 19th Maine Infantry.
Widow's Certificate No. 69603, Mother of Charles Williams, Company H, 69th Pennsylvania Infantry.
Widow's Certificate No. 70669, Mother of Thomas McCready, Company C, 74th New York Infantry.
Widow's Certificate No. 71372, Widow of Kearn Phalen (alias Kearn Fitzpatrick), Company E, 11th Connecticut Infantry.
Widow's Certificate No. 71872, Mother of Martin Noonan, Company K, 64th New York Infantry.
Widow's Certificate No. 74825, Mother of Hugh O'Donnell, Company C, 29th Pennsylvania Infantry.
Widow's Certificate No. 75056, Mother of James Fitzpatrick, Company A, 96th New York Infantry.
Widow's Certificate No. 75830, Minor Sister of Patrick Kinnane, Company K, 155th New York Infantry.
Widow's Certificate No. 76523, Widow of Smith Davis, Company I, 65th New York Infantry.

Widow's Certificate No. 77208, Widow of Thomas Carr, Company H, 20th New York Infantry.

Widow's Certificate No. 77334, Widow of John Wallace, Company D, 63rd New York Infantry.

Widow's Certificate No. 78263, Mother of Cornelius Garvin (alias Charles Becker), Company I, 52nd New York Infantry.

Widow's Certificate No. 79466, Mother of William Martin, Company K, 69th New York Infantry.

Widow's Certificate No. 80051, Mother of James McHugh, Company B, 2nd Battalion, 19th U.S. Infantry.

Widow's Certificate No. 82386, Widow of James Hickey, Company B, 164th New York Infantry.

Widow's Certificate No. 83617, Mother of Daniel P. Collins, Company G, 155th New York Infantry.

Widow's Certificate No. 84143, Mother of Cornelius O'Brien, Company F, 16th Illinois Infantry.

Widow's Certificate No. 84155, Mother of Joseph McConaghy (alias Joseph May), Company B, 73rd Pennsylvania Infantry.

Widow's Certificate No. 84797, Mother of Edward Mooney, Company E, 19th Iowa Infantry.

Widow's Certificate No. 85074, Mother of James Welsh, Company G, 82nd Pennsylvania Infantry.

Widow's Certificate No. 85142, Mother of Patrick Griffin, 6th Independent Battery, Massachusetts Light Artillery.

Widow's Certificate No. 85252, Mother of Mathew McCourt, Company A, 1st Michigan Infantry.

Widow's Certificate No. 86354, Mother of John O'Connor, Company K, 151st New York Infantry.

Widow's Certificate No. 86549, Mother of John Madden (alias John Maitin), Company C, 162nd New York Infantry.

Widow's Certificate No. 86792, Widow of Arthur Mulholland, Company F, 69th Pennsylvania Infantry.

Widow's Certificate No. 87287, Mother of William Maroney, Company B, 164th New York Infantry.

Widow's Certificate No. 88094, Mother of Daniel Dillon, Company D, 10th Illinois Cavalry.

Widow's Certificate No. 88338, Mother of Thomas Keating, Company D, 94th New York Infantry.

Widow's Certificate No. 88894, Mother of Charles Trainor [Traynor], Company F, 69th New York Infantry.

Widow's Certificate No. 88981, Mother of Edward Hanlin, Company E, 12th New York Infantry.

Widow's Certificate No. 89342, Mother of John Finton [Fenton], Company B, 90th New York Infantry.

Widow's Certificate No. 91242, Mother of John Murry [Murray], Company F, 16th Massachusetts Infantry.

Widow's Certificate No. 91465, Mother of Richard Flynn, Company K, 117th New York Infantry.

Widow's Certificate No. 92361, Mother of William Carroll, Company I, 7th Connecticut Infantry.

Widow's Certificate No. 93096, Mother of John Sherry, Company K, 7th Pennsylvania Infantry.

Widow's Certificate No. 93207, Mother of John Dougherty, Company F, 63rd New York Infantry.

Widow's Certificate No. 93487, Mother of John Sheehan, Company H, 94th New York Infantry.

Widow's Certificate No. 94532, Mother of John C. Lynch, Company C, 69th New York Infantry.

Widow's Certificate No. 94716, Mother of Patrick Collins, Company F, 6th Maine Infantry.

Widow's Certificate No. 96027, Mother of James McGee, Company F, 132nd New York Infantry.

Widow's Certificate No. 96255, Mother of Michael McCormick, Company G, 65th New York Infantry.

Widow's Certificate No. 96706, Widow of Patrick McCaffrey, Company F, 69th New York Infantry.

Widow's Certificate No. 96716, Mother of Edmund Ford, Company K, 8th Kansas Infantry.

Widow's Certificate No. 97336, Mother of Garret G. Barry, Company M, 3rd Massachusetts Cavalry.

Widow's Certificate No. 97970, Mother of John Hennessey (alias John Quinn), Company H, 7th New York Heavy Artillery.

Widow's Certificate No. 98455, Widow of John J. Casey (alias John Walker), Company C, 2nd U.S. Infantry.

Widow's Certificate No. 98727, Widow of Farrell Hogg, Company D, 88th New York Infantry.

Widow's Certificate No. 98814, Mother of James E. McGee, Company H, 69th New York Infantry.

Widow's Certificate No. 98996, Widow of Felix Mooney, Company D, 61st New York Infantry.

Widow's Certificate No. 100498, Mother of Archibald Laverty, Company F, 1st New York Infantry.

Widow's Certificate No. 100612, Mother of Bernard Carr, Company C, 79th Illinois Infantry.

Widow's Certificate No. 101875, Mother of John Crowley, Company C, 3rd New Hampshire Infantry.

Widow's Certificate No. 103233, Mother of William Dwyer, Company B, 63rd New York Infantry.

Widow's Certificate No. 103714, Mother of John Boyle, Company I, 38th New York Infantry.

Widow's Certificate No. 103877, Mother of Henry Burns, Company D, 59th New York Infantry.

Widow's Certificate No. 105102, Mother of John Gannon, Company G, 26th New York Infantry.

Widow's Certificate No. 106040, Mother of Joseph E. Sheedy, Company E, 28th Massachusetts Infantry.

Widow's Certificate No. 107142, Mother of Nicholas Mahair [Mahar], Company M, 16th New York Heavy Artillery.

Widow's Certificate No. 107715, Father of Michael Brady, Company A, 75th Ohio Infantry.

Widow's Certificate No. 108486, Mother of James Livingston, Company E, 155th New York Infantry.

Widow's Certificate No. 109749, Mother of Patrick McConnell, Company I, 4th New York Infantry.

Widow's Certificate No. 110019, Mother of James Finigan, Company E, 4th New York Heavy Artillery.

Widow's Certificate No. 114360, Mother of Christopher McGiff, Company A, 119th New York Infantry.

Widow's Certificate No. 114594, Mother of John Kelly, Company C, 16th U.S. Infantry.

Widow's Certificate No. 114954, Mother of James Hand, Company H, 164th New York Infantry.

Widow's Certificate No. 115555, Mother of Timothy Dougherty, Company C, 3rd Wisconsin Cavalry.

Widow's Certificate No. 115828, Widow of Thomas Bowler (alias Thomas Murphy), Company A, 69th New York Infantry.

Widow's Certificate No. 116032, Widow of James Corcoran, Company G, 5th New York Infantry.

Widow's Certificate No. 116156, Widow of Richard Barrington, Company A, 1st Missouri Engineers.

Widow's Certificate No. 116873, Mother of Thomas Madigan, Company I, 69th New York State Militia.

Widow's Certificate No. 117088, Mother of William Flaherty (alias William State), Company K, 6th New Hampshire Infantry.
Widow's Certificate No. 117744, Mother of John Kennedy, Company E, 10th Ohio Infantry.
Widow's Certificate No. 117836, Father of Richard Sheridan, Company E, 82nd New York Infantry.
Widow's Certificate No. 120669, Father of Dennis Larkin (alias William Collins), Company H, 6th New York Heavy Artillery.
Widow's Certificate No. 121011, Mother of John Lane, Company A, 12th Massachusetts Infantry.
Widow's Certificate No. 123070, Mother of Felix Burns, Company E, 13th Pennsylvania Cavalry.
Widow's Certificate No. 124030, Mother of Michael Ryan, Company E, 95th New York Infantry.
Widow's Certificate No. 124498, Father of Charles McKenna, Company I, 3rd Rhode Island Cavalry.
Widow's Certificate No. 124533, Minor Children of Patrick Carraher (alias John Carrier), Company A, 82nd New York Infantry.
Widow's Certificate No. 125192, Mother of James O'Herrin (alias Frank Welch), Company H, 17th Massachusetts Infantry.
Widow's Certificate No. 126148, Widow of John Daly (alias John Ryan), Company A, 51st New York Infantry.
Widow's Certificate No. 126607, Mother of Thomas Reiley (alias Thomas McGory), Company D, 139th New York Infantry.
Widow's Certificate No. 126742, Minor Child of Michael Foran (alias Miles Ford), Company C, 5th Pennsylvania Reserves.
Widow's Certificate No. 127032, Mother of Patrick Galliven, Company D, 10th New York Infantry.
Widow's Certificate No. 127929, Mother of Terrence McFarland, Company D, 182nd New York Infantry.
Widow's Certificate No. 129489, Mother of James O'Neil, Company I, 2nd New York Mounted Rifles.
Widow's Certificate No. 130731, Mother of John G. Slattery, Company H, 12th Massachusetts Infantry.
Widow's Certificate No. 130737, Mother of Jeremiah Dorgan, Company H, 2nd Louisiana Infantry.
Widow's Certificate No. 132012, Father of Edmund Dwyer, Company B, 23rd Illinois Infantry.
Widow's Certificate No. 132926, Widow of Samuel Boyd, Company E, 14th New Jersey Infantry.

Widow's Certificate No. 133177, Mother of Thomas Doyle, Company D, 1st Massachusetts Cavalry.

Widow's Certificate No. 134153, Father of James Henry, Company E, 11th U.S. Infantry.

Widow's Certificate No. 134902, Mother of Francis Cullen, Company H, 24th New York Infantry.

Widow's Certificate No. 137303, Mother of Bernard Curry, Company B, 6th U.S. Cavalry.

Widow's Certificate No. 138484, Widow of John McGillicuddy (alias John McCarty), Company I, 173rd New York Infantry.

Widow's Certificate No. 138689, Mother of Peter Finegan, Company K, 116th Pennsylvania Infantry.

Widow's Certificate No. 138896, Father of William Barry (alias William Porter), Company I, 10th Ohio Infantry.

Widow's Certificate No. 139152, Mother of Charles Graney [Greaney], Company C, 9th Massachusetts Infantry.

Widow's Certificate No. 141783, Mother of Thomas Welch, Company H, 20th Maine Infantry.

Widow's Certificate No. 142303, Widow of Edward Fitzpatrick (alias Edward Honors), Company K, 10th New Jersey Infantry.

Widow's Certificate No. 143339, Mother of Michael Daly, Company A, 7th Illinois Cavalry.

Widow's Certificate No. 144840, Mother of Patrick Dugan, Company E, 39th Illinois Infantry.

Widow's Certificate No. 145128, Widow of John Slattery, Company C, 40th Massachusetts Infantry.

Widow's Certificate No. 161452, Widow of Charles Devlin, Company B, 35th Indiana Infantry.

Widow's Certificate No. 259125, Mother of Frederick Nightingale, Company I, 118th New York Infantry.

Case Files of Approved Pension Applications of Veterans Who Served Between 1861 and 1900

Survivor Certificate No. 266425, Approved Pension File of John O'Brien, Company F, 10th Illinois Cavalry.

Case Files of Approved Pension Applications of Widows and Other Dependents of the Navy

Navy Widow's Certificate No. 1580, Minor Child of Timothy Harrington (alias Thomas Harrington), USS *Cumberland.*

Navy Widow's Certificate No. 1994, Mother of Daniel O'Neil, U.S. Marine Corps.

Navy Widow's Certificate No. 2023, Mother of Peter Campbell, U.S. Marine Corps.

Navy Widow's Certificate No. 2163, Mother of Patrick H. Delanty, U.S. Marine Corps.

Navy Widow's Certificate No. 2196, Widow of Patrick Kellegher (alias John Kelly), USS *Frolic.*

Navy Widow's Certificate 2254, Father of John Sullivan, USS *Underwriter.*

Navy Widow's Certificate No. 2255, Father of Owen J. McGowan, USS *Keystone State.*

Navy Widow's Certificate No. 2286, Mother of James Burns (alias George Lacey), USS *North Carolina.*

Navy Widow's Certificate No. 2318, Mother of Denis Horgan, USS *Sachem.*

Navy Widow's Certificate No. 2356, Father of James Carey, USS *Carondelet.*

Navy Widow's Certificate No. 2390, Mother of George Doherty (alias George Robinson), USS *Horace Beals.*

Navy Widow's Certificate No. 2479, Father of Charles O'Donnell, U.S. Marine Corps.

Navy Widow's Certificate No. 2633, Mother of Dennis Driscoll, USS *Metacomet.*

Navy Widow's Certificate No. 2732, Mother of Patrick O'Brien, USS *Clifton.*

Navy Widow's Certificate No. 2821, Mother of John Riley, United States Marines Corps.

Navy Widow's Certificate No. 2867, Father of Patrick Finan, USS *Wabash.*

Navy Widow's Certificate No. 2901, Mother of William Carroll, USS *Mound City.*

Navy Widow's Certificate No. 2920, Widow of John Crowley, USS *Santiago de Cuba.*

Navy Widow's Certificate No. 2947, Mother of Patrick Dougherty, USS *South Carolina.*

Navy Widow's Certificate No. 3230, Child of Mathew Droney (alias Mathew Callahan), U.S. Marine Corps.

Navy Widow's Certificate No. 3265, Father of Daniel Driscoll, USS *Lexington.*

Navy Widow's Certificate No. 4104, Widow of Thomas Hynes, USS *Cyane.*

Navy Widow's Certificate No. 4180, Father of Henry Clark, USS *Hartford.*

Navy Widow's Certificate No. 4219, Father of John Buckley, USS *Weehawken.*

Navy Widow's Certificate No. 18084, Widow of John O'Brien, U.S. Marine Corps.

Navy Widow's Certificate No. 18243, Widow of John J. Scanlan (alias Charles E. Stanley), USS *Mystic.*

Case Files of Approved Pension Applications of Civil War and Later Navy Veterans

Navy Survivor Pension Certificate No. 5517, William H. Finn, USS *Shawsheen.*

OTHER PRIMARY SOURCES

The majority of these materials were accessed digitally online. Unless otherwise stated, only original scans of original documents were consulted. These primary sources and their repositories of origin are detailed below. These records were largely utilized to confirm ethnicity and add further contextual knowledge concerning the backgrounds of individual servicemen.

National Archives and Records Administration, Washington, D.C.

Record Group 15, Records of the Department of Veterans Affairs.
Organization Index to Pension Files of Veterans who served between 1861 and 1900.
Record Group 24, Records of the Bureau of Naval Personnel.
Weekly Returns of Enlistments at Naval Rendezvous ("Enlistment Rendezvous") Jan. 6, 1855–Aug. 8, 1891.
Record Group 29, Records of the Bureau of the Census.
Seventh Census of the United States, 1850.
Eighth Census of the United States, 1860.
Ninth Census of the United States, 1870.
Tenth Census of the United States, 1880.
Special Schedule of the Eleventh Census, 1890, Enumerating Union Veterans and Widows of Union Veterans of the Civil War.
Record Group 94, Records of the Adjutant General's Office.
Book Records of Union Volunteer Organizations: Descriptive Books.
Compiled Military Service Records of Volunteer Union Soldiers.
Final Statements 1862–1899.
Register of Deaths of Volunteers, Compiled 1861–1865.
Record Group 110, Records of the Provost Marshal General's Bureau.
Consolidated Lists of Civil War Draft Registrations, 1863–1865.

New England Historic Genealogical Society, Boston

1855 Massachusetts State Census.

New York State Archives, Albany

New York State Adjutant General's Office Civil War Muster Roll Abstracts of New York State Volunteers, United States Sharpshooters, and United States Colored Troops.

Pennsylvania Historical and Museum Commission

Record Group 11, Records of the Pennsylvania Department of Health.
Pennsylvania Death Certificates 1906–1963.

ONLINE DIGITAL COLLECTIONS

Ancestry.com: https://ancestry.com/
Fold 3: https://fold3.com/
GenealogyBank: https://genealogybank.com/
Houses of the Oireachtas: https://www.oireachtas.ie/
Illinois, Databases of Illinois Veterans, Index, 1775–1995: https://www.ancestry.com/search/collections/9759/
Irish Newspaper Archive: https://irishnewsarchive.com/
JFK Library: https://www.jfklibrary.org/
Library of Congress Chronicling America: https://chroniclingamerica.loc.gov/
New York State Census, 1855: https://www.ancestry.com/search/collections/7181/
New York State Military Museum Unit History Project: https://dmna.ny.gov/historic/reghist/civil/
Newspapers.com: https://newspapers.com/
The White House: https://www.whitehouse.gov/

NEWSPAPERS

Boston Pilot
Boston Traveler
Buchanan County Guardian (Iowa)
Burlington Daily Times (Vermont)
Cleveland Daily Leader
Cork (Ireland) Examiner
Daily Richmond Examiner
Evansville Daily Journal (Indiana)
Harper's Weekly
Hartford Daily Courant (Connecticut)
Iowa Transcript
Lamoille Newsdealer (Vermont)
Lowell Daily Citizen and News (Massachusetts)
Muscatine Weekly Journal (Iowa)
New Oregon Plaindealer (Iowa)
New York Herald
New York Irish American
New York Times
Philadelphia Inquirer
San Francisco Chronicle
St. Charles City Republican Intelligencer (Iowa)

PUBLIC DOCUMENTS AND PRINTED COLLECTIONS

Bates, Samuel Penniman. *History of Pennsylvania Volunteers, 1861–5; Prepared in Compliance with Acts of the Legislature.* 5 vols. Harrisburg: B. Singerly, 1869–1871.
Gould, Benjamin Apthorp. *Investigations in the Military and Anthropological Statistics of American Soldiers.* New York: Hurd and Houghton for the U.S. Sanitary Commission, 1869.

Kennedy, Joseph Camp Griffith. *Population of the United States in 1860; Compiled from the Original Returns of the Eighth Census, under the Direction of the Secretary of the Interior.* Washington, D.C.: Government Printing Office, 1864.

Massachusetts Adjutant General. *Massachusetts Soldiers, Sailors, and Marines in the Civil War.* 8 vols. Norwood, Mass.: Norwood Press, 1931–1935.

New Hampshire Legislature. *Revised Register of the Soldiers and Sailors of New Hampshire in the War of the Rebellion 1861–1866.* Concord, N.H.: Ira C. Evans, 1895.

New York State Adjutant General's Office. *Annual Report of the Adjutant-General of the State of New York.* 43 vols. Albany, N.Y.: James B. Lyon, 1893–1905.

Ohio Roster Commission. *Official Roster of the Soldiers of the State of Ohio in the War of the Rebellion 1861–1866.* 12 vols. Akron, Ohio: General Assembly, 1886–1895.

Phisterer, Frederick. *Statistical Record of the Armies of the United States.* New York: Charles Scribner's Sons, 1883.

U.S. Congress. *The War of the Rebellion: Official Records of the Union and Confederate Armies.* 128 vols. Washington, D.C.: Government Printing Office, 1880–1902.

U.S. Senate. *List of Pensioners on the Roll, January 1, 1883; Giving the Name of Each Pensioner, the Cause for Which Pensioned, the Post-Office Address, the Rate of Pension per Month, and the Date of Original Allowance, as Called for by Senate Resolution of December 8, 1882.* 5 vols. Washington, D.C.: Government Printing Office, 1883.

SECONDARY SOURCES

Abbott, Henry Livermore. *Fallen Leaves: The Civil War Letters of Major Henry Livermore Abbott.* Kent, Ohio: Kent State Univ. Press, 1991.

Agassiz, George R., ed. *Meade's Headquarters, 1863–1865: Letters of Colonel Theodore Lyman from the Wilderness to Appomattox.* Boston: Atlantic Monthly Press, 1922.

Akenson, Donald H. "Irish Migration to North America, 1800–1920." In *The Irish Diaspora,* edited by Andy Bielenberg, 111–138. Essex: Longman, 2000.

Akhtar, Shahmima. "Learning 'The Customs of Their Fathers': Irish Villages in Chicago's Columbian Exposition, 1893." *Journal of Victorian Culture* 20, no. 20 (2023): 1–25.

Altavilla, Keith. "McClellan's Men: Union Army Democrats in 1864." In *Upon the Field of Battle: Essays on the Military History of America's Civil War,* edited by Andrew S. Bledsoe and Andrew F. Lang, 227–251. Baton Rouge: Louisiana State Univ. Press, 2018.

Anbinder, Tyler. *Five Points: The 19th-Century New York City Neighborhood That Invented Tap Dance, Stole Elections, and Became the World's Most Notorious Slum.* New York: Free Press, 2001.

———. "The Harp and the Eagle: Irish-American Volunteers and the Union Army, 1861–1865 (Review)." *Journal of Southern History* 75, no. 2 (2009): 164–165.

———. *Nativism and Slavery: The Northern Know Nothings and the Politics of the 1850s.* New York: Oxford Univ. Press, 1992.

———. "'We Will Dirk Every Mother's Son of You': Five Points and the Irish Conquest of New York Politics." In *New Directions in Irish-American History,* ed. Kevin Kenny, 105–121. Madison: Univ. of Wisconsin Press, 2003.

———. "Which Poor Man's Fight? Immigrants and the Federal Conscription of 1863." *Civil War History* 52, no. 4 (2006): 344–372.

Anbinder, Tyler, and Hope McCaffrey. "Which Irish Men and Women Immigrated to the United States During the Great Famine Migration of 1846–54?" *Irish Historical Studies* 39, no. 156 (2015): 620–642.

Anderson, Benedict. *Imagined Communities: Reflections on the Origins and Spread of Nationalism.* London: Verso, 1983.

Arneson, Eric. "Whiteness and the Historians' Imagination." *International Labor and Working-Class History* 60 (2001): 3–32.

Ayres, S. C. *Sketch of the Life and Services of Vice Admiral Stephen C. Rowan, U.S. Navy, Read before the Ohio Commandery of the Loyal Legion, April 6, 1910.* Ohio: Ohio Commandery of the Loyal Legion, 1910.

Barnard, Sandy, ed. *Campaigning with the Irish Brigade: Pvt. John Ryan, 28th Massachusetts.* Terre Haute, Ind.: AST Press, 2001.

Barnickel, Linda. *Milliken's Bend: A Civil War Battle in History and Memory.* Baton Rouge: Louisiana State Univ. Press, 2013.

———. "10th Illinois Cavalry at War with Isaac Shepard." *Milliken's Bend: A Civil War Battle in History and Memory* (2013). http://millikensbend.com/10th_illinois_cavalry_at_war_with_isaac_shepard/. Accessed 1 February 2016.

Barr, Rebecca Anne, Sean Brady, and Jane McGaughey, eds. *Ireland and Masculinities in History.* London: Palgrave MacMillan, 2019.

Bateson, Catherine V. "'Forward for Our Homes!': Lyrical Expressions of Home Heard in Irish American Civil War Songs." *Journal of History and Cultures* 9 (2019): 86–100.

———. *Irish American Civil War Songs: Identity, Loyalty, and Nationhood.* Baton Rouge: Louisiana State Univ. Press, 2022.

Beaudot, William J. K., and Lance J. Herdegen, eds. *An Irishman in the Iron Brigade: The Civil War Memoirs of James P. Sullivan, Sergt., Company K, 6th Wisconsin Volunteers.* New York: Fordham Univ. Press, 1993.

Bennett, Michael J. *Union Jacks: Yankee Sailors in the Civil War.* Chapel Hill: Univ. of North Carolina Press, 2004.

Bernstein, Iver. *The New York City Draft Riots: Their Significance for American Society and Politics in the Age of the Civil War.* New York: Oxford Univ. Press, 1991.

Berwanger, Eugene H. *The British Foreign Service and the American Civil War.* Lexington: Univ. Press of Kentucky, 1994.

Bever, Megan L. *At War with King Alcohol: Debating Drinking and Masculinity in the Civil War.* Chapel Hill: Univ. of North Carolina Press, 2022.

Bilby, Joseph G. *Remember Fontenoy!: The 69th New York and the Irish Brigade in the Civil War.* Highstown, N.J.: Longstreet House, 1995.

Bridges, Amy. *A City in the Republic: Antebellum New York and the Origins of Machine Politics.* New York: Cambridge Univ. Press, 2008.

Broomall, James J., *Private Confederacies: The Emotional Worlds of Southern Men as Citizens and Soldiers.* Chapel Hill: Univ. of North Carolina Press, 2019.

———. "Wartime Masculinities." In *The Cambridge History of the American Civil War,* vol. 3, *Affairs of the People,* ed. Aaron Sheehan-Dean, 3–24. Cambridge: Cambridge Univ. Press, 2019.

Brundage, David. *Irish Nationalists in America: The Politics of Exile, 1798–1998.* Oxford: Oxford Univ. Press, 2016.

Burton, William L. *Melting Pot Soldiers: The Union's Ethnic Regiments.* New York: Fordham Univ. Press, 1998.

Byrne, Andrew J. *Memoir of Andrew J. Byrne: Veteran of the American Civil War,* edited by Nicola Morris. Dublin: Original Writing Ltd., 2008.

Carmichael, Peter S. *The Last Generation: Young Virginians in Peace, War, and Reunion.* Chapel Hill: Univ. of North Carolina Press, 2005.

———. *The War for the Common Soldier.* Chapel Hill: Univ. of North Carolina Press, 2018.

Carroll, Dillon J. *Invisible Wounds: Mental Illness and Civil War Soldiers.* Baton Rouge: Louisiana State Univ. Press, 2021.

Casway, Jerrold I. *The Culture and Ethnicity of Nineteenth Century Baseball.* Jefferson, N.C.: McFarland, 2017.

Cavanagh, Michael. *Memoirs of General Thomas Francis Meagher, Comprising the Leading Events of His Career.* Worcester, Mass.: Messenger Press, 1892.

Cimbala, Paul A. *Soldiers North and South: The Everyday Experiences of the Men Who Fought America's Civil War.* New York: Fordham Univ. Press, 2010.

Clark, Dennis. *Hibernia America: The Irish and Regional Cultures.* New York: Greenwood Press, 1986.

———. *The Irish in Philadelphia: Ten Generations of Urban Experience.* Philadelphia: Temple Univ. Press, 1973.

Cooper, Sophie. *Forging Identities in the Irish World: Melbourne and Chicago, c. 1830–1922.* Edinburgh: Edinburgh Univ. Press, 2022.

Conyngham, David Power. *The Irish Brigade and Its Campaigns.* New York: William McSorley, 1867.

———. *The Irish Brigade and Its Campaigns,* reprint, edited by Lawrence Frederick Kohl (New York: Fordham Univ. Press, 1994).

———. *Soldiers of the Cross, The Authoritative Text: The Heroism of Catholic Chaplains and*

Sisters in the American Civil War, edited by David J. Endres and William B. Kurtz. Notre Dame: Univ. of Notre Dame Press, 2019.

Corby, William. *Memoirs of Chaplain Life: Three Years Chaplain in the Famous Irish Brigade, "Army of the Potomac."* Chicago: La Monte, O'Donnell, 1893.

Costa, Dora L., and Matthew E. Kahn. *Heroes and Cowards: The Social Face of War.* Princeton, N.J.: Princeton Univ. Press, 2008.

Costello, Augustine E. *Our Firemen: A History of the New York Fire Departments, Volunteer and Paid.* 1887. Reprint, New York: Knickerbocker Press, 1997.

Crouthamel, James. *Bennett's New York Herald and the Rise of the Popular Press.* New York: Syracuse Univ. Press, 1989.

Curran, Robert Emmett. *American Catholics and the Quest for Equality in the Civil War Era.* Baton Rouge: Louisiana State Univ. Press, 2023.

Curtis, Orson Blair. *History of the Twenty-Fourth Michigan of the Iron Brigade, Known as the Detroit and Wayne County Regiment.* Detroit, Mich.: Winn and Hammond, 1891.

Davis, David Brion. *Inhuman Bondage: The Rise and Fall of Slavery in the New World.* Oxford: Oxford Univ. Press, 2006.

Davis, Graham. "The Irish in Britain, 1815–1939." In *The Irish Diaspora,* edited by Andy Bielenberg, 19–36. Essex: Longman, 2000.

Dean, Eric T. "'We Will All Be Lost and Destroyed': Post-Traumatic Stress Disorder and the Civil War." *Civil War History* 37, no. 2 (1991): 138–153.

Delahanty, Ian. "The Transatlantic Roots of Irish American Anti-Abolitionism, 1843–1859." *Journal of the Civil War Era* 6, no. 2 (2016): 164–192.

Delaney, Enda. "Our Island Story? Towards a Transnational History of Late Modern Ireland." *Irish Historical Studies* 37, no. 148 (November 2011): 599–621.

Denison, Reverend Frederic. *Shot and Shell: The Third Rhode Island Heavy Artillery Regiment in the Rebellion, 1861–1865.* Providence, R.I.: J. A. and R. A. Reid, 1879.

Diner, Hasia R. "'The Most Irish City in the Union': The Era of the Great Migration, 1844–1877." In *The New York Irish,* edited by Ronald H. Bayor and Timothy J. Meagher, 87–104. Baltimore: John Hopkins Univ. Press, 1996.

Douglass, Frederick. *Life and Times of Frederick Douglass.* Boston: De Wolfe and Fiske, 1892.

Doyle, David Noel. "The Irish as Urban Pioneers in the United States, 1850–1870." *Journal of American Ethnic History* 10, no. 1/2 (1990): 36–59.

———. "The Irish in North America, 1776–1845." In *Making the Irish American: History and Heritage of the Irish in the United States,* edited by J. J. Lee and Marion R. Casey, 171–212. New York: New York Univ. Press, 2006.

———. "The Remaking of Irish-America, 1845–80." In *A New History of Ireland VI: Ireland under the Union: 1870–1921,* edited by W. E. Vaughan, 725–763. Oxford: Oxford Univ. Press, 2010.

Doyle, Don H. *The Cause of All Nations: An International History of the American Civil War.* New York: Basic Books, 2015.

Dunkelman, Mark H. *Brothers One and All: Esprit de Corps in a Civil War Regiment.* Baton Rouge: Louisiana State Univ. Press, 2004.

———. *Patrick Henry Jones: Irish American, Civil War General, and Gilded Age Politician.* Baton Rouge: Louisiana State Univ. Press, 2015.

Eagan, Catherine M. "'White,' If 'Not Quite': Irish Whiteness in the Nineteenth-Century Irish-American Novel." In *New Directions in Irish-American History,* edited by Kevin Kenny, 140–155. Madison: Univ. of Wisconsin Press, 2003.

Endres, David J. "'Three Cheers for the Union': Catholic Chaplains and Irish Loyalty During the American Civil War." *Catholic Historical Review* 108, no. 1 (winter 2002): 92–117.

Ernsberger, Don. *At the Wall: The 69th Pennsylvania "Irish Volunteers" at Gettysburg.* Bloomington, Ind.: Xlibris, 2006.

Eva, Phil. "Home Sweet Home? The 'Culture of Exile' in Mid-Victorian Popular Song." *Popular Music* 16, no. 2 (1992): 131–150.

Faust, Drew Gilpin. "The Civil War Soldier and the Art of Dying." *Journal of Southern History* 67, no. 1 (2001): 3–38.

———. *This Republic of Suffering: Death and the American Civil War.* New York: Knopf, 2008.

Ferrie, Joseph P. "The Entry into the U.S. Labor Market of Antebellum European Immigrants, 1840–1860." *Explorations in Economic History* 34, no. 3 (1997): 295–330.

———. *Yankeys Now: Immigrants in the Antebellum United States, 1840–1860.* New York: Oxford Univ. Press, 1999.

Fitzgerald, Patrick. "Mapping the Ulster Diaspora: 1607–1960." *Familia* 22 (2006): 1–17.

Fitzpatrick, David. *The Americanisation of Ireland: Migration and Settlement, 1841–1925.* Cambridge: Cambridge Univ. Press, 2020.

———. *Oceans of Consolation: Personal Accounts of Irish Migration to Australia.* Ithaca, N.Y.: Cornell Univ. Press, 1994.

Floyd, Fred C. *History of the Fortieth (Mozart) Regiment New York Volunteers.* Boston: F. H. Gilson Company, 1909.

Foner, Eric. *Free Soil, Free Labor, Free Men: The Ideology of the Republican Party before the Civil War.* New York: Oxford Univ. Press, 1970.

Foote, Lorien. *The Gentlemen and the Roughs: Manhood, Honor, and Violence in the Union Army.* New York: New York Univ. Press, 2010.

———. "Rich Man's War, Rich Man's Fight: Class, Ideology, and Discipline in the Union Army." *Civil War History* 5, no. 3 (2005): 269–287.

Fox, William F. *Regimental Losses in the American Civil War 1861–1865.* Albany: Albany Publishing Company, 1889.

Frank, Joseph Allan. *With Ballot and Bayonet: The Political Socialization of American Civil War Soldiers.* Athens: Univ. of Georgia Press, 1998.

Fry, Zachery A. *A Republic in the Ranks: Loyalty and Dissent in the Army of the Potomac.* Chapel Hill: Univ. of North Carolina Press, 2020.

Gallagher, Gary W. *The Enduring Civil War: Reflections on the Great American Crisis.* Baton Rouge: Louisiana State Univ. Press, 2020.

———. *The Union War.* Cambridge, Mass.: Harvard Univ. Press, 2012.

Gallman, J. Matthew. *Defining Duty in the Civil War: Personal Choice, Popular Culture, and the Union Home Front.* Chapel Hill: Univ. of North Carolina Press, 2015.

———. *Mastering Wartime: A Social History of Philadelphia During the Civil War.* Cambridge: Cambridge Univ. Press, 1990.

———. *The North Fights the Civil War: The Home Front.* Chicago: Ivan R. Dee, 1994.

Garcia, Christopher M. "The Forgotten Sixty-Ninth: The Sixty-Ninth New York National Guard Artillery Regiment in the American Civil War." Master's thesis, Old Dominion University, 2012.

Garrison, Emma. *A Collection of Brief Poems on Various Subjects.* Baltimore: Sherwood, 1855.

Gerrish, Theodore. *Army Life: A Private's Reminiscences of the Civil War.* Portland, Maine: Hoyt, Fogg and Donham, 1882.

Gilje, Paul A. "The Development of an Irish American Community in New York City before the Great Migration." In *The New York Irish,* edited by Ronald H. Bayor and Timothy J. Meagher, 70–83. Baltimore: John Hopkins Univ. Press, 1996.

Glasco, Laurence A. "The Life Cycles and Household Structure of American Ethnic Groups: Irish, Germans, and Native-Born Whites in Buffalo, New York, 1855." *Journal of Urban History* 1, no. 3 (1975): 339–364.

Glasson, William H. *Federal Military Pensions in the United States.* New York: Oxford Univ. Press, American Branch, 1918.

Glatthaar, Joseph T. *The March to the Sea and Beyond: Sherman's Troops in the Savannah and Carolinas Campaigns.* Baton Rouge: Louisiana State Univ. Press, 1995.

———. "A Tale of Two Armies: The Confederate Army of Northern Virginia and the Union Army of the Potomac and Their Cultures." *Journal of the Civil War Era* 6, no. 3 (2016): 315–346.

Gleeson, David T. "Failing to 'Unite with Abolitionists': The Irish Nationalist Press and U.S. Emancipation." *Slavery and Abolition* 37, no. 3 (2016): 622–637.

———. *The Green and the Gray: The Irish in the Confederate States of America.* Chapel Hill: Univ. of North Carolina Press, 2013.

———. *The Irish in the South, 1815–1877.* Chapel Hill: Univ. of North Carolina Press, 2001.

Golway, Terry. *Machine Made: Tammany Hall and the Creation of Modern American Politics.* New York: Liveright Publishing, 2014.

Gordon, Lesley J. *A Broken Regiment: The 16th Connecticut's Civil War.* Baton Rouge: Louisiana State Univ. Press, 2014.

Gordon, Michael A. *The Orange Riots: Irish Political Violence in New York City, 1870 and 1871.* Ithaca, N.Y.: Cornell Univ. Press, 1993.

Graff, Harvey J. *The Legacies of Literacy: Continuities and Contradictions in Western Culture and Society.* Bloomington: Indiana Univ. Press, 1987.

Greenberg, Amy S. *Manifest Manhood and the Antebellum American Empire.* Cambridge: Cambridge Univ. Press, 2005.

Gümüş, Gamze Katı. "'An Organ of the Irish Race on the Continent': The *Pilot,* Irish Immigration, and Irish-American Identity, 1851–66." PhD diss., University of Kansas, 2018.

Hallock, Judith Lee. "The Role of the Community in Civil War Desertion." *Civil War History* 29, no. 2 (June 1983): 123–134.

Hager, Christopher. *I Remain Yours: Common Lives in Civil War Letters.* Cambridge, Mass.: Harvard Univ. Press, 2018.

Halpine, Charles Graham. *The Life and Adventures, Songs, Services, and Speeches of Private Miles O'Reilly.* New York: Carleton, 1864.

Hamilton, Brendan, and Damian Shiels. "'It Was Not For To Be Soldiers We Came Out': Recruited Straight Off The Boat—Some New Evidence." *Irish in the American Civil War* (2019). https://irishamericancivilwar.com/2019/01/12/it-was-not-for-to-be-soldiers-we-came-out-recruited-straight-off-the-boat-some-new-evidence/. Accessed 25 June 2020.

———. "Recruited Straight Off the Boat? On the Trail of Emigrant Soldiers From the Ship Great Western." *Irish in the American Civil War* (2015). https://irishamericancivilwar.com/2015/10/01/recruited-straight-off-the-boat-on-the-trail-of-emigrant-soldiers-from-the-ship-great-western/. Accessed 25 June 2020.

Handlin, Oscar. *Boston's Immigrants: A Study in Acculturation.* Cambridge, Mass.: Belknap Press of Harvard Univ. Press, 1979.

Harris, Ruth-Ann M., Donald Jacobs, and Emeer O'Keeffe, eds. *Searching for Missing Friends: Irish Immigrant Advertisements Placed in "The Boston Pilot," 1831–1920.* Boston: New England Historic Genealogical Society, 1989.

Hatton, Timothy J., and Jeffrey G. Williamson. "After the Famine: Emigration from Ireland, 1850–1913." *Journal of Economic History* 53, no. 3 (1993): 575–600.

Hearne, John M., and Rory T. Cornish. *Thomas Francis Meagher: The Making of an Irish American.* Dublin: Irish Academic Press, 2006.

Henkin, David M. *The Postal Age: The Emergence of Modern Communications in Nineteenth-Century America.* Chicago: Univ. of Chicago Press, 2006.

Hennessy, John J. *Return to Bull Run: The Battle and Campaign of Second Manassas.* Norman: Univ. of Oklahoma Press, 1999.

Hernon, Joseph M. *Celts, Catholics and Copperheads: Ireland Views the American Civil War.* Columbus: Ohio State Univ. Press, 1968.

Hess, Earl J. *The Union Soldier in Battle: Enduring the Ordeal of Combat.* Lawrence: Univ. Press of Kansas, 1997.

Hodges, Graham. "'Desirable Companions and Lovers': Irish and African Americans in the Sixth Ward, 1830–1870." In *The New York Irish,* edited by Ronald H. Bayor and Timothy J. Meagher, 105–124. Baltimore: John Hopkins Univ. Press, 1996.

Holmes, Amy E. "'Such Is the Price We Pay': American Widows and the Civil War Pension System." In *Toward a Social History of the American Civil War: Exploratory Essays,* edited by Maris A. Vinovskis, 171–195. Cambridge: Cambridge Univ. Press, 1990.

Horan, James D. *Timothy O'Sullivan: America's Forgotten Photographer.* New York: Bonanza Books, 1966.

Ignatiev, Noel. *How the Irish Became White.* New York: Routledge, 1995.

Jacobs, Harriet. *Incidents in the Life of a Slave Girl, Written by Herself.* Boston: Published for the Author, 1861.

Johnson, Mark W. "'Where Are the Regulars?' An Analysis of Regular Army Recruiting and Enlistees, 1851–1865." PhD diss., State University of New York at Albany, 2012.

Johnson, Russell L. "'Great Injustice': Social Status and the Distribution of Military Pensions after the Civil War." *Journal of the Gilded Age and Progressive Era* 10, no. 2 (2011): 137–160.

Joyce, William Leonard. *Editors and Ethnicity: A History of the Irish-American Press, 1848–1883.* New York: Arno Press, 1976.

Judd, David W. *The Story of the Thirty-Third N.Y.S. Vols, or Two Years Campaigning in Virginia and Maryland.* Rochester, N.Y.: Benton and Andrews, 1864.

Kalman, Judy. *Writing on the Plaza: Mediated Literacy Practice Among Scribes and Clients in Mexico City.* Creskill, N.J.: Hampton Press, 1999.

Kane, Michael H. "American Soldiers in Ireland, 1865–67." *The Irish Sword: The Journal of the Military History Society of Ireland* 23, no. 91 (2002): 103–140.

Kaplan, Michael. "New York City Tavern Violence and the Creation of a Working-Class Male Identity." *Journal of the Early Republic* 15, no. 4 (1995): 591–617.

Keating, Ryan W. *Shades of Green: Irish Regiments, American Soldiers, and Local Communities in the Civil War Era.* New York: Fordham Univ. Press, 2017.

Kelleher, Patricia. "Class and Catholic Irish Masculinity in Antebellum America: Young Men on the Make in Chicago." *Journal of American Ethnic History* 28, no. 4 (summer 2009): 7–42.

———. "Flying Dutchmen and Drunken Irishmen: The Myths and Realities of Ethnic Civil War Soldiers." *Journal of Military History* 73, no. 1 (2008): 117–145.

Keller, Christian B. *Chancellorsville and the Germans: Nativism, Ethnicity, and Civil War Memory.* New York: Fordham Univ. Press, 2007.

Kemp, Thomas R. "Community and War: The Civil War Experience of Two New Hampshire Towns." In *Toward a Social History of the American Civil War: Exploratory Essays,* edited by Maris A. Vinovskis, 31–77. Cambridge: Cambridge Univ. Press, 1990.

Kenny, Kevin. *The American Irish: A History.* London: Routledge, 2000.

———. *Making Sense of the Molly Maguires.* New York: Oxford Univ. Press, 1998.

———. "Politics and Race: Editor's Introduction." In *New Directions in Irish-American History,* edited by Kevin Kenny, 101–103. Madison: Univ. of Wisconsin Press, 2003.

Kinealy, Christine. *This Great Calamity: The Irish Famine 1845–52.* Dublin: Gill and Macmillan, 2006.

Kirsch, George B. *Baseball in Blue and Gray: The National Pastime During the Civil War.* Princeton, N.J.: Princeton Univ. Press, 2003.

Klein, Christopher. *When the Irish Invaded Canada: The Incredible True Story of the Civil War Veterans Who Fought for Ireland's Freedom.* New York: Doubleday, 2019.

Knobel, Dale T. *Paddy and the Republic: Ethnicity and Nationality in Antebellum America.* Middletown, Conn.: Wesleyan Univ. Press, 1986.

Kohl, Lawrence Frederick. "The Harp and the Eagle: Irish-American Volunteers and the Union Army, 1861–1865 (Review)." *Civil War History* 54, no. 3 (2008): 313–315.

Kohl, Lawrence Frederick, and Margaret Cossé Richard, eds. *Irish Green and Union Blue: The Civil War Letters of Peter Welsh.* New York: Fordham Univ. Press, 1986.

Kraut, Alan M. "Illness and Medical Care Among Irish Immigrants in Antebellum New York." In *The New York Irish,* edited by Ronald H. Bayor and Timothy J. Meagher, 153–168. Baltimore: John Hopkins Univ. Press, 1996.

Kurtz, William B. *Excommunicated from the Union: How the Civil War Created a Separate Catholic America.* New York: Oxford Univ. Press, 2015.

———. "The Union as It Was: Northern Catholics' Conservative Unionism." In *New Perspectives on the Union War,* edited by Gary W. Gallagher and Elizabeth R. Varon, 91–113. New York: Fordham Univ. Press, 2019.

Lamb, Wilson G. "Seventeenth Regiment." In *Histories of the Several Regiments and Battalions from North Carolina in the Great War 1861–'65,* vol. 2, edited by Walter Clark, 1–13. Goldsboro, N.C.: Nash Brothers, 1901.

Lane, Phyllis. "Corcoran and the Irish Legion: Colonel Michael Corcoran, Fighting Irishman of the Irish Brigade." In *The History of the Irish Brigade: A Collection of Historical Essays,* edited by Pia Seija Seagrave, 13–34. Fredericksburg, Va.: Sergeant Kirkland's Museum, 1997.

Larkin, Emmet. "The Devotional Revolution in Ireland, 1850–75." *American Historical Review* 77, no. 3 (1972): 625–652.

Lause, Mark A. *Free Labor: The Civil War and the Making of an American Working Class.* Urbana: Univ. of Illinois Press, 2015.

Lee, J. J., and Marion R. Casey, eds. *Making the Irish American: History and Heritage of the Irish in the United States.* New York: New York Univ. Press, 2006.

Legrand, Louis. *Beadle's Dime Letter-Writer: A Perfect Guide to All Kinds of Correspondence.* New York: Beadle, 1861.

Linderman, Gerald F. *Embattled Courage: The Experience of Combat in the American Civil War.* New York: Free Press, 1987.

Litwicki, Ellen M. *America's Public Holidays, 1865–1920.* Washington, D.C.: Smithsonian Institution Press, 2003.

———. "'Our Hearts Burn with Ardent Love for Two Countries': Ethnicity and Assimilation at Chicago Holiday Celebrations, 1876–1918." *Journal of Ethnic American History* 19, no. 3 (spring 2000): 3–34.

Lonn, Ella. *Desertion During the Civil War,* reprint with an introduction by William Blair. Lincoln: Univ. of Nebraska Press, 1998.

———. *Foreigners in the Union Army and Navy.* New York: Greenwood Press, 1969.

Luskey, Brian P. *Men Is Cheap: Exposing the Frauds of Free Labor in Civil War America.* Chapel Hill: Univ. of North Carolina Press, 2020.

Lyman, Payson W. *History of Easthampton: Its Settlement and Growth: Its Material, Educational and Religious Interests, Together with a Genealogical Record of Its Original Families.* Northampton, Mass.: Trumbull and Gere, 1866.

Lyons, Martyn. "'Ordinary Writings' or How the 'Illiterate' Speak to Historians." In *Ordinary Writings, Personal Narratives: Writing Practices in 19th and Early 20th Century Europe,* edited by Martyn Lyons. Bern: Peter Lang, 2007.

———. *The Writing Culture of Ordinary People in Europe, c. 1860–1920.* Cambridge: Cambridge Univ. Press, 2013.

Lyons, W. F. *Brigadier-General Thomas Francis Meagher: His Political and Military Career.* New York: D. and J. Sadlier, 1870.

Mach, Andrew. "Claiming America: Irish-Catholic Memory and the Nation, 1865–1925." PhD diss., University of Notre Dame, 2019.

MacNamara, Daniel George. *The History of the Ninth Regiment, Massachusetts Volunteer Infantry, Second Brigade, First Division, Fifth Army Corps, Army of the Potomac, June, 1861–June, 1864.* Boston: E. B. Stillings, 1899.

MacNamara, Michael H. *The Irish Ninth in Bivouac and Battle, or, Virginia and Maryland Campaigns.* Boston: Lee and Shepard, 1867.

Mac Suibhne, Breandán. *The End of Outrage: Post-Famine Adjustment in Rural Ireland.* Oxford: Oxford Univ. Press, 2017.

Manning, Chandra. "A 'Vexed Question': White Soldiers on Slavery and Race." In *The View from the Ground: Experiences of Civil War Soldiers,* edited by Aaron Sheehan-Dean, 31–66. Lexington: Univ. Press of Kentucky, 2007.

———. *What This Cruel War Was Over: Soldiers, Slavery, and the Civil War.* New York: Knopf, 2007.

Martin, Scott C. "'A Soldier Intoxicated Is Far Worse Than No Soldier at All': Intoxication and the American Civil War." *Social History of Alcohol and Drugs* 25, no. 1–2 (2011): 66–87.

Marvel, William. *Lincoln's Mercenaries: Economic Motivation Among Union Soldiers During the Civil War.* Baton Rouge: Louisiana State Univ. Press, 2018.

Maryniak, Benedict R., and John Wesley Brinsfield Jr. *The Spirit Divided: Memoirs of Civil War Chaplains: The Union.* Macon, Ga.: Mercer Univ. Press, 2007.

McCaffrey, Lawrence John. *The Irish Diaspora in America.* 1976. Reprint, Washington, D.C.: Catholic Univ. of America Press, 1984.

McCarter, William. *My Life in the Irish Brigade: The Civil War Memoirs of Private William McCarter, 116th Pennsylvania Infantry.* Edited by Kevin E. O'Brien. El Dorado Hills, Calif.: Savas, 1996.

McCready, Richard B. "Revising the Irish in Scotland: The Irish in Nineteenth- and Early Twentieth-Century Scotland." In *The Irish Diaspora,* edited by Andy Bielenberg, 37–50. Essex: Longman, 2000.

McDermott, Anthony W. *A Brief History of the 69th Regiment Pennsylvania Veteran Volunteers: From Its Formation until Final Muster out of the United States Service.* Philadelphia: D. J. Gallagher, 1889.

McMahon, Cian T. *The Global Dimension of Irish Identity: Race, Nation, and the Popular Press, 1840–1880.* Chapel Hill: Univ. of North Carolina Press, 2015.

———. "Ireland and the Birth of the Irish-American Press, 1842–61." *American Periodicals: A Journal of History and Criticism* 19, no. 1 (2009): 5–20.

McPherson, James M. *Battle Cry of Freedom: The Civil War Era.* New York: Oxford Univ. Press, 1988.

———. *For Cause and Comrades: Why Men Fought in the Civil War.* New York: Oxford Univ. Press, 1997.

———. *This Mighty Scourge: Perspectives on the Civil War.* Oxford: Oxford Univ. Press, 2007.

McWhirter, Christian. *Battle Hymns: The Power and Popularity of Music in the Civil War.* Chapel Hill: Univ. of North Carolina Press, 2014.

Meagher, Timothy J. *The Columbia Guide to Irish American History.* Columbia Guides to American History and Cultures. New York: Columbia Univ. Press, 2005.

———. "From the World to the Village and the Beginning to the End and After: Research Opportunities in Irish American History." *Journal of American Ethnic History* 28, no. 4 (2009): 118–135.

Miller, Kerby A. *Emigrants and Exiles: Ireland and the Irish Exodus to North America.* New York: Oxford Univ. Press, 1985.

———. "Emigration to North America in the Era of the Great Famine, 1845–55." In *Atlas of the Great Irish Famine,* edited by John Crowley, William J. Smyth, and Mike Murphy, 214–227. Cork: Cork Univ. Press, 2012.

———. "'Revenge for Skibbereen': Irish Emigration and the Meaning of the Great Famine." In *The Great Famine and the Irish Diaspora in America,* edited by Arthur Gribben, 180–195. Amherst: Univ. of Massachusetts Press, 1999.

Miller, Randall M. "Catholic Religion, Irish Ethnicity, and the Civil War." In *Religion and the American Civil War,* edited by Randall M. Miller, Harry S. Stout, and Charles Reagan Wilson, 261–296. Oxford: Oxford Univ. Press, 1998.

Miller, Randall M., Harry S. Stout, and Charles Reagan Wilson, eds. *Religion and the American Civil War.* Oxford: Oxford Univ. Press, 1998.

Miller, Richard F. *Harvard's Civil War: A History of the Twentieth Massachusetts Volunteer Infantry.* Hanover, N.H.: Univ. Press of New England, 2005.

———. ed. *States at War,* vol. 4: *A Reference Guide for Delaware, Maryland, and New Jersey in the Civil War.* Hanover, N.H.: Univ. Press of New England, 2015.

———. "The Trouble with Brahmins: Class and Ethnic Tensions in Massachusetts' 'Harvard Regiment.'" *New England Quarterly: A Historical Review of New England Life and Letters* 76, no. 1 (2003): 38–72.

Milner, Dan. *The Unstoppable Irish: Songs and Integration of the New York Irish, 1783–1883.* Notre Dame: Univ. of Notre Dame Press, 2019.

Mitchell, Reid. *Civil War Soldiers: Their Expectations and Experiences.* New York: Penguin, 1988.

———. "Not the General but the Soldier: The Study of Civil War Soldiers." In *Writing the Civil War: The Quest to Understand,* edited by James M. McPherson and William J. Cooper Jr., 81–95. Columbia: Univ. of South Carolina Press, 1998.

———. *The Vacant Chair: The Northern Soldier Leaves Home.* New York: Oxford Univ. Press, 1993.

Morris, David. "'Gone to Work to America': Irish Step-Migration through South Wales in the 1860s and 1870s." *Immigrants and Minorities* 34, no. 3 (2016): 297–313.

Mokyr, Joel, and Cormac Ó Gráda. "Emigration and Poverty in Prefamine Ireland." *Explorations in Economic History* 19, no. 4 (1982): 360–384.

Mulholland, St. Clair A. *The Story of the 116th Regiment Pennsylvania Infantry.* Philadelphia: F. MacManus Jr., 1899.

Murdock, Eugene C. *One Million Men: The Civil War Draft in the North.* Madison: State Historical Society of Wisconsin, 1971.

———. *Patriotism Limited, 1862–1865: The Civil War Draft and the Bounty System.* Kent, Ohio: Kent State Univ. Press, 1967.

Murray, Thomas Hamilton. *History of the Ninth Regiment, Connecticut Volunteer Infantry, "The Irish Regiment," in the War of the Rebellion, 1861–65: The Record of a Gallant*

Command on the March, in Battle and in Bivouac. New Haven, Conn.: Price, Lee, and Adkins, 1903.

National Park Service. "The 1864 Election—A View from the Trenches" (10 October 2017). https://www.nps.gov/pete/learn/historyculture/the-1864-election.htm#_ftn8 (accessed 18 September 2019).

———. "Fort Sumter's Garrison by Nationality" (2 May 2011). https://www.nps.gov/fosu/learn/historyculture/upload/FOSU-Garrison-by-Nationality.pdf. Accessed 19 September 2012.

Neely, Mark E., Jr. *Lincoln and the Democrats: The Politics of Opposition in the Civil War.* New York: Cambridge Univ. Press, 2017.

———. *The Union Divided: Party Conflict in the Civil War North.* Cambridge, Mass.: Harvard Univ. Press, 2002.

Noe, Kenneth W. *Reluctant Rebels: The Confederates Who Joined the Army after 1861.* Chapel Hill: Univ. of North Carolina Press, 2010.

Nolan, Alan T. *The Iron Brigade: A Military History.* First Indiana Univ. Press edition. Bloomington: Indiana Univ. Press, 1994.

Noll, Mark A. *The Civil War as a Theological Crisis.* Chapel Hill: Univ. of North Carolina Press, 2006.

Nugent, Brodie. "Her Exiled Children in America: Irish American Identity and the Civil War." *Flinders Journal of History and Politics* 31 (2015): 76–111.

Öfele, Martin. *True Sons of the Republic: European Immigrants in the Union Army.* Westport, Conn.: Praeger, 2008.

O'Connor, Thomas H. *Civil War Boston: Home Front and Battlefield.* Boston: Northeastern Univ. Press, 1997.

Ó Gráda, Cormac. "The New York Irish in the 1850s: Locked in by Poverty?" *New York Irish History* 19 (2005): 5–11.

O'Grady, W. L. D. "88th Regiment Infantry." In New York Monuments Commission, *Final Report on the Battlefield of Gettysburg,* vol. 2, 510–516. New York: J. B. Lyon, 1902.

O'Malley, Patrick R. "Irish Whiteness and the Nineteenth-Century Construction of Race." *Victorian Literature and Culture* 51, no. 2 (2023): 167–198.

O'Neill, Kevin. "The Star-Spangled Shamrock: Meaning and Memory in Irish America." In *History and Memory in Modern Ireland,* edited by Ian McBride, 118–138. Cambridge: Cambridge Univ. Press, 2001.

Palladino, Anita, ed. *Diary of a Yankee Engineer: The Civil War Story of John H. Westervelt, Engineer, 1st New York Volunteer Engineer Corps.* New York: Fordham Univ. Press, 1997.

Patchan, Scott C. *Second Manassas: Longstreet's Attack and the Struggle for Chinn Ridge.* Washington, D.C.: Potomac Books, 2011.

Peterson, Robert L., and John A. Hudson. "Foreign Recruitment for Union Forces." *Civil War History* 7, no. 2 (1961): 176–189.

Potter, Stephen R., and Douglas W. Owsley. "An Irishman Dies at Antietam: An Archaeology of the Individual." In *Archaeological Perspectives on the American Civil War*, edited by Clarence R. Geier and Stephen R. Potter, 56–72. Gainesville: Univ. Press of Florida, 2000.

Quinn, John F. "Father Mathew's Disciples: American Catholic Support for Temperance, 1840–1920." *Church History* 65, no. 4 (1996): 624–640.

Rable, George C. *God's Almost Chosen Peoples: A Religious History of the American Civil War.* Chapel Hill: Univ. of North Carolina Press, 2010.

Rafuse, Ethan S. *McClellan's War: The Failure of Moderation in the Struggle for the Union.* Bloomington: Indiana Univ. Press, 2005.

Ramold, Steven J. *Across the Divide: Union Soldiers View the Northern Home Front.* New York: New York Univ. Press, 2013.

———. *Baring the Iron Hand: Discipline in the Union Army.* DeKalb: Northern Illinois Univ. Press, 2010.

Reid, Whitelaw. *Ohio in the War: Her Statesmen, Her Generals, and Soldiers.* 2 vols. Cincinnati: Moore, Wilstach and Baldwin, 1868.

Rhea, Gordon C. *Cold Harbor: Grant and Lee, May 26–June 3, 1864.* Baton Rouge: Louisiana State Univ. Press, 2002.

Ridge, John T. "Irish County Colonies in New York City, Part 1." *New York Irish History* 25 (2011): 58–68.

———. "Irish County Colonies in New York City, Part 2." *New York Irish History* 26 (2012): 47–55.

Ringle, Dennis J. *Life in Mr. Lincoln's Navy.* Annapolis, Md.: Naval Institute Press, 1998.

Robertson, James L., Jr. *Soldiers Blue and Gray.* Columbia: Univ. of South Carolina Press, 1988.

Rodgers, Thomas E. "Copperheads or a Respectable Minority: Current Approaches to the Study of Civil War-Era Democrats." *Indiana Magazine of History* 109, no. 2 (June 2013): 114–146.

Roediger, David R. *The Wages of Whiteness: Race and the Making of the American Working Class*, rev. ed. London: Verso, 2007.

Rohs, Stephen. "'The Bold Soldier Boy': Performance and Irish Boldness in New York in 1855." *American Studies* 44, no. 1/2 (2003): 157–182.

Samito, Christian G. *Becoming American Under Fire: Irish Americans, African Americans, and the Politics of Citizenship During the Civil War Era.* Ithaca, N.Y.: Cornell Univ. Press, 2009.

———, ed. *Commanding Boston's Irish Ninth: The Civil War Letters of Colonel Patrick R. Guiney, Ninth Massachusetts Volunteer Infantry.* New York: Fordham Univ. Press, 1998.

———. "Introduction." In Daniel George MacNamara, *The History of the Ninth Regiment Massachusetts Volunteer Infantry*, edited by Christian G. Samito. 1899. Reprint, New York: Fordham Univ. Press, 2000.

Sayler, Lucy E. *Under the Starry Flag: How a Band of Irish Americans Joined the Fenian Revolt and Sparked a Crisis over Citizenship.* Cambridge, Mass.: Belknap Press of Harvard Univ. Press, 2018.

Schrier, Arnold. *Ireland and the American Emigration, 1850–1900.* Chester Springs, Pa.: Defour Editions, 1997.

Shannon, William V. *The American Irish: A Political and Social Portrait,* 2nd ed. Amherst: Univ. of Massachusetts Press, 1989.

Sheehan-Dean, Aaron. "The Blue and the Gray in Black and White: Assessing the Scholarship on Civil War Soldiers." In *The View from the Ground: Experiences of Civil War Soldiers,* edited by Aaron Sheehan-Dean, 9–30. Lexington: Univ. Press of Kentucky, 2007.

———. *Why Confederates Fought: Family and Nation in Civil War Virginia.* Chapel Hill: Univ. of North Carolina Press, 2007.

Shiels, Damian. "A 150 Year Old Missing Persons Case—In Search of a 19-Year-Old Irishman." *Irish in the American Civil War* (2014). https://irishamericancivilwar.com/2014/04/13/a-150-year-old-missing-persons-case-in-search-of-a-19-year-old-irishman/. Accessed 2 June 2020.

———. "'The Blacks Fought Like Hell': Racism and Racist Violence in the Words and Actions of Two Union Irish Cavalrymen." *Irish in the American Civil War* (2016). https://irishamericancivilwar.com/2016/02/05/the-blacks-fought-like-hell-exploring-racism-racist-violence-through-the-words-actions-of-two-union-irish-cavalrymen/. Accessed 6 June 2020.

———. "Charting Desertion in the Irish Brigade, Part 1." *Irish in the American Civil War* (2016). https://irishamericancivilwar.com/2016/08/14/charting-desertion-in-the-irish-brigade-part-1/. Accessed 4 February 2020.

———. "The Crashing Volleys and the Wild Irish 'Hurroos': An Irish Brigade Veteran Remembers Gettysburg, Fifty Years On." *Irish in the American Civil War* (2019). https://irishamericancivilwar.com/2019/02/16/the-crashing-of-the-volleys-and-the-wild-irish-hurroos-an-irish-brigade-veteran-remembers-gettysburg-fifty-years-on/. Accessed 28 June 2023.

———. "A Few Spoke Nothing But Gaelic: In Search of the Irish Language in the American Civil War." *Irish in the American Civil War* (2016). https://irishamericancivilwar.com/2016/04/03/a-few-spoke-nothing-but-gaelic-in-search-of-the-irish-language-in-the-american-civil-war/. Accessed 8 July 2023.

———. "The Fight Was for the Union, Not for the Abolition of Slavery." *Irish in the American Civil War* (2013). https://irishamericancivilwar.com/2013/03/21/the-fight-was-for-the-union-not-for-the-abolition-of-slavery/. Accessed 11 July 2023.

———. "The Forgotten County: Exploring the American Civil War Service of Britain's Irish Communities." *Irish in the American Civil War* (2015). https://irishamerican

civilwar.com/2015/09/03/the-forgotten-county-exploring-the-american-civil-war-service-of-britains-irish-communities/. Accessed 12 December 2019.

———. *The Forgotten Irish: Irish Emigrant Experiences in America.* Dublin: The History Press Ireland, 2016.

———. "In Defence of Substitutes: The Story of Mary and James Ryan of Drogheda, Canada and Vermont." *Irish in the American Civil War* (2020). https://irishamericancivilwar.com/2020/02/18/in-defence-of-substitutes-the-story-of-mary-james-ryan-of-drogheda-canada-vermont/. Accessed 3 June 2020.

———. "Ireland's Forgotten 'Great War'?" *History Ireland* 24, no. 4 (July/August 2019): 30–33.

———. *The Irish in the American Civil War.* Dublin: The History Press Ireland, 2013.

———. "Killed by Torture? The Story of an 18-Year-Old Irishman's Death at the Hands of His Officers, New Orleans, 1865." *Irish in the American Civil War* (2016). https://irishamericancivilwar.com/2016/07/23/killed-by-torture-the-story-of-an-18-year-old-irishmans-death-at-the-hands-of-his-officers-new-orleans-1865/. Accessed 8 September 2020.

———. "The Long Arm of War: Exploring the 19th-Century Ulster Emigrant Experience through American Civil War Pension Files." In *Irish Hunger and Migration: Myth, Memory and Memorialization,* edited by Patrick Fitzgerald, Christine Kinealy, and Gerard Moran, 145–154. West Haven, Conn.: Quinnipiac Univ. Press, 2015.

———. "More Irish than the Irish: The Forgotten Irishmen of Gettysburg's Wheatfield." *Irish in the American Civil War* (2018). https://irishamericancivilwar.com/2018/04/02/more-irish-than-the-irish-the-forgotten-irishmen-of-gettysburgs-wheatfield. Accessed 2 April 2018.

———. "'Our Pickets Were Gobbled': Assessing the Mass Capture of the 69th New York, Petersburg, 1864." *Irish in the American Civil War* (2015). https://irishamericancivilwar.com/2015/12/10/our-pickets-were-gobbled-assessing-the-mass-capture-of-the-69th-new-york-petersburg-1864/. Accessed 4 May 2019.

———. "Preserving the Union? The Irish and the Union War." *Irish in the American Civil War* (2011). https://irishamericancivilwar.com/2011/09/23/preserving-the-union-the-irish-and-the-union-war/. Accessed 11 July 2023.

———. "'Watch the Man's Movements': Illegal Recruitment for the Union in Ireland, Part One." *Irish in the American Civil War* (2013). https://irishamericancivilwar.com/2013/04/03/watch-the-mans-movements-illegal-recruitment-for-the-union-in-ireland-part-one/. Accessed 21 June 2020.

———. "Widows' and Dependent Parents' American Civil War Pension Files: A New Source for the Irish Emigrant Experience." In *The Famine Irish: Emigration and the Great Hunger,* edited by Ciarán Reilly, 85–97. Dublin: The History Press Ireland, 2016.

Silbey, Joel H. *The Democratic Party in the Civil War Era: 1860–1868.* New York: Norton, 1977.

Sim, David. *A Union Forever: The Irish Question and U.S. Foreign Relations in the Victorian Age.* Ithaca, N.Y.: Cornell Univ. Press, 2013.

Sinha, Manisha. *The Slave's Cause: A History of Abolition.* New Haven, Conn.: Yale Univ. Press, 2016.

Slay, David Henson. "New Masters on the Mississippi: The United States Colored Troops of the Middle Mississippi Valley." PhD diss., Texas Christian University, 2009.

Smith, Adam I. P. *No Party Now: Politics in the Civil War North.* New York: Oxford Univ. Press, 2006.

———. The Stormy Present: Conservatism and the Problem of Slavery in Northern Politics, 1846–1865. Chapel Hill: Univ. of North Carolina Press, 2017.

Smith, Malcolm, and Donald M. MacRaild. "The Origins of the Irish in Northern England: An Isonymic Analysis of Data from the 1881 Census." *Immigrants and Minorities* 27, no. 2/3 (July/November 2009): 152–177.

Smith, Michael Thomas. *The Enemy Within: Fears of Corruption in the Civil War North.* Charlottesville: Univ. of Virginia Press, 2011.

———. "The Most Desperate Scoundrels Unhung: Bounty Jumpers and Recruitment Fraud in the Civil War North." *American Nineteenth Century History* 6, no. 2 (June 2003): 149–172.

Smolenyak, Megan. "Joey from Scranton." *Irish America Magazine,* April/May 2013, 56–59.

Spiers, Edward M. "Army Organisation and Society in the Nineteenth Century." In *A Military History of Ireland,* edited by Thomas Bartlett and Keith Jeffery, 335–357. Cambridge: Cambridge Univ. Press, 1996.

Steward, Patrick, and Bryan P. McGovern. *The Fenians: Irish Rebellion in the North Atlantic World, 1858–1876.* Knoxville: Univ. of Tennessee Press, 2013.

Sturtevant, Ralph Orson. *Pictorial History Thirteenth Regiment Vermont Volunteers: War of 1861–1865.* N.p.: n.p, 1910.

Swan, James B. *Chicago's Irish Legion: The 90th Illinois Volunteers in the Civil War.* Carbondale: Southern Illinois Univ. Press, 2009.

Taylor, Paul. *"Old Slow Town": Detroit During the Civil War.* Detroit, Mich.: Wayne State Univ. Press, 2013.

Thernstrom, Stephan. *The Other Bostonians: Poverty and Progress in the American Metropolis 1880–1970.* Cambridge, Mass.: Harvard Univ. Press, 1973.

Thomson, David K. "'Like a Cord through the Whole Country': Union Bonds and Financial Mobilization for Victory." *Journal of the Civil War Era* 6, no. 3 (September 2016): 347–375.

Truslow, Marion A. "The New York Irish Brigade Recruits and Their Families." In *Fight-*

ing Irish in the American Civil War and the Invasion of Mexico: Essays, edited by Arthur H. Mitchell, 37–59. Jefferson, N.C.: McFarland, 2017.

Ural, Susannah J. *The Harp and the Eagle: Irish-American Volunteers and the Union Army, 1861–1865.* New York: New York Univ. Press, 2006.

———. *Hood's Texas Brigade: The Soldiers and Families of the Confederacy's Most Celebrated Unit.* Baton Rouge: Louisiana State Univ. Press, 2017.

———. "'Remember Your Country and Keep Up Its Credit': Irish Volunteers and the Union Army, 1861–1865." *Journal of Military History* 69, no. 2 (2005): 331–359.

———. "'Ye Sons of Green Erin Assemble': Northern Irish American Catholics and the Union War Effort, 1861—1865." In *Civil War Citizens: Race, Ethnicity, and Identity in America's Bloodiest Conflict,* edited by Susannah Ural, 99–132. New York: New York Univ. Press, 2010.

Vinovskis, Maris A. "Have Social Historians Lost the Civil War? Some Preliminary Demographic Speculations." In *Toward a Social History of the American Civil War: Exploratory Essays,* edited by Maris A. Vinovskis, 1–30. Cambridge: Cambridge Univ. Press, 1990.

Voss, Frederick S. "Adalbert Volck: The South's Answer to Thomas Nast." *Smithsonian Studies in American Art* 2, no. 3 (1988): 67–87.

Vronsky, Peter. *Ridgeway: The American Fenian Invasion and the 1866 Battle That Made Canada.* Toronto: Allen Lane Canada, 2011.

Walker, William C. *The Eighteenth Regiment Connecticut Volunteers in the War for the Union.* Norwich, Conn.: Gordon Wilcox for The Committee, 1885.

Walsh, Chris. "'Cowardice Weakness or Infirmity, Whichever It May Be Termed': A Shadow History of the Civil War." *Civil War History* 59, no. 4 (2013): 492–526.

Walsh, Francis R. "The Boston Pilot Reports the Civil War." *Historical Journal of Massachusetts* 9, no. 2 (1981): 5–16.

Warren, Craig A. "'Oh, God, What a Pity!': The Irish Brigade at Fredericksburg and the Creation of Myth." *Civil War History* 47, no. 3 (2001): 193–221.

Weber, Jennifer L. *Copperheads: The Rise and Fall of Lincoln's Opponents in the North.* Oxford: Oxford Univ. Press, 2006.

Weddle, Kevin J. "Ethnic Discrimination in Minnesota Volunteer Regiments During the Civil War." *Civil War History* 35, no. 3 (1989): 239–259.

Weir, Rebecca. "'An Oblique Place': Letters in the Civil War." In *The Edinburgh Companion to Nineteenth-Century American Letters and Letter-Writing,* edited by Celeste-Marie Bernier et al., 271–286. Edinburgh: Edinburgh Univ. Press, 2016.

Wexler, Fred C. *The Tammany Regiment: A History of the Forty-Second New York Volunteer Infantry, 1861–1864.* Bloomington, Ind.: iUniverse, 2016.

Whelan, Bernadette. *American Government in Ireland, 1790–1913: A History of the US Consular Service.* Manchester: Manchester Univ. Press, 2010.

White, Jonathan W. *Emancipation, the Union Army, and the Reelection of Abraham Lincoln.* Baton Rouge: Louisiana State Univ. Press, 2014.

Wiley, Bell Irvin. *The Life of Billy Yank: The Common Soldier of the Union.* Indianapolis, Ind.: Bobbs-Merrill, 1952.

Wittenberg, Eric J. *Little Phil: A Reassessment of the Civil War Leadership of Gen. Philip H. Sheridan.* Dulles, Va.: Brassey's, 2002.

Wongsrichanalai, Kanisorn. *Northern Character: College-Educated New Englanders, Honor, Nationalism, and Leadership in the Civil War Era.* New York: Fordham Univ. Press, 2016.

Woodworth, Steven E. *While God Is Marching On: The Religious World of Civil War Soldiers.* Lawrence: Univ. Press of Kansas, 2001.

Zibro, James. "The Life of Paddy Yank: The Common Irish-American Soldier in the Union Army." PhD diss., Catholic University of America, 2016.

INDEX

www.ingramcontent.com/pod-product-compliance
Lightning Source LLC
La Vergne TN
LVHW091111290126
830469LV00002B/3

* 9 7 8 0 8 0 7 1 8 3 7 0 0 *